Wladimiro Bendazzi - Riccardo Ricci

Ravenna

Guide to the k

mosaics art history archaeology monuments museums

ES

Published by Sirri-Ravenna

Preface

Periodico annuale.
Autorizzazione del Tribunale di Ravenna n. 746 Stampa del 13/6/84
Direttore responsabile: Mari Augusto

Disegni e piantine di Riccardo Ricci
Foto di:
Riccardo Ricci, Museo Nazionale di Ravenna, Mario Francia, Edit. Longo, Scala, Azienda di Promozione Turistica della Provincia di Ravenna, Valerio Maioli Servizi, Domenico Barzagli.
Si ringraziano:
Biblioteca Classense, presso la quale sono stati tratti i disegni di cui alle pagg. 231-245.
Soprintendenza archeologica dell'Emilia Romagna, Soprintendenza per i beni ambientali e architettonici di Ravenna Istituto d'Arte per il mosaico di Ravenna

Redazione grafica: ALCO - Milano
Composizione: Garon, Cremona
Stampa: BSZ, Mazzo di Rho (MI)
Edizione 1993

For further information write to: Edizioni Sirri casella postale n. 242 - 48100 Ravenna

Ravenna as city of art, is universally known for its mosaics. The touristic corporations themselves seem to want to evaluate this image when, on the advertisement posters placed along the roads, they promise tourists sea and pine-woods for health, and mosaics for an aesthetic pleasure.

The image, that has emerged because of the suggestive strength which is part of early christian mosaic art, even if partly true, however reduces very much the complex personality of this city. In Ravenna in fact there aren't only mosaics; for a tourist which has refined tastes there is much more, and for that a large part of tourism that comes from schools and that in spring crowds the Basilicas, we can say that there are documents of the past just as important and suggestive, because framed in a precise historical period.

In order to enjoy the ancient vestiges, expressions of civilizations so far from ours, we need a little information. The mosaic itself which imposes for its fantastic colours wants to be read and understood, so as to be completely enjoyed. On the contrary, its sight doesn't go beyond a superficial consideration that ends only with an exclamation of pleasant surprize.

This guide has exactly the aim of helping the tourist and, why not also the inattentive Ravennati, to read the testimonies of ancient times not only those that are most evident, but also the daily ones, that often are tastier.

Therefore here you won't only find, as occurs in many other guides, the illustration of a famous mosaic, but also the illustration of sarcophagi — another big chapter of the early christian art of Ravenna very often neglected —; in this way the tourist will be

Justinian and Theodora (detail)

guided, even if in the limits of a publication such as this one, through the humble stelae of the «classiari», behind which we can imagine the life of a big naval base; or also in the creations of the Romagnol artistic season of the 15th and 16th Centuries. And he will be given every testimony of artistic, cultural, social life that he will find along his way and that deserves to be considered, maybe only with a rapid glance.

Obviously, this guide has its faults too, because the sediments of two thousand years of history can never be examined in three hundred pages. However we trust to be able to lead the reader into a stimulating discovery of the most interesting aspects of a city that for a certain period had been capital of an empire, and that from the depth of centuries has still something to say to the people of today. We are convinced that the reading of a few pages that we have been able to dedicate to every monument is always remunerative, because only the knowledge of what we are looking at can transform tourism into a valid not ephemeral cultural experience.

The visit of the city is organized on the base of six itineraries all starting from Piazza del Popolo and with returning to it.

In every itinerary one of the greatest monuments of Ravenna or more than one, is included and while going on, the attention of the tourist is directed with brief hints towards other aspects of the city, which can be said minor but certainly not devoid of interest.

At the beginning of every itinerary there is a clear map in which the principal itinerary is indicated with a row of arrows and the eventual variations with a dotting of the roads taken into consideration. In every map only the names of the roads taken in object are indicated.

We advise to carry out the itinerary on foot, both because the itinerary to accomplish is never more than a normal walk (except the visit to Classe that needs a means of transport), and because the centre of town is nearly always closed to car traffic. In every map the zones of parking are always shown, which are quite numerous. We must also underline that parking is admitted at certain hours of the day only

Who would like to follow our itineraries but would like to reach these places directly will find the illustration by consulting the index of the names at the end of the book.

For more complex visits we have widened the written description with other maps with a more topographic character: on drawing them that is, we worried more about the clearness of the information rather than that of the exactness of the proportions.

Unfortunately in our descriptions we couldn't help using numerous technical words, and this could create some difficulties for who isn't specialized; we hope you can excuse us, but these terms couldn't be named other than with their technical terminology.

In the book often there will be some recalls with numbers in brackets, for example: (4). These refer to numbers that you will find on the maps and on other plans of the places of which we shall be speaking of, and they will help you to localize better certain particulars.

The authors.

GENERAL INDEX

Historical outline

We aren't very far from the truth if we imagine the origin of Ravenna's settlement in the following way: a river that flows in the Adriatic sea, a place where we can cross the river, near the sea (a ford), huts around that place, then a village.

When? Let's say about three thousand years ago.

Who? People coming from the East during great population migrations. Later in the 6th and 5th centuries B.C. we can register the introduction of Etruscan and Umbrian populations (and therefore from West and South). Finally, the Celtics (4th century B.C.) from the North.

These were the populations that alternated and mixed in the Romagnol plain, while it seems that Ravenna, starting from the 5th century B.C. had been occupied prevailingly by an Umbrian population.

The ancient world gets to know a decisive divider: the Roman conquest. The history of Europe on the west of the Danube and Rhine, of Mediterranean Africa and of Asia Minor, in different dates, all register the Roman Conquest. Ravenna marks this date between the end of the 3rd and the beginning of the 2nd century B.C. just about one thousand years later than the first appropriation. The Romans don't find a village anymore but a consistent habitat.

The history of the city marks two fundamental moments. The first: the Roman emperor Octavianus Augustus, Caesar's heir decides to build on the narrow beach of Ravenna a very big military harbour. The harbour and the habitat which rose around it, will be called «fleet», in

An image of Ancient Ravenna not based on literary and archaeological references engraved by the geographer Vincenzo Coronelli in the first years of the 18th century.

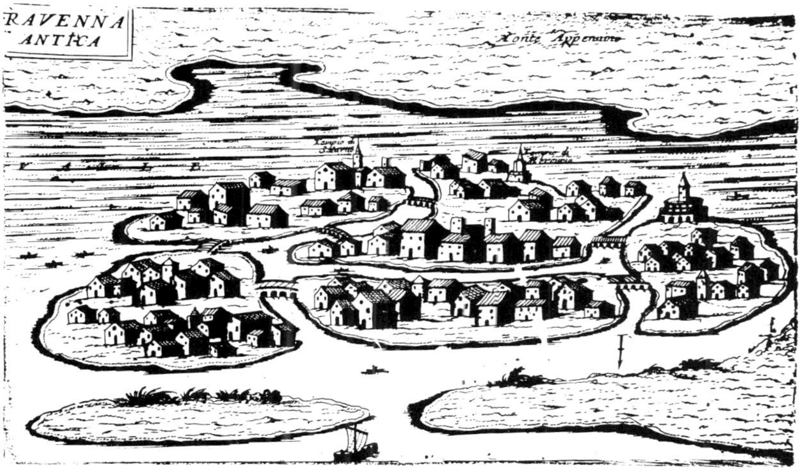

Latin «classis», Classe. A praetorial fleet, the Roman fleet of the East stationed there, which guaranteed the defence of the Adriatic and of the eastern seas of the Empire, with naval squadrons displaced everywhere, till the Piraeus, on the Danube, in the Black Sea. The ships moored in large docks, that stretched even to the habitat, which enlarged to such an extent as to become a single long city divided in three large urban poles: Ravenna, Cesarea, Classe.

As well as the fleet also Christianity gets to Classe, thanks to St. Apollinare, who is placed by legend in the 1st century, and was sent directly by St. Peter, while history places him at the end of the 2nd century.

The city of Classe was surrounded by walls in the 3rd century A.D. Incredibly, the image of the walls, of the harbour and of the city appears on a big mosaic in the basilica of Sant'Apollinare Nuovo, carried out between the end of the 5th and the beginning of the 6th century, when the fleet had already left the harbour.

A second fundamental moment influenced in a very way the destiny of the city: a Roman emperor, Honorius makes Ravenna the capital of the Western Roman Empire.

The Empire had reached its maximum territorial expansion under emperor Trajan who reigned from 98 to 117 A.D., but the vast territory was later on invaded by Germanic populations coming from the east. A first big invasion took place in 376. In order to dominate the situation the Roman emperors provided, in different spaces of

time, to subdivide the Empire so as to govern it better, and frequently changed the capital. The last subdivision of the Empire took place in 395 by Emperor Theodosius. He appointed the eastern part of the Empire, with Constantinople as capital to his son Arcadius and the western half (practically Europe on the western side of the Danube and of the Rhine and the corresponding African coast) to his other son Honorius, with Milan as capital. It was Honorius who in order to escape from the Visigoths of Alaric chose Ravenna later (in 402) as capital of his part of the empire. The city was surrounded by swamps, and was situated near the sea, and it was therefore very difficult for the invaders, men of land, to reach it and it was also open to naval aid from the east.

This was for Ravenna a very flourishing period, thanks both to the Church, that at the beginning of the 5th century moves from Classe to Ravenna and builds its Cathedral (not extant anymore), the Neonian Baptistery (still extant), the archbishopric (of it an oratory of the 5th-6th century still remains); and to the imperial government (Basilica of St. John the Evangelist, Santa Croce, Mausoleum of Galla Placidia). By this time we can see Ravenna surrounded by walls (5th century) and not in the 1st, as has been said for a very long time.

Ravenna was the capital of an invaded Empire. Barbarians had occupied and divided Europe in many territories, starting especially from 406. Then in 451 the Huns with their king Attila arrived. In 455,

◀ National Museum of Ravenna: bas-relief representing, from left to right, a female divinity, general Agrippa, Marcellus (or Germanicus), Livia, Augustus (end of the 1st Century B.C. - beginning of the 1st century A.D.).

Excavations of Classe: Late-Roman and Byzantine portual plant. The road paved with volcanic rock from the Euganean hills, runs parallel to the port canal and divides an area of warehouses destined for the loading and unloading of goods, from a productive area (ceramic-kiln, glass-kiln). The complex can be dated to the 6th Century A.D.

from Africa the Vandals of Genseric pillaged Rome (it had already been attacked by the Visigoths of Alaric). From Ravenna the western emperors govern, if we can say so, only the Italian territory.

Then in 476 the last emperor is deposed and the power is put in the hands of a barbarian, Odoacer, who keeps it for seventeen years. Another barbarian Theodoric, king of the Ostrogoths, dethrones him and kills him and governs Italy for 33 years (from 493 to 526).

This is a new flourishing period for the city, which enrichens itself with the Arian Cathedral and Baptistery, with the church adjacent the imperial palace, then called Sant'Apollinare Nuovo, with the Mausoleum.

Theodoric dies in 526. His successors ten years later must face the army of the eastern emperor (from 527, Justinian), who wants to rebuild a compact Empire by reconquering the territories occupied by the barbarians. The armies of Justinian win (the Byzantines) who occupy Ravenna in 540 and liberate Italy in 553. In the years of the Byzantine conquest the basilicas of San Vitale, Santa Maria Maggiore, Sant'Apollinare in Classe are built. But only 15 years after Italy's liberation, other invaders enter Italy, the Longobards, which deprive the Eastern Empire, in a few years, of quite a good area of Italy, but not Ravenna and a wide territory around it, not Rome, nor the coasts of Calabria and Puglia, nor Corsica, Sardinia, Sicily, and neither the Ligurian coast. And so Ravenna keeps on being capital but only of these strips of Italy and always less effica-

The Mausoleum of Theodoric as it was when Vincenzo Coronelli designed it (end of the 17th - beginning of the 18th century). The building is interred till the arches of the niches (page 167). A sacred building leans against it (page 170).

ciously. The eastern emperor places one of his representatives in it, the exarch who will remain until 751 when the city is invaded by the Longobards. But for very little. In the middle of the 8th century the historical picture changes decisively. From the lands of the Longobards, defeated by the Franks, the city passes in those of the Popes who will reign it by means of local archbishops that were truly dominating the ex-Byzantine territories, often contrasting the Popes themselves. However from the scene of the world history Ravenna enters in the more modest regional ambit.

When, after the year 1000, in Italy the wonderful flourishing of the Municipalities took place as expression of a new world, also in Ravenna this important historical change took place, first under the regency of the local councils, then of a Podesta called from outside (1181).

The period of the municipalities came to an end, as is well known, by means of the affirmation in the cities of Lordships that had come out from bitter struggles between town factions. The phenomenon revealed itself also in Ravenna, the Traversari family prevailed who obtained the seigneury of the city until 1240, followed by the Da Polentas, who governed until the middle of the 15th century, when Venice transformed its influence into a direct dominium.

The Polenta family is famous among other things for having guested Dante who was in exile from Florence and for having given him a solemn burial in 1321.

The Venetians promoted recla-

The most ancient map of Ravenna (second half of the 15th century). The city is surrounded by the Ronco and Montone rivers.

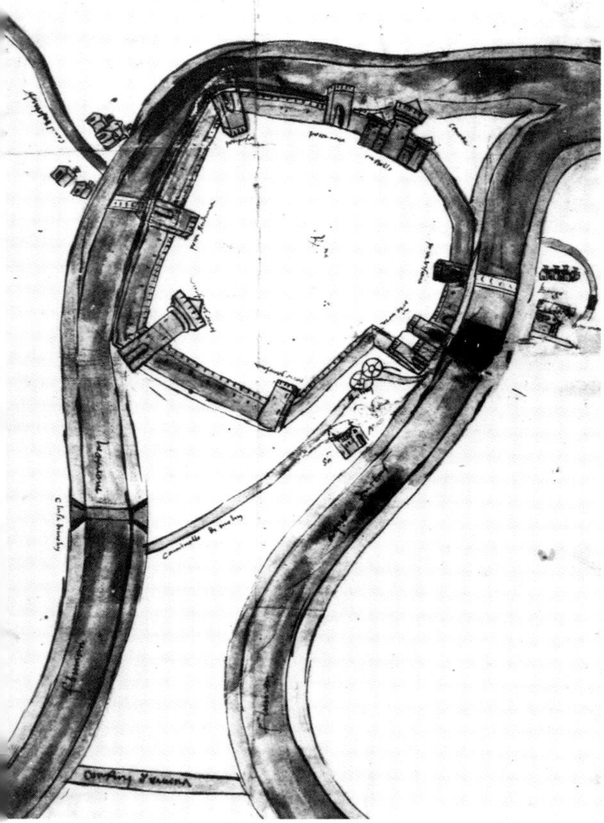

mations to extend the area of agricultural lands: in the last thousand years, in fact, the Ravennate seat has changed physiognomy: the city was only a few kilometers away from the sea and it was still the centre of a vast swampy area but with a growing agricultural vocation. Furthermore the Venetians must receive the merit of having accomplished very important fortification works, among which the great Rocca Brancaleone stands out, and for having left other public works such as the little palace called Venezia-

Galla Placidia.

no in Piazza del Popolo, which had been turned into the seat of the city government. After a few decades, however, the city passed permanently to the Pope after the complex war-diplomatic period that characterized the 16th century. In this frame also the great battle that took place near the city on April 11th, 1512, it was Easter day, between the French and the Spanish, with the Italians that had been variably aligned, must be located. Ravenna, a Pope dominium, was with the Spanish who were conquered by the French, that had been repeatedly pushed back from the walls during the previous days thanks to a heroic defence of the citizens, but with the defeat the conquerors entered and pillaged the town.

In the variable frame of allian-

The first representation of the city in panoramic elevation (17th Century). ▶

Rocca Brancaleone built by the Venetians and finished in 1470 (page 163). Design by V. Coronelli.

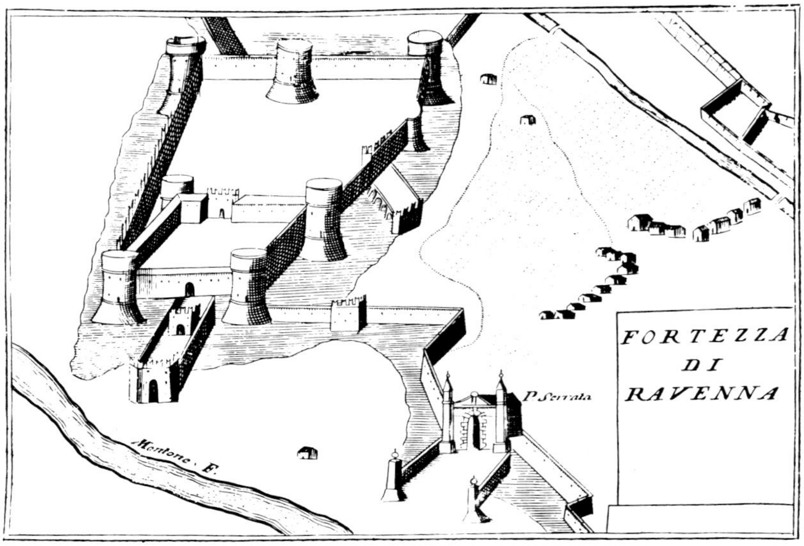

ces however, Ravenna remained to the Pope who kept it as capital of the «Legazione» until 1859, i.e. still for 350 years excluding a very brief period in the 16th century in which it returned to the Venetians, and excluding the Napoleonic period.

The most remarkable fact of these 3½ centuries is constituted undoubtedly by a great work of hydraulic order of the territory: the diversion of the Ronco and Montone rivers which surrounded the city near the walls, and the formation of a new river bed for the Fiumi Uniti till the sea. This work was necessary in order to free the city from the terrible floods that frequently troubled it (famous among all, the one of the 31st May 1636). In the same period also the latest of Ravenna's harbours was opened: the Candiano or «Corsini» canal from the family name of the pontiff Clemente XII that had it built. This canal, later widened, rectified and in recent years provided with modern portual equipment, practically creates a navel cord that unites the city to its sea nearly as if to keep alive, and not only in a symbolic way, an ancient vital communion.

During the 19th century Ravenna participated to the Risorgimento with many of its sons and in this frame it is worthy to mention especially the daring and skilful procedure with which in 1849 the Ravennati Patriots saved Garibaldi who was escaping from the Austrians.

Passed to the Regno d'Italia on the 18th March 1860, after that the pontiff government had been thrown down by an insurrection of common people on the 13th June 1859, Ravenna became the main town of

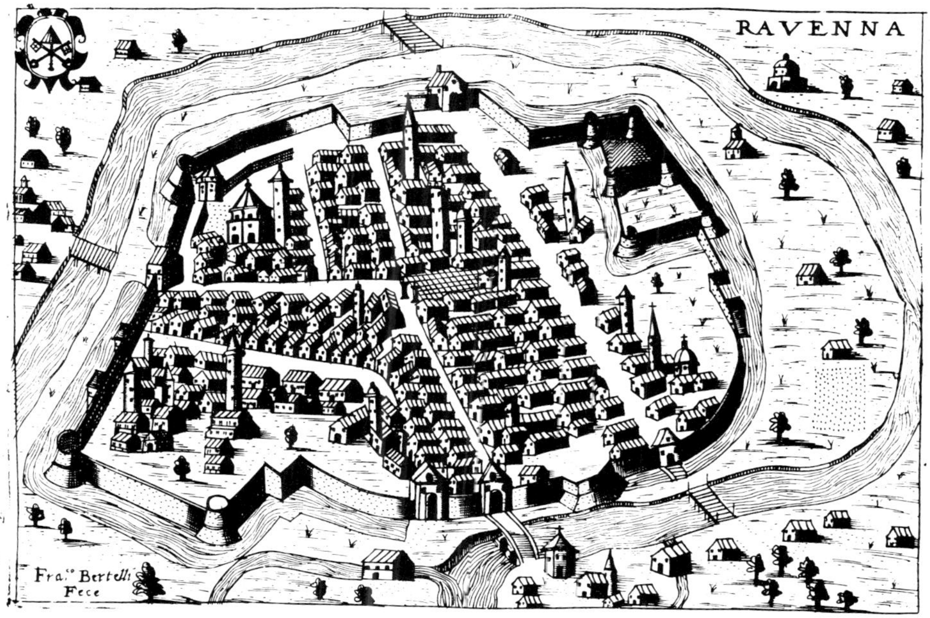

a mainly agricultural province, whose territory was still occupied by vast areas underwater still to be reclaimed and to be turned into agricultural lands. The land reclamation of the major part of these zones marks the history of the territory of the last century: a history in which cooperatives stood out, which also represent a first movement of self-conscience and of redemption of the working classes.

In the second after-war period the city got to know, finally, a great expansion, widening itself out of the walls of the 5th century, especially in virtue of the establishment of numerous big industries that have changed the landscape. In fact from an ancient background of pine-woods and placid valleys now a technological forest of tubes, chimneys and cranes stand out, while big ships coming from every part of the world lazily go up the Corsini canal to the new modern industrial harbour.

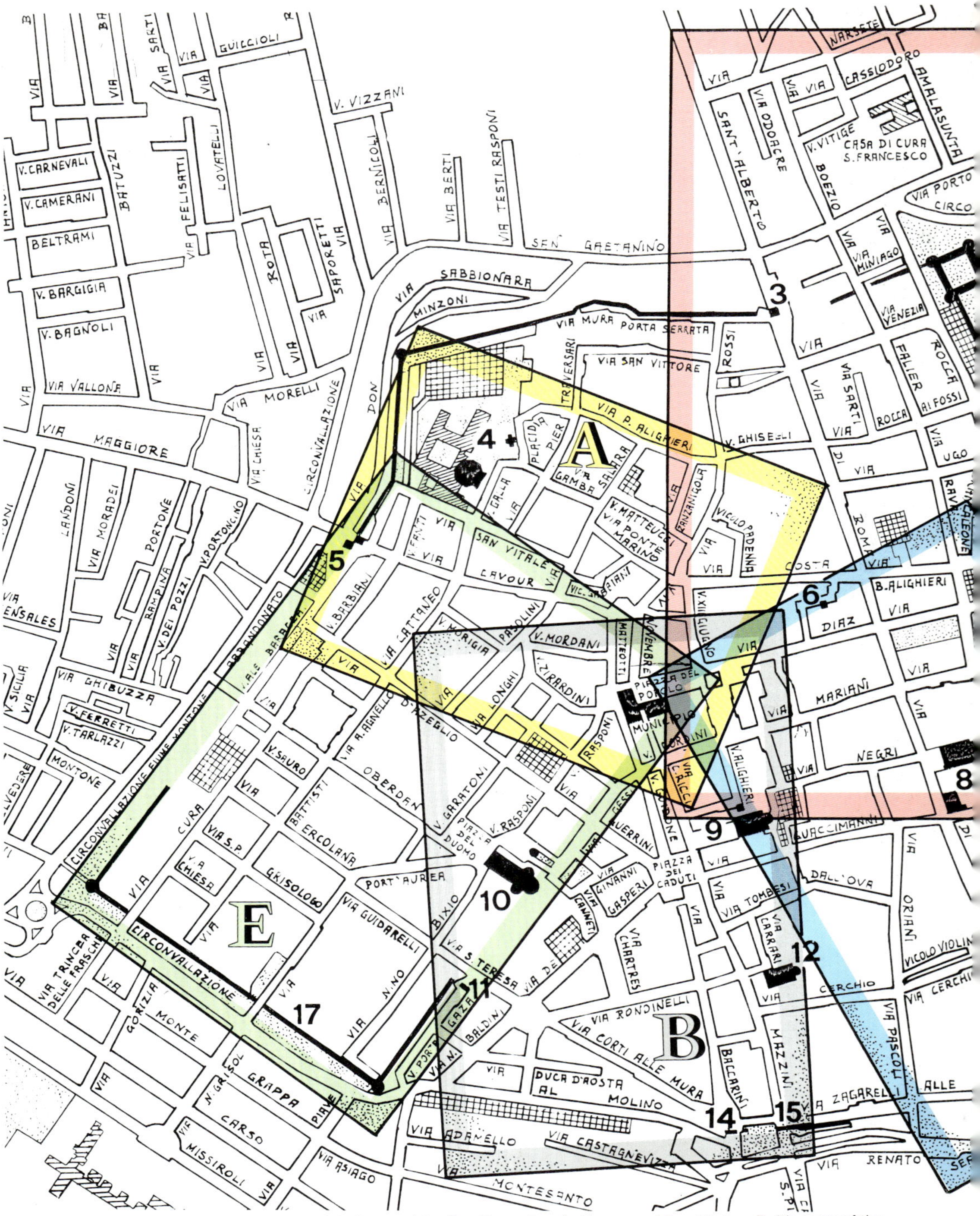

Ravenna - Map of the historical centre: global map of the five itineraries. **A**: Itinerary of San Vitale. - **B**: Itinerary of the Dantesque zone, San Francesco and Sant'Agata. - **C**: Itinerary of San Giovanni Evangelista and of Sant'Apollinare Nuovo. - **D**: Itinerary of Rocca Brancaleone and of the Mausoleum of Theodoric. - **E**: Itinerary of the Cathedral. - 1, Mausoleum of Theodoric. 2, Rocca Brancaleone. 3, Porta Serrata. 4, Complex of San Vitale. 5, Porta Adriana. 6, Baptistery of the Arians. 7, San Giovanni Evangelista. 8, Sant'Apollinare Nuovo. 9, Dantesque zone. 10, Duomo. 11, Porta Gaza. 12, Sant'Agata Maggiore. 13, Santa Maria in Porto. 14, Porta San Mama. 15, Porta Sisi. 16, Porta Nova. 17, Roman walls of the Ist Century.

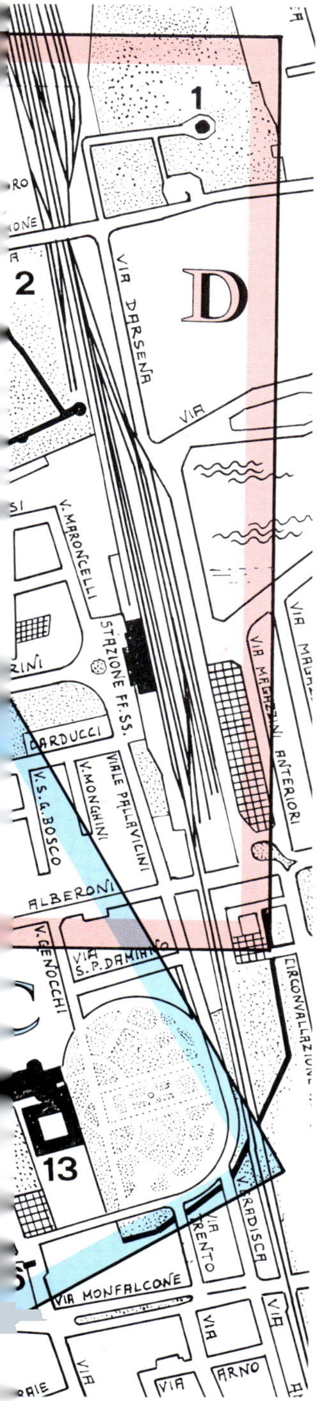

Photo above: The last tract of the port canal of Ravenna. On the background one can notice the habitat Marina di Ravenna and the sea docks.
Photo below: Air view of Ravenna today. We can see the city dock, the Basilica of St. John the Evangelist with the square bell-tower, the Basilica of Sant'Apollinare Nuovo with its Renaissance portico and its round bell-tower.

SAN VITALE ITINERARY

Piazza del popolo - Via IV Novembre - Piazza Andrea Costa - Mercato Coperto - Casa Matha - San Michele in Africisco - Casa Minzoni (*first variation*: Via Ponte Marino - San Giacomo - Palazzo Gamba - Palazzo Cavalli) Via Salara - Via San Vitale - Palazzo Rota - Casa Traversari - **Monastery of San Vitale** - **San Vitale** - **Mausoleum of Galla Placidia** - **National Museum** - - Via Galla Placidia - Santa Maria Maggiore - Santa Croce - Via Mura San Vitale - Porta Adriana - (*second variation*: Via Barbiani - Sant'Eufemia - Santi Giovanni e Paolo - Via D'Azeglio - Via Cattaneo) - Via Cavour - Palazzo Guiccioli - San Domenico - Via Matteotti - Piazza dell'Aquila - Sant'Apollinare in Veclo.

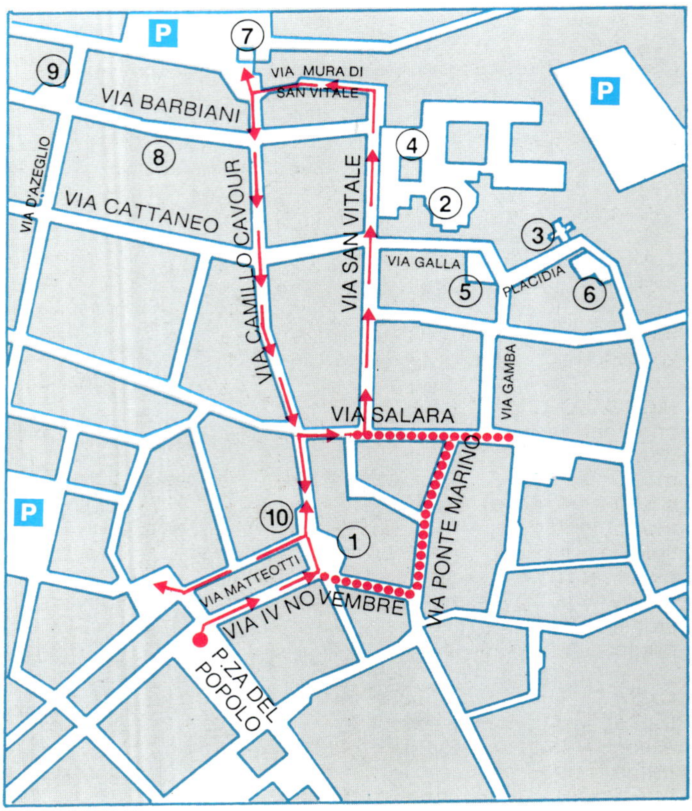

Fig. 1 - **Itinerary of San Vitale**: 1, Mercato Coperto. 2, Basilica of San Vitale. 3, Mausoleum of Galla Placidia. 4, National Museum. 5, Santa Maria Maggiore. 6, Santa Croce. 7, Porta Adriana. 8, Sant'Eufemia. 9, Santi Giovanni and Paolo. 10, San Domenico.

Corner of the Mercato Coperto and Casa Minzoni (ex Cappello Hotel).

Leaving Piazza del Popolo, described at the beginning of the first itinerary, we take Via IV Novembre (north-western corner) and arrive in Piazzetta Andrea Costa where we stop. (See itinerary pict. 1 page 16). The above mentioned street goes on for a hundred meters and follows a layout that once constituted part of one of the river banks crossing the city. The flow of this river, called in ancient times Padenna, is clearly revealed if we look at a city plan by the nearby parallel series of two street lines, one of the banks is marked by the following roads: Girolamo Rossi, IV Novembre, Cairoli, Corrado Ricci, Mazzini; the other one, but in an incomplete way, by the roads: Zanzanigola, Matteotti, Mentana, Guidone, Baccarini (see on page 14).

The small Andrea Costa square is a good look-out point for some interesting buldings: The Mercato Coperto, the seat of Casa Matha, the bell-tower of San Michele in Africisco, Minzoni House, the church of San Domenico.

MERCATO COPERTO - Built on a project by engineer Eugenio Baroncelli, of classic style, was opened in 1922. The ornamentations are made of Istria stone. Metal trestles with trusses sustained by big cast iron columns make up the roofing. Wide windows and sky-lights give light to the inside of the building. After a complete restoration, it was reopened in March 1984. In the hall we find two dolphins made of stone from Istria (first half of 18th century), originally in the old fish market.

CASA MATHA - The building in front of Mercato Coperto guests what was once the «*oldest association of workmen, not only in Ravenna, but in the entire world*» (Bernicoli). Founded in the 10th century it was a corporation organizing the fishermen. Once called «*Schola piscatorum*», it became then Casa Matha or Amata. The origin of the term is controversial: it can be abbreviation of «*ga mazzo*», that is *kamerad* (partner) or *work-companion*, of German origin. It can represent a term meaning *mat or hurdle of paludal rushes*. The latinization *Amata* probably derives from «amo» (hook), the fishermen's instrument. Another interpretation refers to an old way of fishing, in lagoons: «piscare cum matha». The corporation which possessed lagoons and woods and issued orders on fishing and fish trade, also held administrative offices of great importance. The present seat was occupied in 1901. In 1919 the Casa Matha formed a nautical school which operated until the second World War. Today it spreads studies about fishing, ecology, ground and water defence. The marble shell that decorates the ancient seat of the corporation is now on the pediment of the market.

CASA MINZONI - At n. 41 Via IV Novembre there is an ancient building once housing the Cappello Hotel as a proof together with other buildings (Rocca Brancaleone, Palazzetto di Piazza del Popolo, several houses scattered out in the city) of the period during which Venice ruled over Ravenna (15th century). The building still has the main entrance, the little marble balcony, the first floor windows and the little corner pillar while three main doors replace the four windows located on the ground floor.

A popular tradition wants the birthplace of Francesca da Polenta in this house, she was the passionate adultress immortalized by Dante. But it is a certainly groundless rumour as the event took place about two centuries before the building of the house.

SAN MICHELE IN AFRICISCO - Behind the façade of the building, at n. 35-37 Via IV Novembre, we find the square bell-tower (15th century) of San Michele in Africisco church. In a courtyard it is still possible to see the remains of the polygonal apse situated at the bottom of the left nave dating back to the ancient building. There is also a room on the left of the apse but it is contemporary to the bell-tower.

The church was among the oldest of the city. Built by Giuliano Argentario, it was consecrated by the bishop Maximian not before the end of 546. The mosaic of which the apse was adorned, bought in 1843 from the court of Prussia, is now in Berlin, exposed in the State Museums since 1904; it suffered various damages and hardships, among which numerous repairs, the last of these in 1951-52, that have taken away nearly completely its original value.

Etymologically, the term *Africisco* would seem to be in relation with Phrigia, a region of Asia Minor; locally it indicated the section in which the church rose.

Who wishes to reach more quickly the most suggestive part of this itinerary, where the monumental complex of San Vitale is, will go on along Via Cavour leaving on the left the church of San Domenico which we will visit on our return; will then turn right (Via Salara) and then turn the first road left again (Via San Vitale). In such case in order to use this text, you must pass to the paragraph entitled: «Lapide Alidosio».

Who instead has more time available, can follow the alternative here under illustrated.

FIRST ALTERNATIVE - From the little Andrea Costa square we carry on along Via IV Novembre having on the left the Mercato Coperto and, at the end, we turn left in Via Ponte Marino, so called for one of the bridges that here crossed the Padenna River (fig. 1 - the dotted part).

SAN GIACOMO DI PONTE MARINO - At numbers 7 and 9 of Via Ponte Marino we find the side of the church San Giacomo di Ponte Marino (14th century), rebuilt in the 16th Century and in 18th seat of the mint. It then became a home (casa Monghini-Serena). We can admire a few little arches as crowning on the wall.

PALAZZO GAMBA - Having reached the end of Via Ponte Marino we get to Via Salara. We remind that in this Via, right in front of Ponte Marino, already since the 9th century, a church arose, known for its cenoby of Benedictine nuns. Dedicated to Santa Maria in Caelos eo (*in caelos eo* - I go into the sky) it was rebuilt in 1691 and demolished in 1916. We turn right. On the first road on the left (Via Gamba), at number 3 there is the homonymous building built in 1766. On the arched front door there is the family emblem, represented precisely by a leg (gamba). The beautiful windows of the ground floor are provided of an iron grating, those on the first floor are surmounted alternatively by triangular and curved pediments. It is a beautiful example of sober baroque due to the architect Andrea Zumaglini.

PALAZZO CAVALLI - Let's return to Via Salara and, continuing towards left, we get to Marsala Square on which at numbers 40-42, faces the Cavalli building: a construction of the 17th century of great dimensions in which detracting interventions at the beginning of the 20th century have been executed. The main entrance is followed by a hall, followed by a tranquil yard, a second hall and a little garden.

Between the 2nd and the 13th August 1826 Giacomo Leopardi was a guest of the Cavalli family, one of the noblest families of Romagna, in occasion of a visit to Ravenna's antiques. The stay of the poet is remembered by a tablet on the façade.

LAPIDE ALIDOSIO - Let's return on our steps and, returning along Via Salara to the seat of the «Azienda di Promozione Turistica» (local tourist office), we turn right in Via San Vitale, that opens in front of n. 11 of Via Salara. At this point the alternative joins the principal itinerary.

At the beginning of the road, on the left, a little tablet remembers the blood fact in which Cardinal Alidosio was killed.

Francesco Alidosio, Legate Cardinal of Bologna since 1508, not being able to sustain the defence of the city against the French, retired to Ravenna, where Pope Giulio II had already come. Lost Bologna, the nephew of the Pope, Francesco Maria della Rovere, duke of Urbino, accused Alidosio, who retorted the accusation convincing the Pope that the loss of the city was due to the military incapacity of his nephew. The latter strongly resented of this, set off in search of Alidosio and «*unluckily he met the cardinal who from his home was going, accompanied by the captain of the guards and by the guards themselves, to San Vitale to have lunch together with the Pope, that had invited him. The Duke on foot with some relatives of his passed through the middle of the guards that had let him way for respect, and with his left hand took the reins of the mule, on which Alidosio was sitting dressed with a black cloak and with a Spanish hat, and with the right hand thrusted a rapier in the hips of the Cardinal, and threw him to the ground, where Mondolfo Capitan di Cavalli cut his cheek with a dagger, and left him dead on the ground*» (Ginanni).

The fact occurred on the 24th May 1511.

San Vitale - Gate of 17th century.

ENTRANCE TO THE BASILICA
See on page 23

PALAZZO ROTA - At n. 5 we have the Rota building a construction of the 17th century. Ravenna is very rich in buildings of the 17th and 18th centuries, many of which, as this one, have the appearance of forts (compact, massive constructions towerlike and with the façade that falls slopingly) as to testify the fights between various factions, still alive at that time. The sight of the inside garden of the 18th century is very nice indeed.

At numbers 7, 9, 11 we have the Cappi house; and at numbers 22 and 24 a house with elements of the 15th century (cornice with wooden shelves, the door of n. 24 with an architrave).

CASA TRAVERSARI - It is at n. 28. As well as that of the Polentani in Via Zagarelli alle Mura, it can be considered the oldest house in Ravenna because it dates back to the 13th-14th centuries. While certain noble buildings express a sense of strength, power and overbearing, this house, as other ones of hard times too, suggests motivations of a more quiet and compound civilization.

The Traversari family had the supremacy in Ravenna from the end of the 12th century till 1240. Dante celebrated Pietro Traversari and all the rest of his family in the XIV Canto of Purgatory in the verses from 98 to 107 with words of sorrowful regret for the lost virtues of the Romagnol people:

«Where are the good Lizio and Arrigo Mainardi?
Pier Traversaro and Guido da Carpigna?
Oh Romagnol people you have returned
[bastards.»
. . . .
Don't be surprized if I cry, Tosco,
. . . .
the Traversary lineage . . . .»

And the kindness of the women of the family was sung by provençal poets. When Dante was in Ravenna guest of the Polentani, the ancient Traversari family had nearly completely died out, with the survival of a few females, who were nuns at the Santa Chiara Convent.

Today the Traversari house contains the ISTITUTO DI ANTICHITÀ RAVENNATI E PALEOBIZANTINE of Bologna University.

Going on, we reach the portal (of 1622) with lateral niches (of the end 18th century) which served as an entrance, until 1990, to the area with the basilica of San Vitale, the mausoleum of Galla Placidia and the benedictine monastery where the National Museum has its seat. In the crowning of the arch, over the inscription DIVO VITALI MARTIRI there is the figure of San Vitale on horseback with a flag in his hand, coat of arms of the convent. On the top there is an abbatial mitra.

To go into all these buildings we have to walk along Via San Vitale, keeping on the right the part of the monastery which contains the SUPERINTENDENCE FOR THE ENVIRONMENTAL AND ARCHITECTONIC PROPERTIES for the provinces of Ravenna, Ferrara and Forlì and on the left, at numbers 36, 38, 40, 42 the so called houses of San Vitale, built towards the end of the 13th century, used by the monks as guest-quarters.

Finally we come to the gate leading into the courtyard of the Benedictine Monastery.

We are in the area of the MONASTERY. The very recent retrieval and restoration of the

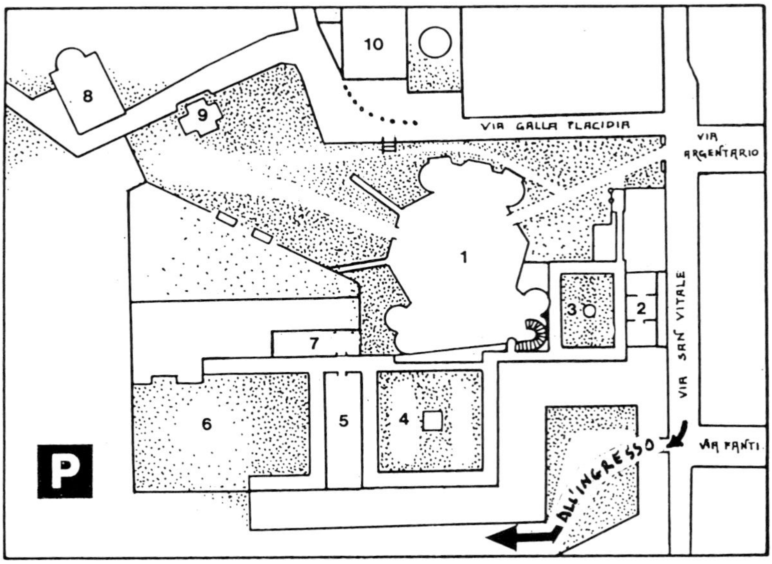

Fig. 2 - **Plan of the San Vitale zone**: 1, Basilica of San Vitale. 2, Show rooms. 3, First Cloister. 4, Second cloister. 5, Refectory. 6, Third cloister. 7, Room with stelae. 8, Santa Croce. 9, Mausoleum of Galla Placidia. 10, Santa Maria Maggiore.

rooms that cointain the NATIONAL MUSEUM invites us to pay attention, as well as to the objects that are exposed also to the building that houses them, which is itself object of great interest.

THE MONASTERY

Near the Basilica of San Vitale, since ancient times a monastery arose, whose origin is not documented, but whose existence is confirmed by testimonies which date back to the 10th century. A diploma of the emperor Otto III is extant, dated 10th, January 999, with which the land next to the narthex of the basilica is granted to the abbot of San Vitale in order to build a cloister; in the State Archives of Ravenna there is the list of names of the abbots of the monastery from the 10th century to 1798; there are historical opinions that date the origin to the 6th century (*Girolamo Fabri*, 1627-1679, to the 9th century (thesis of *Jean Mabillon*, 1632-1707, which assigns its foundation to the archbishop Giovanni IX, 898-904), to the 8th century (thesis of the Benedictine monk of San Vitale, *Benedetto Fiandrini*).

If the origins aren't documented, instead the date (1472) in which the monastery of San Vitale was united to the congregation of Santa Giustina di Padova is known. Since its origin, with every probability the monastery of San Vitale was organized according to the rule of Saint Benedict, which was far off the prevailing rule and nearly the only one of monastic life.

Benedict (Norcia, 480 - Montecassino, in about 547) had established a Rule, composed of a prologue and 73 chapters, which constitued the fundamental and material codex of all the monasticism in the west, essential document for the history of European civilization, origin of any other medieval text of monastic legislation. The monastery was thought of as a little state, as a self-sufficient city both material and spiritually:

«The monastery will arise in a place that will contain all that is necessary i.e. water, mills, kitchen-garden, bakery and different activities that take place in the monastery...».

(Rule of Saint Benedict, chapter LXVI)

And it is in this little city that we would like to lead the visitor, showing little by little as we advance in our visit the monastic function of the single rooms, whilst illustrating at the same time the various pieces.

What we invite you to do is to imagine those places (the long corridors, the cloisters, the refectory, the various rooms, the monks' cells, the cellar, the kitchen, the storerooms, the kitchen-gardens...), still populated by the community of monks, living and operating according to the ancient dictations of the Rule. A community founded on the organization of the various services and on life and property in community, run by a supreme leader, the abbot, assisted by the deans, the prior, by the rector monks, by the forwarder, by the prefect of studies, by the attorney father, by the ministers in charge of the religious activities... An articulated community therefore, that is not so difficult to imagine, if we go through the places where it lived and operated for hundreds of years.

The quiet life of the monasteries, and therefore also the one of San Vitale, underwent a

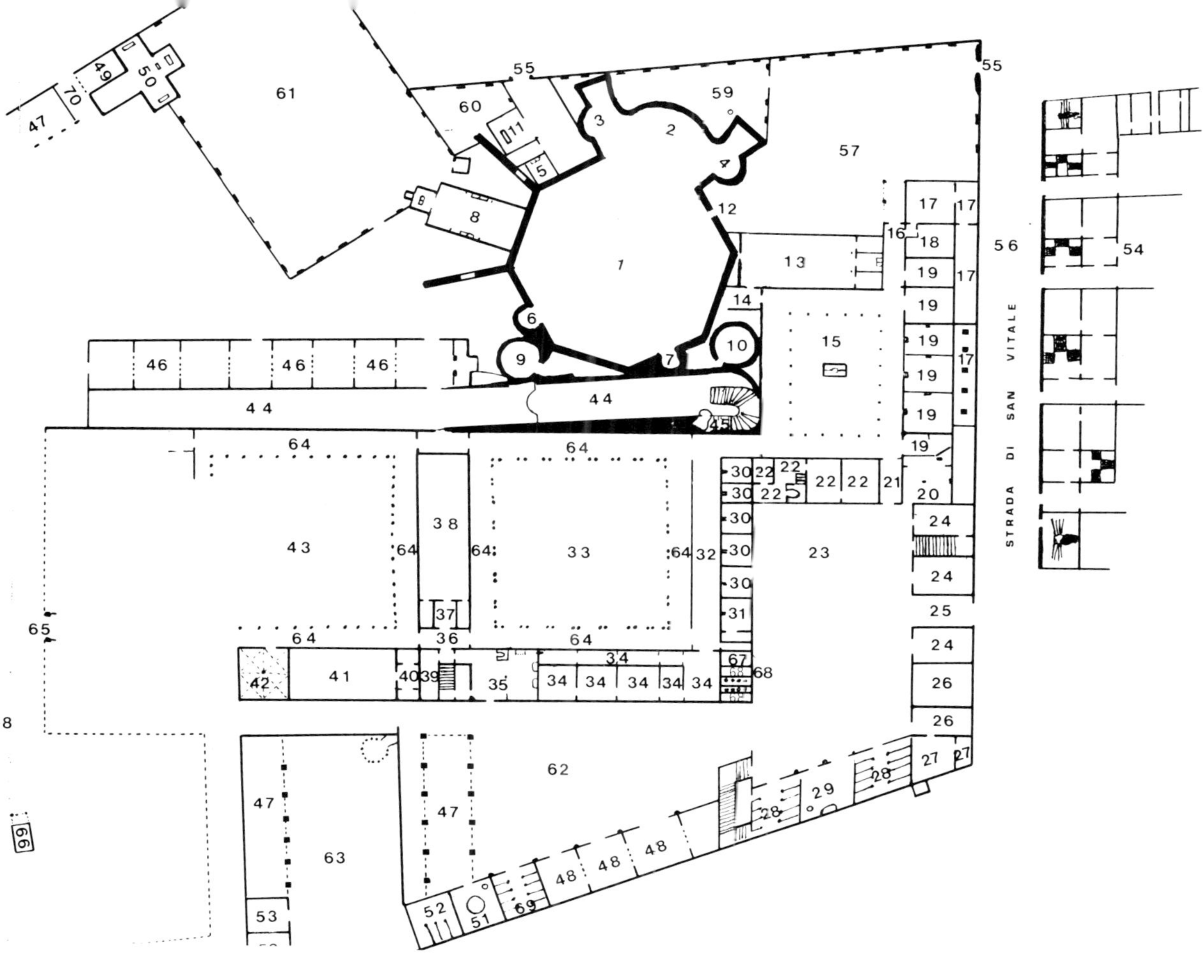

Fig. 11 - DEMONSTRATIVE PLAN OF THE CHURCH AND THE MONASTERY OF SAN VITALE IN RAVENNA. The plan was designed by the Benedictine monk Benedetto Fiandrini, and in the text it is indicated as P.F. 1 - Church. 2 - Choir. 3 - Mary's Chapel, ancient tower. 4 - Chapel called «SANCTA SANCTORUM», ancient tower. 5 - Chapel of Saint Ursicino. 6 - Chapel of Pity. 7 - Chapel of San Vitale. 8 - Chapel of the most Holy Sacrament. Above, choir of the night and chapter of the monks. 9 - Ancient Tower. Above, «Barberia» (i.e. barber). 10 - Bell-tower. 11 - External Chapel. 12 - Doors. 13 - Sacristy. Above, library. 14 - Passage to the sacristy. 15 - Little cloister. 16 - Door and porter's lodge. 17 - Spice chamber. 18 - Porters room. 19 - Storerooms of cheese, ropes, iron and other things. Above 17-18-19, flat of the abbot of Government. 20 - Shop of the carpenter. Above, archives. 21 - Passage. 22 - Baking room, flour pantry etc. Above, cells, and above them, noviciate. 23 - Yard or square for wagons. 24 - Store for coaches and wood. 25 - Door of the wagons. 26 - Dining-room for the servants. 27 - Saddling room. 28 - Horse stables. 29 - Big vault with a well and a drinking trough for the horses. Above the numbers 24-25-26-27-28-29, store-room for pine seeds, of three orders. 30 - Schools. Above cells and over it noviciate. 31 - Room of the forwarder. Above, offices and rooms of the monks. 32 - Corridor of the schools. Above corridor of the noviciate. 33 - Big cloister. 34 - Physic and Surgical Museum. 35 - Kitchen. 36 - Passage to the big refectory. 37 - Hall of the big refectory. 38 - Big refectory. 39 - Passage to the little refectory. 40 - Hall of the little refectory. 41 - Little refectory. 42 - Storeroom for pork meat and oil. Above the numbers 34-35-39-40-41-42, monks' room and dormitory. 43 - Cloister of the kitchen garden. 44 - Cellar. Above new long dormitory. 45 - New staircase. 46 - Cellar for vats. Above, rooms of infirmary and of Forestry. 47 - Wood room. 48 - Storeroom for big marble. Above, hay lofts. 49 - Little store-room for thin marble. 50 - Ancient church of San Nazario and Celso, called Galla Placidia. 51 - Mill. 52 - Stable for the animals of the miller. Above 51 and 52, hay-lofts. 53 - Hen-house, etc. Store-room for gypsum. 54 - New-houses of San Vitale. Above, wheat stores. 55 - Two doors. 56 - Via San Vitale. 57 - Square of the church. 58 - Big kitchen-garden. 59 - Spice kitchen-garden. 60 - Kitchen-garden of the Sacristy. 61 - Novices' kitchen-garden. 62 - Kitchen-yard. 63 - Back garden of the kitchen. 64 - Big cloister. Above, all the rooms of the monks. 65 - Gate of the big kitchen-garden. 66 - House of the market gardener with portico. 67 - Little room. 68 - Lavatories. 69 - Stable for the mules and rural horses. 70 - Passage to Galla Placidia.

sudden arrest in the territories that were occupied by the French armies at the end of the Eighteenth Century. The French entered in Ravenna on the 26th June 1796, and F. Landi says «*In a little more than a year the economical power of the four great abbeys dissolved under the predatory assaults of nobility and of rich local speculators*». The monastery was suppressed on the 4th fructidor of the 6th year of the Republic i.e. on the 21st August 1798. It was turned into barracks in 1796 and it remained such for a century and a half. Since 1909 it housed in the part that was reserved to the abbot's flat the Sovrintendenza ai Monumenti (now Soprintendenza per i Beni Ambientali e Architettonici). Since 1913-14 it started to be turned into a seat of the National Museum.

Occupied partly by families of evacuated people after 1945, handed back in 1968 to the «Soprintendenza», it is now completely and wholly recovered for cultural use and public interest.

In order to make clear our moving in this complicate building we have to refer to the plan on page 21. It is a plan drawn by monk *Benedetto Fiandrini* in 1798, including the monastery, the basilica of S. Vitale and the mausoleum of Galla Placidia.

To distinguish it from others we will call it FIANDRINI PLAN. Following the plan (we came in through the door n. 25 of the plan), we are in the courtyard (n. 23), which acted as SQUARE FOR WAGONS. On the sides of the door there is the STORE FOR COACHES AND WOOD (n. 24), on the right there is the place before occupied by the BAKERY, FLOUR PANTRY AND EVERYTHING CONNECTED to it, on the left the HORSE STABLES (n. 28) with a room for the TROUGH (n. 29) while opposite where now the DIDACTIC ROOM opens, there were the schools (n. 30).

Turning the corner (where there were the LAVATORIES, n. 68), going towards the parking place, we can see on the right the rooms of the lost PHYSICAL SURGICAL MUSEUM that Beltrami described in 1791 this way:

«Before leaving the Monastery you must observe the singular Infirmary, i.e. Medical-Surgical Museum, the first, instituted after the cult of Medicine and of Surgery. This contains and exhibits in various rooms deviced, equipments, instruments, machines and other artful inventions to give humanity the most ready, effective means for recovery from the majority and most difficult and tormentous illnesses or at least to alleviate their gravity. Extraordinary collection indeed, and praised rightly by the most careful visitors. It was started in about 1746, by the well deserving P.D. Ippolito Rondinelli, from Ferrara...».

On the left we have the buildings that contained THE STOREROOMS FOR BIG MARBLES (P.F. n. 48) and after, THE STABLES FOR MULES AND RURAL HORSES (P.F. n. 69), THE PISTRINO (I.E. THE MILL, from the Latin word «pinsere» - to crunch) and the STABLE FOR THE MILLER'S ANIMALS (P.F. n. 51-52) and after a KITCHEN GARDEN, at that time fenced (P.F. n. 63 with the WOOD ROOM (n. 47) HEN-HOUSE and THE GYPSUM STORE-ROOM (P.F. n. 53), the spaces of the BIG KITCHEN-GARDEN (P.F. n. 58) instead of which there is a parking place now.

All the rooms were restored and they are used for cultural and public purposes (State archives, activities concerning mosaic and restoration). So we reach the entrance leading to the BASILICA, the MAUSOLEUM and the MUSEUM.

From the hall we can enter the BIG REFECTORY (see Fiandrini plan n. 38), where the monks had their meals, which according to the Rule, were carried out in silence and listening to the reader.

In the refectory, as two hundred years ago, there is still the big crowded painting of *Gianbattista Bissoni* from Padova, which represents the «*Nozze di Cana*» (Cana's Wedding) (1601) and on the vault of the room a fresco representing «Glory».

In this room a mosaic floor has been placed and it was discovered in 1844 near the Classense basilica of S. Severo and it was placed here after several other collocations. It can be dated after the half of the 6th century and it is 4 metres wide and 12 metres 55 in length. The missing zones have been remade so as to recognize the restoration. A first panel presents in the middle a deer, of naturalistic yield; a second panel shows various geometrical decorations; a third zone follows with two interesting representations: one, lively and fine, shows two peacocks each aside a large vase; a second one shows us a vase to drink in with a deep and thin basin with two handles (càntaro), placed onto two acanthus leaves and grape branches, from which two vine-shoots come out.

A fourth panel repeats the motifs of the second one.

In this room, furthermore, the four segments of the vault of the church of the former convent of Santa Chiara, erected in 1255 and demolished in 1805, are collocated.

The **frescos**, now put on canvas, of Rimini's school, represent, from the left, the first one St. Jerome and St. Matthew, the second St. Ambrose and St. Mark, the third St. Augustine and St. John, the last St. Gregory and St. Luke, i.e. some Doctors of the church and

Basilica of San Vitale.

ENTRANCE TO THE BASILICA

To find the entrance to the basilica see the map on page 21. From San Vitale Street go to the gate (n. 25 on the map) opening into the courtyards of the Monastery. Going through the courtyards (n. 23 and 62 on the map) reach the Entrance (between n. 39 and 35 on the map, where a staircase is drawn and where the Ticket Office is situated). Enter then the cloister (n. 33) and go downstairs into the narthex.

the Evangelists, the latter marked by their symbols. The frescos of the walls of the chapel representing the Nativity, the Adoration of the Three Kings, the Crucifixion, the Announcement and the four figures of the Saints are missing here.

It is the work that the painter *Pietro da Rimini* with some collaborators carried out round about the half of the 14th century and which is one of the most important works of Rimini's school and one of the most significant of the century.

Setting these frescos in their historical background it shows itself the enormous influence which Giotto exerted on the painting, creating especially in Rimini an artistic centre of very high quality. The Riminese school received its work bases from the work of two great unknown artists who worked during the first years of the 14th century in the Church of Saint Augustine in Rimini. One of these, maybe a collaborator of Giotto, fused together typical ways of the master with Byzantine remembrances, the other joined Giotto's lesson with Roman monumental accents. Both of them gave an incredible start to the school of Rimini, which then spread out in the frescoes of the anonymous painter who painted the refectory of Pomposa Abbey (1317-1320). The three unknown masters represent the top of Rimini's school; moved by Giotto's way of painting, they were the pioneers who opened a new way to other artists who, after their discoveries were able to dedicate themselves to elaborate the most vital aspects. The same occurred for the unknown painter in San Pietro in Sylvis near Bagnacavallo and also for Pietro da Rimini in Santa Chiara in Ravenna.

The innovation in these frescos in relation to the style of the school of Rimini is in the research of movement and drama, and this explains the complex articulation of the thrones, from which the figures emerge with great power. In comparison to the calm of the preceeding paintings, here noises and uproars break the enchantment of the ancient silence, and an expressionistic wave puts in agitation the already compact and complete forms (Bottari). Even better this could be seen in the representations of the walls that are here missing.

At the end of the refectory there are two rooms (ENTRANCE OF THE BIG REFECTORY with little rooms, P.F. n. 37; PASSAGE TO THE BIG REFECTORY, P.F. n. 36) which once constituted the entrance to the refectory itself.

From the entrance hall we reach the big cloister (Fiandrini plan n. 33, whose description can be found on page 52). We go to the side of the cloister from which two stairs (eastern side) lead down to the entrance of the basilica, made up by a porch with rectangular plan ending in two little apses (forcep shaped narthex).

SAN VITALE

The narthex as we can notice from the plan of the basilica, doesn't lean against one of the sides of the octagon, but against one of the vertices, we don't know if for pratical reasons of for artistic ones. In such a way two little thin sectors on the extremities of which two round staired towers to reach the women's gallery are placed. The three-mullioned entrance of the

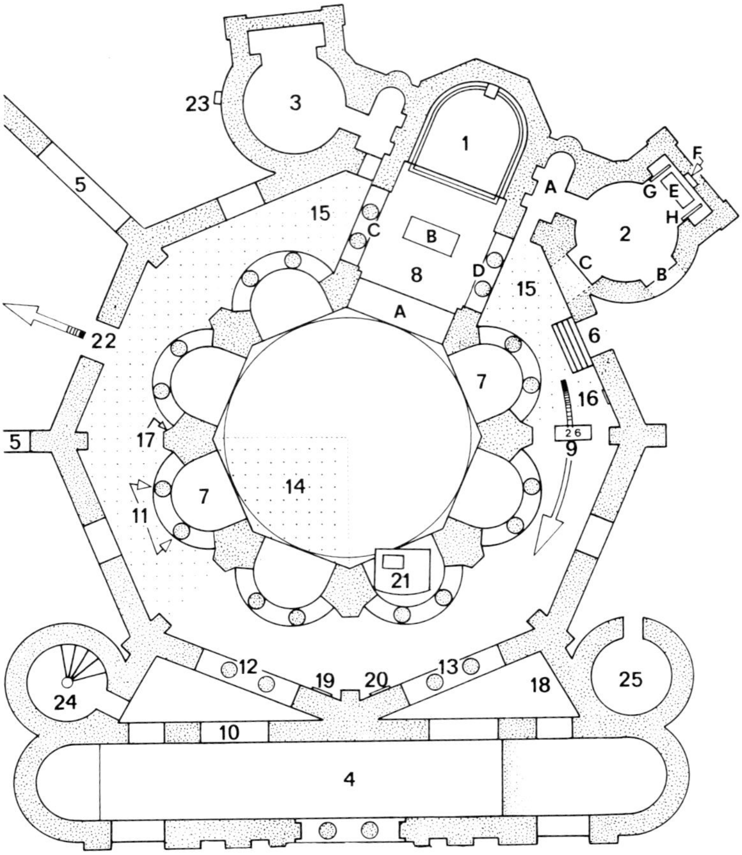

narthex was built in 1929, with columns that were in the store-room of the museum, smoothe pulvinoes deliberately built, and two identical capitals one of which was taken from the museum and considered to be original, the other one was taken from the parish church of Cesato nearby Faenza. In 1929 also the vault of the narthex and the little Northern apse were built while the Southern apse is found in the room of the big staircase which leads to the superior rooms.

We don't have any trace of a great quadriportico which preceeded the narthex, not to be mistaken, it is obvious, with the actual cloister of one thousand years more recent.

Historical outlines about the basilica - The construction had been commissioned by Bishop Ecclesius in 526, on return from a mission in Constantinople, and it is not to be excluded that the idea of a church with a central plan had arisen during a journey in the east where such an architectural model was very diffused.

The church was consecrated by the third successor of Ecclesius, Maximian, on the 17th May of the year 547 or 548. Therefore it took 21 or 22 years to complete the building, and from that time more than one thousand four hundred years have passed. Furthermore, attaining ourselves to dates, the construction of the building had been started under the reign of the Goths and was finished under that of the Byzantines, who had conquered Ravenna in the year 540.

The construction was financed by Giuliano Argentario, a banker of Byzantine origin, who spent for it 26.000 gold coins. Giuliano Argentario financed completely or in part also other sacred constructions of Ravenna, like Sant'Apollinare in Classe, San Michele in Africisco (along with his son-in-law Bacauda) and, may be, also Santa Maria Maggiore. The definition of Giuliano as a banker is given from the adjec-

Fig. 3 - **Basilica of San Vitale**: plan: 1, Apse. 2, *Prothesis - Sancta Sanctorum*. (2A - Apse cell. 2B - Niche in front of the entrance of the chapel called *Sancta Sanctorum*.
2C - Paving mosaic. 2E - The front of Bishop Ecclesius' sarcophagus. 2F - Chapel. 2G-H - Drainers of Ursicino and Ecclesius.) 3, *Diaconicon* - Chapel of the Blessed Virgin.
4, Narthex. 5, External buttresses. 6, Entrance to the basilica. 7, Exedrae. 8, Presbytery. (8A - Intrados of the arch of the presbytery. 8B - Altar. 8C-D - Columns that divide the presbytery from the ambulatory. 10, Ancient entrances to the narthex. 11, Columns of the exedrae. 12-13, Large three-mullioned entrances nearby the narthex.
14-15, Remainders of the original mosaic floor.
16, Remainders of the original coverings. 17, Figure of a monk in the veins of the marble covering. 18, Remainders of the original stuccoes. 19-20, Inscriptions. 21, Sacellum of San Vitale. 22, Exit for the Mausoleum of Galla Placidia.
23, Remainders of a vestibule of the 9th-10th century.
24, Staired Tower. 26, Sarcophagus of Isacio.
◀

tive *Argentario*, which indicates someone who deals, handles money and gets profit out of it. It was also thought, wrongly, that he had been the architect of the basilica. Finally he was thought to be instead an agent of Justinian, emperor of Constantinople, provided with large means with which he could promote in Ravenna spectacular ventures so as to propitiate the Byzantine penetration in view of a real conquest.

Unfortunately we don't know the name of the architect of San Vitale, who certainly was a man of great artistic sensibility and of a daring technical thought.

Architectural Characteristics - San Vitale is a building with a central octagonal plan composed of two bodies: an internal higher one that contains the dome, and an external one that contains the perimetral ambulatory on the ground and the women's gallery on the first floor.

With the external perimeter it is joined the whole of the apse (see on the map, picture 3 - n. 1, 2, 3) and opposite in asymmetrical position, as you can see from the map, the one of the narthex (4) that was one of the sides of the quadriportico, former monumental entrance to the church.

The **dome**, of 16 meters diameter is composed of many rings of fictile tubes stuck one into the other so as to make a strong but light structure. They are the clay tubes, between 15 and 21 centimeters of length, with a diametre between 5-7 centimeters, composed of a cylindrical part finishing into a cone trunk, which were moulded in the lathe and baked. The props of the vaults are reinforced with the insertion of wine amphorae. The dome is covered by a pyramidal roof, independent from the vault, and it serves as protection. In Ravenna such a structure is present also in the two baptisteries, and anticipates that system of crowning that will be used in the Romanesque architecture and that will be called «a tiburio».

The central plan is rare in the ancient Italian churches and San Vitale is one of the most typical and most illustrious examples.

The **walling** is in face-brick, as in all the ancient buildings of Ravenna, in which stone, when it is present, has a more decorative function than a constructive one. The reason of this is due to the fact that stone of any kind doesn't exist here and therefore it was necessary to import it with high costs of transport and with great technical difficulties. Observing the walling of the little apse on the side of the entrance we can see that the bricks used are very long and thin (48 cm of length; 4 cm of thickness) and joined together with clay interstices of the same thickness. We will notice, in the prosecution of the visit, that the bricks used in the Mausoleum of Galla Placidia, and that is about 100 years before, are shorter, bigger and with a very thin clay interstice.

The external characteristics of the building are sober and clean and put in clear evidence the central interpenetration of the two octagonal prisms which form its principal body. We can notice a lively movement of volumes only in the apse part.

The walls are reinforced by pilasters that reach the roof and by strong angular pillars that end with a little triangular tympanum. There are then two big arched buttresses (5) that we shall see later on.

The lateral doors are five: two nearby the

1 2 / 3 — 1, Basilica of San Vitale: apse. 2, Basilica of San Vitale: the inside photographed from the altar area. We can see the mosaics of Abels and Melchizedek offering (on the left) and the scene of Sarar and Abraham. 3, Basilica of San Vitale: the mosaic of the left wall of the presbytery, inferior part.

stairéd towers, two that we shall meet further on and this one, restored in the 16th century.

The internal space - Having gone in the basilica, we find ourselves immersed into an architectural space highly suggestive. In fact, the planner knew how to organize it with a wise game of full and empty, of curved and plain surfaces giving place to alterning lights and shadows, which together with the colour effects of the marble, of the frescos and, especially of the mosaics, gives to the whole an extraordinary lightness, without however concealing the impression of daring and power transmitted by the big polygonal pillars that sustain the vault.

The wings composed of pillars, then, proposing various perspectives increase the deepness of the spaces lying behind, always immersed in the faint light which filtres through the alabastered windows.

To enjoy the fine architectural rythme of the great hall, let's bring ourselves in the centre of the octagon and let's admire, among the great pillars, the loveliness of the colonnades, in two orders, of the seven exedrae (7) that join them: let's give a first look together, finally, to the presbytery (1-8) that from this point of observation seems to sink into an unreal light especially in the morning hours, when the sun shines through the windows exhalting the brilliancy of the colours.

At this first reconnaissance standing still let's follow one in movement, bringing ourselves in the ambulatory and walking through it with our look towards the centre (9): we shall so be able to admire the variation of the perspective and of the backgrounds and their rhythmic coming back as effect of the regular geometry of the construction.

Let's go towards the presbytery and the apse to visit the mosaic part.

Intrados of the great arch of the presbytery: Neptune's throne Fig. 3 (8-A) - Let's go to the centre of the great arch which introduces to the presbytery. At the base there are two Roman reliefs which represent NEPTUNE'S THRONE. Two empty thrones are sculptured on it with the back covered by a cloth, perhaps the divinity's mantel. On the stool something like a sea monster (pistrice), around which several cupids hold the attributes of the God: a shell and a trident. Under the throne there is a sea-monster: in the higher frame there is a motif with dolphins, tridents and shells. The representation of the throne without the divinity will repeat itself in Ravenna in the mosaic of the Neonian Baptistery and the Baptistery of the Arians, and it can be considered as a refusal of the anthropomorphous representation of the divinity that will end up, later, in the iconoclast movement. Images like these in Ravenna whose subject is the throne (here Neptune's, elsewhere of other divinities, such as Saturn, Mars, Bacchus, etc.) acted (whenas we refer to puttos) as patterns for sculptors of the Renaissance. Some scholars antedate now these sculptures from the 2nd to the 1st cent. A.D.

The lateral columns of the reliefs (two for every relief), supported the ciborium of the altar of San Vitale. Three of them are of verd antique and the darker one is of a very rare Egyptian green breccia. The columns and reliefs were composed in the 16th century as they appear now.

Intrados of the great arch of the presbytery: Mosaic strip Fig. 3 (8-A) - Let's start our visit

1 2 3 4
5

1, an open-worked capital.

2, the Divine Lamb on the vault of the presbytery.

3, peacock and doves.

4, presbytery: Moses that grazes the flock.

5, particular of the apse mosaic: the Redeemer and two archangels.

Fig. 4 - BASILICA OF SAN VITALE: graphical scheme of the left wall of the presbytery, inferior part: 1, Abraham's house. 2, Sarah. 3, Abraham. 4, Angels, messengers of God. 5, Oak-tree of the Mambre valley. 6, Abraham that is going to sacrifice Isaac. 7, Isaac. 8, The hand of God. 9, Moses in the solitude of the Sinai receives the Law. 10, Aaron and the representatives of the tribes of Israel. 11, The prophet Jeremiah. 12, Angels that show the symbol of the cross.

Fig. 5 - BASILICA OF SAN VITALE: scheme of the left wall of the presbytery, upper part: 1, John the Evangelist. 2, The eagle his symbol. 3, Luke the Evangelist. 4, The calf his symbol. 5-6, Decorations with vine-shoots. 7, Basket-like capitals with wavy sides. 8, Pulvinoes with monogram of the bishop Vittore.

from the most interesting and spectacular part of the church by observing the intrados of the arch under which we are. The decorative strip that covers it starting from the two thrones of Neptune is surrounded by a very lively frieze and contains fifteen medallions with the portraits of Christ (above in the middle), of the Saints Protasius and Gervasius (below, one per side). On the inside of every medallion there is the name of the character represented. Between one medallion and the other, with a decorative function, are collocated two dolphins which interlace their tails.

The fifteen medallions are work of different people: from the examination of the portraits, in fact, we can suppose the intervention of an artist with great plastic vigour: let's observe for example the wonderful faces of Peter, Mark, of the most beautiful Andrew, of Paul with such a penetrating look. Then a second and less powerful artist worked but gifted with a more delicate painting sensibility, who executed the portraits of Bartholomew, Taddeus, James Alpheus son, John, Philip. Finally there are the portraits of Protasius, Simon, Thomas and other who for their mediocrity are assigned to the work of simple workers.

Presbytery: vault - Let's go on for a few steps till the centre of the presbytery and let's look up the vault. The vision would be much easier with a binocular. In the afternoon hours it is better to switch on the lights.

The decoration of the vault is divided in four sections by means of festoons of leaves and fruit that flow into a central garland, in which the white Divine lamb on a starred background stands out and shows up.

The four sections are occupied by shoots of acanthus that start off from a tuft in the centre of the base and, with always narrower volutes, reach up to the arms of the angel placed at the

Fig. 6 - BASILICA OF SAN VITALE: scheme of the left wall of the presbytery, lower part: 1, Abel. 2, Melchizedek. 3, The hand of God. 4, the young Moses grazing the flock. 5, Moses taking his sandals off before entering in the burning thornbush. 6, the prophet Isaiah.

top of every section. Inside the volutes many species of birds and other animals are represented.

The mosaic that we are observing has been remade for about a fifth in distemper (a very thin white line, slightly visible from the ground with a naked eye, indicates the limit of the remaking) but it hasn't lost anything of its original splendour.

Presbytery: left wall (fig. 4 and 5) - From the centre let's go under the arches of the right wall of the presbytery to observe from a more favourable position the left wall.

Above the great three-mullioned window of the ground floor there is a lunette which, with a narrative solution of a nearly cinematographical kind, contains two scenes of a unique event that symbolize the unshakable faith in the word of God and the obedience without hesitations to his orders: the story of Abraham and his son Isaac.

Keeping our eye on the scheme of figure 4 it will be easy to follow the development of the situations represented.

From the left we see the hut of Abraham (1) on the door of which the sterile wife Sarah appears (2). Abraham (3) offers a tray of food (a calf) to the three characters sitting at the table (4) near the oak-tree of the valley of Mambre (5). The divine messengers have come to announce the Patriarch, who is 99 years old (his wife is 89) a near happy event, considered impossible: the birth of a son.

The branches of the oak-tree have as background coloured clouds which, expanding themselves towards the right, connect the scene now described with its continuation. In (6), infact, there is still Abraham, who, in obedience to the will of God, has brought his son Isaac (7) on the mountain and is going to sacrifice him thrusting him with a sword. But God, as we all know, only wanted to try the obedience of Abraham, and prevented the sacrifice to take place: therefore we see his hand (8) that comes out of the clouds to stop the hand of the patriarch that is going to strike. At Abraham's feet there is the ram, not entangled in the branches of a shrub as instead is said in the Genesis (XXII, 2, 13), that will substitute the human victim.

All the scene is very lively, both for the brightness of the colours and for the quantities of landscapes that move it.

Outside the lunette, high on the right (9), there is the figure of Moses young who, in the solitude of the Sinai, represented with a fantastic matching of colours, receives the rolls of law from the hand of God, who once again comes out from the clouds. Lower (10), in a compact group, Aaron entertains the representatives of the twelve tribes of Israel that are nearly waiting for a new covenant with God.

High on the left, the prophet Jeremiah that opens in his hands the big roll (11). In the centre (12), two angels show the symbol of the cross. Looking up above the lunette now described, we see the opening of the big three-mullioned window that from the women's gallery looks into the presbytery. On its sides there are two wide panels: on the one on the left (scheme fig. 5) is represented John the Evangelist (1) with the eagle his symbol (2): on the one on the right Luke the Evangelist with a calf that symbolizes him (4).

The realistic atmosphere of the two scenes is rich for agreeable particulars: Let's observe, for example the elegant little heron below the figure of Luke.

The mosaic decorations of the wall are com-

Fig. 7 - BASILICA OF SAN VITALE: scheme of the right wall of the presbytery, superior part.
1, Matthew the Evangelist.
2, The angel, his symbol.
3, Mark the Evangelist.
4, The lion his symbol.
5, basket-like capitals.
6, Pulvinoes with monogram of Giuliano Argentario.

pleted by two series of volutes of vine shoots that expand from two vases on the sides of the three-mullioned window (5 and 6).

On this wall, as on the opposite one that we shall describe with attention the variety of the friezes, of the frames and of the smallest decorative particulars, which witness a fervid fantasy must be observed. We can moreover affirm that one of the most notable richnesses of the mosaic cycle of the presbytery is exactly in the meticulous care of the particulars of contour and background.

The ancient and unknown mosaicist, so sure and, lively in the solution of the movement of the figures, in giving the changing tones in shining vibrations, in filling the backgrounds up without making them too heavy in spite of more significant ones, appears rather awkward, instead, when the representation implies linear perspective solutions. Let's notice for example, the table at which the angels sit, the sacrificing altar of Isaac and Abraham's hut: they are represented with a primitive perspective, similar to the one used by children in their drawings.

On the table notice three loaves that from a perspective point of view, instead of being laid on top of the table are represented frontally, as if they were standing upright. This, while it doesn't take any beauty away from the scenes, moreover, it enriches them with a touch of naivety, mustn't surprize us; infact, many centuries have still to pass before certain formal solutions, like the linear perspective, are considered by the artists an important element in their representations.

Presbytery: right wall (fig. 6 and 7) - The composing scheme of the right wall is exactly the same as that of the wall we have already observed (scheme Fig. 6).

On the lunette there are two sacred scenes which both carry out the theme of offering: on the left Abel (1), dressed as a shepherd with a red cloak, comes out of his hut and offers a lamb before an altar covered by a white cloth with embroided hems, on which there are two loaves and a chalice with handles containing wine; on the right, Melchizedek (2), coming from a rich temple in solemn paludaments, offers a bread. The hand of God (3) coming out from these clouds seems to accept the offer. On the grass some lilies bloom.

On the left of the lunette there are other two scenes; on the low side there is Moses young that grazes the flock of sheep (4) and, higher, Moses again that unties his shoes to enter into the burning bramble-bush, represented by the crown of flames that surrounds the white figure of the legislator. Of great pictorial effect is the representation of Mount Horeb. High on the right, the prophet Isaiah, represented with the nimbus and with a volume rolled up in his hands. Next to him there is an exedra on which a crown is placed.

Next to the three-mullioned window of the women's gallery (scheme fig. 7), on the left Matthew the Evangelist (1) with the angel his symbol (2), and on the right Mark the Evangelist (3) surmounted by a lion that symbolizes him.

Presbytery: arch of the apse - Let us now go towards the apse after having returned to the centre of the presbytery.

On the external façade of the arch which lets us into the apse the cities of Jerusalem and of Bethlehem are represented ideally. The walls of the two cities are adorned by vivid gems. In the centre, two flying angels show an iridescent disc carrying an alpha in the centre.

Fig. 9 - BASILICA OF SAN VITALE: scheme of the left wall of the apse: 1, Emperor Justinian. 2, A group of soldiers. 3, Maximian. 4, Giuliano Argentario or maybe, the praefectus praetorio. 5, Maybe Belisarius, the conqueror of Ravenna.

◀ Fig. 8 - BASILICA OF SAN VITALE: semi-vault of the apse: 1, The Redeemer. 2-3, Two archangels. 4, San Vitale. 5, The bishop Ecclesius.

Presbytery: altar (fig. 3 8-B) - In the presbytery a very ancient altar is collocated, whose wide and splendid table is made of a thick slab of alabaster (with an electric torch placed underneath we would see its warm opalescence). Even the three sides are in alabaster.

On the front a latin cross is sculptured bordered by two lambs; two festoons come down from two crowns. Mazzotti writes: «*as date I have no doubt that the altar can be assigned to the sixth century; I wouldn't answer with the same security if it was made with the basilica; that is, if it is the altar that consacrated Maximian of Pola in 548*». The great altar, that in centuries suffered various shiftings and of which we had lost news, was placed here again at the end of the last century, and since 1930 it is supported by four angular little columns of verd antique marble with bases and capitals.

Apse: semi-vault (fig. 8) - On the semi-vault of the apse (scheme fig. 8) the classical scene of theophany or manifestation of appearance of God in a sensible form.

In the centre a young beardless Redeemer (1), dressed in purple, sits on a blue globe between two archangels (2 and 3). From the rocks below flow stylized, the four rivers of Eden (Phison, Ghihon, Tigris, Eufratis) which symbolize the four Gospels.

Christ holds in his left hand the roll of the seven seals and gives with the right the crown to the forthcoming Vitale (4) who is wearing a very decorated military cloak.

Fig. 10 - BASILICA OF SAN VITALE: scheme of the right wall of the apse: 1, Empress Theodora. 2, Dignitaries of court.
4-5, Maybe Antonina and Giovannina wife and daughter of Belisarius.

On the right bishop Ecclesius (5) is represented, founder of the basilica, who presents the model of the construction. The figure of the founder of churches who presents the model of the construction to the divinity or to the saint is an iconographical model very frequent in all the Christian art nearly till our days.

Lower, rocks and multi-coloured flowers; on top some clouds. But, the figures stand out directly on a golden background without any landscape sign.

The scenes of the presbytery, as we have seen are rich of naturalistic elements, they are placed in a well defined reality, even if it is stylized and poetically transfigured; in the apse, on the contrary, the scenes take place in a rarified atmosphere and place themselves as if they were out of space and time.

As so radical contrast of representative conception can't be simply explained with the fact that the two mosaic complexes are work of several artists. Infact, in reality, more than several artists, we find ourselves in front of two different artistic-cultural traditions: of Roman-Western Tradition the «concrete» mosaicist of the presbytery; of Eastern-Byzantine tradition the «abstract» artist of the apse. A kind of encounter-clash, to come to the point, between two figurative civilizations, that is like saying between two different conceptions of life, not exempted, however, from mutual exchanges.

The wall of the apse below the semi-vault was covered in 1903 by marble inlays with a large use of porphyry. In the same year also the seat of Greek marble was built.

Apse: left part (fig. 9) - Let's now look up to the left on the big rectangular panel that represents the emperor Justinian (scheme fig. 9 n. 1) with his suite. The figure of the ruler of Byzantium stands out for the richness of his purple garments and for a halo which surrounds his face a symbol of his power of divine origin. The emperor carries a big golden paten as offer for the sacrifice of mass.

The characters that accompany the emperor are represented frontally and reduced to pure rigid outlines and without volume, according to the Byzantine tradition. The scene, of chromatic intonation rather monotonous, is livened up by the colours of the garments of the soldiers on the left (2).

On the left of Justinian (on the right of who is looking) the figure of the archbishop Maximian (3) stands out, the only character whose name is on the background, who holds a gemmed cross in the right hand. Notice the exceptional artistic quality of his face, obviously it is his portrait, full of truth and life. Maximian was consecrated bishop of Ravenna at the age of 48, in 546. He arrived in Ravenna at the end of 546 or at the beginning of 547. He became archbishop between 551 and 554 (he was the first archbishop of the west), he died in 556.

Between the emperor and the archbishop, in the second row, there is a character (4) whose strongly characterized physionomy makes us think of a portrait; maybe it is Giuliano Argentario, the maecenas, or maybe the *Praefectus Praetorio*. Being the latter the governor of Italy, he represented at the consecration the imperial couple, who never came to Ravenna.

As for the other dignitaries we don't have sure elements of recognition. The one on the right of Justinian (on the left of who is looking), could be Belisarius (5), the conqueror of Ravenna, victorious on the reign of the Goths.

Apse: right wall (fig. 10) - In front of the panel with the suite of the emperor there is the panel with the suite of the empress Theodora (scheme fig. 10 n. 1), recognizable for her stature, the richness of her garments, of her jewels and for the diadem and the golden halo that surrounds her head. The empress carries a chalice for the celebration of mass. On the inferior hem of the garment there is an embroidery with another offer: the arrival of the three kings with gifts for Jesus. The decorative motif of the embroidery will be also found more developed on the sarcophagus of Isacio, here in San Vitale, and then on the side of a little marble box now at the archiepiscopal Museum and, in all its possible opulence, in the big mosaics of Sant'Apollinare Nuovo. On the left there is a little column surmounted by a calice that emanates a gush of water.

The suite is preceeded by two dignitaries (2 and 3) and it is composed of seven ladies who follow Theodora. The first two (4 and 5), who have somatical characters quite different, could be Antonina and Giovannina, Belisarius' wife and daughter, who seemed to be very close friends of the empress. The other five have faces nearly all the same and have no other function than that of filling the picture, giving the impression of a very numerous suite. This mosaic is, from a chromatic point of view, much livelier than the one in front, thanks to major fantasy and polycromy, which distinguishes the female fashion from the male one.

Basilica of San Vitale: Justinian and Theodora.

Also here the figures are deprived of any material thickness and reduced nearly to symbols of aristocratic humanity.

Both the scenes, as well as their artistic value, have a documentary one really extraordinary. From them in fact, although the stylizations, we can deduce the splendour of the Byzantine court, the fashion of the garments, the colour and the decoration of the materials used.

As we have already said, Justinian and Theodora never came to Ravenna, therefore the two pictures don't represent a ceremony that really took place, but they are a symbolic image of the oblation of imperial gifts to the church of Ravenna. The theme of the two mosaics is the offer of the chalice and of the paten for the Eucharist.

The frescos - Having finished visiting the mosaics, we can dedicate ourselves to the discovery of other aspects of the church, less striking but not less important and less pleasant.

Let's start from the frescos that cover the vault of the central body. Executed between 1780 and 1782, even if they are not connected to the spirit of the architecture in which they are, and to the spirit of the primitive mosaic decoration - the agitated barocco doesn't agree well with the severity and the composure of the Early Christian Art - contribute to create a soft golden atmosphere in which we are immersed.

Considered then on their own are the valuable works of the painters Ubaldo Gandolfi and Iacopo Guarana and of the Bolognese decorator Serafino Barozzi. The Gandolfi painted the central disc. At his death Guarana took his place, he did the figures of the clouds, which show ciboria, harps, chalices, crowns, books etc. Barozzi painted the frames, the balustrades, the loggias, the columns, the lacunars, the festoons, the leaves, the flowers, the fruit. The pictures are bright until the height of the big arches and in the vaults of the exedrae, soft lower, till the pulvinoes of the fourteen columns and till the marbles of the pillars. Before the present paintings the dome, that was never covered by mosaic, accommodated other paintings. The first ones in a period between 1000 and 1400, the following ones in the years 1541-1543, work of Giacomo Bertucci and Giulio Tonduzzi from Faenza.

At the bottom of the paintings, above the arches we notice two of the eight niches which constituted nearly a third order, after the ambulatory and the women's gallery, which alternated the windows placed a little higher.

A fragment of the ancient painting appears above the door which leads to the chapel on the right of the apse.

The capitals - One of the characteristics of this church is given by the openworked capitals. Among them are particularly notable for their beauty especially those of the columns which divide the presbytery from the ambulatory and those of the columns of the two overhanging three-mullioned windows (fig. 3 n. 8 C-D).

The first ones have an upside down pyramid shaft and slightly swollen, as if it were for effect of the weight. Observe the four faces: they are opendecorated by a ribbon of leaves, branches and flowers which, twisting in regular volutes, finish to close five circumferences arranged in such a way as to form a cross.

The capitals of the three-mullioned windows of the women's gallery are in a basket-like form; those on the right wall (fig. 7 n. 5) have the faces adorned by a cantharus or by one or

◀
Basilica of San Vitale: floor.

▶
Basilica of San Vitale: particular of the mosaic of the floor of San Vitale memorial chapel: cantharus and peacocks.

two cornucopias from which vine branches come out. The faces are delimited by a frame of vegetable motifs; in the centre of one of them there is a disc on which maybe a monogram had to be sculptured.

The capitals of the three-mullioned window on the left have wavy faces (fig. 5 n. 7). The columns are made of onyx.

The fourteen columns on the ground floor of the exedrae (fig. 3 n. 11) are topped by lotus leaf type impost-capitals with stylized palmettes flanked by lotus leaves. It is a decoration with flat relief, without any plastic sign: a drawing engraved in stone.

The capitals that we have observed have the pleasant and surprizing aspect of stone lace: of works, that is in which a patient work of chisel and drill have been able to subtract from the materials its natural heaviness. The openwork, already pictorial on its own, is here and there enrichened by golden heighteners, by crimson shades and touches of green, not very visible now, but which must have conferred originally to the reliefs a very lively aspect.

On one of the two great three-mullioned doors which lead to the narthex (12) there are composite capitals with acanthus made in big indents, the same as those of the fourteen columns of the women's gallery. On the other three-mullioned door (13) there are capitals with acanthus leaves but indented thinly.

On the **pulvinoes** of the columns of the exedrae on the ground floor, on both faces - towards the inside and towards the ambulatory - there is in flat relief, a monogram in Greek letters that is interpreted as VITTORE, one of the four bishops which succeeded each other during the building of the basilica. The same monogram is on the pulvinoes of the columns of the three-mullioned window of the women's gallery which opens on the left wall of the presbytery (fig. 5 n. 8). Instead on the two pulvinoes of the columns in front (fig. 7 n. 6) there is a monogram, graffito and not relieved, assigned to GIULIANO, the financer of the basilica.

On the pulvinoes of the columns of the exedrae in the women's gallery, on the face that looks towards the centre of the church there is a cross bordered by two big leaves of acanthus.

The beautiful four pulvinoes in the presbytery show, on the face towards the ambulatory, a cantharos with peacocks; on the face towards the presbytery, two lambs with a paw lifted on the sides of a Latin cross coloured in gold, and two cypresses on the background; on the long sides, two ornamental motifs composed by a tuft of acanthus (fig. 3 n. 8 C-D).

The floor - The floor of the central octagon is of the 16th century, except the two sectors which date back to the time of the construction of the basilica, i.e. 6th century. These sectors are in mosaic (fig. 3 n. 14), while the more recent parts are in marble inlay. Notice that the floor level of the basilica of San Vitale is the only one of the ancient churches of Ravenna still at the original quote.

Also in the ambulatory, on the left and on the right of the presbytery (fig. 3 n. 15) there are large tracts of floor in mosaic with a big variety of ornamental motifs. They are in major part redone on the traces of original fragments existing in loco.

The floor of the presbytery is of the beginning of our century, designed on the prints left by the original marbles and mosaics. Also the floor of the apse is of recent times, and even if it inspires to ancient motifs, it is completely invented. Recently a remarkable work of restora-

tion of the floors of the basilica has been done; pieces have been repaired and put back again and integrative interventions have been carried out with lighter tesserae, and separating the original parts from the completing ones, marked by rows of glasses and tesserae put sideways.

Vault of the ambulatory - In origin the covering of the ambulatory was made of wood with lacunaries. A thesis (C. Ricci) wants that the substitution of the wood with bricks happened not long after the construction of the church to avoid danger of fire; another thesis (Gerola) wants the operation to have been done in the Romanesque Age, with the consequent construction of the big external arched buttresses (fig. 3 n. 5) so as to counterbalance the new thrusts.

Coverings - On the perimetrical wall there are the remains of the ancient covering. Once, starting from the floor, there was a marbel skirting-board on which, divided by a fillet of rectangular section, there was a band of African marble slabs alternated with Greek slabs. A frieze followed about forty centimetres high with inlays of porphyry, serpentine and mother-of-pearl, delimited by marble fillets. Over the inlaid band there was another one of marble slabs, surmounted by a second fillet and by a last band of Greek marble about sixty centimetres high. The visitor can rebuild this covering helping himself with white substantial fragments still existing (fig. 3 n. 16).

On an independent panel a fresco of the 15th century has been put back, on the wall on the left of the entrance, which was torn and repaired in 1976.

The covering of the great poligonal pilasters was collocated during the repair finished in 1869, and it repeats more or less the original one.

A curiosity: on the pillar marked on the plant with n. 17, in the position indicated by the arrow, high up, the veining of the two marble slabs opposite to one another form the figure, vague but still well perceptible, of a monk wrapped in a wide soutane.

Here and there on the pillars, some people see other figures. The research can be rich of possibilities: a little as if it were lead on mutable game of clouds or on the test tables of Rorschach.

Plasters - The space over the marble covering, till the primitive ceiling made of lacunars, was anciently covered by plasters. The beauty of this decoration can be revealed by what is left of it in the underarches of the two inferior three-mullioned doors of the presbytery (8-C), on the back wall and on the vault of one of the triangular rooms between the narthex and the body of the basilica (18), and on the underarches of the two three-mullioned doors which lead into the above mentioned rooms.

On the two three-mullioned doors of the presbytery there is a rich decoration in which also the colour takes part. The plasters of the wall and of the vault of the triangular room are made up by tufts of acanthus, branches, flowers and leaves, candlesticks with long stalks with leaves and branches, shoots that come out from a cantharos, little panels with a leaf, etc. On the underarches of the three-mullioned doors that lead to the narthex there is a double motif carried out with volutes, with leaves and flowers in the empty spaces, and birds.

Inscriptions - Hung up on the walls there are

◄
Basilica of San Vitale: presbytery. Great ornamental motif above the three-mullioned window of the women's gallery.

►
Basilica of San Vitale: Isacio's sarcophagus.

two slabs (19 and 20) sculptured in 1947, one thousand four hundred years after the consecration of the church, which reproduce two already existing inscriptions according to the testimony of the historian Agnellus.

The one that starts with: «ARDUA CONSURGUNT VENERANDO CULMINE TEMPLA...» which translated means: «*The great temple with a praising dome arises, sacred to God under the name of Vitale, and Gervasio with Protasio occupy this dwelling, united in birth, in faith and in temple. To these sons the father while escaping the infections of the world, was example of faith and martyrdom. Ecclesius was the first to entrust this dwelling to Giuliano, who executed the work wonderfully*».

The one that starts: «BEATI MARTYRIS VITALIS...» says: «*the temple of the blessed martyr Vitale, under the will of the bishop Ecclesius, Giuliano Argentario built, adorned and inaugurated, consecrating it to the very reverend bishop Maximian*».

Windows - In the apse, on the windows of the galleries and on the big ones of the dome there is modern alabastered glass supplied by the firm Quentin of Florence.

Sacellum of San Vitale (fig. 3 n. 21) - According to the legend from the pseudo Ambrose, already famous at Ecclesius's time, Vitale fought in the Roman army under the rule of the emperor Nero. Finding himself garrison in Ravenna and on discovering his joining to the Christian religion, it seems he was thrown into a well then covered by stones. The well of martyrdom seems to be in the place where now a basin full of water opens, in which, the tourists like to throw a good-wishing coin. In that place, in remembrance of the martyrdom, a sacellum was erected, which originally consisted of a rectangular room of m, 8,48 of length. The mosaic floor has been recently recomposed and collocated near the sacellum, on a metallic framing. On it there are swastikas and a *cantharus*. In loco the basement of the original altar still exists. It shows the seats of the four little colums which sustained the table and, in the middle, the little groove for the relics, we don't know if it was incorporated in a cippus. The sacellum is previous to the construction of the basilica and it doesn't date back beyond the last years of the 5th century.

The basin also serves for the draining of the water that otherwise would invade the basilica, whose plane is now under the level of the water - bearing stratum; from it infact, a piping starts off through which, by means of a pump, the water is sucked up when it reaches a pre-arranged level. The suction plant is contained in a little container that you can see leaned against the wall of the yard on the left going towards the Mausoleum of Galla Placidia.

Sarcophagus of Isacio - In the ambulatory, recently the sarcophagus of Isacio has been collocated (fig. 3 n. 26) (before it was in the chapel on the right of apse), which dates to the first years of the 5th century (De Francovich: end of the 4th century). It is so called because not long before the middle of the 7th century it was reused to contain the mortal remains of the Armenian governor Isacio, who died in 643, as is said by the Greek and Latin inscriptions on the lid, which is not the original one. On the *front* there is an adoration of the three Kings of clear and vigorous relief; on the left there is the Blessed Mary sitting down, with the child on her lap who stretches out to receive the gifts, above, there is a star. The Three Kings go on with their cloaks fluttering over the oriental costume

(Phrygian cap, trousers and a short tunic) carrying in their right hand the gifts. On the left *side* Daniel in the lions' pit is represented, on the right one, the resurrection of Lazarus. On the *back*, in flat relief, there is the Constantinian monogram bordered by two peacocks, behind which there are two palms. On the whole it is a work of very high quality.

Chapel on the right of the apse - (plan fig. 3 n. 2) - To get to the chapel on the right of the apse, called «Sancta Sanctorum», you must get the guardian to open the gate.

You enter into a little room (apse cell) (2-A) in which on the left, there are two niches that were used to place the vases and the objects used for daily functions. In this place the monks had made a stair to get to the women's gallery, which was taken away in 1863. From the cell you pass into the ancient prothesis, coeval to the basilica. Here the sacred vessels and vestments were collocated and here the priests prepared themselves for the liturgical functions.

The accesses to the prothesis were two, the actual one and an external one, from which today we see the niche in front of the entrance (2-B).

This place was then changed into a sepulchral cell, dedicated to the Saints Nazario and Celso, and it contained the bodies of the bishops Ecclesius, Ursicinus and Vittore. To collocate the sarcophagi, the two entrances which we spoke about a little were closed and a door which lead directly into the basilica was opened. On the plane of this recess there is a little tract of pavement mosaic left (2-C).

The place, maybe in the 15th Century, was dedicated to the Saints Gervasio and Protasio substituting Nazario and Celso; therefore the denomination «Sancta Sanctorum» appears. Destructing interventions occurred in 1731, but in 1905 everything was re-established as it must have been originally.

Turning towards the left, we see a rough altar of cement (fig. 3 n. 2-E) in which, on the front façade, the front of bishop Ecclesius's sarcophagus is inglobed, he was the one who ordered the construction of the basilica. It is a fragment which presents in the middle, a cross on whose sides there are two beautiful peacocks and under which there are two deer; on the extremities, two palms. The relief isn't very emphasized, and if we compare it with the more stressed one of Isacio, we have an example of the evolution of taste during the 5th and 6th century. On the right side of the same altar there is another fragment of Ecclesius's sarcophagus, with part of the inscription (...LESIUS EPISC...).

On the left side there is a third fragment, coming from the sarcophagus of the bishop Ursicinus, dating back to the first half of the 6th century.

Mausoleum of Galla Placidia: outside.

In a little niche beyond the altar there is a very little shrine made of marble, which contained the relics of the Saints and on which there is the inscription: IULIANUS ARGENT(arius) SERVUS VEST(er) PRAECIB(us) VEST(ris) BASI(licam) A FUNDA(mentis) PERFEC(it). It is of the 6th Century and it recalls the financer of the basilica (fig. 3 n. 2-F).

On the left of the altar there is the marble drain on which in the sarcophagus the body of Ursicinus was laid (fig. 3 n. 2-6), it is on the floor on one of the long sides, and it is leaning against the wall. On the opposite side there is the drain of Ecclesius (fig. 3 n. 2-H). On the left niche there is the sepulchral slab of a Domenico priest. On the North of the presbytery there is another apsidal cell with another chapel (called of the Blessed Virgin), that was the ancient *diaconicon*.

Treasure wells - The basilica has some treasure wells. You can see them from the women's gallery, to which we reach from one of the two staired towers (fig. 3 n. 24) restored round about the end of the last Century when the helicoidal flight of 67 steps was reconstructed on the trace of some original ones. The wells were used to hide the treasures of the church.

From the basilica to the Mausoleum of Galla Placidia - Going out of the basilica (fig. 3 n. 22) we go towards the Mausoleum of Galla Placidia.

In the ground that divides the two constructions in 1912 the foundations of a Roman house with mosaic floor were found, but they have been buried again; in this zone, they started building at least in the 4th century, i.e. before the Placidian buildings, and the remains of the Roman house, with a few mosaic floors, prove it.

Going towards the Mausoleum, the two sarcophagi on the left are of the middle of the 5th century; the first one presents on the front two

Mausoleum of Galla Placidia: mosaic decoration of the vault on the wing in front of the entrance. Particular.

lambs which face the *chrismon*. Above the lambs there is a flower. On the left side a wreath with *chrismon* is sculptured, on the right a cantharus, nicely reliefed.

The second sarcophagus carries two lambs (behind which there are two palms), that face a wreath with *chrismon*. On the corners, there are two little pilasters with Corinthian Capitals. On the left side a disc with a cross, from whose arms the apocalyptical letters *alpha* and *omega* hang.

MAUSOLEUM OF GALLA PLACIDIA

Historical outlines - It was built within the first half of the 5th century probably by Galla Placidia (425-450). The construction, therefore, is about one century previous to San Vitale.

Galla Placidia led a very adventurous life: daughter of the emperor Theodosius, she was born around the year 386, when the empire, even if it was kept firmly by the father, was already under the continuous menace of the barbarians.

In 395, at the death of Theodosius, the brothers of the ten years old Galla Placidia, Arcadius and Honorius, succeeded their father respectively in the East and in the West. At the same time the barbarians became more dangerous. The Visigoths of Alaric devastated Italy until they were driven away by Stilicho, Honorius' general and tutor, by means of a few lucky battles.

But Alaric confined in Illiria, returned quite soon in Italy and in 410, after having occupied and pillaged Rome, took with him as prisoner Galla Placidia, sister of the emperor, moving towards the South. Honorius in the meanwhile, had taken shelter in Ravenna, which was now the real capital of the empire.

In the same time Alaric died in Cosenza, and the brother-in-law Ataulfus, who had succeeded him, having come to pacts with the empire, led his hordes, towards Gallia and Iberia. In Narbonne, in 414, the king of the Visigoths married the young imperial prisoner. In this way, Galla Placidia became queen of a barbaric population, but only for a short time. The year after, in fact, she became a widow and Wallia, successor of Ataulfus, sent her back to Ravenna.

Here, in 416 or 417, she married Constantius, patrician of Honorius and an excellent general.

From Constantius, Galla Placidia had two sons: Honoria and Valentinian.

In 421 the uncertain Honorius joined to his throne the brother-in-law Constantius, therefore Galla Placidia, already queen of the Visigoths became Roman empress. But once again only for a little: in fact in the same year Constantius died.

Galla Placidia then tried to influence the choice of the successor and having come into strong contrast with her brother, fearing his hostility and the one of the Roman court, she escaped to Constantinople with her children.

When in 423 Honorius died, Galla Placidia managed to obtain, from Constantinople the recognition of her son Valentinian as Emperor of the west. Since he was only five years old, she was entrusted the regency, which started in 425.

The already expert sovereign then proved to be able to handle the court plots and the difficulties of her government and managed to hold the throne for her son until he came of age. She

died in Rome on the 27th November of the year 450, and was nearly certainly buried in the mausoleum of the Theodosian family at the basilica of Saint Peter in the Vatican. Later sources of information refer that she was then transferred to Ravenna, but this seems to be very improbable.

The mausoleum of Ravenna, now isolated, was initially put onto one of the extremities of the portico of the church of Santa Croce built by Galla Placidia herself and that we can see, strongly reduced and rearranged, on the other side of the little road which borders San Vitale. On page 234 it is represented the original situation.

Architectural characteristics - The mausoleum is a little construction with sober and not pretentious outlines. Since its original plan is 1 metre 50 below the actual plane of site, it now appears without any slenderness and rather squat.

The plan is of a Latin cross; the limb that looks towards the entrance, infact is a little longer than the other three. The construction is all of brickwork. The external walls have a series of little blind arches, not very much projected, originated by means of strong pilasters that lie onto a base that is now buried. The four limbs of the cross have barrel-vaults and three of them end with tympana. From the intersection of the four limbs a square tower arises covered with four slopes. The whole as it is represents a neat and sharp geometry and gives the impression of a strength that the blind arches, with their rhythm, make so dynamically live. Above the entrance door there is a Roman frieze in which we can recognize panthers, vine-shoots and rods. Of the original door the shutters are still visible. It was narrowed into a door with arch, of which we can still see trace above the actual architrave.

Inside: general characteristics - On entering at first we are impressed by the magnificence of the decorations and of the mosaic scenes, by the richness of the marbles, and especially by the unreal atmosphere in which we find ourselves suddenly immerged, so that the architectural characteristics tend to lose any projection and to dissolve into pure chromatism.

The mosaic covering starts off from the bottom of the barrel-vaults of the four limbs and covers all the high part of the building. The walls are covered with yellow marble from Siena, collocated from 1908 to 1912, considering a fragment of yellow marble found on the wall. The marble band, that is now 2,54 metres high, was four metres high, since the floor was lower. The actual floor in marble marquetry dates back to the 16th century, when its raising took place. In the right corner, just as you enter, you can see a tract of the buried wall, which shows a decoration alternating in Greek marble with rhombs and rectangles. This decoration went all around. Another decoration just the same winded round higher up.

Inside: lunette above the door - Go under the dome and look towards the entrance.

The lunette in front of you is one of the most beautiful mosaics of Early Christian art.

It represents the Good Shepherd among his flock. Christ, without beard, is dressed with a golden tunic and with a purple cloak: he leans onto a high golden cross and has his face surrounded by a halo which is gol-

1 2 3
4

1 - Mausoleum of Galla Placidia: particular of the mosaic decoration.

2 - Mausoleum of Galla Placidia: mosaic of the barrel-vault.

3 - Mausoleum of Galla Placidia: mosaic of the Good Shepherd (particular).

4 - Mausoleum of Galla Placidia: the mosaic of the Good Shepherd.

Mausoleum of Galla Placidia: doves on the brim of a vase full of water.

Mausoleum of Galla Placidia: lunette of St. Laurence.

Mausoleum of Galla Placidia: so-called sarcophagus of Constantius III. ▶

Mausoleum of Galla Placidia: mosaic decoration of the arch. Vase with fruit. ▶

den too. He is sitting on a rock with a very lively attitude: the inferior part of the body, infact, is turned left, while the bust is turned in the opposite sense; the face, then, returns towards the left and his crossed feet complete this kind of twirl. It derives therefore that the figure, soft and round, even if sitting is rich of contained strength.

On the sides of Christ there are six sheep, three on each side, with various attitudes and expressions, but all with their muzzles looking towards the centre; one of them comes, nearer to receive a pat from the Shepherd.

The idyllic scene takes place in a scenery of low hills profiled on the background by trees and shrubs.

The chromatic general intonation is soft and warm: the contrasts of colour are resolved with well graded passages of tone.

Inside: the lunette of Saint Laurence - It is the lunette at the end of the limb in front of the door. Saint Laurence, who had been worshipped very much in ancient times, is represented while going towards martyrdom carrying a cross on his right shoulder and a book on the left forearm.

The figure, wrapped in twisted and fluttering garments, appears nervous and moved. In the centre, there is the grill on the burning brazier, which for tradition was the instrument of martyrdom. On the left, an open cupboard with four gospels.

Inside: the lunette of the deer - The wings of the transept end with two lunettes whose decorations are nearly the same. In the centre, under the little window, there is a little lake bordered by flowers and grass to which, nearly extricating themselves laboriously from wide volutes of acanthus, two thirsty deer make their way. The acanthus volutes, with a decorative function, fill the rest of the lunette.

The scene has a symbolic meaning which is found again in other places of the primitive Christianity: it recalls to the similitude of the Psalm, according to which the soul of man seeks God just as the deer seeks a source of fresh water.

Inside: the dome - It rises from four big lunettes that occupy the extrados of the arches over the four wings of the building.

A night sky is represented made of concentric circles of stars which, tightening towards the top, increase the distance effect of the perspective of the dome. In the middle, a cross: on the four corners the symbols of the four Evangelists. The effect of this night sky, that seems to shine of its own light, increases when moving around it slowly, we can see the alternate lighting up and turning off of the thousand reflections which quiver in it. The phenomenon is due to the fact that the tesserae of the mosaic of Ravenna, pushed into the mortar bed with the tip of the thumb, remain fixed with very varied inclinations, so that the light is reflected very varied too according to the place from which you look.

Inside: the big lunettes under the dome - The big lunettes are delimited by a large red band inside which a blue ribbon with a white hem twirls.

In the middle of every lunette there is a small window on whose sides there are two characters in white garments that raise their hands for acclamation. They are the apostles, not individually recognizable, except the two of the lunette above the wing on the left of who en-

ters. One of them infact has a key and it can't be but Peter: in front of him there is Paul, recognizable for the somatic characteristics assigned to him from tradition, (long face, pointed beard and semi-baldness).

Since the lunettes are four and the decoration of the mausoleum rigidly symmetric didn't permit to introduce a third figure because of the window, we have only eight apostles. However, the other four might be the severe figures that we see on the vaults of the two lateral limbs.

Under the little windows there is the symbolic motif of the pidgeons which approach a fountain (on two opposite lunettes) or that rest on the edge of a vase full of water (on the other two opposite ones).

Above the figures of the Apostles big umbracula like shells stretch out, which in ancient art showed the sublime dignity of the characters below.

Inside: vaults of the four limbs - Let's start off by admiring the liveliness of the bands below the sustaining arches of the lunettes and delimiting the decoration of the vaults.

In the one that delimits the entrance wing there are opulent festoons of leaves and fruit which, on a white enamel background, start off from two baskets and surround a cross on the top of the arch. In the arch of the back wing there is a Greek-fret very elaborated and complexed carried out with an extraordinary chromatic richness. On the two lateral arches, a simpler motif: little shaded panels, nearly a scale of colour and light.

The two vaults of the entrance wings and the one at the back are covered by fantastic carpets of stone and enamel, on which, from the dark blue background, the little golden

▶
Fig. 12 - **National Museum; plan of the first cloister**
1 - Well-curb. 2 - Bridge cordon. 3 - Military column. 4 - Altar. 5 - Portal of the 16th century. 6 - Tombstone of Caius the son of Zobone. 7 - Double portal of the 16th century. Little room of the Roman Villa of Russi. 8 - Portal of the 16th century - of «Porta Aurea». 9 - Fragments of the 1st Century, B.C. - 1st century A.D. 10 - Stele of Longidienus. 11 - Stele of gubernator (helmsman) of the Galeata ship. 12 - Stele of Publius Arrius Montanus. 13 - Stele of the petty officer Atenione. 14 - Stele of the freedman Caius Marius.
15 - Stele of the freedwoman Paccia Elpide. 16 - Stele of the Firmia Latronia family. 17 - Honorary base of Marco Apicio Tirone. 18 - Inscription of the centurion Titus Flavius Rufus. 19 - Front of Olia's sarcophagus.
20 - Front of Marcus Aurelius Macedo's sarcophagus.

globes emerge, light blue corollas, big white daisies, pink-orange flowers, etc.

To enjoy completely this marvel it's worth to observe with analytic attention some particulars so as to extend the vision to the whole.

The vaults of the two wings of the transept, nearly the same, present four characters which, as we have already said, could complete the number of the apostles. The figures are placed among blooming curls of vine-shoots and recall the decorative planning of the lunettes at the end, the ones with the deer.

Also the vine-shoot, with vine-leaves and grapes is a symbolic motif that found reference in a passage of John's Gospel.

«*As the shoot can't give fruit on its own if it doesn't remain attached to the vine, so can't you if you don't remain united to me. I am the vine, you are the shoots*».

Inside: the sarcophagi - In the back wing and in the two lateral ones there are three big sarcophagi.

In the one in front of the entrance, according to the tradition, Galla Placidia should rest but as we have observed, this is improbable. It is a rather rough unfinished sarcophagus, without sculptures and inscriptions, maybe pagan, which belonged to a noble character. The span roof like lid has acroteria on the four angles. The dimensions of this sarcophagus are really imposing (the length of the lid m. 2,75 width m. 1,40: the whole sarcophagus is more than two metres high). In it there was an unidentified body sitting on a cypress throne. The body was visible through a hole of about 20 centrimetres, placed on the back of the sarcophagus. On the 3rd May 1577 some boys, throwing some candles into it, burnt the body. The hole was closed after a short time with plaster; in 1899 it was closed with Greek marble. On the back the traces are still visible.

On the left wing there is a sarcophagus said without historical basis, of Constantius III, Galla Placidia's husband. The tipology is on the scheme of the one already examined i.e. coffin with the lid shaped like a span roof and acroteria. The decoration is very important because it marks nearly a stage along with the other coeval sarcophagi, of the evolution which showed up in the sculpture of Ravenna towards the end of the 5th century: that is to say the gradual passage from a naturalistic representation to one tending to symbolic abstraction.

Here then, the motif of Christ between two Apostles present on other sarcophagi (look at the cathedral-Duomo), here it resolves in pure allegory: not human figures, but symbols: the haloed lamb on the mountain from which the four biblical rivers gush out is Christ, the two lambs on the side are the Apostles. In the halo of the Divine lamb there is the monogram of Christ, expressed by the Greek letters X and P interlaced. Two palms complete the scene.

The left *side* represents a vase with handles from which the water flows: two pidgeons, symbol of the souls who longing for divine grace, quench their thirst. The sarcophagus dates back to the end of the 5th century.

The third sarcophagus is said of Valentinian III, son of Galla Placidia and emperor, or of the emperor Honorius brother of the empress. Also in this case it is an assignment due to tradition but that is not supported by any proof. From these arbitrary assignments, however, the desire of popular pity to join together again in eternal peace some of the most conspicuous components of a family which were a leading character in such a difficult historical moment seems to shine through.

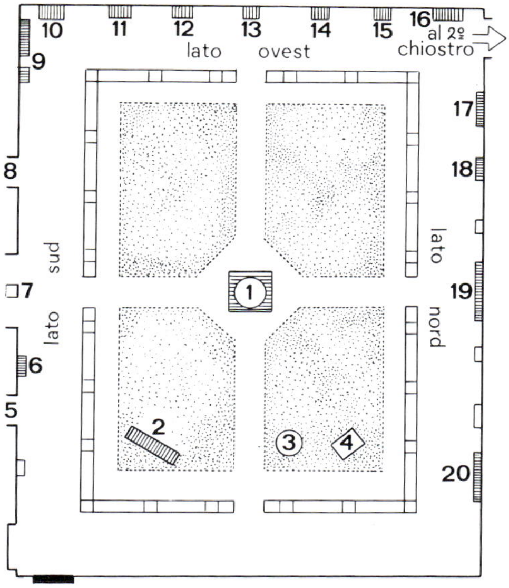

The lid is semi-cylindric, that is to say of the «trunk» or «barrel» kind. The decoration is all laid on the symbols contained in three niches: cross with shell on the two lateral ones delimited by spiral columns; the Divine lamb on the mountain with the four rivers, and a cross with two pidgeons resting on the limbs in the centre (this niche has no arch, but two slopes). The «*retro*» (back) is like the «*recto*» (front) but the sculpture is only rough-hewed. On the *sides* there is a large vase with handles; on the one on the left side there are two pidgeons which quench their thirst. Very beautiful are the interlaced decorations of the left lunette of the lid. On the right lunette there are two sheep that seem to sniff the fruit of a palm. This sarcophagus is of the beginning of the 6th century and presents a relief still well emphasized.

According to some experts the three sarcophagi weren't originally in the mausoleum; they must have been brought there at the beginning of the 14th century. According to others (De Francovich) they must have been instead built for the mausoleum.

Our itinerary now forecasts a visit to the National Museum. We have to go back, again through the basilica, into the great cloister from which we came.

THE NATIONAL MUSEUM

A first museum collection took place thanks to the «Camaldolesi» of Classe, on the initiative of Pietro Canneti, founder of the Classense Library. Bought by the Municipality in 1804, the collection became national in 1885, by means of the convention between the ministery ofPublic Education and the municipality of Ravenna. With that act the municipality handed over in perpetual deposit the materials it possessed. To these legacies of private citizens were added and pieces taken away from buildings and monuments of Ravenna. At first collocated in the rooms of the monastery of Classe, in town, the National Museum was transferred in the rooms of the monastery of San Vitale since 1913-14. The main protagonist of the birth of the National Museum was the Ravennate sculptor *Enrico Pazzi.*

National Museum: capital.

National Museum: **a** - sacrificial slaves which lead a bull to be sacrificed; **b** - National Museum: stele of Paccia Elpide. ▶

National Museum: big marble patera from Port'Aurea. (1st Century A.D.)

We shall visit it taking in consideration the map drawn by the Benedictine monk *Benedetto Fiandrini* in 1798, that you will find at page 21. The numbers with which the rooms will be marked correspond to those of the map which, to distinguish them from others we shall call PIANTA FIANDRINI (P.F.).

To facilitate the reading of some parts of the museum, the guide is accompanied by other maps (of the ceramic and majolic rooms, of the 1st cloister, of the 2nd cloister, of the rooms around the 2nd cloister), with indication of the single localizations we shall indicate these last maps with the page number in which they turn up.

THE CLOISTERS - We are in the great cloister (second cloister), see fig. 11, n. 33. Close to this one there is a smaller cloister (fig. 11, n. 15), and to respect the chronological order in which the pieces are exposed, we must now go to the smaller one.

FIRST CLOISTER - (let's now follow plan fig. 12 here above). Of the Renaissance period (in P.F. n. 15 it is indicated as LITTLE CLOISTER OF THE CISTERN) it is a rythmic rectangle of 24 columns. In the centre of the lawn, a well-curb of Istria stone of the 16th century (n. 1 plan). Still in the lawn there is a bridge cordon (2), a milestone of the 4th century (3), a travertine altar on which the inscription: «ARAE VETER CHRISTIANORUM» that was engraved in the 14th century (4).

From the cloister we can see the **bell-tower** of the basilica which arises over one of the stair towers (fig. 3 n. 25). Built for the first time in the 10th century, destroyed by the earthquake of 1688, it was rebuilt in 1696. It ends with a dome surmounted by a ball with a cross.

On the **southern side** of the cloister the elegant **portals** open (5-7-8), of which the central one is double. It was sculptured in the 16th century and was transferred here, in 1910, from the cloister of the monastery of Classe, into town. On the double portal (7), Saint Michael weighs up the souls while tramping on the demon. On the lateral portals, the reliefs represent the coat-of-arms of the «Camaldolesi».

Between the first and the second portal we notice, on the wall, a sepulchral slab (6) which carries two inscriptions; one, high up, with lapidary characters well drawn and one, below, with very rough characters. On the high part we notice some cancellations carried out with the chisel. This is the explanation: a pagan, Pomponius, had the tombstone sculptured for his wife which had died at the age of 20. Later, in the 4th century, a Christian wanted to utilize the tombstone again, and so he cancelled the face of the woman, on the upper part, and cancelled some signs of paganism and of idolatry and that is D.M. (*Dis Manibus*; to the Gods Manes), with which the pagan sepulchral epigraphs started; he also cancelled Pomponius's name which was Hermes, a Greek God, finally he put his inscription, in which we read that he was Caius, son of Zobone, originary from an African city called Kasae (De Lo-(co) KASENSE).

In the second room, which we reach through the double portal, the findings of the **Roman** Villa of Russi are exhibited. They are the remainders of a big complex of rooms housing land-owners, they were found in 1938 in Russi, a city 16 kilometres from Ravenna on the s.s. n. 302 which leads to Faenza and to Florence.

The excavations were widened at the end of the post-war period. The most ancient parts of the Villa date back to the 1st century B.C., otha

b

National Museum: stele of Longidienus (particular).

er parts to the 1st century A.D Many floor mosaics are still «in loco».

In the last room we find all that is left of **Porta Aurea**, erected in 43 B.C. by the emperor Claudius, which opened in the surronding wall of the 1st century. Among the remainders, the two big paterae stand out, with a first external ring made of little spindles, a second ring of oak leaves and a third big strip with palms. At the time of the monastery the two rooms that we have just visited were used as store-rooms for CHEESE, ROPES, IRON and other things (P.F. n. 19). Above them there was the abbot's apartment.

At the end of the corridor, on the left (9) two very beautiful fragments of a same **bas-relief** very famous and very studied about, it was sculptured between the 23 and the 12 B.C. The date is however object of discussion, and several experts indicated the first decades of the vulgar era (Tiberian or Claudian Age).

The first fragment represents some victimarii slaves, one of which armed with an axe which lead a bull to be sacrificed; the second from left to right, a young female divinity, General Agrippa, a young man who died at the age of twenty, Marcellus or Germanicus, loved very much by Augustus, Livia as procreating Venus (Amoretto on her left shoulder), and finally Augustus as Jupiter (with lightning in his left hand, and the left foot on the celestial sphere, the right hand high leaning onto a lance which is missing).

On the **western side** we find seven funerary stelae, leaning against the wall, with the portraits of the dead.

The first one (10) is the sepulchral stele that Publius Longidienus, while he was still alive, had got sculptured (SE VIVO CONSTITUIT). Carpenter (FABER NAVALIS) of the Roman

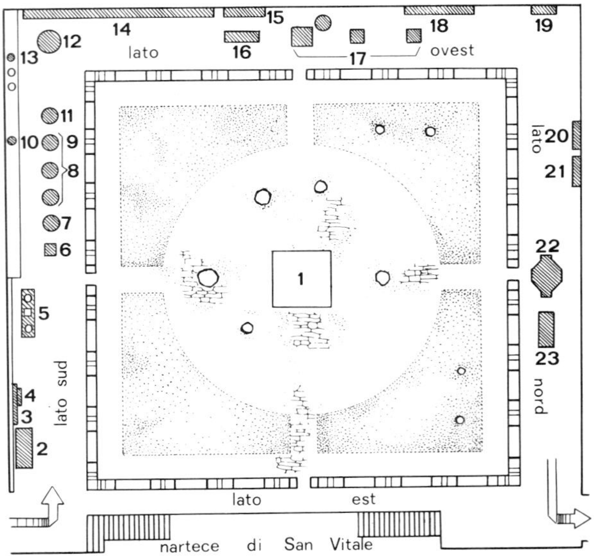

Fig. 13 - **National Museum: plan of the second cloister**. 1 - Monument to Clemente XII. 2 - Sarcophagus of *Traditio Legis*. 3 - Corpse drain. 4 - Fragment of Ambo. 5 - Capital with *ionic imposts*. 6 - Pulvino. 7 - *Theodosian* capital. 8 - Capitals of the type *leaf moved by the wind*. 9 - Capital with Theodoric's monogram. 10 - Capital of *lyre* type. 11 - Capital of the *acanthus leaf thinly indented* type. 12 - Great Capital. 13 - Basket-like Capital. 14 - Zone of marble fragments. 15 - Terra-cotta zone. 16 - Sarcophagus of the two lions. 17 - Street crosses. 18 - Little statues of Saints and Prophets. 19 - Bas-reliefs of the Madonna and God. 20 - Coat-of-arms and bearings of monasteries. 21 - Portal frieze in brickwork from the so-called house of Guidarello. 22 - Well-curb of the Monastery of Classe. 23 - Sarcophagus of Caius Sosius Julianus.

National Museum: the front of the sarcophagus of Olia Tertullia - particular (1st or 2nd century A.D.).

National Museum: The sarcophagus of Traditio Legis. On the side: Daniel among the lions.

fleet in Classe, Longidienus got himself portrayed while working with an axe; the little inscription infact, so as to dispel any possible error of interpretation of the image even if eloquent, precises: P. LONGIDIENUS P.F. AD ONUS PROPERAT (Publius Longidienus son of Publius is intent on his fatigue).

Above Longidienus and the freedwoman Stacte are represented, having side by side two winged funerary genii leaning against a torch, placed on two altars decorated with a festoon; under, the freedmen Rufius and Pilades. The stele is of Augustan epoch (beginning of the 1st century A.D.).

The second stele (11) carries the bust of the pilot (GUBERNATOR) of the Galeata ship.

We give, as example to the reading of an epigraph the explanation of the last two lines of this one: IN FR PVI IN AGR P XV; they are the measures of the sepulchre. Extensively we read: IN FR(onte) P(edes) VI, IN AGR(o) P(edes) XV. We translate: In front six feet, towards the field 15 feet. Flavian Age.

The third stele (12) is of Publius Arrius Montanus and family (first half of the first century A.D.).

The fourth stele (13) is dedicated by the petty officer (CORONARIUS) Atenione of the trireme Danae, to his wife Aufidia (middle of the 1st century A.D); the fifth (14) is of the freedman Caius Marius and family (beginning of 1st century A.D.); the sixth (15), of the freedwoman Paccia Elpide of which it presents a very beautiful portrait.

The last stele, in travertine (16), is of the family Firmia Latronia and it dates back to the middle of the 1st century A.D. The arrangement of the figures is hence interpreted: the grandmother, purchaser of work, is represented in the panel above, on the right, as well as the son and the grandaughter which turns her head towards her father. On the top we have the daughter-in-law alone. More under, two brothers: Latronius Secundus and Saturninus still alive when the stele had been sculptured (the letter V engraved on their chests). Finally, at the bottom a «verna» i.e. a slave born in the house of the slave owner.

In the **northern part** we notice the honorary base of Marcus Apicius Tiro (17) whose grades and charges reached during his career are listed: he made part of the first maniple of the XXII Legion Primigenia Pia Fidelis, prefect of the XII Legion Gemina, Centurion of the XV Legion Apollinaris, Curator of the registers of the Military Jails, Patron of the municipality of Ravenna, Pontiff (middle of the 2nd century A.D.); an inscription in honour of the centurion Titus Flavius Rufus follows (18), military architect and soldier who received the password (2nd century A.D.).

In the middle of the portico there is the front of the sarcophagus of Olia (19) of which we develop the inscription made up of beautiful characters (Ist or 2nd century A.D.).

OLIAE P(ublii) F(iliae)
TERTULLAE
V(ixit) ANN(os) XV M(ensis) VIII D(ies) X
OLIUS TERTULLIANUS
Fil(iae) PIENTISSIMAE ET SIBI

from which we learn that the very tender Olia lived 15 years, 9 months and 10 days while we feel the contained grief of the father in having had his sepulchre built for himself and for his daughter so as to rest near her.

Big granite rock with the inscription IN AGRUM found (1901) embedded in the foundations of a tower in Andrea Costa square, in front of Mercato Coperto.

Finally, the front of the sarcophagus of the Dalmatian sailor Marcus Aurelius Macedo (20) on which two little genii lean onto two upside-down torches; it is of the 2nd century A.D.

The eastern side carries other inscriptions.

SECOND CLOISTER - (look at plan fig. 13 at pag. 50. In P.F. it is called BIG CLOISTER). We reach it going through a passage on the side of the Firmia Latronia family's stele. Having gone up four steps, on the right there is the entrance to the superior part of the museum.

The second cloister has for width and richness, extraordinary monumental characteristics. Built in 1562 on design of Andrea da Valle, it has on every side of the big square, eight pairs of columns. In the centre of the lawn, among a group of trees there is the **statue of Clemente XII Corsini** (1) sculptured in Carrara marble by Pietro Bracci. It testifies the gratitude of the city to the pope who had opened the channel harbour to which he gave the name (Porto Corsini, Canale Corsini), which had joined together the rivers Ronco and Montone digging them a new bed to the sea, moving them away from the populated area for which they constituted a continuous menace, and which on the new course of the Fiumi Uniti had built the Ponte Nuovo. The statue, originally collocated in Piazza del Popolo was taken away from it in 1867 and after placed here.

In this cloister we find a great quantity of fragments and monuments of different epochs, from the Greek epoch, to the Early Christian, to the Byzantine, Romanesque, Gothic, Renaissance, Baroque.

In the Southern part, right on the left while entering, we meet a very interesting **sarcophagus** that in front has a bas-relief with the **Traditio Legis** (the giving of the law); Christ in the centre, on the left Paul (bald head, pointed beard), on the right Peter with veiled hands so as to receive the roll of the law.

Behind the palms, the leaves of which seem to be invested by the wind, we find husband and wife purchasers of the work. On the left side, the resurrection of Lazarus very well done; notice the tree on the left and the decorative taste with which the foliage on which a bird lays itself is rendered. On the right side, Daniel between two lions, with a Persian suit; tight trousers, rolled up tunic, cloak with a clasp, Phrigian cap. The sarcophagus dates back to the end of the 4th - beginning of the 5th century and it is one of the most ancient Early Christian specimens extant in Ravenna (2).

On the right of the sarcophagus, hung on the wall, we notice the so-called **corpse drain** (3) with hollows for the heads of the dead of the beginning of the 5th century. Till the 7th century the dead person was placed in the sarcophagus on a stone slab with crossed grooves and perforated at every intersection, through the holes the liquid humor would flow out.

Under the drain there is an ambo fragment of the 6th century.

In the corridor many **capitals** are collected and since it isn't frequentely possible to see them so near, it is convenient to examine them with attention.

Let's start from the two capitals in the middle of which there is the fragment of a pillar (5). The two capitals, that are of the second half of the 6th century are of the type called «*of ionic impost*»). They are so called because in the inferior part, here very reduced, there is the ionic motif (the volute) above which there is an impost, in a unique block, that here, on the short sides, between two acanthus leaves, presents a cross that seems to arise from the leaves themselves. On the long sides there are lanceolate leaves, intervalled by a kind of an oblong stylized lily. The superior part (abacus) is smoothe and of remarkable thickness. The two capitals come from San Pietro in Vincoli, locality near Ravenna.

Between the two capitals there is a pillar fragment with a cross of very weak relief, with an internal drill and, below, five vertical pod-like decorations (middle of the 6th century).

Of the following seven pieces placed on brick bases, the first (6) is a pulvino of the second half of the 6th century, which presents above an edge decorated with a singular motif of stylized palms upright and upsidedown. Underneath there is a central, vertical fillet, on the sides of which there are vegetable racemes. On the edge there is an acanthus leaf. On the minor sides, worn out, there is a circular zone that maybe was the head of a lion.

The first capital placed onto a cylindric base (7) is of the type so-called *Theodosian*, with acanthus very thinly indented. The presence of acanthus leaves would indicate it as a *Corinthian* capital, but since above the leaves there are also volutes like in the *Ionic* capital, the capital is said «*composito*», i.e. the result of the combination of Ionic and Corinthian. This that we are examining is called *Theodosian* because it was very diffused during the epoch of Theodosius II. From the inferior part (torus), that is a ring with a rope-like motif, a circle of eight acanthus leaves arises, above which other eight acanthus leaves stay. Every leaf is divided in seven lobes, of which the superior one stretches out towards the outside. The superior body of the capital has winding volutes and prominences with vegetable ornamental motifs (little branches and palmettes). The abacus (the superior layer) is adorned by bay-leaf motifs. It is of the middle of the 5th century.

A group of three capitals follows (8) of the type with acanthus leaves «*moved by the wind*», because every leaf seems to be contorted by a turbinous air, current that moves it towards the right or towards the left. On the capitals of these three kinds there are two circles of leaves each made up of four pairs of leaves. In every pair, a leaf bends towards the left and the other towards the right making you think of butterfly wings. Every pair is divided by a row of little holes which mark also the central nervation of the two leaves. From every central nervation three lobes divide which once again subdivide in other three little lobes. Above the two rings of leaves there are some prominent volutes, therefore also these three capitals are of «composite» order. All is crowned by a thin abacus.

In the third capital of this group there is Theodoric's monogram, unfortunately very worn out. We find it on a high face above the leaves in the middle of the ovule rings. The three capitals are of the Theodorican period (493-526) and they should come from the church of Sant'Andrea dei Goti, built by Theodoric and demolished by the Venetians in the 15th century to use its ruins in the foundations of Rocca Brancaleone or, according to another hypotesis, from a public building. Other capitals of the same origin were placed by the Venetians above the columns of the little palace built by them at the end of the 15th century, and that we can admire in Piazza del Popolo.

Behind the capital with a monogram, leaning against the wall, there is a Corinthian capital said «*lyre type*» (10). It is made up of two circles of four acanthus leaves. The abacus has a central flower by side. The flower goes downwards, towards the leaves from which it is separated by a «V» form (or lyre). It is of the first half of the 6th century.

The second last capital (11) dates back to the second half of the 6th century and it is of the type of acanthus thinly indented. It is very ruined.

The last capital (12) that for its dimensions can be monumental, is of the 6th century. It is of «composite» order with big indents. Every leaf is divided into two lobes by side and finishes going forwards. The ribs are marked by deep grooves. The abacus is decorated with bay-leaves.

On the low wall, near the capital now described, the last of a group of three (13), is a capital called «basket-like» of the second half of the 6th century, with vegetable decorations made of thorny acanthus leaves, reliefed but not going towards the outside, with nervatures. The abacus is tall, decorated with palmettes.

On the **western side** several marble fragments, decorated with crosses, twirls, knots fretwork of the 8th and 9th centuries are exhibited (14). In this zone we underline, behind the big capital, a pluteus with knotted festoons which form eight circles in which there are rosettes, interlacements, crosses; it is of the beginning of the 9th century. Near it, there is a fragment of archivolt of ciborium, of the 8th century. Between the first two windows there is an altar piece of the 8th century which carries in the middle a Latin cross with rope-like extremities and on the sides a decoration of vine-shoots. Under there is a well with figures of lions followed by a sarcophagus of the Rasponi family with a lid that doesn't belong to the coffin. Under the first window there are some little pillars of the 8th and 9th centuries. They are «pergula» pillars i.e. used for enclosures, variably decorated on which we notice, in one of the sides, the groove for the placing of the slab.

The Romanesque terra-cotta zone follows, with animal figures and Christian symbols, of the 10th-11th centuries (15). Under the terracottas there is the sarcophagus of a child with two lions that lift a paw towards a palm (16) of the second half of the 7th century; it wasn't finished, as you will notice especially from the frame. Near it there is a Romanesque capital of the 10th century, on which panthers, rough human faces, and in the corners, animals' heads with very curved horns have been sculptured.

Some Romanesque street crosses (17) follow placed on columns, three of which with a blessing hand. The second column with a cross, the one grooved vertically and with an inscription on the base, is the so-called «**Crocetta**», which indicated the place of the demolished church of San Lorenzo in Cesarea. In the column zone there is a travertine cippus with a big round motif connected with a cross motif and four leaves. It was part of an altar, and on the superior part it presents a little well for relics. On the wall behind the «crocetta» there are three paterae with birds (after the year 1000).

Little statues of prophets and Saints (18) follow, used as portal decorations (12th century). Between two columnholder lions, one coming from San Pietro in Vincoli, the second from San Vitale, there is the base and the central column of an altar, which comes from the church of Santa Maria in «Coeloseo».

On the wall there is an archivolt in brick-work of the 14th century. On its left there is the fragment on the front of an altar or of a sarcophagus, representing maybe Saint John the Evangelist with a cross in his hand, work of Venetian creators of the 14th century. Remarkable, at the end of the corridor, the warrior carrying a shield, maybe he also made part of the front of a sarcophagus, dressed in a classical armour. It can be attributed to the hand of Antonio da Rigesio, called Bregno who made similar pieces in the Ducal Palace in Venice and in the Borromeo monument in Isola Bella. Furthermore we indicate two bas-reliefs (19) of the

15th century representing one God who is blessing, the other the Madonna on a throne with the Infant, drawn from the prospect of the churches of San Sebastiano and San Marco.

Among the material placed on the **northern side** we underline at the beginning the ciborium, coming from the church of Godo, with angels of the 15th century. On the lunette above there are two angels holding a chalice with the host, and below we see some coat-of-arms, one of the Rocchi family, of 1547. Further on there are different coat-of-arms with weapons and bearings of monasteries; a portal frieze with a pointed arch, in brickwork decorated with cones, indents, crosses (21), drawn from the so-called house of Guidarello built in 1490 and demolished in 1934; an octagonal well-curb (22) of the Camaldolese Monastery of Classe, in Istria stone, of the 16th century, with a very low and delicate relief made of acanthus leaves, monograms, various little figures, a skull, a mask.

Remarkable the sarcophagus that follows the well-curb (23). It is of Caius Sosius Julianus, oculist, who got himself portrayed on the left side, while curing a patient (but Bermond Montanari interprets: Memphius sitting down, woken up after the unction of an oculist). The two objects of bell form are cupping glasses and they allude to the medical profession. In front a woman who is playing a cithara, another holds an unfolded roll; along the frieze and the lateral bas-reliefs there are two Greek epigraphs. It is of the 3rd-4th century A.D.

The **eastern side** is completely occupied by the original entrance of the basilica of San Vitale, that we have already described.

THE THIRD CLOISTER - We can enter it through a gate standing in the corner made up by the porches in the eastern and northern sides. On Fiandrini plan it is called CLOISTER OF THE KITCHEN GARDEN (P.F. n. 43) and it is not always possible to visit it.

Designed by *Soratini*, it is of the second half of the 18th century, and one of the four sides is missing but since origin (it was interrupted in 1745). In this third cloister the bronze statue of Alessandro VII Chigi has been placed. It is a not very beautiful work of *Francesco Maria Bandini* of Urbino, it was finished in 1672 and had many vicissitudes; first it was collocated in the square, then in the church of S. Sebastiano, then in S. Francesco square from which, after having been thrown down by unknown people in 1867, it was taken away and put into a warehouse. It was then brought to Rome in «Palazzo Chigi» and after world war first it was brought back to Ravenna and placed in the Museum.

In the cloister now some marble pieces have been placed. Let's notice che sarcophagus of VIBIUS PROTUS. The inscription on the tabula ansata tells us that the sarcophagus was placed by the captain of the fleet, the prefect VIBIUS SENECA, for a freedman of his. On the sides of the tablet there are two aediculae surmounted by a pediment. It is of the middle of the 3rd century. Let's also see the inferior part of a sarcophagus, of which we can make out two little angular pilasters on the extremities, a figure of a woman (on the left) and of a man (on the right), both with a «cista» at their feet. On the «cistae» the numbers XL e LI are engraved, maybe the years of life of the two. The bases of two little columns follow.

For the destination of the rooms of the monastery, let's say that at the extremity of the shortest wing of this cloister there was the STOREROOM FOR OIL AND PORK MEAT (P.F. n. 42). Near it there was the LITTLE REFECTORY (P.F. n. 41) preceeded like the big refectory, by a PASSAGE (P.F. n. 39) and a HALL (P.F. n. 40).

MUSEUM: SUPERIOR FLOOR - Going along the narthex of San Vitale, let's return in the passage between the two cloisters and, on the left, we go towards the superior rooms of the Museum.

The marble bust that we find in front is the portrait of Innocenzo X Pamphili, the pope who in the middle of the 17th century opened the canal which permitted to sail from the ancient harbour Candiano to Porta Nuova or Pamphilius and that as the «porta», was called Pamphilia in his honour. The bust was, originally, in fact on the arch of the Porta (gate) from which it was moved in 1757 because it threatened to fall; placed back again in 1780, it was definetely taken away a few years later. It was attributed to *Bernini*.

The big staircase, executed between 1791 and 1793 in the place of another one is *Benedetto Fiandrini's work*. The stucco-works and the two statues (Saint Benedict and the Madonna with the infant) are of *Paolo Trifogli* and *Paolo Giabani*. On the top there are two Greek marble columns that come from the pronaos of San Vitale. In P.F. it is indicated as NEW STAIRCASE (n. 45).

Before the entrance to the room that were all monks' rooms (P.F. above 64) there is a **Byzantine capital**, very beautiful indeed, dating a little before the middle of the 6th century, coming from the church of San Michele in Africisco.

It is of the basket-like type, decorated with open-worked interlacements and palmettes. It is a very well conserved piece in which with the alterning and interpenetrating of light and dark, results a very soft pictorial effect. The numbers in brackets which follow refer to the plan pag. 58 figure 14. Opposite there is a plaster copy of the sarcophagus of archbishop Theodore. The

National Museum, Room of bronzes: Above, fantastic animal of paduan school datable back around 1500. Below, little cup from Egypt of the 16th century.

1 2 5 6
3 4 7 8
9 10

National Museum: Small bronzes and plaquettes: 1, Shell shaped ink pot with male figure holding a candlestick (end of the 15th century). - 2, Emperor Marc Aurelius on horse; the shell on the base serves as an ink pot. - 3, Atlas holding a terrestrial globe, which acts as on oil-lamp (middle of the 16th century). - 4, S. Cecilia and four Saints. - 5, Four-footed shaped jug. - 6. Satyr with a vase acting as an ink pot. - 7, Challenge on music between Pan with the flute and Apollo with the lyre; in the middle god Tmolo as a judge. - 8, Argus asleep, Mercury playing the flute transformes him into a heifer (1st half of the 17th century). - 9, Hercules chokes Anteus; the bow, the quivers and the hide of the nemean lion hang on a tree trunk (end of the 15th century, beginning of the 16th century). - 10, Two little angels with the symbols of the Passion: bandages and veronica; it is a work of G. Campagna (beginning of the 17th century).

Fig. 14 - **National Museum: Plan of the little rooms that go onto the second cloister, to the upper floor.** Room A - prehistoric findings in the province of Ravenna. B. 1 - brick-work draw-plate to make glasses and little vases. C. 2 - Glass vases of the Roman epoch. C. 3 - Little engraved early Christian gem. D. 4 - Portrait of a man and a young woman. D. 5 - Portrait of a young girl. G. 6 - Five herms. D. 7 - Sarcophagus of a child. D. 8 - Base and head of a statue of Apollo Medico. E - Findings of the Roman Necropolis «Palazzette». F. 9 - Bronze grating of the crypt of S. Apollinare in Classe. F. 10 - Side of a sarcophagus, of the beginning of the 5th century, with the scene of Thomas' incredulity. F. 11 - Hercules and the deer. F. 12 - Chancel-screen maybe from San Michele in Africisco. F. 13 - Three chancel-screens of the basilica of San Vitale. F. 14 - Mosaic fragment of the vault of the Presbytery of San Vitale. F. 15 - Bronze cross already on the roof of the Basilica of San Vitale. G - Fragments from the «palace of Theodoric». H - Ancient cloths. I - Ivory room L. 16-17 - Pastorals of the 14th and 15th centuries. M - Cabinet from Brussels. N-O-P - Cabinets.

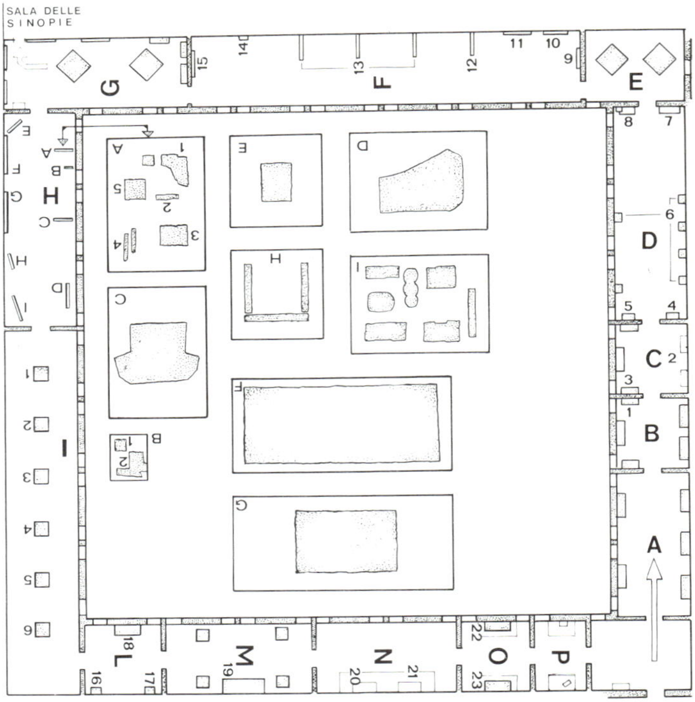

National Museum: the furniture of a pharmacy of the end of the 18th Century, with pharmaceutical jars.

original of the 5th century is in the basilica of S. Apollinare in Classe.

Before starting our visit to the rooms that run around the second cloister we enter into the corridor in which a precious collection of little bronzes and plaques are exhibited and where the furniture of an eighteenth century Pharmacy has been placed.

Among the little bronzes, of Medieval Renaissance and Modern epoch, we must point out an Aquamanile (13th century) used by the prelates for the ablution of the hands during religious functions (n. 1), a beautiful Marcus Aurelius on horse-back (n. 6), (of the beginning of the 16th century) a Satyr with a vase (n. 11), the Head of a Youth (n. 30), a Female figure (n. 46) (See pages 55-56-57).

Among the plaques we point out n. 29 (a fight among some cavaliers, 15 th century), n. 39 (Pity), n. 74 (St. Cecilia and Saints), n. 75 (Paris' judgement, of the middle of the 16th century), and n. 82 (Argus charmed to sleep by Mercury of Flamish school, dating to the first half of the 17th century).

The plaques decorated clothing, headgears, objects, they imitated gems and money and were collected.

The pharmacy of which the furniture is here exhibited, was in Ravenna (via Mazzini) and it dates back to the last years of the 18th century. It has been completed by pottery furnishings made up of 139 chemist jars coming from Verona, in order to recreate the atmosphere of a pharmacy that in past times had been significant under cultural and civil points of view.

Let's now enter the MONKS' ROOMS.

In the entrance hall the superior part of a three-mullioned window in walling has been rebuilt, coming from the bell-tower of Sant'Apollinare Nuovo, with two ceramic ornamental basins (XIIth-XIIIth Centuries).

ROOM A (look at plan figure 14) - Prehistoric findings in the province of Ravenna. In this room we have pieces of the bronze Age, that in Emilia Romagna goes from 1800 B.C. to 900 B.C. The presentation distinguishes among various periods in which the Bronze Age is subdivided (ancient Bronze, 1800-1450 B.C.; medium Bronze, 1450-1100 B.C.; final Bronze, 1100-900 B.C.).

ROOM B - Materials coming from stratigraphic wells South-West from Ravenna and in Via Morigia. This material recovered during excavations carried out in 1968-69, that demonstrate the presence of Ceramic work-shops and that have also revealed, at the depth of seven metres, traces of settlings on pile-dwellings which can be dated, on the base of Etruscan and Attic ceramics, to the end of the 5th century and to all the 4th century. In particular, in the wells South-West from Ravenna a great quantity of

National Museum: side of the sarcophagus with Saint Thomas' incredulity.

National Museum: Hercules capturing a deer.

National Museum: chancel-screen maybe from the Church of San Michele in Africisco. ▶

Roman ceramic has been found, among which fragments of terra sigillata vase matrixes in relief. In the show-case of the wall at the bottom of the room, on the left side of the door (1), there is a very interesting stamp of a certain kind of glass, which under the rim is decorated by a strip of little leaves, under which there are geometric motifs with rhombuses and triangles very closely dotted. It was used for the production of a glass of the type called ACO. This (pressing) moulding tecnique, apart from the use of machinery, was like the one of today; the only difference maybe is the fact that, nowadays are made of gypsum. In the mold or matrix or stamp they would press a foil of tender clay until it would take the internal shape of the glass or vase; on contact with the absorbing surface of the terra-cotta matrix, the clay lost part of its dampness, and would withdraw detaching itself from the matrix and after a few hours from pressing the piece could be taken out of the mold, be completed (the rim or eventually mould handles) and be set to dry for the cooking process. On the external surface of the so formed piece obviously, the decoration would be right (positive), decoration which of course in the matrix was of the wrong side (negative). Observe for this research, for its clear evidence, the little matrix fragment with a flower whose petals are obtained (in negative) with a punch shaped on purpose.

ROOM C - The first cupboard on the right wall (2): contains glass vases of the Roman epoch, coming from excavations carried out in the surroundings of Ravenna. They are majorly containers for oils and perfumed essences, of various form; bottles, little flasks and glasses of current and daily use, and which appear often in the tombs of the Roman epoch. Notice, on the middle shelf, a cinerary urn with two handles of dark green colour, of the 1st-2nd Century A.D., and on the upper shelf a green glass with blue tablets of the 4th-5th century. On the lower shelf, a dark green glass amphora of bulb shape, maybe from Egypt, which was used for wine or perfumes (4th-5th century A.D.); second cupboard on the right wall: as well as a bronze bell (4th-5th century A.D.) a little Serapis head of terra-cotta, in this show-case a collection of bronze and terra-cotta lamps are presented. Below, an amphora of Ravennate production and a stone mortar with three holders.

In the other show-cases there are necklaces, glass, three dice, the fragment of a comb, lamps, coins.

In the little show-case of the entrance wall on the left (3), through a lens, one can see an engraved Early Christian gem with a cross and 2 fishes.

ROOM D - (some herms and the sarcophagus of a child) - Entrance wall: on the right, Roman portrait of a male figure, of the end of the 1st century B.C., with a strong and resolute expression and with a compact structure.

— Portrait of a young woman, with the so-called melon hairstyle, made of tubolar elements, which in Roman epoch, for its simplicity, was preferred by young girls (beginning of the 3rd century A.D.) (4).

— On the left there is another portrait of a young girl (5) and a fragmentary head (middle of the 2nd century A.D.), representing maybe a personification of the city.

In the room **five herms** (6) are exhibited, they were found in the sea between Marina di Ra-

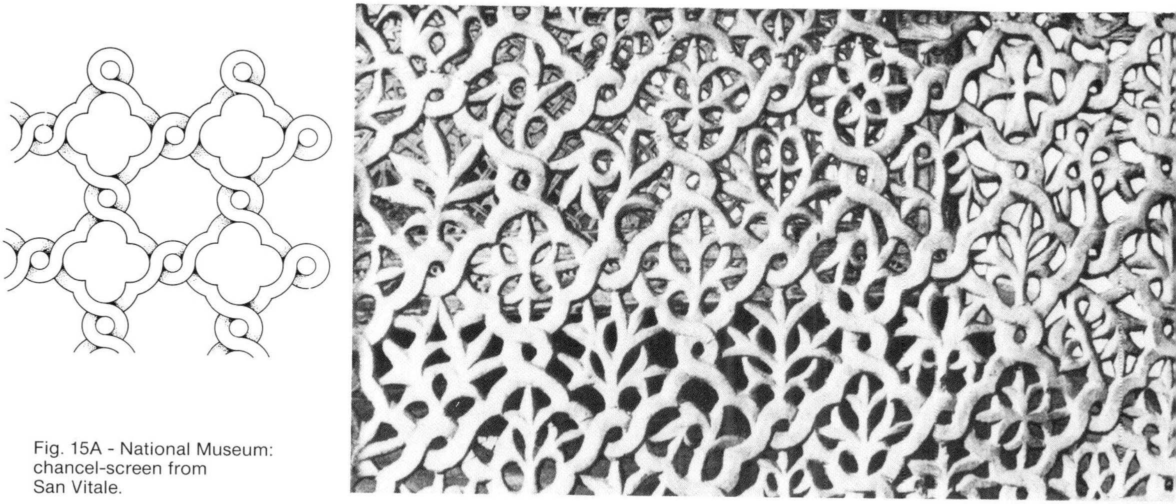

Fig. 15A - National Museum: chancel-screen from San Vitale.

venna and the Rhine outlet, maybe they made part of the cargo of a wrecked ship, cargo which had been sent off by the cardinal Ippolito II d'Este from Rome to the Este court of Ferrara. On the right wall we see in order: Bearded head representing Dyonisius or Hermes of the so-called Dyonisius-Platon type, the nose is missing. It is of the first half of the 2nd century A.D. Herm representing the Greek philosopher Carneades, of the 2nd century A.D. Herm representing the Greek philosopher Epicurus, of the 2nd century A.D. Herm representing Miltiades, as indicated on the epigraph, which carries a bilingual inscription with nearly all the letters engraved again. The piece of the «Antoninian» Age, has gone through various restorations of the 16th century. Second herm of Miltiades, on the left wall, nearly in front of the preceeding one, it also belongs to the Antoninian Age.

These five herms are copies derived from the original ones dating back to different epochs.

— Front wall on the right: **Sarcophagus of a child** (7). This little sarcophagus with a beautiful deep relief, was brought from Rome to Ravenna round about 1760, to enrichen the Classense archaeological collection, and it is of Roman style and iconography. Its date is uncertain: the experts sway in the limits of the 3rd century A.D. because of the «flame» hair on the head of the Good Shepherd, Bovini places it between 250 and 275, recognizing in this hair style a characteristic of that period.

In front, in the middle, a young man is sitting on a chair; at his feet he has some rolled untied books. His face was only sketched. A woman is looking at him, and leaning against a column, is holding her face in her hand. It is a teaching scene in which the young man who is sitting is the teacher. On the left of this scene there are three figures: a girl with a dove and two adults, maybe the parents. On the right there is the Good Shepherd with a stick. On the sides of the sarcophagus the relief is less marked. On the left side there is a winged putto who is rowing looking backwards. On the right side there is a shepherd with a cloth wrapped around his hips, with the right foot on a rock and a little basket slipped in his arm. He is fishing a hooked fish from the water.

— Bottom wall on the right: head base of a statue known as «Apollo medico» («Apollo doctor») of the end of the 3rd century A.D. (8). The first fragment is limited to the legs of the god near to whom, on the left, there are the remainders of a tripod with a snake, while on the right there is a snout. The head is surrounded by a bay-leaf crown.

ROOM E - Two cubic showcases containing findings of the Roman necropolis «Palazzette» in Classe, dug in 1970. The necropolis is in the zone of the annular road South of Sant'Apollinare in Classe. The show-cases contain lamps, necklaces, vases, little vases of green glass (balsamaria) of different forms, tube-like with drop-like tummy, spheroidal tummy, conic tummy. The findings can be dated from the Ist to the 4th-5th centuries A.D.

ROOM F - (some chancel-screens) - Entrance wall on the right: hung upon it is a **bronze grating** with semi-circular motifs one over another and alterned with crosses in the resulting spaces, which closed the external window of the crypt of Sant'Apollinare in Classe (6th century A.D.) (9).

— Right wall: **Side of a sarcophagus** of the be-

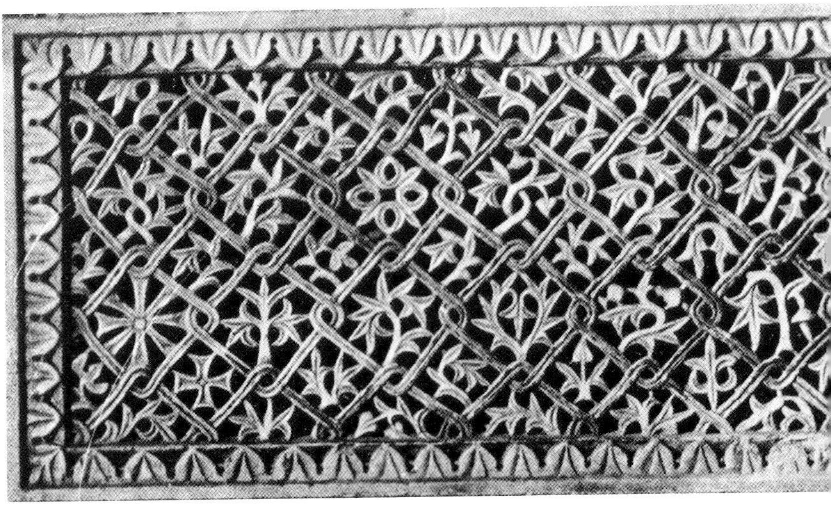

Fig. 15B - National Museum: chancel-screen from San Vitale decorated with leaves, leaf twirlings and intertwinings.

ginning of the 5th century in which the incredulity of Saint Thomas is represented. The scene occurs in the moment in which Thomas puts his hand on the wound, while Jesus lifts his left arm. This subject is very rarely found in ancient Christian sculpture (10).

— Great **bas-relief** representing the third of Hercules' labours, the capturing of the deer, with golden horns and bronze hooves (11). It is of the 6th century A.D., and «in its scheme it inspires to the Greek art models of the 4th century B.C., but in the effect reveals what was the essential spirit of Byzantine art: transform plastic into painting sculpture. This is how the figures flatten and how the relief forms practically another parallel plane to the background» (Bovini).

— Four beautiful Byzantine **chancel-screens** of Greek marble, of the first half of the 6th century follow. The first (12) maybe comes from the church of San Michele in Africisco and in the middle it has a golden cross. The other three (13) come from the basilica of San Vitale. To enjoy fully these chancel-screens, after a first global look it is necessary to discover the basic motif which carries them, the regular geometric structure with which the sculptor, releasing his fantasy, has inserted leaves, flowered branches, other geometric motifs, birds. Just to give an example in fig. 15 A-B we have the scheme of the third and fourth chancel-screens, look at the original, let's now try to recognize and isolate this scheme and we shall see clearly the turning up also of the variety and grace of the motifs inserted in its empty spots.

— The **mosaic** fragment that follows (14) is a head that belonged to one of the angels holding the garland within which there is the Divine Lamb, in the presbytery vault of San Vitale. It was detached in 1881 because tattering. It has been restored very much, it dates back to short time before the middle of the 6th century.

— Bottom wall on the right (15): big **bronze cross** that until 1911 was collocated on the roof of the basilica of San Vitale. The holes in the arms most probably contained some gems. In the mosaic of the apsidal conch in San Vitale, this cross appears in the representation of the model of the basilica which bishop Ecclesius presents.

ROOM G - Room dedicated to the fragments dug up in 1908-1914, in the area of the Theodoric palace (Palazzo di Teodorico). The numerous captions in loco are sufficient to make out the various fragments. Numerous elements of architectural decoration, reliefs, frames, fragments of capitals and column bases, fragments of plutei (5th century) and chancel-screens (5th century), sculptures, etc. are revealed. On the entrance wall on the right, there are two lead fistulae of the aqueduct restored by Theodoric, found in 1938 in the crossroad between Via Roma and Via Alberoni.

On the right wall there is a show-case with four shelves. From the upper shelf:

— Cups and plates of the 1st and 2nd Centuries A.D. In the middle a plate with a stamp of the 3rd-4th century;

— Fragments from the necropolis of Marabina, among which a glass vase with blue bubble decorations.

— Fragments of plates with seals;

— Bricks with stamps and names of emperors (Adrian, Antoninus Pius, Commodus, Septimius Severus), of the 2nd-3rd century A.D.

In the central show-case we notice a satiresque mask, with the typical characteristics of

National Museum: silk pall placed under the head of St. Julianus in Rimini.

the wrinkled forehead, snub-nose, open mouth, long ears; near it a lyre (end of the 1st - beginning of the 2nd century A.D.). Let's also notice a terra-cotta torso, very beautiful indeed maybe of the first imperial age, and a dressing scene, where a woman sitting on a little foldable stool with a cushion ties a band around the hips of a girl standing up.

On the middle of the right wall there is the plan of the Palace of Theodoric according to the relief carried out during the excavations of Ghirardini (1908-1914), followed by a watercolour of G. Azzaroni representing the paving mosaic of a room with three apses.

We also underline on the bottom wall on the right, the little frame above with double «*himation*» of the 1st century. On the upper part the leaves form a continuous ribbon, while in the longitudinal fissure which divides the leaves there is a triangular little leaf (*himation* of the continuous type). Under, instead we have a threelobed *himation*; the decorative little arches are gone through by a groove, forming on the top an eyelet in which the point of a lance hangs. Among the little arches bilobed flowers develop.

Under the little frame there is a beautiful pilaster capital of the 5th century: an external pair of leaves frames a cantharus on which we find two dolphins; among them there is a thin and tall stalk ending into a cup.

On the small-case at the bottom on the left wall there are four pieces among which the fragment of a frame on which we read the letters N V and a very little tract of an S, the ending of a name «...NUS» (5th century). At this point we interrupt temporarily going through the perimetral rooms of the second cloister to go, on the right to

THE ROOM OF THE SINOPIES - In this room various pieces found in the period 1973-1976: some stelae and fragments of stelae, a slab with inscriptions, two little sarcophagi, the sinopies of a mosaic decoration not carried out in Sant'Apollinare in Classe, some tracts of paving mosaics, various objects in some showcases.

Stelae: They were found in 1976, during excavations carried out inside Sant'Apollinare in Classe. Starting from the first one, we see the stele of LUCIUS PETRONIUS CELERE, Egyptian, who died at the age of 53, after having served in the fleet for 28 years: of GAIUS SEIUS VITTORE, Dalmatian, who died at the age of 50, after 26 years of military service (end of the 3rd century A.D.); of ANTONIA MARCIA and LUCANIUS DECIMUS, and of MARCUS AURELIUS SIRONE, who lived for 60 years, 7 months and 13 days, both of the end of the 2nd century A.D. The fragment of an epigraph, the fragment of a slab and the fragment of a pluteus, maybe of the 7th century A.D. follow.

Slab: Written on both sides. It is an original and important finding of 1976, on a side (side A, towards the wall), it carries a text composed of 65 readable names, probably the list of the «fabri» of the naval fleet of Classe. On the other face (side B, towards the centre of the room) there are 92 names of persons who belong to a college.

The list is subdivided, considering an internal hierarchy, in PATRONI, MATRES, AMATORES, SCRIBA, ORDO, and that is on the base of the position held by the single person inside the college: the authorities (*Patroni, Matres*), the «sustainers» (*amatores*), the simple components (*ordo*).

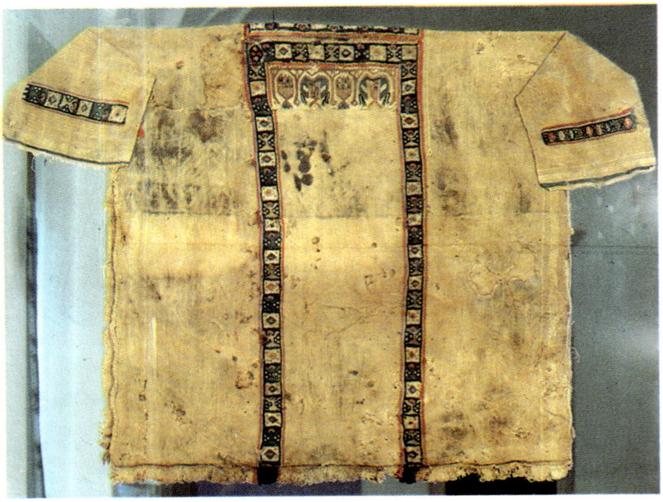

National Museum: linen tunic for a child of the 6th century.

▶ National Museum: Ivory room. Central part of the «Murano Dyptych». Christ between four Saints or Apostles.

Above the frame that holds this text there is a dedication that referring to the consolate of Diocletian and Maximian, dates the slab between 287 and 304 A.D. On the short sides it is said that the patron Domitius Felicissimus made the epigraph at his own expenses.

Two little sarcophagi of children, both of the 4th century A.D.

Sinopies: the most interesting piece of this room is constituted by the presentation of the sinopies found in Sant'Apollinare in Classe. The sinopia is a drawing of red soil, that is necessary to the artist to prepare the execution of mosaics and frescos. In the consolidation process of the mosaics of Sant'Apollinare in Classe the mosaics representing sheep, at the feet of the figure of Sant'Apollinare, were detached and it was discovered that the bricks underneath, instead of sheep, presented peacocks. Most probably the first project had been thought over and therefore we have a different representation.

That project provided pairs of peacocks, males and females, which were in front of a basket with grapes. Between each pair of peacocks a shrub appears. On the ground, near the scrawls of the animals, there are some lilies, while above the peacocks a frieze with festoons. With a particular technique it has been possible to take away both the coloured mark and a very thin layer of brick, that is what we see here.

Paving mosaics: under the sinopies three fragments of the primitive floor of the basilica Sant'Apollinare in Classe with original parts and integrations with clearer tesserae have been placed.

Show-cases: there are three show-cases, in one of which coins are collected, dating between the end of the 2nd and the beginning of the 6th century A.D., found during the excavations of 1976 in Sant'Apollinare in Classe. In the central show-case there are various fragments that can be referred to the 5th and 6th centuries A.D., among which the finding of a part of a horn is remarkable, it belongs to one of the capitals that are in the archbishopric museum. In the third show-case there is the fragment of an epigraph and a beautiful little capital of Greek marble, maybe belonging to a «pergula». Four angular leaves dotted with a drill that frame a cross, show up. Above the show-cases there is a sinopia on a plaster, representing a sheep.

Let's continue on the route that we had temporarily abandoned, and let's enter in

ROOM H - (cloths) - Left wall: the first three glass panels (A-B-C) present coptic materials acquired by the museum in 1968. With the term «coptic cloths» we indicate materials produced in Egypt at the beginning of the vulgar age till the Arab conquest (1-7th century A.D.).

Panel A - (look at plan fig. 14 pag. 58) 1 - Fragment of raw, black linen material, part of a «tunic». A hunting scene is represented on it (5th century). 2 - Piece of wool of very live colours blue, red, yellow, black with a stylized human figure and an imaginary animal. 3 - Piece of linen of blue background, with a yellow band and two lines of human figures and quadrupeds, with live colours, green, yellow, red (6th-7th centuries). 4 - Two narrow bands with stylized warriors among vegetable elements

(6th-7th centuries). 5 - Piece of linen on which a round piece of wool called «orbicolo» is sewed. The «orbicolo» is a decoration that was placed at the height of the shoulder. In the centre here is a woman's head (6th century).

Panel B - 1 - Piece of wool of the 5th century, on which a vase from which an ellipsis with a sitting cupid comes out. Above two winged cupids; below, near the vase, two dancers. 2 - Piece of wool and linen of the 6th century. In the middle a figure comes out of a vase. Around there are four geniuses. On the outside a decoration of vegetation and of imaginary animals.

Panel C - Linen tunic for a child, of the 6th century. It is a unique piece of a rectangular material, cut and not sewed, decorated with red and green woolen pieces.

Panel D - Half a chasuble of blue velvet on

Tablet representing «Apollo and Daphne». Egypt, Hellenistic art.

Tablet representing the «Dormitio Virginis».

Birth of Jesus.

Deposition and threne.

Wooden casket covered with ivory, with representations of animals.

Tablet with a scene of a tourney.

a

◀
National Museum: Collection of icons.
a - Glycophilousa Virgin.

National Museum: Collection of icons.
b - Glycophilousa Virgin;
c - Odighitria Virgin.
d - Glycophilousa Virgin;
e - Virgin and Infant. Cretan-Venetian school 16th century;
f - Adoration of the shepherds. Cretan-Venetian school, 17th century;
g - Tablet divided in 9 parts: Christ Pantokrator, the marriage of St. Catherine, Annunciation, Crucifixion, Resurrection, theories of Angels and Saints. Cretan-Venetian school 16th-17th century.
h - Nativity. Cretan-Venetian school, 17th century.

pink background, of the end of the 16th century. A motif of peacock feathers is repeated.

Panel E - White cloth with satin background with velvet motifs of amaranth colour of rampant lions, eagles and plants, on the latter touches of blue and yellow are inserted.

Panel F - Big cloth of yellow silk with narrow blue and white strips, which wrapped the body of San Giuliano in Rimini (beginning of the 9th century).

Panel G - Silk cloth, with two lines of «orbicoli», on each of which a lion is represented. It is a very beautiful piece in the conception, in the position and drawing of the lions, whose stylization derives from «sassanide» model. It was placed under the head of San Giuliano in Rimini (9th-10th centuries).

Panel H - So-called «**veil of Classe**» of the second half of the 8th century. They are three embroided strips on which the busts of the Veronese bishops are represented (the upper disc on the right presents the hand of God) woven for the altar of the relics of the Saints Fermo and Rustico in Verona, and then brought to Classe. It is a precious piece for the fine embroidery with silk and various colours and golden threads.

Panel I - Coptic materials with very live and strong colours. We admire several decorative motifs, human and animal representations and especially a head in frontal position very well drawn.

ROOM I - (ivories) - It contains a precious collection of ivories, full of very valuable pieces.

Show-case 1 - Very famous little tablet of the end of the 5th century - beginning of the 6th, representing «Apollo and Daphne», according to the legend that tells us how Apollo, who had fallen in love with the nymph Daphne while reaching her sees her transform into bay-leaf. On the tablet Apollo holds the zither in the left hand, with the right the plectrum. Daphne is already beginning, in the inferior extremities, to change. Above there is an armed cupid, below a swan attribute of the god.

— Beautiful Gospel covering called «**Diptych of Murano**», because it comes from the Camaldolese monastery of San Michele in Murano. It is a table composed of five pieces. In the middle there is Christ among Peter, Paul and two apostles; underneath the three Jewish children in the burning furnace are represented, they are saved by an angel; on the sides we have four miracles of Jesus (on the left «the healing of the blind», «the liberation of the obsessed»; on the right «Lazarus' resurrection», «the healing of the paralized». On the superior part of the tablet there are two angels that sustain a crown with a cross. On the inferior part on the right Jonah that is going to be thrown in the sea while a fish is ready to swallow him, is represented; on the left Jonah on the body of the fish, rests under a pergola of pumpkins, near an angel. It is a work of Egyptian origin that dates back to the end of the 5th-beginning of the 6th century.

— In the show-case are also two wooden little coffers covered of ivory, destined to contain necklaces, rings etc... they are boxes of Byzantine art, diffused during the 12th century, which carry various decorative motifs and real or imaginary animals are in front of one anoth-

b

c

d

e

f

g

National Museum: Collection of icons. Nativity. Cretan-Venetian school, 17th century.

er or while fighting. On the lid of one of the two there are some jugglers carrying out some exercises.

Show-case 2 - In this one, as in the following ones, as well as various little pieces, there are some wooden rectangular coffers, with the exception of the one of the last show-case, octagonal, composed of historiated bone lamellae. They are beautiful works of art, executed by carvers belonging to the school of the Embriachi (or Embriaci), famous family of ivory carvers maybe original from Genoa, who worked in Venice from the end of the 14th century to the middle of the 15th century.

— Square panel with the bust of the Redeemer, of the 9th century. The Redeemer holds a book in his left hand, and keeps his right hand on his chest. His image is inserted in a circle decorated with little cones. The external square frame is decorated with little palmettes that fill the corner spaces.

— Square panel with the bust of an angel, symbol of Saint Matthew, of the 9th century. Similar to the preceeding one in decorations, here the angel has a halo around his head and a book in his hands. Some parts are painted.

— Little tablet with images of four Saints, fragment of a book covering, dating back to the 12th-13th centuries. In an interlacing of vine-shoots there are four busts of the Saints Steven, Vitus, Modestus, Cassianus.

— Little tablet of «**Dormitio Virginis**»: Christ accepts in his hands the soul of Mary, represented with human resemblings, while the body lies on a high catafalque surrounded by decorating figures. Above, two angels (Constantinople, Byzantine art of the 12th century).

— Little tablet of «**Maiestas Domini**: Christ is represented on a throne with a cushion. Four angels sustain a shield that carries the representation (Byzantine art of the 12th century).

— Scenes of Jesus' birth: it is represented the scene of the Crib with angels, shepherds, sheep, the Three Kings, the Child, the ox and the little donkey. Below there is a well-known scene of the Child's bath (12th century).

— Scenes of Jesus' burial: Christ is taken away from the cross, surrounded by the pious women and by the angels (Byzantine art of the 14th century).

Show-case 3 - Little tablet with a tournament scene: two horsemen face each other while above the judges and spectators with shrills of trumpets observe the scene. On the sides of the tablet two ladies give the weapons to the two horse-men (14th century).

— Tabernaculum representing in the middle the Madonna sitting with the infant, while an angel hands her the crown. On the doors other scenes are nicely worked (French art of the 15th century).

— Little statue of a king on the throne, with a crown, sceptre and a hawk in the left hand, surrounded by warriors. It is a work of the 13th century, and it would represent the emperor Fredric II or Henry the Fowler.

— Bone panel on which a woman crowns a young man (French art of the 14th century).

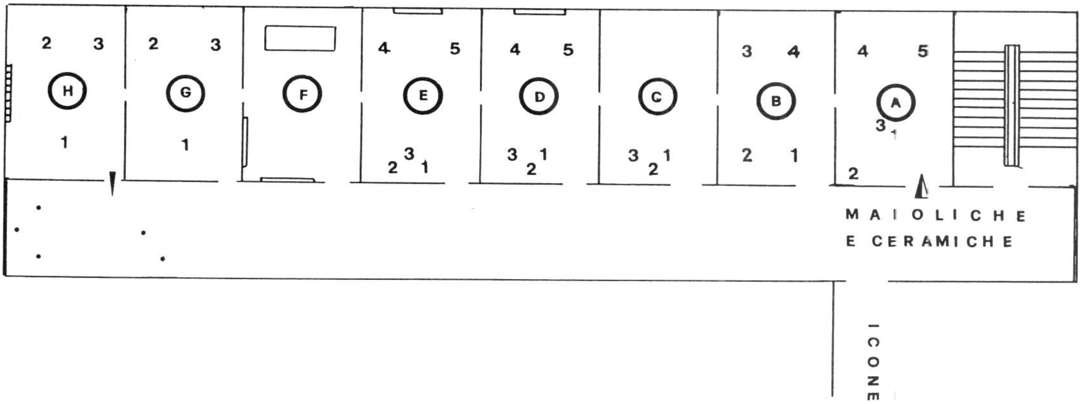

Fig. 16 - Plan of the ceramic and majolica rooms.

— Diptych on which the crucifixion and the arrival of the Three Kings are represented (14th century).

Show-case 4 - Little tablet rich of decorations obtained with tanglings and interlacings of plants, on which figures of animals appear and, in the middle, a warrior on the ground bitten on the legs by a hyena. (Arabic art of the 13th century).

Show-case 5 - A big coffer, two smaller coffers and various pieces that make part of coffers.

Show-case 6 - Beautiful octagonal coffer of the Carthusian type (manner of the Embriachi), rich of various and beautiful scenes worked in a masterly manner.

— Two little painted tablets: on one Christ carrying the Cross. and the Nativity; on the other, Jesus in the garden and the presentation to the Temple (14th century).

— Little tablet, divided in two compartments, with traces of colour, on which high above the Crucifixion is represented, and below the Announcement (14th century).

— Little square tablet of Russian art divided in seven compartments with scenes of the New Testament, practically miniaturized.

ROOM L - Pastoral (first on the right) (16) of enamelled copper with a deep blue background covered with golden lilies (Venetian art beginning of the 15th century.

— Pastoral (second on the right) (17) with pieces of ivory and wood painted in miniature (14th century). On the stick an ivory curl of preceeding age, which ends with a dragon's head and closes in the volute the «Agnus Dei». Above we read, in Gothic letters, the word PHILIPPE.

ROOM M - Cabinet of the 18th century, made in Brussels (19). In the central part there is an architectural motif with tortile columns sustaining pediments. On the sides there are five orders of drawers decorated with glasses on which landscapes with human figures, castles and ruins are painted.

ROOM N - Cabinets of the 17th century and 18th century.

ROOM O - Work cabinet with a flap, of the 16th century (Northern Italy).

ROOM P - Cabinet of the second half of the 15th century and little coffer of the 18th century.

Now we must still visit an important section of the Museum i.e. the COLLECTION OF ICONS, THE COLLECTION OF MAJOLICAS AND CERAMICS, THE COLLECTION OF COINS.

In order to reach this side of the museum we must return to the ROOM OF THE SINOPIES, from which we get to two corridors and where we find the collection of icons. The visit must start from icon n. 1, at the beginning of the corridor on the right.

COLLECTION OF ICONS

This collection is of municipal property, deposited at the museum, it is made up of 192 pieces exposed in 29 windows.

With the term «icon» we intend the sacred image painted on wood with the aim of vener-

ation. At the base of the icon there is theology «which explains and makes worthy its deep meaning, it gives an explanation of the correlation between image as appearance and image as substance, i.e. between the religious affirmed principle and the artistic module consequently elaborated» (P. Angiolini Martinelli).

The icons are classified according to precis conventional terms. Therefore we have the kind of the «Madonna that protects you along your way» (VIRGIN ODIGHITRIA); the «Madonna of tenderness» (VIRGIN GLYCOPHILOUSA); the breast-feeding Madonna (VIRGINA GALAKTOTROPHOUSA) etc...

We remind futhermore that here real icons of Byzantine subject and style of Cretan origin are exhibited; paintings which show local influences, firstly from Venice, but also from Bologna,

A B E F
C D G H
I K

National Museum: ceramics and majolicas.

- a - Majolicas and ceramics. Room A, show-case 3: Plate of Deruta majolica, representing the bust of an armed warrior.
- b - Majolicas and ceramics. Room A, show-case 4: Cup with Diogenes near the barrel before Alexander and cavaliers.
- c - Room A, show-case 4: trencher with the scene of Scipio's embarkation towards Spain.
- d - Room A, show-case, 3: profile of a woman. Deruta majolica.
- e - Room B, show-case 2: little basin with a man closed in a cage.
- f - Room B, show-case 2: The Tiburtine Sibyl that announces to Augustus the birth of the Saviour. Plate from Faenza.
- g - Room B, show-case 4: plate in majolica of Castelli with scene of triumph.
- h - Room B, show-case 4: plate in majolica of Castelli with an emperor and his army.
- i - Room D, show-case 4: bottle and jug.
- k - Room F: majolica jugs from Ravenna.

ANCHOR
IO SPERO

LIMARIE
MAR: SIMP:

Ferrara, Romagna; other tablets which can't be classified as icons.

This is not the seat to describe every single piece. We shall therefore limit ourselves to describe the grouping, advising the visitor a personal and careful consideration of the various paintings, that are numbered from 1 to 192.

First two show-cases (number 1 to 15): icons of the 15th-16th-17th centuries, representing the Madonna and the Infant in a tender attitude, with their heads and cheeks near to one another (VIRGIN GLYCOPHILOUSA).

Third, fourth, fifth, sixth, seventh, eighth show-cases: n. 16 Virgin NICOPEIA (Madonna on the throne with the Infant on her lap, of the 14th-15th century); n. 17 MADONNA PLATYTERA (Madonna with Christ represented on a shield (clipeus) that lays on the bosom, to express the Immaculate Conception, of the 16th century); numbers 18 to 50, VIRGIN ODIGHITRIA. The Virgin is represented while holding the Infant on the right arm (centuries 15-16-17).

Ninth show-case: n. 51, Crowned Virgin; n. 53 Virgin «ROSA SEMPITERNA» (Virgin with rose and palm, Infant with sceptre and the world), of the 18th century.

Tenth show-case: mystical mariage of St. Catherine and various Saints (14th-15th centuries).

Eleventh show-case: various paintings with the VIRGIN ODIGHITRIA and Saints.

In **show-cases 12-13-14-15-16-17** (numbers 71 to 111); VIRGIN GALAKTOTROPHOUSA: The Virgin breast feeds the Infant holding him in the left arm. Sometimes Saints such as Catherine, Saint Sebastian, San Rocco etc... appear (centuries 15-16-17).

In the corner room, icon n. 113; in front Saint Peter and Paul, on the back the Annunciation (16th century). N. 154 Triptych of Christ, of the 15th century.

Eighteenth show-case: (numbers 112-114-116): Announcements.

Show-cases 19-20-21 (numbers 117-136): icons all representing the Nativity or the adoration of the Three Kings. They belong to the 16th century - 18th century. N. 118 belongs to the 18th century and 135 and 136 to the 18th and 19th centuries.

The remaining show-cases (from 22-29 for the numbers that go from 137-192) present icons with different subjects. We underline n. 137: Introduction to the Temple (and of the 16th century); n. 138: Deesis (intercession of the Virgin Mary and of the Baptist before Christ the Supreme Judge, 16th century); n. 142: Saint George and the Dragon (second half of the 17th century); n. 144: Crucifixion among Mary, John and four Saints (first thirty years of the 16th century); n. 146: Saint Parasceve, 16th-17th centuries (Parasceve i.e. preparation: Friday for the Jews when they prepare all that is necessary to celebrate Sabbath); n. 154 Triptych of Christ (15th century); n. 165: Daniel in the lion's pit (17th century); n. 191: Madonna between Saint Catherine and Saint Jerome.

Let's go along the two corridors of the icons and get to the LONG NEW DORMITORY (Fiandrini map, above n. 44) in which, on the right the eight rooms of FORESTRY AND INFIRMARY open, which are above the cellar for vats (Fiandrini Map above n. 46). From the windows of the big corridor we can see the staired tower of which at n. 24 of the plan at page 24, the roof of the narthex of the basilica (n. 4, plan at pag. 24), the bell-tower.

Let's enter the first of the eight beautiful rooms where the collection of

MAJOLICAS AND CERAMICS is located - Majolics are ceramic products of porous pasta, opaque, not as fine as china. Ceramic consists of a mixture of clay and other substances, which undergo the action of fire. The word «majolica» derives from Majorca Island.

What we shall say on visiting the rooms will be sufficient enough to make out the majority of the pieces exposed, considering the plan on page 00.

The first two rooms contain majolicas of the Renaissance and Baroque epoch, coming from the Classense Museum.

ROOM A

Show-case 1: two very beautiful majolica plates of Hispano-moresque art, maybe from the Spanish town «*Manises*» (in the province of Valenza, famous since the 5th century for its ceramics). The two plates of the second half of the 15th century, are decorated with concentric rings of little leaves, flowers and vine-tendrils. In the centre, one of the two plates carries a heraldic shield with a hilly-goat and star, the other with a ram according to the kind of the *Agnus Dei*.

Show-case 2: cup, plate and vase of Deruta, from the first third of the 16th century. In the plate the crucifixion and a crowd of 67 figures is represented. On the edge there are 16 little circles with episodes. The town of Deruta is famous for the majolica schools that flowered there.

Show-case 3: four majolica plates of Deruta, first third of the 16th century..., in one of which the bust of an armed warrior is represented, while in the other three a woman seen in profile is drawn, in front of which there is a ribbon with a distinct inscription: IN CHOR GINTILE NON REGNA INGRATITUDINE - SOLA LA MORTE ISTINGIE EL VERO AMORE - LA VITA EL FINE EL DI LODA LA SERA.

Show-case 4: Three cups and a trencher (plate, tray) in majolica of Urbino. On one of the cups the scene of Cronos and Filira is presented. We can see Cronos, who caught by Rea, under the form of a horse leaves Filira, one of the Oceanines, loved by him. The centaur Chirone thus is born. On another cup you can see Diogenes near the barrel, in front of Alexander and the cavaliers. On the third cup the episode of Pan and Syrinx is painted. Syrinx, nymph of Arcady, while chased by Pan transforms into a reed. After this Pan made an instrument of reeds of different lenghts, called for this reason *syrinx* (panpipe).

On the trencher we can see the scene of the embarking of Scipio who from Rome is going to Spain to fight against the Carthaginians, as the long inscription on the back explains. In the centre, a majolica plate, from Forlì, representing in live colours Scipio's triumph. It is of the 4th decade of the 16th century. On the back the inscription: FU FATE IN FORLI.

Show-case 5: A majolica jug of Faenza stands out, that dates back to 1435-1540, in which two of Hercules' labours are represented (the fight against Anteus and against the Nemean lion, and the adoration of the Three Kings. The city of Faenza, which is 32 Kilometres from Ravenna, is universally known for its ceramic production. Two trenchers of Urbino, of the second half of the 16th century, on which the scene of Muzio Scevola who burns his hand in front of Porsenna is represented, on the other, the camping scene with tents and soldiers. A majolica cup of Forlì, of 1545, in which Parnassus (Apollo and a group of Muses) is represented. Another majolica element (1530-1540) in which the rage of Juno had broken out against Aeneas: «I shall...» Neptune doesn't continue his invective, and in this form the «*quos ego*» has remained a famous, effective, proverbial example of reticence full of obscure threats. This scene is interpreted also as Aeneas and Acate, brave and faithful companion of Aeneas, who meet Venus.

In the room there is a fire-place with stucco-works and four octagons with putti.

ROOM B

Show-case 1: two majolica cups, of the second half of the 16 century..., one represents Jesus Christ mocked with his thorn crown. In the inscription: AVE.REX.IUDEOURM.FORUM LIIVII (Forlì), 1563. On the other one we have the representation of Daphne, who chased by Apollo is going to be transformed into bay-leaf. A majolica epergne of Urbino, of the end of the last 20 years of the 16th century. The epergne is a tray with several shelves. «Crespina» (a cup with a short foot with a wavy edge), of the second half of the 16th century. David playing for king Saul is represented.

Show-case 2: Two plates of Faenza, one of which dating 1563, representing the baptism of Christ in the Jordan River with the signature of the author: «Iacomo timimoteo 1563 adi 13 de novembro» the other of the last 30 years of the 16th century represents the Tiburtine Sybil who announces Augustus the birth of the Saviour. A little basin of Forlì production, in which a man closed in a cage is represented, iconic visualization of the motto: ANCHOR IO SPERO - 1562. The cage could be a «travaglio», which is a means of keeping together and still horses or other animals.

Show-case 3: a majolica coffee-pot of Faenza, of 1740-1750, surrounded by Castelli plates, all of the 18th century, with landscapes, rural scenes and personification of different sciences. The Castelli town, in Abruzzo is famous for its ceramic industry, particularly prosperous from the 16th century to the 18th century.

Show-case 4: four majolica plates of Castelli, of the middle of the 17th century one of which with a triumph scene, another with the emperor and his troops, the third with a hunting scene, the last one with a woman and a monkey under a tree.

Rooms C and D present pieces bought after the passage of the Museum to the state.

ROOM C

In the three show-cases little jugs and «albarelli» are exhibited. The «alberello» (more often called «albarello»-little tree) is a painted majolica vase which gets its name from the fact that often these vases, used by the druggists, were made of poplar wood, that before were derived from reed bamboo containers cut in nots. These pieces, as those of show-cases 4 and 5 of room D, are chemist vases and carry the relative inscription to what they contain.

In the room, as in the following ones, there is an inlaid Renaissance chest.

ROOM D

Show-case 1: in the lower part we notice a Castelli plate of the 17th century and a Faenza epergne of 1644, both from the conventional typology of the «*whites*», a sauce-boat and an

1
2 3
4 5

National Museum: 1, Constantinople's Mint, emperor Manuel 1st (1123-1180) on the left, who holds a cross on a globe together with another character. - 2, Constantinople's Mint, busts of Constantius 7th (905-959) on the left and of Roman 2nd (939-963) with a crown on which there is a cross. - 3, Constantinople's Mint, Constantius 2nd (630-668). - 4, Ravenna's Mint, Galla Placidia (388-450). - 5, Ravenna's Mint, Valentinian 3rd (419-455) with the sceptre in his right hand, while trampling on a snake with human head.

espergne of Pesaro, a plate of Faenza of the end of the 17th century (typology of the whites). On the stem, a coffeepot of Faenza of the 18th century, a fruit-bowl, a little cup and plate, of the 18th century.

Show-case 2: it presents several pieces of Ferniani factory of Faenza, factory which recovered the situation of the Faenza production, which had gone down at the end of the 17th century. There are plates, a tray, a sauce-boat, little cups and plates, all in majolica, of the 18th century.

Show-case 3: the portrait of Enrico Pazzi, a sculptor, born in Ravenna in 1818, died in 1899, author of many remarkable sculptures, here he is reminded only as the promoter of the Museum, and by the statue *Venice Chained* (see p. 81). His most famous work is the statue of *Dante Alighieri* which was placed in Santa Croce square in Florence.

Show-cases 4 and 5: «albarelli», jugs, pill containers, vases, bottles of the 17th and 18th centuries. They are all pharmacy containers, some of which carry signs of their provenance. A few examples: show-case 4, bottle n. 54 coming from the San Domenico Pharmacy, with the image of the Saint. Show-case 4, bottle n. 50, coming from the Pomposa pharmacy, with the inscrition POMPOSIA, around an eight pointed star above which there is the abbatial hat, of blackish colour, and from which plaited ropes fall down. On this vase the inscrition LINARIE appears, which refers to the medicine contained, which generally was a vegetable extract. The «linaria» is a grassy plant that in some species is similar to linen, from which it derives the name. Show-case 5, «albarello» n. 42: here the provenance is indicated by initials, formed by the interwining of the letters CLS, initials of the monastery of Classe.

Rooms E and F contain archaic ceramic (the ceramics produced until the beginning of the 15th century are called archaic) of Ravenna's production found during excavations (in Sant'Agata church and Caduti square - Piazza dei Caduti). They are interesting for their sober decoration with two colours, and because they document the first attempts to use «stannifero» glaze. Generally they are decorated with big Gothic letters, with stems, and animal figures.

ROOM E

Show-case 1: bowls, little plates, fragments.

Show-case 2: big vase with two handles, little plates, saucers, bowls, jugs. A few pieces are marked with the initials S.V. (San Vitale).

Show-case 3: plates, bowls, fragments. Big vase with a pouring spout and a pilgrim's flask.

Show-case 4: vases, pots, pilgrim's flask, trivet, basin, jug. Little kitchen vases (centuries 15 and 18).

Show-case 5: basin, bowl, various fragments (16th century).

As well as a Renaissance chest, in this room there is a big painting of a local painter of the end of the 16th century representing the *Madonna with the Baby and Saints*.

ROOM F

The big window contains: below, several jugs coming from furnace discarding, because they had turned out faulty during the cooking phase and therefore thrown away; higher up, a group of jugs which can be dated back to the end of the year 1300, with Gothic letters and various drawings. Let's simplify indicating the jug n. 154 (heraldic mount and star), n. 156 (man's profile, rather rare as a subject), n. 157. with a deer.

All together there are about fifty jugs, water and wine containers, with a three lobed spout decorated with flowers, religious, geometrical motifs.

In the room two chests, two chairs, and two paintings of *Bernardino Guarini*, dated 1601.

ROOM G

Didactic room, that in three show-cases develops the theme: *From the manipulation of clay to the ceramic object*. The demonstration presents the successive phases of its processing with complete explanations «in loco».

Between the two windows, stucco-work ornaments. On the walls, a very ruined fresco of a Romanesque-Byzantine painter of the 13th century and a fresco of a painter from the Romagnol school, representing Saint Paul, Anthony abbot and maybe Saint Apollinare. Two lunettes of *Francesco Longhi*, on one of which Galla Placidia during a thunderstorm is represented, while on the other we can see the consecration of the church of San Giovanni Evangelista, built as grant to the vow.

ROOM H

Various pieces are exhibited, among which we notice (*show-case 1*) half a brick with a mould for the production of lead pellets for harquebus (near it, a leaden slab). In *show-case 2*, plates and vases of the centuries 15 and 16 of Faenza and Ravenna. In *show-case 3*, a love cup on which there is a female figure that holds in the right hand a book and in the left hand a cup with two eyes. The latin inscription says: FACIAT UNUSQUISQUE QUOD VULT SIVE... CUNCTOS SORTE GENERAVIT) The inscription is remarkable and curious, and it makes use partly of musical notes (re-mi-fa-sol-la)

Light-weight cuirass (breastplate) (around 1550).

Corset for tourneys. We can notice the rest and three screws (around 1575).

Helmet (around 1540).

Pair of armlets for tourneys (around 1560).

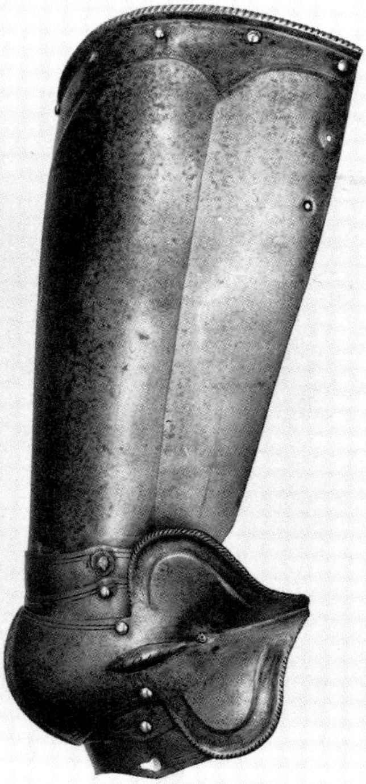

Jamb (around 1560).

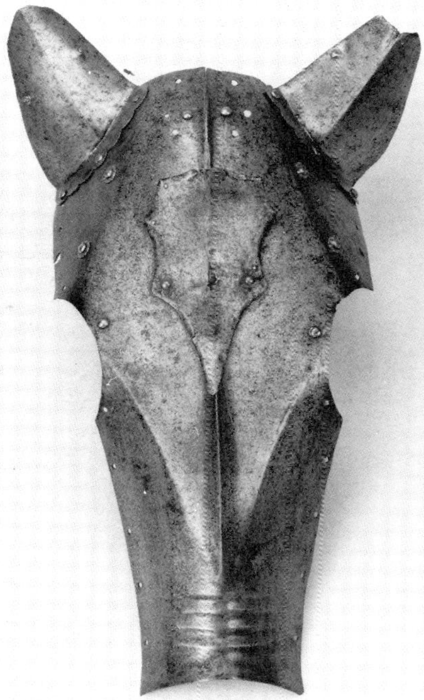

Round shield (small wheel) (first half of the 16th century).

Horse's armour (crown-piece) (second half of the 15th century).

Shoulder plate (16th-17th centuries).

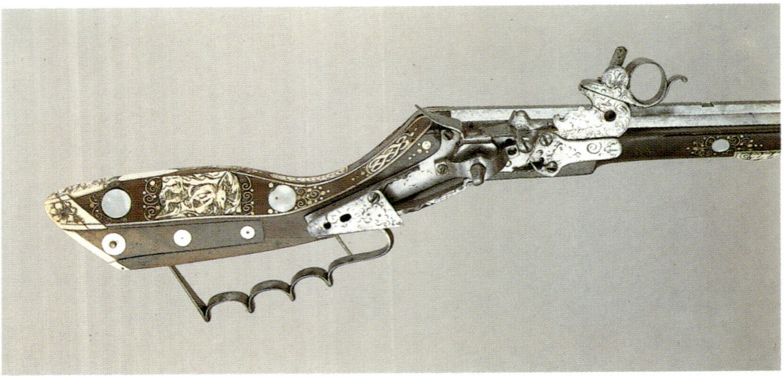

▲
Wheel locked small arquebus (around 1660-1670).

Wheel locked pistols (around 1590).
▼

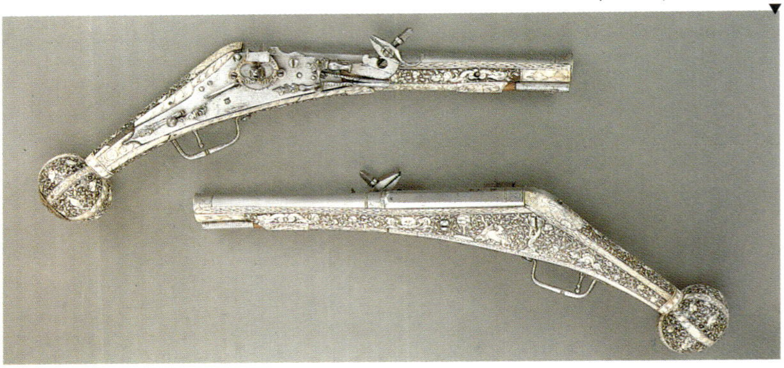

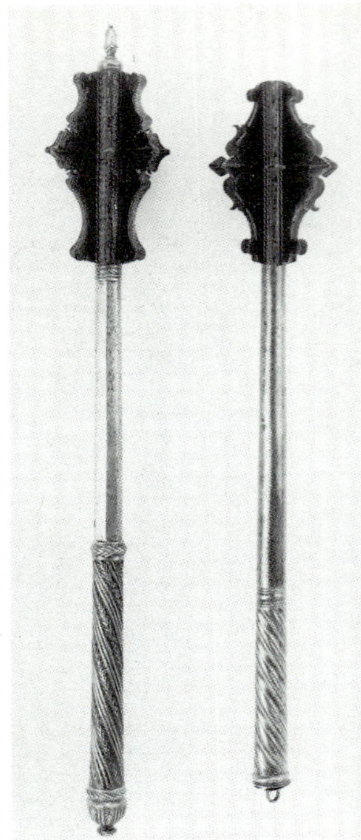

▲
Sledge-hammers (16th century).

◀
Sword blade with the inscription WEILMKLEIN (the author) SOLINGEN (the town) (around 1630-1640).

Powder flask (beginning of the 17th century).
◀

▶
Part of armour-plated doublet (beginning of the 16th century).

which together with the words, give the following clause (the syllables made up of one note are in cursive): «Tu **solla** sei che *mi* fai *la*ngui*re* cum la tua *fare*tra che *mi* passato il co*re sol fa mi*o possente amo*re* già nol posso abandona*re*». Let's notice that the musical line is of four lines. This cup, found in the excavations of Sant'Agata in 1914, is of Faentine art of the 15th century. The love cups were offered to young women and girls in occasion of matrimonies, dances and parties.

Between the two windows, stucco-work decorations. On the walls, paintings of Ravennati painters (16th-17th centuries), a copy of the paintings of the dome of San Vitale, a painting of Domenico Cignani (18th century) and one of a painter from Rimini of the 17th century.

In the room there is also an altar complex, which also comprises a ciborium, angels and six candeliers. It is a work of *Bartolomeo Borroni*, carried out in the years 1737-1739 for the church of San Romualdo on design of *Giampaolo Pannini*.

Let's return to the corridor, where the wide window allows us to see the space which was once occupied by the BIG KITCHEN GARDEN (P.F n. 58) of the monastery, and in which the house of the gardener arose. The area is now used for parking.

Near the window we find three show-cases. One of them contains a model of the Mausoleum of Theodoric, complete of the circle of columns which composed the higher open-gallery. The other two present a study of the space of the Neonian baptistery, work of the architect *Raffaello Trinci*. Other two show-cases present material found during excavations carried out in the church of Santa Croce.

A few little doors in the corridor lead to offices, which once were the MONKS' ROOMS.

Let's go down to stair flights that bring to a mezzanine floor, where a precious **COLLECTION OF COINS** is exposed. The corridor which houses this collection, with a low vault ceiling, goes onto the third cloister of the monastery.

The collection consists of several thousand coins, which cover a period that goes from the 4th century B.C. to Modern times. In this seat we can only determine the great periods in which the complete collection can be subdivided, revealing that the visit is facilitated by an excellent arrangement of material.

— Greek coins.
— Roman coins of the Republican period; pieces that go from the end of the 4th century B.C. to Anthony and Julius Caesar.
— Roman coins of the Imperial period, from Augustus to Theodosius.
— Coins of the Roman Emperors of the West, period during which Ravenna was seat of the Imperial Court (coins of Honorius, Galla Placidia, Valentinian III, Maggicriano...).
— Coins of the Barbarian kings: Odoacer, Theodoric, Athalaricus, Theodahat, Vitiges, Baduela (Totila).
— Coins of the Byzantine emperors, from Arcadius to Justinian to Alessio III Angelo, who died in 1203.
— Medieval and Modern coins.
— Medals, seals and plaques.

The Byzantine coins belong majorly to Italian mint issues and to Ravenna's mint.

Going down the last flight of stairs we reach a long room that the monks used as a TINNAZZARA (Flandrini plan n. 46), called in dialect of Romagna TINNAZZERA or TINAZERA and in Italian TINAIA, which was the place where the vats stood.

The large room where we can see eight big arches on each side, with dome vaults, held «8 vats with four iron hoops... other 15 vats with three iron hoops» (taken from an inventory of the end of the 18th century). A part of this room was raised short time ago in order to build some toilets.

Collocated in favourable position, we can finally see a statue representing **Venice chained**, valuable work of the sculptor *Enrico Pazzi*. Venice, a woman of great beauty, with her fallen cloak held by the left arm expresses pain, on her face, on which also hope shines through.

She is sitting on the back of the lion of Saint Mark, and she lays her right hand on its mane, while the ancle is chained and the bare foot touches the sea (notice the shells). The lion with its folded wings holds with its paw the ducal horn, ceremony headgear and insignia of the doges of Venice, very elegantly adorned, it expresses a collected, detained strength. The author writes that this Venice was to remind «its past power, the actual oppression and misery, the awaiting for its recovery».

The clay model of the statue was executed in 1865, when Venice was still under Austria, but since war broke out (3rd war of independence, 1866) and Venice became Italian, the theme lost actuality and the model was made in marble only in 1884, under request of the Rasponi family.

Whilst going towards the exit on the left we can see the sarcophagus of Tiberius Claudius Felix Victorinus (first decades of the 3rd century A.D.), decorated on three sides, with a roof-like lid, provided with acroteria made up of youth busts. The inscription referring to a boy who died at the age of three years, 5 months and 13 days presents on its sides two male characters dressed in togas. On the right hand side of the corridor there are: an architectural element of a Roman building of the 2nd-3rd century A.D. and a Byzantine capital of the 6th century made like a truncate upside-down pyramid, decorated with a cluster and thorny leaves. Farther on the left there is an iron bombard, found in the Rocca Brancaleone, of the end of the 15th or of the beginning of the 16th century.

Finally on the right we can see the relief map of the excavations carried out in 1980 at the new seat of the Banca Popolare di Ravenna, with three levels (A: the Medieval phase from 0,70 m. to 3,5 m of depth; B: the Byzantine and Medieval phase, from 2,30 m to 3,90; C: the Roman, Republican and Imperial phase from 4,40 to 5,50 m).

The raised part of the room contains a

COLLECTION OF ARMOURS - The museum houses a valuable collection of arms, of the 16th and 17th century, but at present (end of 1993) not exhibited. We are going to describe in any case the pieces which were before exposed, in their placing now eliminated. The pieces were distributed in five double rectangular windows, on the left side of the room; in three cubic show-cases in the central part; while on the right two sustains with cuirasses, six mannequins with armours, and some pieces of armours lined up. On the walls lances and halberds.

As it is impossible to describe every single piece of this interesting testimony of a time that has definitely come to an end we shall point out:

Left wall - *Window 1*: A frontal of a horse armour with protection for the ears. Fire-arms. *Window 2*: Crossbows and pistols with ivory inlaid cases. The two pistols higher up have ivory inlayds which represent volutes, birds, little geniuses and monsters (18th century). Near the pistols a little flask for gun-powder with ivory inlayds is exposed. On the visible part, on a little mother-of-pearl disc, a ministral playing the liute is represented; on the non-visible part a Spanish cavalier in a gala suit (18th century). On the back a few maces. *Window 3*: Three shields. The one on the left is a light shield of steel with leaf and flower decorations, in helicoidal radiuses. In the middle, a little round shield with the central part very convexed and sometimes, as here, provided with a point, decorated with nine radiuses and a brass rose-window. On the right, a light shield of chiselled steel, divided in four concentric zones. *Windows 4 and 5*: Various swords, one of which, with a long blade, with the inscription WEILM KLEIN SOLINGEN (Solingen is a German city, already famous in the Middle Ages for its sword factory).

Central part - *First cube*: pieces of armour and swords. *Second cube*: as well as a few weapon-models, remarkable is the Serravezza marble head, maybe a work of *Tullio Lombardo*, author of the statue of *Guidarello Guidarelli*. It represents the face of a dead young man, maybe Gastone di Foix. *Third cube*: It contains five sallets (war helmets different from others because they have no crest). The one in the middle, has the shape of a sparrow's beak decorated by chisel. The two thin opening so as to permit visibility are to be noticed.

Right wall - Among the cuirasses, we underline the second one on the wooden support, which on the right side is supplied with «rest», i.e. a bar on which the lance butt was laid, during fighting. On the left side of the same cuirass there are three big screw keys. The helmet is supplied with throut defence, the visor is hood-like. An oblong opening allows the combatant to see. Notice also the little round rectangular holes placed on the fold of the hood, that are necessary for breathing. Six mannequins with armours follow, beyond which, on the walls, parts of armours are hung, such as shoulder, elbow, arm and thigh coverings.

Let's pass the room with lowered vaults of the CELLAR (P.F. 44), in which the barrels were placed (15 casks with four hoops containing about 4 barrels, for red wine; 13 barrels with 4 iron hoops, for white wine...) (taken from an ancient inventory). Now it houses the findings carried out near S. Martino in Gattara, locality in the Lamone valley on the boundaries between Romagna and Tuscany. These findings of the 6th, 5th, 4th centuries B.C., coming from tombs, would testify the existence of Celtic populations in Italy starting off at the end of the 6th century B.C., confirming the news of Titus Livius according to which the Celtics had arrived in Italy during the reign of Tarquinius.

In the same room there are also other archaeological findings from excavations (cinerary vases and stelae) carried out in the Necropolis of Via Romea Vecchia, 300 metres South of the church of S. Severo. It was a necropolis of sailors of the imperial fleet stationed in Classe, dating back to the 1st century A.D.

Let's notice on the left the stele of Anarius Felix who was discharged from his military service carried out on the ship «Sphynx» with two oar orders (liburna). The open V sign pointing to the right, placed after the word «MISSICIO» indicates that Anarius was a non-commissioned officer. This is confirmed also by the knotted rod, below, insignia of the command that the centurions held on the right hand and that they used for punishments. Let's also notice the stele of Plator, son of Abacalli, carpenter as we can suppose from the sculpture under the inscription. On the frontal edges there are two little columns with Corinthian capitals and, in the centre of the pediment, a flower. It is of the 2nd quarter of the 1st century A.D.

Let's then see the stele of Apella (the fifth on the left) GUBER (nator), i.e. helmsman of the ship Neptune, with a beautiful realistic portrait and the representation of the rudder. It dates back to the 1st century A.D.

Let's also notice (in the back corner) the stele of Velageno Gralis, son of Caronio, a carpenter (DOLATOR), with beautiful decorative motifs such as two semi-circles in the centre of which a flower and behind, three acanthus leaves. The Vicus Clablus remembered in the inscription is an unidentified place (1st century A.D.).

Finally the stele with the little portraits of two women who are combed with a middle parting.

On the wall at the end there are cinerary vases of terra-cotta a few of which painted, glass and lead cinerary vases, oil-lamps and coins (necropolis of Via Romea Vecchia).

Once this cellar extended in lenght beyond the extremity where cinerary vases are now lined up, until occupying the narthex of the basilica and joining the subsequent staircase.

Going out of the museum, on the right in the open air you can see the so-called

Baths of the clergy - Here some parts of the wall structures that were found while digging for the widening of the Banca Popolare, near the «Duomo» and the «Neonian» baptistery have been rebuilt. They made part of the architectural complex of the bishopric, the construction of which was started in the 5th century. We received news of the existence, in this place, of baths, by the protohistorian of the Ravennate church Andrea Agnello, who wrote in the 9th century. We can see two semi-circular baths, one of which with a marble coating, the other with traces of a heating implant under the floor. The recomposition of the structure was executed by disassembling the parts and with the aid of resin moulds.

Having finished our visit to S. Vitale with the mausoleum and to the National Museum, le'ts go out just walking near the basilica, along the iron gate that encloses the area. We can admire the strong buttresses build up around 1000, and the lively look of the side with the apse.

Near the counter-fort immediately on our right there is a sarcophagus of the first half of the 6th century, used later by the Cavalli family, as we can read from the inscription.

From this point we can see on the wall of the circular chapel on the side of the apse (chapel of the Blessed Virgin), under the crowning, a little column which sustains a «crutchlike» capital (fig. 3 n. 23).

It is the remainder of a vestibule built in the 9th-10th century in front of one of the five perimetral doors of the basilica. The vestibule was thrown down in the second half of the last century, in the wrong convinction that it was an arbitrary adding of recent times.

The two circular chapels ending with a little rectangular lower chapel placed on the sides of the apse, and one of which we have visited the inside, are the «prothesis» and the «diaconicon».

Beyond the basilica we can see, on the right, the wall with narrow windows and arches that open on the level of the floor, under which there are some sarcophagi. It was part of a building preceeding the present one and it is certainly in connection with the former monastery. A beautiful bricky cornice of the 16th century, that was at n. 19 of Via Guaccimanni, has been put here. But we suppose it originally decorated a palace of the Rasponis' demolished in 1581.

Farther on, on the right, there is an elegant Renaissance portico with little columns of Veronese marble, tied in the middle by a ring. One of these is variably fluted.

The inscription «PROCUL O PROCUL ESTE PROPHANI», that we find on the architrave on the door, reproduces the formula used in the «eleusinian» mysteries which Virgil puts in the mouth of the Sybil when he introduces Aeneas in the Avernus excluding his mates (Aeneid, book IV, v. 258):

«. . . . . . Away, away profanes
shouted in the prophetess, go far away from [the wood,
and you enter with me»

(vv. 381. Translation Annibal Caro)

Now we are in a courtyard with lawns, bay shrubs, pines and holm-oaks, surrounded by an iron gate that substitutes a wall demolished in 1890, where we can see several sarcophagi. Along the gate ther are seven of these, with lids of various kinds, on the right there are four uncovered sarcophagi, two of which adorned with festoons, one is next to the basilica.

The sarcophagi of Ravenna constitute a remarkable chapter of early Christian Art, those that we see here haven't much sculptural value, but they are very ancient, even if sometimes they have been used again in more recent epoches. Among them we underline the last one on the left which constitutes a beautiful example of sarcophagus ready to be sold, in the awaiting that the buyer would decide which type of decoration was to be effected. Infact the parts destined to be sculptured (the sides of the space that is to be dedicated to the epigraph; the sides, the back) are deliberately roughed out. The fourth sarcophagus of the seven on the left has the lid like a barrel, adorned, on the right lunette, by a little cross closed between two palmettes, and on the left lunette by a Chrismon; it is of the 5th century. On the right we underline the sarcophagus immediately before the Renaissance portico, shattered in front, that carries a monogrammed cross, and it dates back to the first half of the 6th century.

The sarcophagus, known as Bonifacio's, next to the basilica, is of the end of the 5th century, with the inscription on it engraved much later. The two coats-of-arms on the sides of the panel that carries the inscription substitute two crosses. At the back, a monogrammatic cross with the pendulous letters (alpha and omega), motif that repeats itself also on the lid where, on the front side, is bordered by two peacocks. On the lunette of the lid there is a cross inserted into a lion mask, bordered on the right lunette, by two doves and on the left on by two lambs.

Let's go out through the arch, already described on page 00, and, for a visit to the churches of Santa Croce and Santa Maria Maggiore, let's turn left immediately into Via Galla Placidia that borders the fence of S. Vitale and in which there are the two very ancient churches of Santa Maria Maggiore and Santa Croce.

SANTA MARIA MAGGIORE - The church is on a little square beyond the apse of San Vitale. It was built by bishop Ecclesius in the years 525-532, that is at the same time in which they were working to build San Vitale, it was originally a church of great beauty. It was rebuilt in 1671 by Pietro Grossi according to some baroque models, it now presents itself externally with a very modest aspect and internally very much redone, with a few remainders of the primitive construction. The bell-tower is of cylindrical form, as others in the Ravenna zone. It shows on the bottom traces of an original door. It presents two rows of narrow windows, two of tall and large ones, one of six windows with two lights. It has been assigned to the 9th-10th century.

The ancient church had three aisles, subdivided by 16 columns of Greek marble, provided of a transept in which the triumphal arch opened held by two big columns. In the apse there was a mosaic representing the Madonna with the inscription «VIRGINIS AULA MICAT» (the room of the Virgin shines). On the inferior part there was a marble covering. Maybe the mosaic extended also to the front of the triumphal arch, with the representation of Ecclesius who offered Mary the model of the church. The mosaic got ruined in 1550.

Today the church, that is the one of 1671, maintains the ancient apse that now serves as presbytery. From the first reconstruction, other twelve columns of Greek marble have been used again with Byzantine capitals of the 6th century. The bases of the columns, instead, were sculptured in 1671 by *Domenico Cerchioli*.

The three aisles are divided on each side by four arches, divided by a piece of wall for support and reinforcement.

Three windows for each wall of the central aisle and one of the lateral aisles, give light to the inside. The ceiling is trussed.

Above the entrance door there is a bust representing Ecclesius with the inscription «B. ECCLESIUS ARCHIEP HANC AEDEM EREXIT A.D. DXXVII» («*the blessed archbishop Ecclesius built this church in the year of God 527*»). On the sides of the door two terra-cotta medallions are placed, they were in the church of San Romualdo. On the right, entering, at man's height there is a brick taken from the Porta Santa di San Pietro in occasion of the sacred year 1650. The holy water stoup, sustained by a column, comes from the disappeared church of Santa Maria *in Coeloseo*.

In the middle of the right aisle there is the canvas of an unknown painter of the eighteenth century representing the Crucifixion; on the transept there is an ancient fresco representing the Madonna with the Infant. At the bottom of the aisle the Roman sarcophagus used by the Rasponi family. Above it there is a long epigraph with the epitaph of the architect Camillo Morigia, here buried. This chest-like sarcophagus is dated at the beginning (2nd century A.D.) of the production of sarcophagi in Ravenna. The iconography (a tabula ansata held by two winged victories) symbolizes the apotheosis of the soul.

In the apse, behind the altar, there is a marble statue representing the Virgin with the Infant, work of *Giovanni Toschini*, which with the angels of the major altar, of the same author, comes from the basilica of San Vitale. The apse conch has the form of a big shell. In the chapels of the transept the stucco-works are of *Antonio Martinetti*. In the one on the left a Gothic station crucifix is placed.

At the end of the left aisle there is a painting of *Luca Longhi* which represents Saint Paul visiting Saint Agatha in prison.

On the aisle wall there is a painting recently restored with the Blessed Virgin Mary of the snow, Baby Jesus, Saint Joseph and Saint Jerome. In the middle of the aisle there is a fresco of the sixteenth century representing the Madonna with the Infant called «Madonna della Tosse» restored and brought back to canvas in 1977. It is placed over the ancient door that led to the cemetery. At the beginning of the aisle, another painting with Christ's baptism.

On the floor, in the middle of the church, the

epigraph «CAMILLO MORIGIA ULTIMO DI SUA FAMIGLIA SI RACCOMANDA ALLE VOSTRE ORAZIONI, MORÌ IL 16 GENNAIO 1795 IN ETÀ DI ANNI 51 E QUATTRO MESI» (CAMILLO MORIGIA LAST ONE OF HIS FAMILY RECOMMENDS HIMSELF TO YOUR PRAYERS, DIED ON THE 16th JANUARY 1795 AT THE AGE OF 51 AND FOUR MONTHS).

SANTA CROCE - Leaving Santa Maria Maggiore, we continue on the right along the fence of San Vitale until we reach a construction placed at the height of the Mausoleum of Galla Placidia. This is what is left of the very ancient church of Santa Croce, which had been erected by Galla Placidia (first half of the 5th century) who, as the historian Agnellus in a very suggestive piece tells us, used to go there to pray:

«*... they say that Galla Placidia herself ordered to place chandeliers on four bases of red marble, and during the night and during the day she would throw herself on the floor to pray to God, and would spend the night, praying with tears in her eyes, until the candles gave light*».

The excavation of Santa Croce, with its various metres of deepness, gives us the opportunity to remember that if we dug all around the surrounding zone we would find, as have been found in various occasions, evidence of the existence of a vast residential area of Roman epoch, at an inferior quote and therefore preceeding the sacellum of Galla Placidia and naturally the basilica of San Vitale.

The church of Santa Croce was built on the remainders of a big Roman building of the 2nd-3rd century A.D. This building like also the whole Roman residential area, was thrown down between the IVth and the beginning of the 5th century. It is in this period that the imperial court moves from Milan to Ravenna (Honorius leaves Milan and moves to Ravenna because of the invasion of Alaric, in 402) and probably there is a relation of cause and effect between this transfer and the throwing down of the Roman area (Cortesi). The region became a cemetery area, and always following the traces of Cortesi, we present the hypothesis that the basilica of Santa Croce had funerary aims (another hypothesis less believable wants the basilica to have been the church of the imperial palace). Its construction must have occurred between 417-421.

As we can notice from the ruins put in evidence by the excavations, the church was much longer, with a quadrangular apse and with two transversal arms (transept). Also the façade was more advanced than what it is now, because it underwent a shifting back in 1602 to make place to the present day's street called Galla Placidia. The excavations also permit us to make out the porticos (we can see the bases of a few columns and the mosaics of the floor of the Southern portico) which bordered the unique aisle, and two rooms on the side of the apse, of which one, the one on the South, with the function of pastophorium. We must furthermore consider that the basilica was preceedec by a narthex which extended itself beyond the façade on both sides, and which ended with two sacella of cross shape, the one on the South being the Mausoleum of Galla Placidia, and the one on the North the «monasterium Sancti Zachariae», whose remainders are under the yard of the police (Comando del Gruppo Guardie di P.S.).

What we see today is a façade of the seventeenth century, shifted backwards, in respect to the primitive one, of 7 metres; an apse of the fifteenth century, which arises out at the height of the ancient crossing between the aisle and the transept; the lateral walls, with original parts of the 5th century and with redoings of the Medieval Age (10th-13th century). The basilica was redimensioned at various intervals: the lateral porticos were demolished during the Romanesque Age; the transversal arms and the quadrangular apse between the end of the 14th century and the beginning of the 15th century; the façade, in 1602. The little bell-tower is of the eighteenth century.

Let's return on our steps towards Galla Placidia and let's turn right into Via San Vitale following it until the end.

Having reached the end of the street, we are compelled to turn left into a little via called Mura di San Vitale. A few low ruins show us the remainders of the town-walls in that point.

Having reached the end of the little slope the street ends, on the left we have via Cavour, on the right Porta Adriana.

PORTA ADRIANA - It opens the city at its hinterland. Until 1735 in front of the Porta the Montone river flowed which lapped the walls starting from Madonna del Torrione until Rocca Brancaleone the actual ring-roads Fiume Montone Abbandonato, San Gaetanino and Rotonda follow the course of the ancient river. The river was crossed before the Porta by a bridge which, when the new bed had been dug far from the city, buried itself and in 1774 it was demolished. The name of the Porta is very ancient and its origin is uncertain.

The actual construction is of 1583.

Some marbles of the ancient Port'Aurea which had been demolished the year before were used. Furthermore the two big paterae that we already saw in the National Museum were brought there. Maybe for the use of ancient marbles the Porta was called AUREA NOVA, as we read on the pediment, but this name didn't oust the ancient one.

The two venetian lions were mutilated in the period of the Cisalpina Republic when the Jacobins destroyed all the public emblems of the fallen powers, all the symbols of ancient oppression and cancelled and modified the laudatory tablets of popes and cardinals.

In 1857 Pio IX visited the city, and during that occasion the gate was restored and embellished with the adding of two lateral columns on the basement of which a pine-tree is sculptured, symbol of the city of Ravenna.

The two narrow pedestrian passages between the columns were opened in recent epochs like in other gates of the city. On the two central arches, inside, there still are some hinges of the ancient doors.

On the sides of the gate there were in origin, two semi-circular crenelated towers; in the 18th century they were substituted by the two actual squared bastions, which preceed the door of about twenty meters to increase the efficaciousness of defence in case of attack.

Of the ancient towers only a few «brackets» on a piece of wall that stretches towards the city from the bastion on the right of who is looking externally, remain. They are three ogival little arches with thin friezes in brick-work.

Who wishes to complete the itinerary without delay will continue along via Cavour full of shops. In such case pass to the paragraph «Via Cavour». Otherwise you can follow the second variation that we hereunder propose.

SECOND VARIATION - Go down along via Cavour for about fifty meters then turn in via Barbiani, the first one on the right.

CHURCH OF SANT'EUFEMIA - At about half way of via Barbiani, on the left, behind a railing of wrought iron made at the beginning of the 20th century, preceeded by a green open space, there is the church of Sant'Eufemia, built between 1742 and 1747 on design of Gian Francesco Buonamici, the architect of the Duomo.

The place was occupied by a very ancient church, with three aisles, separated on each side by six columns, of which we don't know the precise date of construction.

Legend however, hasn't worried about the prudence of the experts, and declares that in this place the most ancient church of Ravenna and the whole Cispadana rose. This legend says that Saint Peter, in the year 46, consecrated bishop of Ravenna one of his disciples Apollinare, and sent him in the territories of his mission.

Having arrived in Cesarea, at the doors of the city, and being guest of an oriental man called Ireneo, a soldier, Apollinare cured his blind son; having been introduced to the Tribune of Ravenna, he cured his wife Tecla. To these miraculous facts many conversions followed. Apollinare taught the new Christians and administred the Sacraments in one of the most hidden rooms of the tribune's palace and under his and the local protection, reduced it to a Christian chapel, it was the first oratory or church of the city and of the region. In that same place then the primitive church of Sant'Eufemia rose, so called because Apollinare passing through Aquileia, had himself handed over as sacred relic the body of the young girl who had died not long before.

To strengthen the legend, we have the fact that, in 1686, in the church the relics of Saint Eufemia and Saint Agatha were found. In the sacristy there is a little well on which, in the 18th century was written: «COEPIT HIC FIDES RAVENNATIUM» (*«Here the faith of the people of Ravenna started»*). As to the epoch in which Sant'Apollinare lived, it must be noticed that the experts collocate it between the end of the 2nd century and the beginning of the 3rd. It is the «Passio» of Sant'Apollinare, written between the 5th and the 6th century (Mazzotti) which places it retrospectively between the disciples of Peter. The church has a round plan, with three altars. Behind the high altar there is the choir. The sacristy is drawn from the oratory of *«Santa Maria libera nos a poenis inferni»* belonging to the congregation of the hundred priests that has its seat here.

In 1686, in occasion of the finding of the relics of the two saints, placed in the little sarcophagus in the altar, the Bolognese painter *Antonio Burrini* (1656-1727) received the task of painting a picture representing the death of the Saint. It is one of the best works of the artist. It shows Valens that has already killed the daughter Dorothea and the nieces Erasma and Tecla (but on the ground there are only two bodies) and that is going to thrust, with ferocious determination, the mortal stroke on the neck of his daughter Eufemia. The painting is in the choir, behind the altar. On the right, always in the choir, there is a beautiful work of *Andrea Barbiani* that represents «Sant'Apollinare baptising the Tribune».

In the left chapel there is the «Announcement» of the Ravennate painter *«Giovanni Capaci»* painted in 1747. In the right chapel there is the «Visitation» in which another painting is inserted with the Madonna and the Infant. In the sacristy there are various lunettes assigned to *Barbiani*. In the third bell-tower there is one of the most ancient bells of Ravenna dated 1358.

Porta Adriana: the remainders of the ancient towers.

CHURCH OF SAINT JOHN AND SAINT PAUL - Having reached the end of via Barbiani, on the crossing with via Massimo D'Azeglio we can see the little church of Saint John and Saint Paul called also «Degli Angeli» (of the Angels) for a popular feast that takes place on the 2nd October, celebration of the Guardian Angels.

The **little bell-tower**, square at the bottom, round on the top, is one of the most ancient bell-towers of Ravenna (Galassi, 8th century; Serafini, 9th century; Pavan, «the original implant is of the 11th century»). On it windows, loopholes, four mullioned-windows open and on the top part remade in the 18th century, four long windows instead of preexisting mullioned-windows. A source of the 6th century testifies the existence of a church in this place. The one we see was built in 1758 by *Domenico Barbiani*, and has inside, arches and columns of Neoclassical style. The actual church occupies maybe the place of the central aisle of the original church, and therefore it had three aisles, larger and longer than the one we see.

In old times the church opened on the side of the walls from which it was distant only a few metres, since they went along the little street slope that concludes Via D'Azeglio. Today the entrance door is where the apse was. An ambo of the 6th century that was once here is now in the Archbishop Museum.

Let's continue along via Massimo D'Azeglio leaving behind us the church until we reach the first road on the left (via Cattaneo).

At n. 38 of via D'Azeglio we find **PALAZZO BACINETTI** restorated in the middle of the eighteenth century, whose entrance and stairs are of the architect *Soratini* and it has beautiful painted and decorated rooms.

At n. 10 of the same road the remarkable Istria stone door of **PALAZZO PRANDI**, later **VICARI**, stands out, its arch is overhung by a shell connected to the window-sill of the upper window by means of volutes. At the sides of the shell some festoons come down which end with two masks. The sills of the windows and the cornices are of the eighteenth century. The building dates back to the 17th and 18th centuries and carries paintings of the 19th century.

Going along via Cattaneo we notice at n. 34 an old patrician house that from 1675 to 1810 became a monastery under the Santa Chiara rule (since 1814 the convent moved to via Pietro Alighieri). At n. 22 we see a building constructed in 1860 with door and arch marble balcony, a beautiful cornice which is work of the architect *Romolo Conti*.

Most probably the streets Carlo Cattaneo, Andrea Agnello, Cesare Battisti constitued a secondary Decuman of the Roman Ravenna. From where we are we can valuate visually the size of square-like Ravenna because we have via Cavour a few steps away, and turning on the opposite sense, we can see the green scarp of the remaining walls.

Going further we are again in via Cavour through which we shall now run until the end keeping right.

VIA CAVOUR - At numbers 78, 80, 82 (via Cavour crossing - via Cattaneo) we can observe a house of the eighteenth century, with a Renaissance pilaster in the corner, walled traces of doors and windows, a semicircular balcony in via Cattaneo.

At n. 72 a house of the seventeenth-eighteenth century.

At n. 73 a house with the coat-of-arms of the Rota family and a Baroque balcony.

At n. 60 a house of the seventeenth century, with a baroque balcony and a cornice of the nineteeth century.

At n. 51 a house with the coat-of-arms of the Pignata family (pot and crown).

PALAZZO GUICCIOLI - We find it at n. 54. Lord Byron lived here, in 1820-1821. He was the guest of Alessandro Guiccioli and had a tender relation with his young wife Teresa Guiccioli. In this building several works of the English writer were carried out.

The building is of the seventeenth century, and it is incomplete on the right side, with a high door overhung by a balcony of the eighteenth century; it still has decorated rooms. The entrance has the ceiling with a vault and a brick floor with two other stone lanes for the passing of the coaches. A two-storeyed building follows the yard, its architecture is of the eighteenth century and it has a portico and an attic with a railing. Another service-yard follows.

LAPIDE DELL'INONDAZIONE (FLOOD TABLET). Continuing along via Cavour, we meet on our left via Salara, that we went through before going towards San Vitale. Immediately at the beginning of the via, on the right there is a little commemorative tablet not very easy to read, with the inscription «A DI 28 MAGGIO 1636 SIN QUI L'ACQUA ARRIVÒ» (On the 28th May 1636 water arrived till here). It indicates the water level reached by the most terrible among the recurring floods of the Ronco and Montone rivers that at that time lapped the city, surrounding it.

LAPIDE DEL PONTE DI AUGUSTO - A little further, always in via Salara, on the left another tablet indicates the place where the bridge crossing the Padenna River was: «È QUI SOTTERRA IL PONTE DI AUGUSTO O DI AUSTRO, SUL GIÀ FIUME PADENNA» (Here underground there is the Augusto or Austro bridge, that crossed the Padenna River). This Padenna river mustn't be confused with the homonymous one of which we have already spoken about. This one is instead the so-called «*flumisellum Padennae*». Most probably the wall of the 1st century ran along this river. The bridge was brought back to light in 1983, during works connected with the new sewerage network, and it was covered again while waiting to decide for a better collocation of it. Here a gate (Porta Asiana) that looked onto the bridge opened. Porta Asiana was one of the two endings of the «decuman» 720 metres long that went from where we are standing to Port'Aurea.

CHIESA DI SAN DOMENICO - Returning to via Cavour after the short digression, we go leftwards and after a few metres we find on our left preceeded by a little square delimited by twelve pillars, the church of San Domenico.

The dark unfinished façade, shows a big door, a tondo, a window, a little window. Two pilaster strips go from the ground till the windows.

This church was built in 1269 and it was widened in 1374, on the façade, it had some arches where the burials were placed. Of the ogival arches, we can see a trace on the sides of the entrance door (three on each side); and so we notice the traces of two windows on the sides of the tondo. The church was nearly completely remade during the first years of the eighteenth century on design of *Giambattista Contini*.

The inside is constituted of a unique wide nave, with barrel-vault, in which three chapels on each side open.

First chapel (on the right) - Commemorative tablet of the Parish priest Giuliano Berti, who died in 1880, learned man and researcher of the ancient memorials of Ravenna.

Between the first and the second chapel, we have the Latin inscription that was on the tomb of the painter Luca Longhi (1507-1580), buried in the cloister of the church.

Second chapel - It is a work of *Camillo Morigia*, with marbles, sarcophagus and painting of *Gaetano Gandolfi* (1796) representing the Madonna, Saint Dominic (San Domenico) and an angel who is throwing down heresy.

Third chapel - It has beautiful tortile columns. The painting is the last work of *Luca Longhi* and represents the «Finding of the cross». The woman in the foreground is Saint Helen, mother of Constantine, who is contemplating with two dames, the real cross found among others, recognized because it raises a young boy from death. On the background we see Jerusalem, and the unearthed crosses that the old Judah, here holding the found cross, told of and indicated the place where they were buried only when taken by hunger.

Apse - There are seven paintings among which the four big temperas of *Nicolò Rondinelli* (1460-1545) are worth paying attention to, they represent «An Angel», «The Annunciation», «Saint Dominic» and «Saint Peter». The four paintings were four organ doors. Rondinelli was a pupil of Giovanni Bellini in Venice, and according to Vasari he was an excellent painter.

At the bottom of the apse there is a second rate painting of the Ravennate painter *G.B. Ragazzini*: «Madonna in glory among a flight of angels, Saint Dominic and Saint Catherine from Siena, Saint Margaret and Saint Giacinto and Saint Peter Martyr and Saint Thomas

D'Aquino and in the middle Raymond that is ploughing the waves on a cloak».

In the presbytery, on the left there is a good tablet of *Benedetto Coda*, representing «The Virgin, the Infant and the Saints Joseph and Dominic and Francis of Assisi.

Chapel of the Crucifix - It opens near the left apse. It was built on design of *Domenico Barbiani* between 1746 and 1755 the dome it has, was painted by *Andrea Barbiani*. A wooden crucifix is collocated here, placed behind a gate, with the cross of «Y» form. It is a crucifix of the 13th century. Christ is «*of empty wood on the back part then plastered and covered in front with canvas, then plastered again and painted so as to seem made of skin*» (Ghigi). One of the fires set in Ravenna during the pillage of 1512 by the soldiers of Luigi XII and Alfonso D'Este invested also this crucifix it is thought was exposed to public in the zones of via Zanzanigola - Pietro Alighieri. The miracle was as far as we know, that the feet drew back and that the fire dried out, leaving carbonized the inferior part of the cross; the image sweated blood. It was object of veneration and homage for a very long time and in various occasions.

The two lateral statues of the Virgin Mary and of Saint John, are of the Venetian *Giuseppe Torretti*.

Central chapel on the left - 15 tondos on wood of *Luca Longhi* representing the 15 mysteries of the Rosary are collocated here, placed into a rich framework of marbles: the joyful mysteries (the Announcement, the Visit, the Birth of Jesus, Presentation at the temple, Discussion with the doctors), the painful mysteries (Jesus in the garden of Getsemani, the scourging, the coronation of thorns, the way of Christ to the Calvary), the glorious mysteries (Resurrection, coming of the Holy Spirit, Ascension of Christ, Assumption of Mary).

In the ***last chapel*** there is the blackened, ruined «San Michele Arcangelo» of *Bernardo Zuccaro*.

In the convent attached to the church Angelo Ghislieri lived and taught for a few years, he became pope in 1566 with the name of Pio V and made effective the Tridentino Council and created the Holy League against the Turks.

It seems that in the zone now occupied by San Domenico during the Roman epoch the **Campidoglio** (which contained the reliefs of the thrones that are now in San Vitale), the equestrian statue called **Regisole**, and the **Prisons** rose.

Having left the church we continue along via Matteotti. At a certain point, on the right, we notice the little portico of the second half of the 15th century, on the side of the church of San Domenico. A little further on, in the road that we find on the right (via Mordani), we notice the trees of the garden of the Pasolini dall'Onda building, the façade of which looks onto the square XX Settembre (already called piazza dell'Aquila), in which via Matteotti brings us.

A forgotten church: Sant'Apollinare in Veclo - Between No. 8 and No. 4, via Pietro Alighieri, at the end of via Salara, there is a church from the 18th century (1763) built by the architect *G.A. Soratini*, which belongs to the cloistered nuns of the Capuchin order, who live here. The church has replaced an ancient *monastery*, the name of which was Sant'Apollinare, that certainly already existed in the 7th century. It was probably one of the small sacella or monasteries (we could say «little churches») lying around the basilica of Santa Croce (according to what Cortesi maintains), therefore it dates back to the 5th century. That little church was called, we don't know when, Sant'Apollinare *in Veclo*. «Veclo» in Latin spoken in the Middle Age means ancient. In Ravenna there is, as everybody knows, a Sant'Apollinare *nuovo*. This church, built at Theodoric's time, was dedicated to Sant'Apollinare in the 9th century (originally it was dedicated to Our Lord Jesus Christ). So there were at least three holy places dedicated to Sant'Apollinare in the 9th century: the one in Classe and the other two in Ravenna. From these facts we can just conjecture about the existence of these two opposed adjectives (new, old), because we have no certain elements.

ITINERARY OF THE DANTESQUE ZONE, SAN FRANCESCO AND SANT'AGATA

Piazza del Popolo - Palazzo Comunale - Palazzetto Veneziano - Palazzo dell'Orologio - Venetian Columns - Via Cairoli - Via Corrado Ricci - Santa Maria Maddalena - Palazzo Rasponi-Bellenghi - **Dante's Tomb** - Franciscan cloisters - Dantesque Museum - Quadrarco di Braccioforte - Piazza San Francesco - **Church of San Francesco** - Casa Oriani - Piazza dei Caduti - Palazzo della Provincia - Via Mazzini - S. Carlino - **Sant'Agata Maggiore** - Casa Polentana - Porta Sisi - Porta San Mama - Via Baccarini - Chiesa di San Nicolò - Monastery of Classe - **Classense Library** - Church of San Romualdo - Via Guidone - Via Mentana - Piazza XX Settembre.

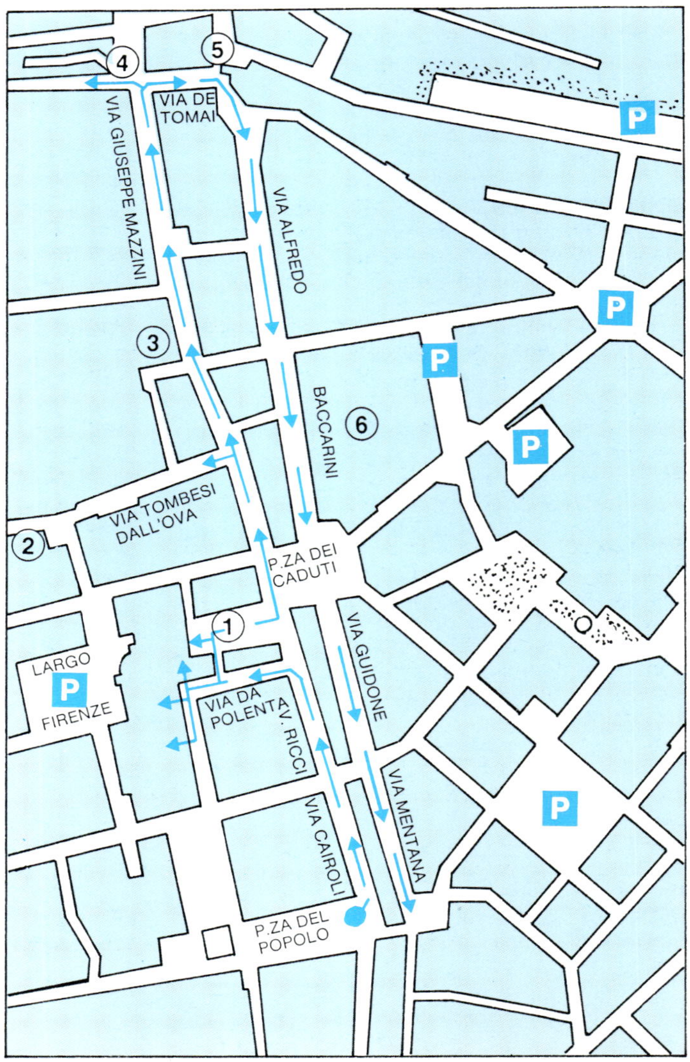

Fig. 17 - **ITINERARY OF THE DANTESQUE ZONE, SAN FRANCESCO, SANT'AGATA.** 1 - Dantesque Zone. 2 - San Carlino. 3 - Sant'Agata. 4 - Porta Sisi. 5 - Porta San Mama. 6 - Monastery of Classe - Classense Library.

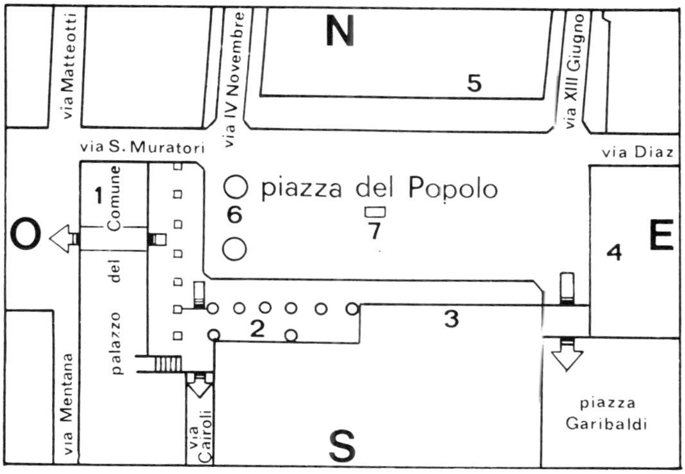

Fig. 18 - **Map of Piazza del Popolo**.
1 - Palazzo del Comune (Town-hall).
2 - Palazzetto Veneziano.
3 - Prefecture. 4 - Building of Banca Nazionale del Lavoro, once Churches of San Marco and San Sebastiano.
5 - Credito Romagnolo, Rasponi del Sale building. 6 - Venetian Columns.
7 - Tablet of the tree of liberty

PIAZZA DEL POPOLO

The square, of quadrangular form, of noble aspect, is the ideal centre of the city and daily meeting place for the people of Ravenna. Six streets go into it: via Diaz, via XIII Giugno, via IV Novembre, via Santi Muratori, via Cairoli, and the passage that leads to piazza Garibaldi. In the immediate neighbourhood there are other two squares: piazza XX Settembre (piazza dell'Aquila). With this last square there is a connection, as well as through via Santi Muratori, also through a passage under the «palazzo comunale» (Town-hall).

The following buildings look onto Piazza del Popolo: the palazzo del comune (Town-hall) on the West (fig. 18-1, at pag. 79), the palazzetto Veneziano (2), the Prefecture building (3) on the South, the building seat of Banca Nazionale del Lavoro overhung by the clock-tower (4) on the East, the building seat of the Credito Romagnolo (5) followed by houses on the North.

Palazzo del Comune - Once on the place now occupied by this building the Padenna River flowed; then we know of having been there the house of Bernardino da Polenta, as well as other little houses. Finally in 1681 this building was constructed, which through various widening works, reached in 1761 the size and slowly the aspect of today.

Six octagonal pillars with marbles coming from Santa Maria Maggiore and two rectangular ones, at the extremities sustain the arches, two of which pointed-arches. On the first floor there are five windows and a big balcony, higher up five windowed tondos. The crenelation, which is a false Medieval one, was placed in 1857 to hide the roof, in occasion of the coming to Ravenna of Pius IX.

Against one of the pillars of the portico there is a fountain of 1870, against the nearby pillar there is a kind of tabernacle with its sides adorned by beautiful candlesticks in bas-relief of the 16th century, surmounted by a marble pine-cone. The vault of the covered passage which unites the piazza del popolo to piazza XX Settembre was decorated by Gaetano Savini in 1873 with decorative motifs and medallions representing renowned people of Ravenna and some monuments and aspects of the city. The two squares are connected by a passage of the end of the 15th century. The access stair to the building, placed under the portico, dates back at least to 1411; of the same time are the semi-column and the pine-cone; the gate is of Bellotto (1921).

At the top of the staircase, on the right in a corridor, the model of the public measures are sculptured (TRUE MATRIX OF THE PUBLIC MEASURES), in Istria Stone; they date back to 1625 and are a work of Giacomo Bellabarba. The measures are indicated in the following way: GAVALO MAGGIORE - GAVALO MEZZANO - GAVALETTO to measure wheels; BRICK - TILE - HOLLOW FLAT TILE for elements in brickwork; BRAZZO for the lengths; LAND SURVEYING FOOT, which formed the tenth part of the Ravennate perch; HAND FOOT (P. DA MARANO), to measure wood. Measure of «CARRO DEI ZOCCHI» to measure big logs of wood for fire, that was sold in wagons (CARRI). A CARRO DI ZOCCHI of oak of pine-wood was equivalent to mã 3,650.

For the inside of the building we only limit to say that the vault of the «Sala del Consiglio» was painted by Savini 1882. The allegorical figures of Science, of Industry and of Commerce are of prof. Alessandro Guardassoni. The bust of the walls represent Giuseppe Garibaldi, Giuseppe Mazzini, Luigi Carlo Farini, Vittorio Ema-

Piazza del Popolo: Town-hall and Venetian columns.

nuele II, Gioacchino Rasponi and Alfredo Baccarini.

Palazzetto Veneziano - After various building vicissitudes, constructions and reconstructions, it owes its actual aspect to works carried out in the first decade of the Venetian possession of the city (second half of the 15th century), these works and interventions however didn't cease with the return of Ravenna back to the Holy See. It rises in a zone where also before there were the offices of the podesta, since 1288. Time before the Town-hall was in the zone of Banca Popolare Cooperativa (once Malagola House) in Via Guerrini, 14; the news is taken from a document of 978. It is formed of five big arches with the archivault in terra-cotta, decorated. On top there are three beautiful mullioned windows, a balcony and two tondi.

The palazzetto Veneziano doesn't comprise of the big vault, that was built a little before 1534, from which we pass in via Cairoli and which is formed by a very wide lowered arch. The façade above the arch shows a mullioned window and it is crowned by a crenelation.

To build the portico of the palazzetto eight granite **columns** and **capitals** of the Theodorican Age were used (493-526). The first capital on the left is of the composite type with thinly indented acanthus, the others are always composite with acanthus leaves moved by the wind, of the «butterfly» type. Four of them carry the monogram of Theodoric not very easy to be seen, for example, on the last one on the right. Columns and capitals are thought to derive from the church of Sant'Andrea dei Goti, built in the Theodorican Age and demolished in 1457 to use the material in the construction of Rocca Brancaleone. A second hypothesis assigns the provenance from a public building like the portico of a market, and exedra or something else. In the palazzetto there are some municipal offices.

Palazzo della Prefettura (Prefecture building) - It was built in 1696, and it occupies the space that first was of the Apostolic and Legation building. The façade has a noble and austere aspect that adapts very well to the atmosphere of the square.

Building of the Banca Nazionale del Lavoro - This side of the square was occupied by two singular churches, San Sebastiano the oldest one, on the side of via Diaz, and San Marco built in 1419, they were so near that it was possible to pass from one church to another through three arches opening on the divisory wall. The two façades were practically fused together and the complexive aspect towards the square was not very different from today. On the top of the building there was the clock-tower with bells, while the clock-face was in the central panel a little lower and carried the indication of all the twenty four hours of the day. This clock-face is now in the yard of the «Palazzo della Provincia».

In 1783 the façade with the tower and the clock as we see them now was built according to the project of *Camillo Morigia*. The façade is composed of six big panels and a light ashlar-work, with a beautiful Sansovinian balustrade, and it is harmonic and elegant. On the six lower panels, on the sides, there are two doors, and in the middle there is a tablet which carries the names of the partisans who died while fighting or for reprisal in the period from September 1943 to April 1945. Above, on the sides, two windows with tympanum and in the middle an architectural motif with columns and a curved pediment.

Piazza del Popolo: base of a Venetian column.

The two churches after desecration, served for several uses (the puppet theatre of the famous Campogalliani (in 1905), the first cinema in Ravenna (1907), a chicken market, tobacconist shop, a butchery, a garage); they were demolished in 1925 and the actual building conserving the Morigia façade was built. The building is now property of Banca Nazionale del Lavoro.

Building of the Credito Romagnolo **-** It is the Rasponi del Sale building, and it was built in 1770. The side which looks onto the square presents a beautiful portal of recent construction whose ornamentation comprizes the window above. On the architrave a relief with the birth of Christ is inserted. On the sides of the windows of the second floor above the entrance two coat-of-arms of recent collocation appear (initials of the bank and the emblem of the city of Bologna).

Venetian Columns (6) - The two columns in front of the Town-hall were erected by the Venetians in 1483 with the base and the steps sculptured by *Pietro Lombardo* (father of Tullio author of the famous statue of Guidarello), as can be read on the inscription sculptured on the top of the highest step (OPUS PETRI LOMBARDI 1483). The bas-reliefs carry ornamental drawings, particularly beautiful are those of the middle step, and the twelve zodiac signs (aries, taurus, gemini, cancer, leo, virgo, libra, scorpio, sagittarius, capricorn, aquarius, pisces) on the superior step of the Northern column. On the panel under the date 1483 of this column the **colossus of Ercole Orario**, called by the population Conchincollo. It was a very big statue placed in the Roman basilica of Hercules. It represented the semigod with a knee on the ground holding above his head a dial of semispherical shape on which there was a stylus from which the time lines divided. It was in fact a solar and lunar clock. The statue collapsed and shattered in 1591 because of an earthquake and some of its base marbles were used for the column base now in Piazza dell'Aquila, while the shattered statue was given to an architect whose heirs undid it for other use. A foot of the statue is kept in the National Museum.

Originally on the top of the two columns there were the statutes of Sant'Apollinare (North) and the lion of San Marco (South). The lion was taken away in 1509 at the end of the Venetian dominium. In 1644 the statue of Sant'Apollinare was moved to the Southern column, and on the Northern one a statue of San Vitale was placed, work of *Clemente Molli*. On the latter, a sun-dial was engraved.

Tablet of the tree of liberty (7) - In the middle of the square there is a tablet on which there is the following inscription: «L'ALBERO DE LA LIBERTA FU QUI PIANTATO IL 15 FEBBRAIO DEL 1849 E IL MUNICIPIO DI RAVENNA A RICORDO POSE IL 15 MAGGIO DEL 1904» (The tree of freedom was planted here on the 15th February of 1849 and the municipality of Ravenna placed this in memory on the 15th May 1904). This was a period of revolutions in all Europe, and Ravenna didn't lose time to do her part with the conquest of an ephemeral freedom.

VIA CAIROLI - VENETIAN HOUSES - Let's leave piazza del Popolo from the South Western corner passing under the big vault on the right of the palazzetto Veneziano, and let's set off through the narrow and characteristic via Cairoli which preserves two interesting examples of Venetian house. The first one is at n. 12, original in the superior part with the four arched windows, the higher little windows and the cornice; the second one is at n. 25, it is also original on the

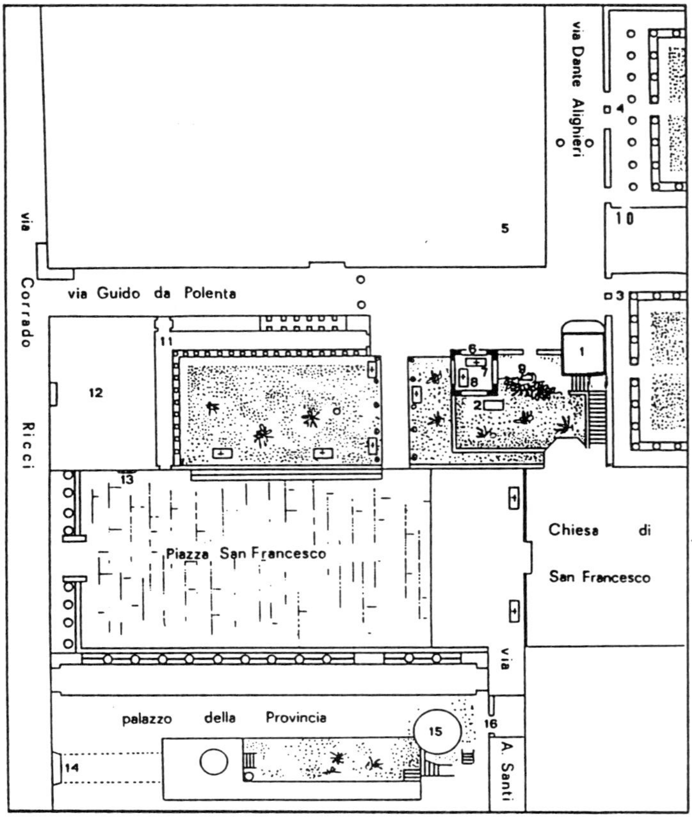

Fig. 19 - **Plan of the Dantesque zone**.
1 - Sepulchrum of Dante. 2 - Seat where the bones of Dante were hidden from 1810 to 1865. 3 - Cloister of the cistern. 4 - Cloister of the double portico. 5 - Scarabigoli house. 6 - Quadrarco di Braccioforte. 7 - Sarcophagus of prophet Elyseus. 8 - Sarcophagus of Pier Traversari. 9 - Grave where the bones of Dante were placed from 1944 to 1945.
10 - Access to the Dantesque Museum. 11 - Portico already of the monastery of Porto. 12 - Oriani House-Library. 13 - Byron tablet. 14 - Entrance to the «Palazzo della Provincia». 15 - Rasponi Crypt. 16 - Arch formed with the dial of the clock which had been on the churches of San Marco and San Sebastiano in piazza del Popolo.

superior part of the façade (cornice, little windows, window of the balcony, two mullioned-windows with a marble column). They both date back to the 15th century. This street, called in origin «strada del Ponte Coperto», had also other denominations, such as: «Palserrato» or «Palchiavato» and «delle Drapperie».

LITTLE CHURCH OF SANTA MARIA MADDALENA - From via Cairoli we enter via Corrado Ricci where the little church dedicated to Santa Maria Maggiore must be noticed, it is preceeded by a gate and it is a little higher in respect of the street level, it was built between 1748-50 by the architect *Fausto Pellicciotti*.

It rises on the seat or in the neighbourhoods of an ancient church which appears in the documents right since 1076 with the name of Santa Maria Luminaria. It is of Baroque style, with one nave only, decorated by several pictures and by a painted apse. Above the entrance door there is the choir.

The high altar was designed by *Domenico Barbiani* and it is adorned by chosen ancient green, white, black oriental marbles. The latter, could have belonged (according to C. Ricci) to the loggia that surrounded the superior floor of the Mausoleum of Theodoric. The ciborium that rests on the altar is of *Giulio Costa* from Ravenna.

Domenico Corvi (1721-1803) painted the first two pictures, starting from the entrance, on the right and on the left («Magdalene at the sepulchre», «Magdalene and Jesus in Martha's house»). In the two chapels there are the paintings of *Andrea Barbiani*: on the right, «Sant'Apollinare and San Romualdo»; on the left, «the Virgin, Antonio da Padova and Francesco di Paola». Beyond the chapels, on the right, there is the painting of *Marcello Leopardi* (who died in 1795-96) «Magdalene comforted by the Angels»; on the left the painting of *Tommaso Sciacca* (born in 1734) «Magdalene in the house of the Pharisee». The painting at the end is of *Filippo Pasquali* and represents «The Saviour who appears to Magdalene with the aspect of a gardener».

BENELLI - CASADIO HOUSE - It is a Neo-classical construction (19th century), at n. 14. We can take a look at the reliefs under the cornice: they contain dancing female figures very well drawn with the inscription «TACITO PEDE CURRUNT IUGITER» (without stopping they go on with silent foot).

PALAZZO RASPONI - It is the big building on the corner with via Guido de Polenta (nn. 20-22-

24 of via Corrado Ricci), and it was rebuilt in 1541 by Giovanna Rasponi, it has a corner balcony sustained by five brackets. It was built as a fortalice or tower (it was called «tower of Saint Francis») to face the fightings in which the Rasponi family was engaged. It was then the seat of an inn (Osteria della Corona) in the Seventeenth and Eighteenth Centuries; 1877 a famous drugstore opened here (Bellenghi), and finally, since 1975 it is the seat of a winery (**Ca de vén** - house of wine) which presents on its nineteenth Century shelves a good assortment of Romagnol wines and publications on Romagna. This is a very nice place for who wishes to drink wine and eat «piadina» in a very picturesque environment. In the same building, at n. 22, there is the seat of the «Circolo dei Ravennati e dei Forestieri».

DANTESQUE ZONE TOMB OF DANTE DANTESQUE MUSEUM

Let's turn on the left for via Guido da Polenta and enter in the so-called «Dantesque zone» which comprizes the little temple called «Tomba di Dante» (Dante's tomb). The two Franciscan cloisters, the Quadrarco di Braccioforte, the green zones with sarcophagi and portico, the square and the church of San Francesco. It is a zone rich of interesting monuments dominated by the presence of the great poet and reserved, in silence and isolation, to his memory and his cult. The project of the arrangement of the zone is of Giorgio Rosi; the works were started in 1933, the inauguration took place in 1936.

Tomb of Dante - (look at plan fig. 19 n. 1, at pag. 94). The little temple contains the sarcophagus in which the bones of Dante are conserved. Built in 1780 by the architect *Camillo Morigia*, it is a discussed and however modest and inadequate work for the role to which it has been destined (we can however excuse this good architect by considering that he was commissioned to build a construction of these dimensions and characteristics).

The outside of Neo-classical style is composed of a façade with an arch in which there is an entrance door, surmounted by the inscription «DANTIS POETAE SEPULCHRUM» and by the coat-of-arms of the cardinal Luigi Valenti Gonzaga, commissioner of the work. Above the lunette of the arch there is a jutting out tympanum inside which a snake who is biting its tail is sculptured, it is the symbol of eternity. The little temple is covered by a little dome surmounted by a pine-cone.

In the square room inside, we can see the sarcophagus where we can read the Latin inscription dictated in 1327 by Bernardo Canaccio: «*The rights of the Monarchy, the supreme inhabitants of the sky, the Flegetonte river and the frozen lake of Hell I sang, until my mortal life. But since my soul went to better places and happier reached among the stars its Creator, here I am closed, I, Dante, exiled from Earth where I was born, who generated Florence Mother of little love.*»

Above the sarcophagus, the bas-relief of Pietro Lombardo, sculptured in 1483, representing Dante near a reading desk. The marble around the bas-relief is «Africanone». On the lunette the motto of Cardinal Bembo: «VIRTUTI ET HONORI». On another marble, that is now on the wall of the cloister on the left of the little temple at about three meters of height, the same motto is expressed with «VIRTUS ET HONOR» and it is accompanied by a second motto: «HIS NON CEDO MALIS», literally «I DON'T SURRENDER TO MISFORTUNE». Of Virgil derivation: «Tu ne cede malis, sed contra audentior ito» («Don't give in to misfortune, but courageously go against it» verse 95 of the 6th canto of the Aeneid), it is translated by Annibal Caro: «Ma il tuo cor non paventi, anzi con l'animo supera le fatiche e gli infortuni» (verses 141-142 of the translation).

Above the bas-relief of Lombardo there is a golden cross given as donation by the Pope Paolo VI, placed in 1965. The garland at the feet of the sarcophagus, gift of the victorious army in the war 1915-18, was taken here in 1921, sixth centenary of the death of the poet. In the middle of the temple a lamp of the Eighteenth Century burns, in substitution to the one offered by the people of Florence in 1908; it is kept burning with oil of tuscan olive trees, which is given in donation by the municipality of Florence on the second Sunday of September, in memory of the death of Dante, which took place during the night between the 13th and the 14th of the same month. On the right there is a silver cruet for oil, modelled by *Giovanni Mayer*, which represents the five provinces of Venezia Giulia and Tridentina: Tergeste, Histria, Gorizia, Dalmatia, Tridentum.

The coverings of the walls in onyx and base of cipolin, and the floor in porphyry and verd antique are of 1921.

The epigraph on the right wall: «O Dante, tu giacevi qui in un piccolo tumulo...», was placed by Bernardo Bembo in memory of the works promoted by him. The epigraph of the left wall is of 1921, it remembers Bembo, the works wanted by Luigi Valenti Gonzaga, and the Italian government which decorated the sacellum with works of bronze and marble.

In 1321, after the death of the poet (the funerals were celebrated in the near church of San Francis), his body was closed in a rough sarco-

Dante's Tomb: the bas-relief sculptured by Pietro Lombardo.

Dante's Tomb.

phagus of Greek marble, which was collocated on the outside of the wall of the cloister near the church, in the place where the temple rises.

In 1483 around the sarcophagus a little chapel was built under order of the captain and podesta of Ravenna Bernardo Bembo (father of Pietro), and Pietro Lombardo was appointed and was he who made the sacellum and the bas-relief.

In 1519 the people of Florence obtained from Pope Leo X the permission to take the bones of the poet and bring them to Florence, but, when they reached Ravenna and opened the sarcophagus, they found it empty. The bones, in fact, had been stolen during nightime by the monks of the church of San Francis who from the inside of the cloister had made a hole in the wall and in the the sarcophagus. In the inside of the cloister the place in which the monks made the hole is marked by a tablet, it is visible also from the outside through the narrow space between the temple and the wall of the cloister. The monks kept the relics first in the monastery and in 1810, having to leave the place in obedience to the laws of soppression of the religious orders, they buried them at the threshold of an old door that was in a wall extant at that time between the «Quadrarco di Braccioforte» and the church; the bones were in the little box in which, in 1677, the monk Antonio Santi had put them. The box was found in that place in 1865 during preparation works for the celebration of the sixth centenary of the birth of Dante. Then the bones were placed back into the primitive sarcophagus, in a walnut coffin closed in a lead coffin.

Cloister of the cistern (3) - This cloister (whose entrance is near Dante's tomb) as the one we

Dantesque Zone: the cloister of the cistern. ▶

Dantesque Zone: cloister of the cistern and bell-tower of San Francis. ▼

shall see later on was part of the convent built by the Franciscan monks when in 1261 they received in concession the church of San Francis. Both the cloisters, restored and in part rebuilt in 1954, aren't the original ones, but are of the 15th century with interventions of the 17th century.

The cloister is formed in the first order by arches sustained by 28 columns (seven on each side); on the superior order it is open only on the side which leans against the left nave of the church. On the western side notice the tablet which remembers the stealing of Dante's bones in 1519; on the Southern part the wall of the Polentani chapel that we shall see inside the church, and the remains of the wall paintings of the 14th century; on the Eastern part a door which leads to the library of the monks; all around there are many coats-of-arms of Italian cities that in this way have paid homage to Dante. In the middle of the lawn there is a beautiful cistern rich of marbles (1639). The «puteal» (a low circular wall on which the roe to pick the bucket up ran through) is of stone: the two little pillars in Greek lean on the plinths of Veronese red and pedestals of Greek marble. The very beautiful capitals topping the pillars are of the «composite Byzantine» type and they can be dated to the 6th century. The architrave, in Greek marble, is crowned by two Baroque volutes which carry on the extremities and in the middle spheres of Veronese red marble.

Cloister of the double portico (4) - We enter n. 4 of via Dante Alighieri. The cloister has unequal sides, and the one towards the road has a double portico sustained by two rows of columns. The side towards the road was taken from rooms that till 1936 existed on the side too. The corridors have cross-vaults. The third

and eighth column of the Southern side with hollows for little crosses were to belong to a ciborium. In the superior order only one of the sides is open and articulated by little columns of brickwork. In the middle of the lawn recently an ancient well-curb with the coat-of-arms of the Pignata family has been placed.

The two cloisters, for the peace that reigns in them, deserve a pause for rest and meditation.

From this cloister we can get at the

Dantesque Museum - It was established in 1921 and, after its closing for many years, it was reopened in 1990; it is divided into five rooms. On the first landing there are four plaster busts of Dante. On the wall we can see the project by Adolfo de Carolis for the frescos in the apse of Saint Francis.

— *First room*: A big allegoric bas-relief of marble by Archimede Campini. A drawing with verses by Z.P. Pieromaldi in Beatrix's honour.

— *Second room*: On the right the wings of the door from the 18th century of Dante's tomb. Four lateral stucco-pillars which belonged to the tomb before the setting (1921) of polychrome marbles. Left wall: reproduction of drawings and engravings describing the story of the tomb. Drawings by the winners of the competition that the Board of Education organized in 1920 for the decoration of St. Francis' church, never carried out. The winners were: Adolfo de Carolis, Guido Cadorin, Carlo Wostry, Arduino Berlam, Rodolfo Villani. Right wall: pictures from the recovery of the box with Dante's bones, that happened in 1865. Other drawings relative to the competition. In the middle of the room there are two models representing two moments of the placing of Dante's grave. Some other drawings relative to the competition. The one representing the apse is very impressive.

— *Third room*: One more project relative to the competition and, in the middle, plastic model of the project by architect Roberto Papini for the «Silence area». Sacks containing laurel leaves gathered and sent by Gabriele D'Annunzio to the mayor of Ravenna in 1921. On the wall a xylography by De Carolis with autographical dedication by D'Annunzio: «To Ravenna, forever illuminated by this "holy lamp".».

— *Fourth room*: The so called Montevideo's room, because of the decoration by the Milanese Giovanni Buffa offered by the Italians from that city. Garlands and wreaths of wrought iron, which contain plates with the dedications of the presenting committees, complete the decoration, painted with a series of laurel leaves. In the middle of the room we can see the bronze model of Dante's monument in Trento, a work by Cesare Zocchi and a lamp given by the Italian Dantesque Society, influenced by Indian art. Below, a silver hammer and a trowel used for the laying of the foundation-stone of Dante's monument in Rio de Janeiro.

— *Fifth room*: Wooden box that contained Dante's bones from 1677 to 1865. Small room to the right: plaster mould of the Madonna with the Infant, perhaps coming from Dante's former tomb, now in Louvre Museum. Now we are arriving at the MUSEUM OF THE DANTESQUE MEDAL AND SMALL BRONZE, situated in the southern, eastern and northern passages of the cloister (at the beginning of the southern pas-

Dantesque zone: cloister of the double portico. Foreshortening.

sage, from which we have a good view of the cloister of the cistern, there is the fine masonry of the outside part of the Polentani's chapel), where over 300 small bronzes representing Dante or scenes from Dante's works are exposed, together with over two thousand medals, coins, tondoes, plates dedicated to Dante, paintings and xylographies. In the third passage, to the left, Rodolfo Villani's study for the decoration of Saint Francis. On the back-wall a plaster representing Dante by Angelo Biancini.

From here we get at the DANTESQUE LIBRARY, established in 1963 by Severino Ragazzini, who founded and directed the DANTESQUE CENTRE. In the library there are over 20,000 volumes and it has also archives with microfilms of codices belonging to other libraries all over the world. Since 1981, according to a departmental order, the preservation of the library has been bound to Ravenna.

***Scarabigoli house* -** Let's return on the road and observe the corner building between via Dante Alighieri and via Guido da Polenta (5) which was partially rebuilt after the last war. It has origins of the fourteenth century. It didn't belong, as is often thought, to the Polentani family and it wasn't a dwelling of Dante; it was instead property of the Rasponi's for a very long time. On the entrance door, in via Guido da Polenta n. 6, there is an oriflamme with the monogram of Christ. The house next door, at n. 4 (Fabri house), also belonged to the Rasponi's, it has in the yard a Renaissance gallery after which a garden with a marble column follows.

Quadrarco di Braccioforte (6) - On the right railing of Dante's tomb (built in 1921 as work of the Venetian *Umberto Bellotto*), a passage which leads into a garden rich of suggestive remembrances, opens. First of all the so-called Quadrarco di Braccioforte imposes itself to the visitor, it was a very ancient oratory once connected to the church by means of a portico that doesn't exist anymore. The origin of the denomination «BRACCIOFORTE» is connected to the invocation that two believers must have made towards the «braccio forte» (strong arm) of the Saviour, whose image was painted in the place, as guarantee of a contract of theirs. It is a legend quoted by the historian Agnello (9th century).

Under the quadrarch there are **two sarcophagi** of which the most remarkable is the one of **Prophet Elyseus**(7) used later by the Pignata family; it is of the first years of the 5th century (De Francovich: 390-400). In the *front*, in beautiful relief, there is Christ represented on the throne pressing a lion and a dragon (Christ the winner against evil powers); on the sides Peter and Paul and two palms with dates. On the *left side* there are two sculptured figures, that are seen by some people as the characters of the legendary invocation to «braccio forte», but that maybe are Joseph and Mary. Others instead see in it the visit of Mary to Elizabeth (Visitation), or else the trial of the bitter water which Joseph and Mary underwent and which proved that «they had no sin» (from an apocryphal Gospel). Here Joseph undergoes to the trial. On the *right side*, very beautiful indeed, the announcement of the angel to Mary who is busy spinning; on the *back*, with a less emphasized relief, but pictorially softer, two deer quenching their thirst are represented. In «Francesca da Rimini» of D'Annunzio the sarcophagus is described in the following way:

«Il Redentore
ha sotto i piedi il leone e la serpe;
Elisabetta visita Maria;
L'Annunciatore appare a Nostra Donna;
i cervi si dissetano alla fonte».

The second sarcophagus (8), destined in 1225 to the burial of **Pietro Traversari**, has *in front* a «tabula ansata» with two crosses on the sides. *The roof-like lid* has in the «acroteria» some peacocks. On *the sides*, on one side the cross with alpha and omega, on the other the monogram of Christ and it also has the apocalyptic letters. It is of the end of the 5th century.

In the garden the ruin of the ancient wall (2) is preserved in which, as we already said, the box with the bones of the poet was placed, and, before the entrance, a grave covered with ivy under which the bones of Dante were placed from the 23rd March 1944 to the 19th December 1945, to preserve them from possible war damages (9). In the little garden, behind the temple, there is the staircase which leads to the entrance of the Dantesque Museum (10) and the bell, in a little bell-tower at the top of the stairs, which was given by the Italian municipalities. The inscription says: «A RIEVOCARE IN PERPETUO IL RICORDO DEL POETA NELL'ORA CHE VOLGE IL DISIO AI NAVIGANTI QUESTA SQUILLA I COMUNI D'ITALIA DONARONO A LA VESTALE DEL SUO CULTO - RAVENNA XIV SETTEMBRE 1921».

Every evening, while dusk is falling, the bell rings thirteen times which renews the memory of the triplets of the 8th Canto of Purgatory:

«Era già l'ora che volge il disio
ai naviganti e 'ntenerisce il core
Lo dì c'han detto ai dolci amici addio;
E che lo novo peregrin d'amore
punge, se ode squilla di lontano
che paia il giorno pianger che si more;
.....................».

Leaving the little garden, we reach piazza San Francesco turning into the cypress zone that leaves on its left the Quadrarco di Braccioforte.

San Francesco Square: the Church of San Francesco and the portico of the Palazzo della Provincia.

Portico of the Monastero di Porto (11) - The cute portico (1522) that closes the two sides of the garden on the right of the cypress zone, made up of 29 Sixteenth Century columns with Lombardesque capitals variously decorated in the «lyre», is taken from the Monastero di Porto. It was transferred here and recomposed in occasion of the settlement of the zone.

In the garden there are some sarcophagi which, as well as the trees, make the environment severe and tranquil.

San Francesco square - We reach the square by going down some steps, since the level was lowered after 1935 as regards to the street level. In that occasion, the Garibaldi monument that was seated here, was brought to piazza Garibaldi, where it is still today.

San Francesco square - called before Garibaldi - was opened in 1679, and delimited by the church of San Francesco on the East, by the side of the Palazzo della Provincia (Province Hall) on the South, by two little gardens and by a side of the Oriani house on the North. On the West there is via Corrado Ricci, beyond which the building of the «Istituto Nazionale delle Assicurazioni» rises.

SAN FRANCESCO

Historical hints and external characteristics - The church was built by bishop Neone (and therefore after 450) with the name of Basilica or Church of the Apostles (Peter and Paul). Called also San Pietro or San Pietro Maggiore, it was then called San Francesco having in 1261 passed in concession, with houses, kitchen gardens and porticos, to the Franciscans who, having abandoned it in 1810, returned in 1949.

Nearly nothing remains of the ancient construction, considering the redoings and the many restorations of the 10th, 11th, 18th centuries. In 1793 it was practically rebuilt by Pietro Zumaglini.

The simple, rustic, serene façade, is made up of a central body which carries the entrance door and a mullioned window, and by two lateral bodies. Something about the history of the church can be read also on the façade, from the arch trace, behind the marble sarcophagus on the right of the entrance door. It shows the upper part of ancient door whose base lies at more than three meters of depth and therefore indicates a remarkable change in the structure of the building.

The square **bell-tower** emerges from the right side of the façade, lightened in the terminal zone, by three rings of openings: mullioned windows, three mullioned-windows, four mullioned-windows. The date of the bell-tower oscillates between the 9th and the 11th century, with a certain propensity for the 9th. The zone of the four mullioned windows was redone during the restorations of 1921.

The sarcophagus on the left of the entrance, of the first half of the 6th century, is decorated on the right side of the lid by a cross which carries three candles. The one on the right of the entrance has a lid of the first half of the 6th century, while the urn is pagan.

A portico, demolished in the 17th century, joined the façade of the church with the Quadrarco di Braccioforte.

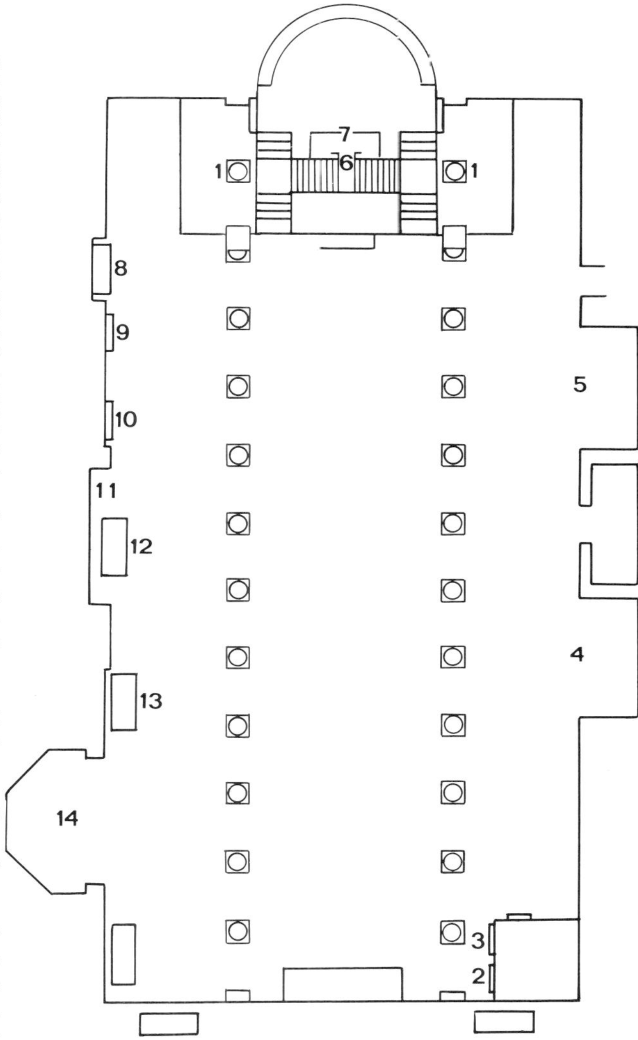

Fig. 20 - **Basilica of San Francesco**: 1 - Columns based on a preceeding level than the actual one. 2 - Fragments of the first quarter of the 6th century. 3 - Tablet with inscriptions. 4 - Chapel with arch and pillars of Tullio Lombardo. 5 - Chapel with the gable of Bernardino Saluteri, frescoes of Andrea Barbiani and altar-piece of Gaspare Sacchi. 6 - Window of the crypt. 7 - High altar - Sarcophagus of bishop Liberius III (end of the 4th - beginning of the 5th century). 8 - Sepulchral monument of Luffo Numai. 9 - Tombstone of father Enrico Alfieri, general of the Franciscan order who died in 1405. 10 - Tombstone of Ostasio da Polenta who died in 1396. 11 - Chapel of the Polentani family with frescos. 12 - Sarcophagus of the end of the 4th century. 13 - Sarcophagus maybe of the 3rd century with the sides maybe worked in the IVth Century, inscription of the 18th century. 14 - Animated Christian crib.

Inside: right nave - The inside made up of naves separated by two rows of twelve columns of Greek marble with capital and pulvino, is naked on the windowed walls and in the apse. The capitals of the columns, in part hammered away in the 17th century, were completed in gypsum according to the original model. The last two columns near the apse (plan fig. 20, n. 1), one on each side, even if they stand at 1.70 meters (floor level of the 11th century) under the level of the others, don't start off from the original level, that is instead at 3.60 meters. The last elevation of the floor took place in the 16th century.

Restorations of 1921 eliminated several baroque superstructures bringing the church back to its original ancient austerity.

On the right whilst entering, at the base of the bell-tower four fragments dating back to the first quarter of the 6th century (2) have been placed. The two inferior ones, pieces of a sarcophagus (De Francovich) or of a chest-altar (Mazzotti), carry a cross inside a niche with tortile little columns and an inscription. The two superior fragments, one of which damaged by the violent insertion of a cross, present a grooved vase with handles bordered by two peacocks which are on tendrils. Above there is a wicker basket from which vine-shoots with two grape bunches on the sides of a pine-cone come out, while on the rim of the basket two figs hang out which are pecked by two pidgeons.

Below there is a tablet that wrongly assigns the erection of the church to San Pier Crisologo, according to the thesis of the monks. The inscription is of 1651 (3). The tablet, however once an altar table, is more ancient, as is proved by the inscription placed on the cut which starts with: «ANNO DOMINI...» and which commemorates the enterprize of the Ravennate archbishop Gherardo who in 1188 took part in the third Crusade, where he died.

The fragment of a detached fresco, above the tablet, is part of the crucifixion painted by *Pietro da Rimini*, who left also in this church a testimony of his great art.

On the adjacent side of the bell-tower there are mosaic fragments, maybe of the 8th century, one of which should come from the church of Sant'Agata, and the fragment of a Byzantine painting.

On the wall of the nave two big chapels of a certain interest open, and between them a smaller one that we reach through a door with a marble lintel.

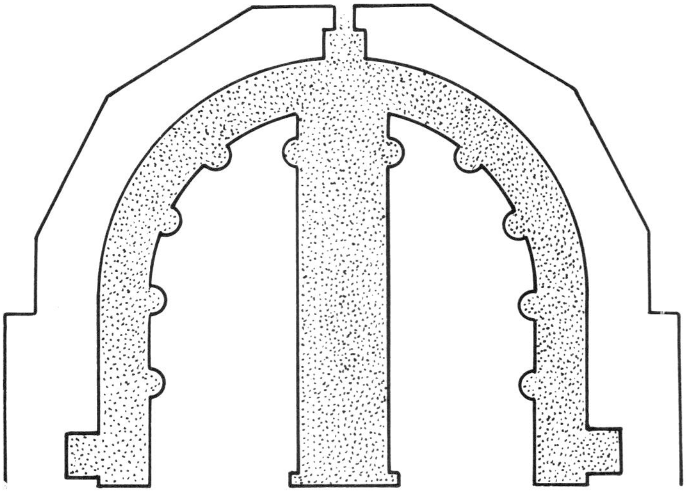

From left to right:

Fig. 21 - Plan of the semiannular crypt.

Basilica of San Francesco: the crypt.

Basilica of San Francesco: high altar-sarcophagus said to be of the bishop Liberius III - particular (end 4th - beginning 5th century).

In the extrados and in the intrados of the arch of the first big chapel (4) *Tullio Lombardo*, in 1525, collocated the capitals on two columns of Greek marble and the pillars of Istria stone beautifully sculptured. Inside the chapel, on the right, there is a niche with the remains of a painting of the Fourteenth Century representing a Saint.

The second big chapel (5); beyond the central body is of 1532; we get to it through an elegant gable, work of *Bernardino Saluteri* from Como on design of the Milanese *Filippo Mariani.* The dome is frescoed by *Andrea Barbiani* (1755) while the painting above the altar is of the Imolese *Gaspare Sacchi* and represents «The Madonna with the Infant, Saint Sebastian, S. Rocco, Saint Francis and Camilla Dal Corno». Of this last one, who was the purchaser of the chapel and of the painting the painter gives us a beautiful profile portrait.

Inside: apse and crypt - The apse, semi-circular in the inside, eptagonal on the outside, was restored in 1920, the level higher as regards to the one of the church, hides a crypt built round about the end of the 10th century. The crypt is well visible through a window (6) which opens below between the staircases built in 1918-1921 in forms attaining to the original ones: the light in the inside is by command and it lasts about two minutes.

The vision isn't devoid of suggestion, because the room is full of water. On the bottom semi-circular wall there are altogether ten columns and pillars, and in the middle as sustain of the vault there are four columns which stand on the primitive plan of the church. Here was preserved the tomb of bishop Neone who at his death was buried in front of the altar of the basilica. His bones were then brought, during the first half of the 9th century, in the place where later the crypt was built: they had been placed in a stone sarcophagus found in 1926 and which is still under the crypt. Actually the relics of the bishop are kept in a little sarcophagus coming from Sant'Agata, that can be found in front of the central window of the crypt.

In January 1977 the mosaics found in the floor were arranged, they are made up of a Greek epigraph which commemorates the offerers Esichio and Gemella, and from the epigraph in three hexameters which refers to Neone's tomb and which says: «(is) TE LOCUS SANCTI COMPLECTITUR (ossa Neonis) (hui-)US CANA FIDES ALTUM PER SAICULA (caelum) POSSIDET (et) TOTOS GAUDET SECURA P(er annos)». («This place contains the bones of Saint Neone, for his immaculate faith he has reached heaven forever and forever rejoices in peace»).

Before this crypt which is so well visible, it is convenient to say a few words in general on the crypts of the churches of Ravenna. There are four: in Sant'Apollinare in Classe, in Sant'Apollinare Nuovo, in San Francesco and in Basilica Ursiana (Duomo). Among these, only the first one can be walked through, because the other ones are constantly invaded by water.

The crypt we are looking at now is of the «oratory» type; it is formed, that is, by a normal room with the vault sustained by columns; those of the two Sant'Apollinare, instead are very different from this one, because they have the shape of a semi-annular corridor, from the centre of which a wing opens following the direction of the axis of the church (fig. 21). The crypt of Ursiana is very

similar to the «oratory» type, but it also has some of the semi-annular type characteristics, being made up of a double corridor that in the central part is covered by two cross-vaults.

The crypts of Ravenna, built to keep the relics of the Saints, are a few centuries posterior to the churches which house them.

Inside: high altar (7) - The altar placed in the apse is a beautiful **sarcophagus** said to be of bishop Liberius (**Liberius III**). In the front, as at the back, it presents five figures in shelled niches, divided by several spiral columns with Corinthian capitals; it is the representation of «Traditio legis», that in *front* represents Christ on the throne facing Peter and at the back facing Paul, the latter with veiled hands. Paul is well characterized by the beard and by the bald forehead, according to tradition. The other characters, including the ones on *the sides*, are Apostles. As regards to this sarcophagus, De Francovich speaks of «elegance of craving and lirical emotion that pervades the faces of the characters». The sarcophagus dates back to the first decades of the 5th century or, according to De Francovich, round about the year 380.

Behind the altar, around the apse, a wooden choir is placed.

Inside: left nave - Going along the left nave, from the apse towards the entrance, we notice a trace of an ancient room followed by an ark inside an arcosolio. It **is the sepulchral monumento of Luffo Numai**, secretary of Pino Ordelaffi, whose family kept the dominium of Forlì, with alternate events, for about two centuries (8). The sculpture is work of *Tommaso Fiamberti* who was born in Campione, on Lugano Lake, and who worked in Forlì and Cesena. Numai worked in 1508 and the sepulchrum was finished in 1509; it is similar to another one that had been ordered to the sculptor by Numai in Forlì. This one of Ravenna seems unfinished in the superior part: the pendentives and the lunette, in fact, are naked and the arch is too simple. The inferior part, instead, appears very well completed. Above there is the inscription: «THOMAE FIAMBERTI SCULPTORIS OPUS 1509». On the sarcophagus a bird and a camel, with the words ABSTINE PATERE (Abstain and refrain yourself), are sculptured.

Further on there is the tombstone of Father Enrico Alfieri, general of the order of San Francesco who died in 1405 (9), followed by the tombstone, in Veronese red, with the hands and the face in white marble, of Ostasio da Polenta who died in 1396 (10).

A wide ogival arch of the fourteenth century follows with two windows and traces of frescos which are now illegible. It was the private chapel of the Polentani family (11). Another fresco was discovered during the restorations of 1921 on the lateral wall of the nave near the end; it represented a figure sitting and thinking and considered to be the portrait of Dante. Both this fragment and the one of the chapel representing the crucifixion, are of Pietro da Rimini.

In the room of the chapel, which isn't deeper than the intrados of a normal arch, a very beautiful **sarcophagus** (12) is placed, it is of the end of the 4th century with a roof-like lid, worked only on three sides with a very emphasized relief nearly completely round; it shows in the niches divided by little Corinthian capitals and columns Christ sitting on a throne with a cushion, dressed with a short-sleeved tunic and a pallium, who hands a roll to Saint Paul, having near to himself Saint Peter and a few Apostles. Also the decoration of acanthus leaves, vine-shoots and grapes is very beautiful. On the sides other Apostles in niches. Another **sarcophagus** (13) follows, which carries on the *sides* lambs facing the «*Chrismon*» with alpha, omega and a star and on the front two winged puttos that hold the inscription. The sarcophagus was used again by the Del Sale family. The fact that the acroteria are sculptured with two busts makes us think that it is of the 3rd century, worked on the sides in the 4th century while the inscription is of the 18th century. The cross of the tympana of the lid is oblique.

In a room a little further on a Modern Christmas Crib finds place (14), which can be animated and enlightened by the visitors, it is a work of *father Lambertini*, remarkable for its grace, the property of its movements, the game of lights, the beauty of the statues (of the Graziani-Dalmonte school). Finally, in a corner, a last sarcophagus, it is Roman and it was used by the Rasponi family. The ceiling, like the keel of a ship, was remade in 1918-21 on the remains of the one of the Fourteenth Century.

ORIANI LIBRARY (fig. 19 n. 12, at pag. 94) - Let's return to piazza San Francesco, let's cross it until via Corrado Ricci and let's turn right and carry on a few steps until n. 26 where we have Oriani house, which houses a remarkable library specialized in Modern history and political and sociological studies. From 1978 a newspaper and periodical library of the Classense and Oriani Libraries. The seat is on the place where the Rizzetti house rose, dating back to the Sixteenth Century, and demolished to make space for the new building. Rizzetti house had also been turned into an inn and in it between 1819-1820, George Byron lodged; later on, there was «caffé Byron», which was the most aristocratic café of the town. To commemorate the stay of the English poet, who in Ravenna received cordial accommodation and love, on the side of the Oriani house towards Piazza San Francesco there is a tablet with the following inscription: «QUI ERA LA CASA OVE DIMORÒ NEL 1819 LORD BYRON, SOMMO POETA INGLESE, AMICO DEI PATRIOTI RAVENNATI» (13) (This is the house where in 1819 Lord Byron the great English poet, friend of the Ravennati patriots stayed).

PALAZZO DELLA PROVINCIA - RASPONI CRYPT - Let's now go to the near piazza dei Caduti where, beyond the «Palazzo della Provincia» (fig. 19 n. 14) onto which some buildings in the heavy style typical of the fascist period look, like the curved one at the bottom on the right, built in 1939 to house the «casa del fascio» (fascist house) and that was provided of a lictorian tower, later demolished.

Remarkable is the Palazzo della Provincia, work of the architect G.U. Arata, which rises on the place where there was a Rasponi building which had been turned into the luxurious Hotel Byron at the end of the Nineteenth Century. Then, from 1918, it was the seat of the «Federazione delle Cooperative», burnt by the fascists in 1922. On the ruins the building of a hotel had been started. During the works, the destination of the building was changed and the work continued as «Palazzo della Provincia».

The new building, finished in 1928, adapts to the austere environment of the Dantesque zone with the monumental portico on the Southern side of piazza San Francesco, with the alternate use of stone and bricks and of varied architectural elements such as square windows, cubic capitals, short towers.

In the inside there is a beautiful garden in which, among the high walls that close it, a suggestive atmosphere reigns, particularly notable in the ending part, which is pensile, and which can be reached by means of a few flights of stairs. Immediately after the entrance there is a fountain and a little further there is a column with a ball on top.

At the bottom on the left we reach a little tower that in the inferior part has a crypt, called *Rasponi crypt* (15) formed by a room covered by a semi-spherical vault carried out by means of concentrical rows of bricks in the middle of which there is a stone ball with the inscription «SIC VITA PENDET AB ALTO» (the light switch is near the entrance). In the little articulated room there are arches, niches, little recesses with commemorative inscriptions of the Rasponi family. The mosaic floor, with decorative motifs and figures of various animals comes from the Classense church of San Severo, as is remembered in an inscription placed in the centre, and which dates back to the second half of the 6th century.

Under one of the external arcades of the tower there is a Byzantine pulvino decorated with crosses.

Leaving the crypt we continue to go up the stairs until the belvedere from which we can see piazza San Francesco. We are in a garden from which we can pass to the contiguous terrace, built in 1839, that goes over via Antonio Santi and which served to connect Palazzo Rasponi to the stables and to the storehouses. The entrance arch to the terrace is rather unusual: it is, in fact, **the marble dial of the clock** (16) that was on the front of the churches of San Sebastiano and San Marco in piazza del Popolo before Morigia changed their façade in 1783. The dial, as we have already said, marked all

Basilica of Sant'Agata Maggiore: vestibule and bell-tower.

the twentyfour hours and here we find twelve on one side and twelve on the other side of the arch. At the end of the terrace there is a beautiful façade of brickwork with a little pointed mullioned window.

PIAZZA DEI CADUTI - Let's return to piazza dei Caduti in which, under the flower-bed placed in the middle, recent excavations discovered wall structures relative to the water-course of the Padenna River. In this zone, in fact, once the Padenna River and another water-course called «fossa Lamisa or Amnis», which lapped against the buildings of the bishop's residence, joined together (look at the plan fig. 45 at page 181).

CHURCH OF SAN CARLINO - From piazza dei Caduti let's take via Mazzini and after a short while we can turn left in via Tombesi Dall'Ova to reach, at a few hundred meters from the road-crossing the Church of San Carlino, now preceeded by a little square that constituted the church-square.

The church rose in 1062, and it was dedicated to the Apostles Simon and Judah and to the martyrs Fabiano and Sebastiano. It was then called San Carlino because, in 1583, was founded there a brotherhood of laymen under the patronage of San Carlo Borromeo. Of the ancient church we still have the little apse with windows decorated in brickwork and the crowning; these however maybe date back to the 13th century.

The actual church was practically rebuilt in 1756: from here the Eighteenth Century façade of Doric order with the door bordered by granite columns.

The inside reserves a nice surprise by offering vision of the paintings of the little dome, fresh and live, they are due to the brush of *Domenico Barbiani*, and of the stucco-works of the apse by *Giuliano Garavini*. Of the dome especially remarkable are the four «chiaroscuro» red medallions.

On the left wall we find the marble **bas-relief** that served also as Tabernacle of the Madonna del Sudore, in the Duomo. It is a perspective with a barrel vault and columns, which carries in the middle a beautiful and elegant relief of the Madonna with the Infant which however, didn't make part of the tabernacle which, instead, should be completed with an Ecce Homo now kept elsewhere. Above there is a Resurrecting Christ and on the sides, from behind the columns, two figures carrying a flaming vase show up.

The tabernacle was ordered to a Lombard sculptor by the archbishop Filiasio Roverella at the beginning of the 16th century and, as the inscription says, it was brought here from the Duomo after that the Dal Cornos patrons of the church, bought it.

The painting behind the altar represents San Carlo Borromeo.

On the left wall there are three epigraphs. The bottom one is the original epigraph of 1062 that gives the act of birth of the church and says that it was built by a certain Oddo that provided it of some plots of agricultural ground placed in Gambellara (Massa Camillaria) and in other places. Above we have the funerary epigraph of Gurlino Tombesi, Ravennate soldier, general captain of the Venetians, who died in 1501. The epigraph comes from the church of San Nicolò. High up there is an inscription of 1762 in which it is specified that Oddo, founder of the church, was of the Tombesi dall'Ova family.

Under the three tablets there is a little interesting marble engraving, with the use of colour, which represents the map of a farm of Piangipane, that the Dal Corno family, which were the owners, gave to the church.

On the floor, as also on the walls, the emblem of the Dal Corno family appears. The floor is yellow and red and near the entrance it is composed of fragments of ancient marble on which also a few mosaic tesserae appear.

Returning in via Mazzini, at n. 44, we notice the **Donati house** built in the Eighteenth Century and at n. 55, 53, 49 **Pignata house**, that already existed in 1485. In 1560 Torquato Tasso was guest here, as is remembered on a little tablet not very readable above the arch of the gate. Now the building is seat of the Consorzio Agrario Provinciale. In front of Pignata house there is the church of Sant'Agata Maggiore.

SANT'AGATA MAGGIORE

Historical hints and external characteristics - Founded at the end of 5th century (when it was built the Padenna River flowed in front of it), during the centuries gone by it underwent many modifications, more than any other basilica in Ravenna. However the church has maintained its ancient fascination. It rises quite far from via Mazzini and it is rather lower than the street level; in fact we must go down eight steps until the lawn that preceeds it and we must go up five to enter in it. The lawn is surrounded by a railing and crossed by a pavement; several sarcophagi have been placed here and a few columns and a round bell-tower rises here. This space, since the construction of the church, was used as a cemetery and it was maintained such until the 16th century. It was surrounded by a little quadriportico, which maybe had been added at the time of bishop Agnello (557-570), that reached till via Mazzini in continuation of the lateral walls of the church, with columns on the inside and walls on the outside.

The excavations carried out between 1913 and 1918, following the demolition of some houses, brought to light the sarcophagi that are placed here and the tombstones and marbles that we'll find inside the church. Then also the façade was restored by placing the 15th century protirus (fig. 22, n. 1) taken from the side of the church of San Nicolò. It is a light and elegant architecture and the beautiful mullioned-window formed by marbles which is above it increases its charm. The columns which sustain the vault rise from a strong marble balustrade. Even if the façade is in rough brick without any other ornament than six pure brickwork pilasters, this elegant element of such different style however integrates perfectly. Notice the capitals very delicately worked, the frieze of the great arch and the elegant candlestick reliefs of the pillars against the wall on the sides of the door.

Fig. 22 - **Basilica of Sant'Agata Maggiore: plan**. 1 - 6th century vestibule. 2 - Sarcophagus of the 6th century. 3-4 - Imposts and remainders of ancient half buried doors. 5 - Bell-tower. 6 - Sarcophagus of the end of the 6th century. 7 - Gothic fragments and of later on. 8 - Pluteus with chrismon. 9 - Pluteus with clipeus and side of a sarcophagus with the Annunciation chiseled. 10 - Bricks with the trade-mark. 11 - Monogram of the bishop Peter II. 12 - Trace of the primitive impost of the arches. 13 - Traces of the arches of the ancient doors. 14 - Corpse drain. 15 - Niche with ancient paintings. 16 - Ambo of the 6th century. 17 - Big marble canopy. 18 - Big canopy of the 16th century, sarcophagus-altar of St. Sergius and of the Archbishop Agnellus. 19 - Big Renaissance canopy. 20 - Big canopy with altar-piece of G.B. Barbiani.

Altogether the sarcophagi are fourteen, of various epochs, and some preceed the construction of the quadriportico; the first on the right of the stairs, for example, with a cross sculptured on the front, is of the 6th century (2).

On the left of the vestibule we can notice the impost of a walled door surmounted by an architrave of shaped marble and by the trace of an arch (3); on the opposite side, on the right of the vestibule behind the bell-tower, there is the impost of a second ancient door that still has the left door-post of worked marble (4). The two doors are for two quarters of their height buried and give a precise idea of the difference between the original level and the actual one.

The **bell-tower** is of the 16th century (1560). Dotted by many little holes, with some windows and, above, with four mullioned windows, it is a little higher than the church.

Inside: space which preceeds the big arch - The inside is made up of three naves, with some columns reinforced by brick pillars and by a big arch at the height of the second column. The columns are ten on each side, very unequal, some of them in two pieces, and the capitals and the pulvinoes are various and different. For example, in the second column incorporated in a pillar of the Southern nave there is an impost capital with frame on the sides, of Justinian epoch; on the fifth column on the left there is a Corinthian capital with two rows of four big acanthus leaves

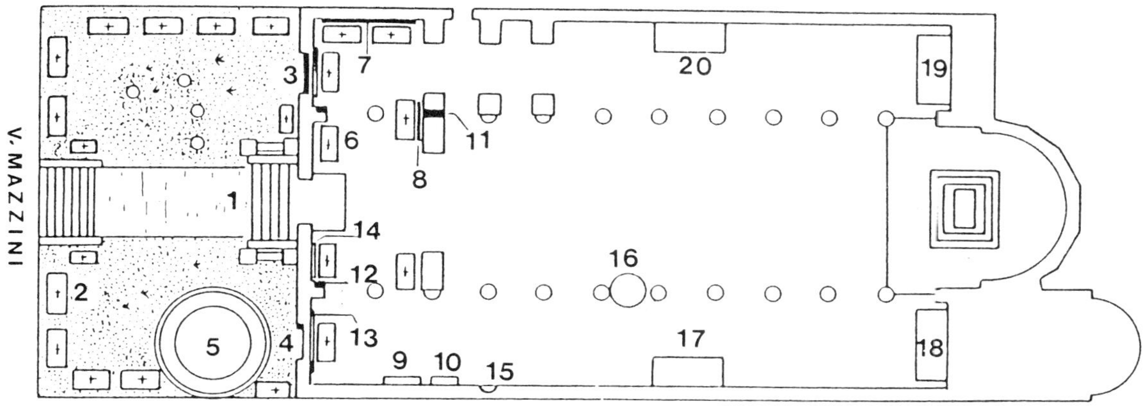

and a two band abacus (5th-6th century), on the third column on the left, incorporated in a pillar, there is a Corinthian capital «of lyre» type of the end of the 5th century, and on various other columns (sixth on the left, fifth and seventh on the right) there are Corinthian capitals of «lyre» type, all different from one another; other four capitals are of the Renaissance period etc... It was thought (Mazzotti) that not all of the ancient columns and capitals were put back in use when, between the end of the 15th century and the beginning of the 16th century, the floor was made higher.

The roof of the three naves is made of trusses. In 1980-81 nearly all the old trusses were redone with new material. Nine windows on each side above the arch gives light to the inside.

In the space that preceeds the big arch the findings of the excavations of 1913-18 have been placed. There are eight unadorned and rough sarcophagi. The first on the left of the entrance (6), with a cross on the front, is of the end of the VI century.

On the inside wall of the façade, on the left while entering, and on the contiguous wall of the nave many fragments and Byzantine inscriptions, and Gothic fragments and others of later on have been placed (7).

On the two pieces of wall which sustain the arch there have been placed fragments of plutei and an intact pluteus (8) that carries in the middle a *chrismon* from which two «lemnisci» that end with a leaf depart.

Onto the wall of the right nave a pluteus with a clipeus in the middle is fixed, it was used as an altar's table, it is of the middle of the 6th century (9); on top there is the side of a chiseled sarcophagus in which the Announcement can be seen: it is of the end of the 4th century.

On the left of the pluteus we must notice a «manubriato» brick (i.e. a brick with a hole that permits to hold it) and brick fragments with the furnace trade-marks on them (10).

Before proceeding in the visit of the church, let's lift our eyes on the piece of wall on the left of the arch: in a little window deliberately left at the height of the columns we can see a pulvino of the epoch of Peter II (494-519) with a complex monogram meaning *Petrus Episcopus* (11).

Let's observe finally, on the two pillars of the first arch, against the inside wall of the façade (12), the trace of the junction point of the original arches that, as we can see, is much lower than the actual one. Notice also, behind the two sarcophagi placed along the internal wall of the façade, the trace of the two arches of the original doors that we saw also on the outside (13); they are very low too and give the idea of how much the floor has been raised, making higher correspondingly the columns and obtaining arches at the expenses of the overhanging wall, therefore the whole construction has lost slimness. Notice, finally, fixed on the wall above the sarcophagus on the right while entering, a corpse drain (14).

Inside: right nave - Little beyond the pilaster of the big arch, on the wall of the right nave there is a little niche (15) with a very ruined painting, representing a bishop, near which there is a Saint Sebastian of the fifteenth century.

Between the fifth and the sixth column on the right there is an **ambo** of the 6th century (16) in Greek marble veined grey and green which has the aspect of the shell of an enormous column grooved by nine very little slim niches on each side. Above the little arches there is a frieze with ovules, pearls and leaves. The niches are divided by columns ending in little capitals. Curious particular: the columns are unequal in height; their base, is placed at different levels. The ambo stands onto a massive cylindrical base.

A little further there is the first of the four elegant **canopies** (17) with which the church is adorned. Among them, the most interesting is, maybe, the one placed at the bottom of the nave (18). It is of the 16th century and is over an altar formed by an ancient sarcophagus that contains the ashes of San Sergio Martire and of the archbishop Agnellus. At the extremities of the front, under two crosses, there are two monograms that should mean: «SERGIUS» the one on the left, «DIACONUS» the one on the right. The painting above the altar represents Sant'Agata who accepts martyrdom so as not to succumb to Quinziano, governor of Sicily. The other saints are Catherine and Cecily the hill landscape wants to represent the neighbourhoods of Catania. It is of Luca Longhi and belongs to his second period.

Inside: apse - The original part of the church, that is the one which dates back to the last quarter of the 5th century, is constituted by the inferior part of the apse and by the walls of the Northern nave. The apse has five windows, opened again in 1964; during these works fragments of the primitive mosaic decoration which covered, as well as the apse exedra, also the triumphal arch and part of the contiguous walls, appeared. The mosaics were all destroyed because of earthquakes and they were substituted by frescos which also disappeared. The mosaics represented Christ on the throne clothed in purple, a roll in the left hand, two archangels clothed in white on the sides, on a ground covered with flowers. The fragments left in the intradoses of the windows are very beautiful. On the inferior part of the apse fourteen century paintings emerge.

On the altar a beautiful tablet of the 6th century is incorporated in which two peacocks facing the *chrismon* are represented.

Inside: left nave - At the bottom of the left nave there is a Renaissance canopy with columns of Greek marble (19). The painting, of *Andrea Barbiani*; represents Saint Apollonia and Saint Lucia. A painting representing the «Madonna del Buon Consiglio» (Madonna of Good Advice) is inserted too. Nearby there is the trace of the arch of a door, whose threshold is 2.80 meters as regards to the actual level, which led to one of the «*pastophoria*».

The canopy in the middle of the nave overhangs a canvas of *Giovan Battista Barbiani*, representing the Madonna, Jesus, Saint Peter and Magdalene (20).

Apse: outside - To see the outside of the eptagonal apse we must return in via Mazzini, turn right and right again into via Carrari, enter through the little door at the bottom on the side of the church, cross the yard, go past a second little door; you will find yourselves in a wide yard of a modern block of flats which makes part of the new Sant'Agata district. Going on until the end of the yard, you can easily see, inside a green zone, the recently restorated apse.

South of Sant'Agata, during the Roman Age, the **Circus** rose and via Cerchio commemorates it in its name.

Continuing along the via Mazzini route, we notice a subway that joins via Mazzini with via Baccarini. In the subway, near the entrance at n. 57, some little marble fragments discovered in the Ronco river-bed near S. Bartolomeo, in Longana, have been placed, among the remainders of the Trajan aqueduct restored by Theodoric. We find then at n. 75, the **Lovatelli building**, of the Eighteenth Century, seat of the Tavelle Institute, they are a religious group of nuns that take their name from sister Adriana Tavella who established the order in 1586.

At n. 78 another **Lovatelli building** with a high portal. The staircase opens in the hall on the left, while at the bottom the green space of the garden opens.

At n. 84, a house of the Seventeenth Century.

CASA POLENTANA - At the end of via Mazzini, on the left, the narrow via Zagarelli alle Mura opens where, at n. 2, we find one of the most ancient houses of Ravenna. It dates back to the 13th century and it belongs to the Da Polenta family. This family had the supremacy in Ravenna, starting from 1275 when Guido Minore da Polenta, head of the Guelphs (and father of Francesca), drove all his political opponents away from the city. After 166 years the Polentani gave their command up to the Republic of Venice. On the rustic and unadorned façade little windows open, some of which are pointed, others are walled. The entrance door is very simple, with a brick-arch. On the façade a little tablet with the bearings of the canons of Porto who owned the house in the 15th century is walled. Legend indicates it as Francesca's house.

In front of the house the traces of the ancient city-walls are still visible. A little beyond, in the space widened in the Nineteenth Century, people played football, and the place is still known and called by the old «Ravennati» as «Il giuoco del pallone» (The football game). The place used to be closed at the two extremities and people would enter by paying.

Porta Sisi: foreshortening.

PORTA SISI - Returning to via Mazzini, we observe the entrance gate to the city, called anciently Porta Ursicina. The actual name was probably formed as a dialect corruption of the original one.

In the beautiful form of nowadays it was remade in 1568 and restored in 1649. The ray lunette, of wrought iron, that we find in the arch, was placed in 1885; it was once in the arch of the Monastery of San Vitale in via San Vitale n. 21, that was reduced to architrave. In the middle there is San Vitale on horseback, now very worn away.

The two columns are made of grey granite.

THE PORTONACCIO - Beyond the gate, at about two hundred meters, we can see the arch of the Portonaccio, that takes its name from an ancient crenelated arch that rose in that area.

It was built in 1785 on design of Camillo Morigia. It isn't a gate of the city, but a celebrative arch for the rearrangement - nearly a reconstruction - of via Ravegnana which leads to Forlì, which had reached such a deteriorating state to be impracticable for coaches. The road, had been wanted by cardinal Valenti Gonzaga, pontifical legate.

CHURCH OF SAN ROCCO - Between porta Sisi and the Portonaccio, on the seat of the church built in 1583, the church of San Rocco rises, its construction was started in 1828 on design of Antonio Sarti who wanted it under the form of a Pantheon. After having collapsed many times during construction, the church's construction was carried on by engineer Luigi Bezzi, who modified deeply the designs of Santi.

The parish priest Angelo Montanari had the parsonage built and the clock-tower. The beautiful marble altar was transferred here in 1921 from the church of San Francesco.

Let's return on our steps and go through Porta Sisi again so as to enter on the left into via de' Tomai which leads us into via Baccarini.

PORTA SAN MAMA - On reaching via Baccarini, looking towards the left we notice another gate that, for the shortness of via De' Tomai is very near to the preceeding one. The presence of two gates so near to one another may be explained by the fact that they were divided by the Padenna river, of which via Baccarini and via Mazzini constituted the two opposite banks.

The name of the gate originates from the church of San Mamante that was nearby but outside the walls. It is a very ancient gate (11th century) but the actual construction dates back only to 1613. Between the two lions of the attic there was, it seems, the coat-of-arms of the pontiff Paolo V that was reigning at that time.

The place is remarkable because on the 9th April 1512, a few days before the battle of Ravenna, the artilleries of the Duke of Ferrara, alley of the French, opened a hole in the walls on left of the gate. Nevertheless the assault of the French that day didn't succeed: the citizens, infact, defended themselves tenaciously, while a bronze culverin, placed on the walls near porta Gaza, hit the attackers sideways slaughtering them.

Before the deviation of the rivers Ronco and Montone and the formation of the actual riverbed of the Fiumi Uniti (1736), the Ronco river reached the walls right in front of this gate from the direction of via San Mama, then it turned right towards porta Sisi. In this place, then, the river received on the left the channel «del Mulino» and the drain Lama, therefore we can

Porta San Mama: base of the impost of the arch with Christ's monogram.

imagine how picturesque and various the scenery was, with the waters, the mill (Mulino), the wooden and wall bridges, the bastion which preceeded the gate for its defence. And we can see how everything has changed.

CHURCH OF SAN NICOLÒ - Let's go along via Baccarini entering more and more into town. Having reached n. 70 we notice high on the left the bell-tower of S. Romualdo and between n. 68 and the subway, we notice the top of the bell-tower of what was the church of San Nicolò, the side of which runs along an enlargement of the road. The primitive church was built in 768, and was officiated for various time by the hermit fathers of Sant'Agostino.

A brief deviation on the left through via Nicolò Rondinelli allows us to see the rustic high façade of the church, once supplied with a circular window onto which a cross was over-exposed, now supplied of five big windows, and of two cloisters of the convent of the Augustinean fathers, restored in the 18th century by Camillo Morigia.

The convent rose on the side of the church and now the offices of the «Intendenza di Finanza and of the Direzione Provinciale del Tesoro» find seat here. We enter at n. 6.

The actual church which rose between 1356 and 1359, was suppressed in 1866 and it became a military riding school from 1885. A single wide nave, contained many beautiful paintings of Cesare Pronti. Now it is used as military deposit. On its side there was the vestibule that we saw in front of the near church of Sant'Agata.

MONASTERY OF CLASSE CLASSENSE LIBRARY CHURCH OF SAN ROMUALDO

The remaining piece of via Baccarini, on its left side, is nearly entirely occupied by the great complex that constituted the monastery of the Camaldolesi monks. The monastery had had origin by means of the intervention of the Polentani family, and it rose outside from the city, near the basilica of Sant'Apollinare in Classe. From this first dwelling the monks moved to town in 1515 due to the destructions suffered by their seat in the French-Spanish war of 1512. The famous battle of Ravenna, furthermore, took place in the territory placed near the basilica.

Coming to Ravenna, where they already had the church of San Bartolomeo in Turricola with the hospital of San Lazzaro joined to it, both given to them by the Polentani in 1433, the monks started off the construction of the great monastery that continued with successive widenings, for not less than three hundred years. The whole includes the church of San Romualdo, the cloisters, the monastery.

Our visit starts from the little entrance at n. 3. It is a beautiful Renaissance portal, totally devoid of decorations and frills, clean in its lines and harmonic in its proportions. Above the architrave, that carries the date of 1523, there is an inscription: IGREDIETIB' ET BONVFACIETIB' SEPITERNA GLA MDXXIII (To the one who enters and he's right eternal glory 1523).

First cloister - After a little hall we reach a cloister with the construction of which the monks started the erection of the monastery

Monastery of Classe, refectory: Luca Longhi, «Le nozze di Cana» (particular) (Cana's wedding).

as soon as they came to Ravenna. It is composed by 24 columns of which 22 on three sides, being the fourth nearly entirely occupied by a big Baroque pediment in the middle of which an arch surmounted by a tondo opens and by a big balcony window with a marble balustrade. On the sides, two ogival windows. Above, in a little niche, the bust of San Romualdo.

Of the three sides with columns, two have walled arches.

In the middle there is a well, whose marble curb was once in piazza del Popolo. Around the well, some big trees.

At the bottom of the Southern corridor, on the left, in March 1977 the lending library of contemporary literature «PONTI» has been placed, the library was founded by the countess Maria Pasolini Ponti, to honour the memory of her father.

The bottom door leads to a passage that brings you to the second big monumental cloister.

Second cloister - Unlike the first one, which is rather dark, this one is wide and full of light. It was built between 1611 and 1620 on design of the Tuscan *Giulio Morelli*, it is made up of thirty-two Istria stone columns. The arcade is very wide and it is divided from the open space by means of a wall. In the middle there is a beautiful **cistern** of white Istria stone, high up on three steps.

Two pairs of columns sustain an arch surmounted by a little dome and a crown with four bronze angels with little pyramids and a bronze star. From the arch a big bronze pulley hangs down with a chain onto which two buckets in bronze too, very elegantly worked hang.

The design of the cistern is of *Gian Paolo Pannini* (1691/92-1765). *Domenico Barbiani* in order to execute this work developed such a design.

Numerous big trees create around the well a thickness of shadows, and nearly hiding the buildings that overhang the porticos give us the impression to be in a forest.

Refectory - Let's return to the first cloister and let's go through the door with a glass wrought iron gate placed correspondingly to the arch of the façade. Let's enter into a vestibule and from this one into the second one that can be reached from the monk's refectory, finished at the end of the 16th century. The **door** is a remarkable carving work of 1581, of *Mario Peruzzi* from Ancona. On the sides there is an architecture of the 16th century with telamons. In this vestibule there are also two lavabos, also of the 16th century, with animals that sustain a basin and an urn, above which there are the little statues of San Benedetto and San Romualdo.

We enter into the magnificent refectory: a big room in which we find the stalls carved in the Sixteenth Century by M. Peruzzi. The ceiling, with many panels, lunettes, tondi, groins, is frescoed by Longhi's pupils.

Close to the entrance door there is a pulpit from which the reading father during the meals, read chapters of the Rule or of the ascetic works. Worked in 1581-82 by the brother-in-law of Luca Longhi, Jacobo Baranzello, it was redone in 1781 by the carpenter Agostino Gessi, from Ravenna.

The windows, work of the beginning of the Eighteenth Century of father *Giuseppe Grimani*, are rectangular, divided in compartments, with interlacements with multiple knots, geometrical and decorative compositions.

Monastery of Classe, sacristy of the church of San Romualdo now «Sala Muratori»: decoration of Cesare Buti (particular).

The big painting of *Luca Longhi* «Le nozze di Cana» occupies all the bottom wall, it is remarkable for its equilibrium and harmony. It is the second last work of the Ravennate painter.

Jesus, in the centre, has on his left Simon Peter who is speaking to his elder brother Andrew. Two disciples follow: Philip (in which one of the sons of Luca, the painter Francesco, is portrayed) and Bartholomew (in which Pomponio Spreti is portrayed) as well as a pilgrim (self-portrait of Luca Longhi) to whom a Moorish pours something to drink. On the right of Jesus there is the Madonna, then the groom and the bride. In the woman in the fore-ground, who is the mother of the groom, Barbara the paintress daughter of the author is portrayed.

The big painting is ruined and faded below because of the 1636 flood while on top the colours are live and the drawing is clear, thanks also to a recent restoration. The room, destined from 1921 to the reading of Dante, is called «Sala Dantesca».

Classense Library - Let's return to the first vestibule. We have to go onto the higher floor that leads to the rooms of the library going up three staircases which bring to a very long corridor in which, as well as two canvases and different oval paintings which represent various characters, there are two big paintings of the 16th century. Alfredo Panzini talks about the one nearer to the entrance door in the following way.

«*The corridor is adorned with a beautiful fresco. In the middle of it, with a thick beard, white tunic, sits a very austere old man. It is San Romualdo. Around him, with joined hands, some adolescent monks are kneeling: their heads are shaved and look towards the ground with great humbleness. San Romualdo rises his hand and says the greatest of words: "Quiet". Everything is still.*

The hundred year old man seems to teach those monks the religion of all religions: silence on the human things.

"If only senses didn't awaken" those monks seem to say.

"Quiet" answers San Romualdo».

The doors which open in the corridor lead to

Church of San Romualdo: particular of the marble pilaster strip.

the consulting and reading rooms, to the offices and to the book deposits. Here the HISTORICAL MUNICIPAL ARCHIVE finds its seat, inaugurated in 1913, whose principal nucleus is made up by the administrative correspondence of the municipality from 1512 to 1919. It starts from 1512 because in the pillage of the town during that year the French destroyed nearly all the old archive. Let's look towards the beautiful hall designed by the «Camaldolesi» architects *Giuseppe Antonio Soratini* and *Fausto Pellicciotti*. Two stairs lead to the main room. On the left there is the monument in memory of the abbot Guido Grandi, a mathematician. Work of the stuccoworker *Domenico Piò* who did it in 1747.

The **main room** is magnificent, big, full of light, richly decorated in Baroque and Rococo style. The shelves on the walls were carved by *Fausto Pellicciotti*. On the ceiling the painter *Francesco Mancini* (Sant'Angelo in Vado 1679-1758) represented «The Divine Wisdom which orders Theology and other sciences to destroy the scisma, heresy, and ignorance». The two canvases at the entrance door («Union of the Latin church with the Greek one», and at the bottom of the room «the Camaldolese Graziano and pope Gregorio IX compiler of the Sacred Canons») are also works of the painter Mancini. The stucco-works are of *Antonio Martinetti*. This room is above the refectory. The two big globes are work of Vincenzo Coronelli.

Going up a stair at the end of the main room, we reach a higher room. This room designed by Camillo Morigia, presents stucco decorations and a canvas of the Sicilian *Mariano Rossi*, representing «Fame which leads Virtue and Glory showing them the temple of Eternity» (1779). This **room** is said «**delle scienze**» (of science) because it contains scientific books. The stucco decorations are of *Giacomo* and *Giovanni Bonesani, Paolo Giabani, Paolo Trifogli*. The carver of the shelves is *Carlo Montanari*. As well as this one there are several other rooms, added in 1764, with book deposits.

The actual library was founded in 1707-1711 by the Cremonese abbot Pietro Canneti. We have moreover the news of a library of the monastery since 1556. In 1791 there was «*the most plentiful and beautiful library of the city*» (Beltrami). With the Napoleonic suppression of the religious orders, in 1804 the library became municipal. The municipality, then absorbed books from other convent libraries which had been suppressed and increased and still increases with continuous purchases the library patrimony. The library has famous codices, among which the one that contains eleven comedies of Aristophanes; it is a membranaceous codex, in folio, of the 11th century, bought in Pisa in 1712. Among the printed books, it contains several hundred incunabula. On the whole, the endowment of the library is now more or less than 600.000 volumes. A recent restoration has allowed to use some spaces of the ground floor as exhibition rooms.

Church of San Romualdo - It is on the corner between via Baccarini and via Rondinelli; its side runs in front of the façade of San Nicolò.

The first stone of the church was placed in 1630, on project of the Ravennate architect *Luca Danesi* (1598-1672). It was dedicated to San Romualdo (who died in 1026) founder, in the mountains of Casentino, of the hermitage of Camaldoli, which gave the name to the Camaldolese Benedictine order.

The church was rich of paintings, sculptures and stucco-works works of *Giovan Battista Barbiani, father Cesare Ponti, Michelangelo Cerquozzi, Marcantonio Franceschini* («Saint

Bartholomew and Saint Severo»), *Cignani* («Saint Benedict»), *Guercino* («San Romualdo»), *Vasari* («Deposizione»). The last paintings are now in the Civic Picture-gallery.

Also *Morigia*, the stucco-worker *Martinetti*, the sculptor *Giovanni Camino da Venezia* worked here.

As we can understand, it was a sumptuous church: but when the Camaldolesi were sent away in 1798, little by little it deteriorated: it was museum, gymnasium... Santi Muratori in 1926 defined it *«a ship of superb size and beauty, bogged down. Men and weather both competed in tearing its boards, break its keel, root out its foundations»*.

Fortunately the temple was turned into SACRARIO DEI CADUTI IN GUERRA E IN PRIGIONIA (SACRARIUM FOR THOSE WHO DIED IN WAR AND AS PRISONERS OF WAR) and this permitted a dignified restoration.

The church has one nave only, with three chapels on each side, and a triangular choir. Actually it still presents, in a little lowered dome with the lantern, the frescos of *Giovan Battista Barbiani*, which represent «The Immaculate among Saints, Apostles and choirs of Angels» and on the lunette of the choir «The extasy of San Romualdo», always of the same author.

On the vault of some chapels there are tondi and panels with painted scenes. Remarkable are the two little portals of the transept, of pink marble, in a compound Renaissance style.

The high altar, rich of precious marbles, was designed by *Morigia* as a table standing onto a marble swollen urn destined to contain the relics of San Severo; on the two sides the table is sustained by two bronze putti designed by *Morigia* and accomplished by *Giuseppe Baroni*.

On the two sides of the presbytery two bulletins of the declaration of war and of the victory of World War I are placed. In the choir the tablets with the names of the fallen are walled.

Connected to the vast **sacristy** (we enter at n. 5 of via Baccarini) now called «Sala Muratori», from the name of the Ravennate Santi Muratori (1874-1943), famous director of the Classense library and humanist, has been turned into a conference hall. The big painting of the wall at the bottom represents «The resurrection of Lazarus» and it is a beautiful work of art of *Francesco Zaganelli*. The two beautiful columns are made of porphyry. The decorations of the vestibule, which was used to prepare Mass, are of *Cesare Pronti*.

The side of the church of San Romualdo, divided by eight grooved marble pilasters with sculptured capitals, should be the wall of San Bartolomeo in Turricola used by the monks for the new church (Savini).

Finally let's remember that the building now described housed one of the four great abbeys of Ravenna, and that in 1650 it had a hundred rooms for 44 monks and 31 people among servants and work-men.

Returning into via Baccarini, at the end on the left, after n. 1, we can see what remains of the building which had been adapted to house the Academy of Fine Arts (Accademia di Belle Arti), now transferred to the Monastero di Porto. It is a beautiful, simple and elegant façade, of Ionic order, designed by *Ignazio Sarti* and built between 1827-1829. It had nine arches (now there are only three) with the entrance in the central one.

Let's then leave Piazza dei Caduti, where we have already been, and through via Guidone and via Mentana let's return to Piazza del Popolo.

ITINERARY OF SAN GIOVANNI EVANGELISTA AND SANT'APOLLINARE NUOVO

Piazza del Popolo - Via Armando Diaz - Banca del Monte - Casa Guaccimanni - **San Giovanni Evangelista** - Via di Roma - Palazzo Grossi - Palazzo Serena Monghini - **Sant'Apollinare Nuovo** - Palazzo Malagola - so called Palazzo di Teodorico - Palazzo Spreti - Casa Bezzi - Palazzo Rasponi-Bonanzi - Santa Chiara - **Santa Maria in Porto** - **Monastero di Porto** - Modern mosaics - Ornithological and Natural Science Museum - **Civic Pinacotheca** - Porta nuova - Public Gardens - **Loggetta Lombardesca** - Via Mariani - Palazzo Corradini - Teatro Alighieri - Piazza Garibaldi.

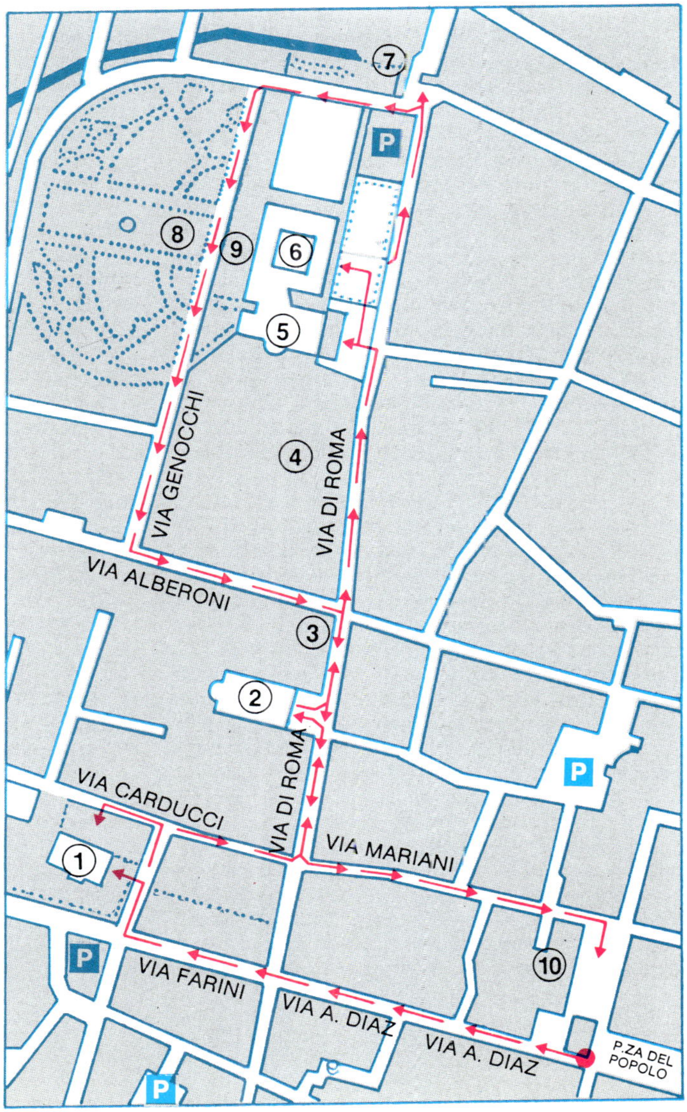

Fig. 23 - **Itinerary of San Giovanni Evangelista and Sant'Apollinare Nuovo.**
1 - San Giovanni Evangelista. 2 - Sant'Apollinare Nuovo. 3 - So-called Palazzo di Teodorico. 4 - Santa Chiara. 5 - Santa Maria in Porto. 6 - Monastero di Porto-Ornithological an Natural Science Museum-Civic Pinacotheca. 7 - Porta Nuova. 8 - Public Gardens. 9 - Loggetta Lombardesca. 10 - Teatro Alighieri.

War memorial: particular.

This itinerary, starting from Piazza del Popolo, extends to the zone that was once called *Regio Caesarum*: a vast territory between the first Roman city and the sea, surrounded by swamps, from which it distinguished itself for being solid and suitable for building. Seat of various buildings since the 2nd century A.D., this territory was inglobated in the town walls of the 5th-6th century. It extended to the zone around the actual via di Roma.

Let's leave the square from the Eastern side, getting into via Diaz, which was opened by the Venetians between 1467-1469, that in the first piece runs along the church of Suffragio and the building seat of the Banca Nazionale del Lavoro.

Behind the Bank the little Luigi Einaudi square opens, obtained by means of the 1925 demolishion of various houses, onto which also the back part of the Alighieri Theatre looks.

SEAT OF BANCA DEL MONTE - It is at numbers 4, 6, 8 of via Diaz, the place in which in 1492 the mount of Pity was established, that is one of the most ancient of Italy. This singular institute of credit permitted to who needed money not to have to go to Jewish money lenders, who were accused of asking too high rate interests. From the Mount (Monte), in fact, people could obtain little loans without interest leaving as guarantee a pawn. These operations were possible because the Mount obtained the necessary capital by means of free contributions, collection of money, legacies and various donations (therefore the term «Monte»).

Of the original construction very few traces remain, and that is the architrave of the entrance door at n. 6 with the inscription «S. MONS PIETATIS ET DEPOSIT(orum) PIO-(rum)», («Sacred Mount of Pity and of the pious deposits»), the marble oval of the sixteenth century above the inscription (beautiful relief of the Redeemer taken down from the cross sustained by an angel, work of *Girolamo Bertos*), the wooden roof of the inside, portraits of bishops and Saints.

In the meeting room a fresco of the Ravennate painter Nicolò Rondinelli representing the Madonna with the infant is kept.

CASA GUACCIMANNI - At n. 15. It was built at the end of the 15th century. The portal is overhung by a pointed arch and by a balcony with Gothic elements. The cornice is original, while of the primitive windows on the ground floor there remains only a few traces above the actual ones. The trace of the big arched opening with two little columns of cylindric bricks at n. 13 indicates the existence of a hall. Characteristic is the yard with the loggia of Lombardesque style. The superior part of it can be seen from the little lane on the side of the theatre, passing through the gate in the North-east corner of Piazza Einaudi.

A little further on, on the right there is via Antica Zecca and from this point via Diaz changed deeply because of recent constructions.

MONUMENT OF THE FALLEN - Via Diaz ends crossing via di Roma, beyond which we have the road that leads to the station. Let's walk along this road and reach on the right the monument to the fallen during the national wars, it is a work of *Cesare Zocchi*, inaugurated in 1888.

The attitude of the four lions expresses the atmosphere of the great dates of the Italian Risorgimento (1831-1848-1859-1870). On the central base, there is a standing, female figure, that symbolizes the city of Ravenna, and places a bay leaf crown onto a dead soldier. On the

Basilica of San Giovanni (St. John): vestibule and bell-tower.

bronze reliefs, Anita Garibaldi on horseback while crossing the river Canavas, and the scene of the death of Anita.

At the back of the monument there is the building Liceo-ginnasio, in front there is the seat of the House of Commercio, Industria, Artigianato and Agricoltura.

SAINT JOHN THE EVANGELIST

Historical hints - As we see it now, the church has been rebuilt quite a lot, having the bombing of the last war reduced to ruins all the front part and part of the apse.

The reconstruction was made attaining to the original forms, in this way we can still be fascinated by this building, which was built by Galla Placidia in a period that goes from 424 to 434 so as to release herself from a vow during a sea tempest.

Galla Placidia had taken refuge in Constantinople because of contrasts with her brother Honorius. After his death, she returned to Ravenna to hold the regency of the Western Empire in the name of her little son Valentinian III, while the «primicerio» John who had proclaimed himself emperor had been defeated in Aquileia. During a furious tempest in the sea she made a vow to build a church dedicating it to St. John if she escaped from this serious danger; after this, as the historian Agnellus says, «*liberata est a furia maris*». The church was built and in the original mosaic (see fig. 26, pag. 121), the empress had an inscription inserted so as to remember the releasing of the vow, a quotation from the Bible in which it is affirmed that kings and queens must offer gifts to the Lord, and an exhaltation of John the Evangelist.

The journey of Galla Placidia most probably followed this itinerary: Constantinople - Thessalonica (Salonicco) - Durazzo - Salona (near Spalato). From here the Empress tried to cross the Adriatic sea unsuccesfully, and so she continued by land passing through Aquileia (Deichmann).

Medieval portal (fig. 24 pag. 118) - The church is preceeded by a wall that we get to, through a beautiful Medieval Gothic portal (14th century) with pointed arch, decorated by tortile columns and strips with a rich sculptured decoration, among which 24 little niches are inserted with statues of Saints now very worn out.

The reliefs of the cusp show the Redeemer (1), Saint John with an emperor (maybe Valentinian III) (2), Galla Placidia with some soldiers (3), Saint Barbaziano with some priests (4).

On the two «peducci» on the side of the ogival arch there are the archangel Gabriel (5) and the Madonna (6); the two figures, even if

Fig. 24 - San Giovanni Evangelista: graphical scheme of the Gothic portal. 1 - The Redeemer. 2 - Saint John the Evangelist with an emperor, maybe Valentinian III. 3 - Galla Placidia with soldiers. 4 - San Barbaziano with priests. 5 - 6 - The archangel Gabriel and the Madonna: scene of the Annunciation. 7 - Apparition of Saint John and Galla Placidia prostrated. 8 - 9 - Groups of Angels.

they are far from one another, make up the scene of the Annunciation. In the lunette we find Galla Placidia who is prostrating herself at Saint John's feet, who had appeared to her the night before the consecration of the basilica while she was praying with the blessed Barbaziano; whilst disappearing, the Saint leaves the empress a sandal as a relic (7). On the sides (8 and 9) two groups of angels.

Very beautiful is the architrave decorated with volutes closing little animals.

The enclosure was built in 1959 and on it, in the same year, the magnificent portal was placed back.

External architectural characteristics - Let's now walk around the outside of the church to the apse. On the left side we notice, above, eleven windows in the middle of blind arcades, while below the windows open onto the comparments delimited by pilasters that run until the crowning of the wall. About the big double arch between two vertical lanes of protruding bricks, before the windows of the ground floor we shall talk about later on. The body of the basilica is interrupted by a wide projection of a fourteenth century chapel.

Let's reach the back of the church where, among the nearly squared chapels, of the diaconicon and of the prothesis, there is a penthagonal apse in the inferior part but heptagonal in the superior part; this fact is rather curious. We can think that the construction was started as pentagonal with three windows of which we see the walled arches, and then became heptagonal i.e. with seven sides (or nine if we consider also the two extremities onto which the lateral chapels lean) with a «loggetta», by means of the work of an architect who, having succeeded the first one, during the construction must have changed the original project. Some suppose, that the substitution of the three windows with the loggetta must have occurred in the 8th century.

Let's now return to the front of the basilica and let's enter into the squared space closed by the wall which sustains the portal. It is a space that re-proposes the one already closed by a quadriportico from which we know the church was once preceeded.

Basilica of San Giovanni Evangelista: Gothic portal - particular.
◄

Basilica of San Giovanni Evangelista: loggetta of the apse - particular.

The façade presents a **prothyron** of Medieval conception, very high in which the entrance door and a little window open.

Bell-tower - It is 42 meters high, and rises from the body of the church using its walls for two sides; the internal corner is sustained by a column. It finishes with a conic cusp covered by majolica white and green tiles.

Until the height of the roof of the church the bell-tower rises compact with some windows not lined up, then it opens, on every side with two mullioned windows one on top of the other, a three-mullioned window and a little finishing mullioned window. Until the height of the three-mullioned windows excluded, the construction has been dated back to the 7th (Galassi) or to the 9th century (Gerola). The presence of the eyebrow contours of the three-mullioned windows assigns them to a period around the year 1000. The zone of the mullioned windows, and the spire are of the 14th century.

In the bell cell we find four bells, two of which were cast in 1208 by *Roberto Sassone*. They are called «*Marzia*» and «*Dolorosa*» and their names express the character of their voice: a martial and shrill tone the first (now it is out of use because of a long crack), with accents of mourning and sadness, the second one, just as the melter wanted it to accompany the grief of his daughter Berta, who was unconsolable for the death of her lover. The legend wants the sadness of the sound to derive from the fact that the girl during the melting process let many tears fall in, as well as the necklace that her beloved future husband had given her.

It is suggestive to think that such a real phenomenon and the same time so caducous as the sound, and the feeling that can derive from it, may be heard and lived by us just as it was by Dante who certainly must have listened to these tolls.

Inside - The inside, wide and full of light, is made up of three naves subdivided by 24 columns of grey marble with composite capitals (a hint of volute with two orders of acanthus leaves underneath) and pulvinoes (all coeval to the church) decorated with leaves, chrismon and cross, which, in some, is inserted in a garland.

The original floor is about two meters below the actual one. In the 16th century a section of wall above the arches was taken away. These were made higher, with their columns, except the granite one, with capital of the 6th century, onto which the bell-tower stands, and those on which the triumphal arch which leads into the apse stands.

In this way a higher floor level was obtained so as to avoid frequent water infiltrations. The same operation was effected in other churches of Ravenna.

We shall start our visit of the church from the right nave, observing in particular the floor mosaics, placed on the walls, which come from excavations at various depths carried out in the inside. The floors that followed one another during the passing of the centuries are four, the original one of the 5th century maybe in marble (*opus sectile*) of the 6th-7th century, of the 11th and 13th centuries (1213).

Inside: right nave - On the right of the entrance door there is a mosaic with a semi-circular writing under which there is another fragment with some letters (fig. 25, n. 1).

On the wall of the right nave, as in the position corresponding the left nave, there are traces of two arches one on top of the other: the internal one obviously is a reinforcement.

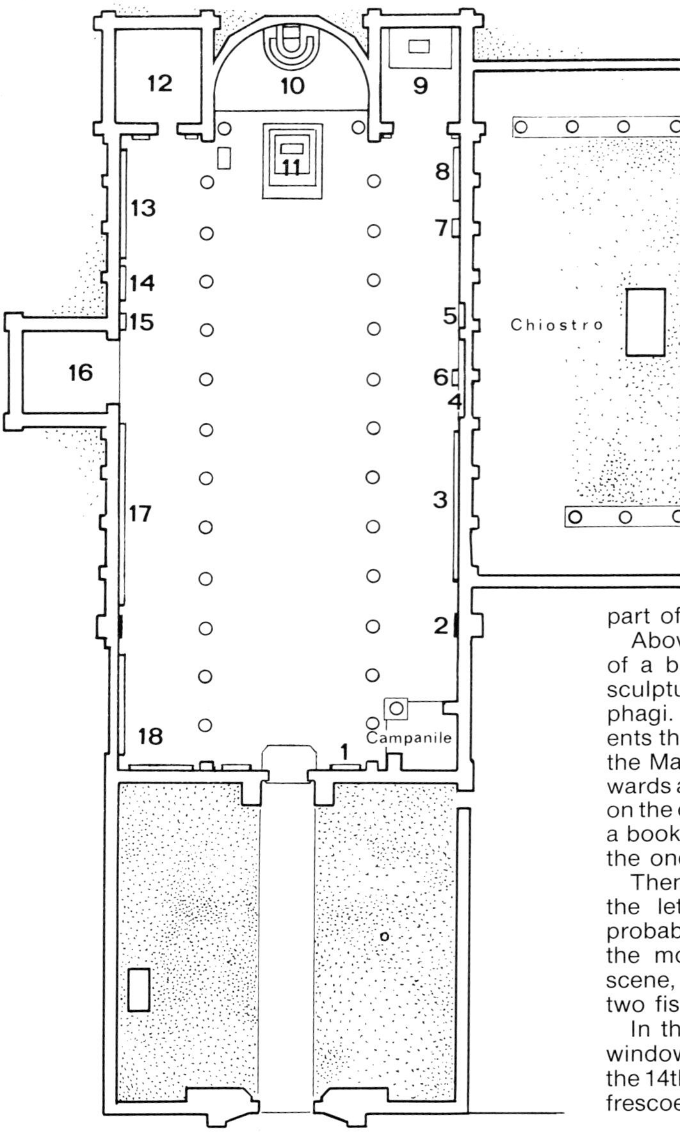

Fig. 25 - **San Giovanni Evangelista: plan**.
1 - Mosaic fragments. 2 - Trace of the junction points of the primitive façade. 3 - Fragments of floor mosaics. 4 - Big arch. 5 - Superior part of an ancient lateral exit. 6 - Fragments of a bas-relief of the 14th century. 7-8 - Floor mosaics. 9 - Prothesis with a cippus altar of the 5th-6th century. 10 - Throne of the abbot Benvenuto. 11 - Chest-like altar with elements of the 5-6th century. 12 - Diaconicon. 13 - Fragments of floor mosaics with animals. 14 - Two fragments of floor mosaic with the funeral of the fox. 15 - Fragment with the unicorn animal. 16 - Chapel of the fourteenth century with frescoes. 17 - Eleven panels of floor mosaics with scenes of the fourth Crusade. 18 - Fragments of floor mosaics with figures and vegetable and geometrical decorative motifs.

In front of one another, there were here the lateral openings of the narthex with which the church was provided, therefore originally it was shorter. The wall of the façade, in fact, ran little beyond the two arches and we can still see the junction points on the wall (2). In order to widen the church, the space occupied by the narthex was englobed to the construction of a new longer façade. The widening took place not long after the primitive construction.

Proceeding along the nave, we can see some mosaics, one of which with two big animals fighting against a snake (11th century) and others with ornamental motifs (3).

In the middle of the wall of the nave there is a big arch of which we don't know the destination (4). The other smaller arch (5) is the superior part of a lateral exit of the church.

Above the big arch let's observe the fragment of a bas-relief of the fourteenth century (6), sculptured on the back side of a drain for sarcophagi. Between two horizontal freizes, it presents three niches: on the one on the left we see the Madonna with the Infant that leans out towards an offerer, maybe one of the Three Kings; on the one in the middle an angel that is handing a book, the Apocalypse, to its author John; on the one on the right, Peter with the keys.

Then we have a mosaic (7) in which we read the letters «DECEN... OM... BER... VBER», probably these fragments are of the names of the months. Other mosaics carry a hunting scene, a strange representation of a woman, two fishes, ornamental motifs (8).

In the intrados of the second last and third windows we notice a hint of painting anterior to the 14th century: maybe once all the church was frescoed.

Inside: apsidal part - At the end of the nave the room of the prothesis opens: inside it there is a beautiful **cippus altar** of the 6th century. In this altar the «*fenestella confessionis*» is drawn on marble, with eight panels divided by a cross which must have carried, in the grooves now empty, marbles or precious stones. Above the door, formed by two spiral columns and arch, there is a shell. All is framed by a frieze in which a branch of ivy embinds.

At the bottom of the apse a marble throne has been placed (10): it is the cathedra of the abbot Benvenuto, done in 1267. The cross on the back is of the 6th century.

Remarkable is the **chest-like altar** (11) for some elements which compose it (the four angular pillars, the back slab and the little door

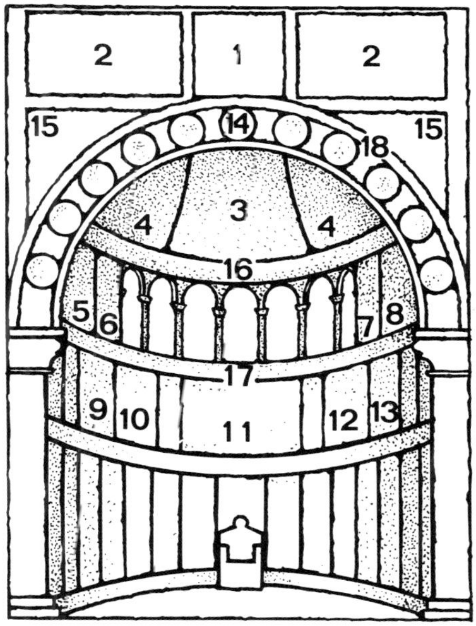

Fig. 26 - **San Giovanni Evangelista: hypothesis of reconstruction of the destroyed mosaic decoration of the apse and of the triumphal arch**. 1 - The Redeemer gives the book to St. John the Evangelist - Apocalyptical symbols. 2 - Ship during the sea-tempest led by St. John the Evangelist with Galla Placidia and her suite. It illustrated the episode that gave origin to the vow of building a church dedicated to the Evangelist Saint. 3 - Christ in throne with an open book in his hands. 4 - Books of the Apostles. 5 - Eagle and St. John the Evangelist. 6 - Calf and St. Luke the Evangelist. 7 - Angel and St. Matthew the Evangelist. 8 - Lion and St. Mark the Evangelist. 9 - The empress Eudossia. 10 - The emperor Arcadius. 11 - Angel with San Pier Chrisologo who celebrates the mass of the consecration of the temple. 12 - Theodosius II emperor. 13 - The empress Eudocia. 14 - Symbol of the cross. On the other tondi, the clypeate images of ten emperors of the Theodosian house. 15 - Decorative motifs. 16 - Inscription on two lines: «SANCTO AC BEATISSIMO APOSTOLO JOHANNI EVANGELISTAE GALLA PLACIDIA AUGUSTA CUM FILIO SUO ET FILIA SUA JUSTA GRATA HONORIA AUGUSTA LIBERATIONIS PERICULUM MARIS VOTUM SOLVENT». 17 - Inscription: «CONFIRMA HOC DEUS QUOD OPERATUS ES IN NOBIS TEMPLO SANCTO TUO JERUSALEM TIBI OFFERENT REGES MUNERA». 18 - Inscription: «AMORE CHRISTI NOBILIS ET FILIUS TONITRUI SANCTUS JOHANNES ARCANA VIDIT GALLA PLACIDIA AUGUSTA PRO SE ET HIS OMNIBUS VOTUM SOLVIT».

with the inscription: «SCE IOHANN ARCHAM. XPI ACCEPTA TIBI SIT ORATIO SERVI TUI»: it is an invocation to Saint John so that the prayers of his faithfuls would be well accepted). On the left of the apse, the «*diaconicon*» room (12) which presents as the prothesis, six low arches in the inferior part and four windows. On the wall, a beautiful Madonna with the Infant of the Fifteenth Century, and a Renaissance basin with lion heads.

Inside: left nave - Going up the left nave we meet mosaic fragments with animals: chimera, gryphon, panther, bull, dog, deer, goose (13). The scene of the following fragments is rather curious it represents the funeral of the fox (14): two cocks carry a fox hanged to a chain. This subject, the fox that pretends to be dead so as to attack suddenly its victims, is very exploited in the Medieval iconography. On the following panel there is another fragment of the funeral; a duck carrying a thurible in its beak, while a pidgeon carries a twig. Finally, there is a panel with an animal with one horn (15).

Let's now meet the chapel of the Fourteenth century of which we already saw the outside (16). The ceiling is divided in four sections and it shows fragments of frescos with Saint John and Saint Ambrose, Saint Augustine and Saint Matthew, Saint Jerome and Saint Luke, Saint Gregory and Saint Mark; the combination between Doctors of the church and Evangelists which, with some formation variant, is also in the coeval frescoes of Pietro da Rimini in Santa Chiara, now at the National Museum.

On the bottom wall, now very worn out and in some parts illegible there is a fresco with a Magdalene that stretches out her arms to the cross and other people praying. Below, the image of the Madonna and the four offering people.

Salmi sees characters of the Riminese school in the frescoes of the vault and behaviours of late Giotto imitation in the fragments of the bottom wall.

Beyond the chapel, towards the exit, there are eleven panels with episodes of the fourth Crusade (17): we can make out scenes relative to the seizure of the city of Zara (IADRA AD... CEDEM) and of Constantinople (COSTANTINOPOLIM), scenes of the beseiged that leave the city, the winners with weapons in their hands, a ship with a vedette sailor on the top. These are fragments of the 1213 floor, a little later, therefore, than the elements that it describes, since the Fourth Crusade took place in 1202. Zara was captured by the Venetians, against whom it had rebelled, with the help of the Crusaders, who in this way paid the freight of the ships they needed to go to the East; Constantinople was captured and the Latin Empire of the East started.

Other mosaics represent a woman that offers a flower, a woman with an olive branch and fragments with vegetable and geometrical drawings.

Reconstruction hypothesis of the ancient mosaics of the apse - A tablet on the inside wall of the façade informs us about the inscriptions that were inserted in the mosaics of the apse of which the last fragments were destroyed in 1568 during some redoing works, were rebuilt by various authors with different hypothesis. We shall present, for curiosity, the reconstruction of those who accept the thesis that the «loggetta» of the apse is original. More than a description we think it is better to rely onto a scheme; keeping an eye on it and transferring it to the apse, we shall get an idea quite clear of the primitive aspect of the church (fig. 26), without forgetting that the actual floor is about two meters higher than the original one.

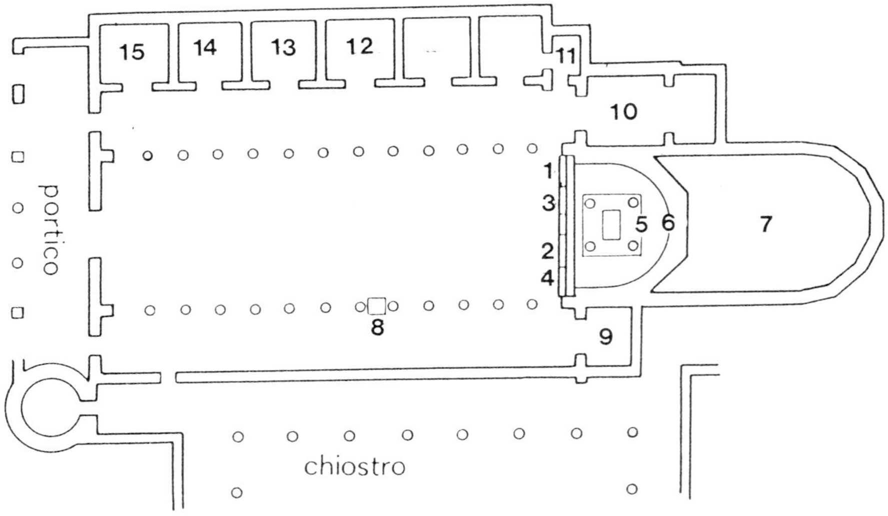

Before going out let's reserve a little of our attention to the beautiful big canvas placed above the door: it is of the painter *Carlo Bonone* (1569-1632) from Ferrara, and it represents the banquet of Assuero.

Cloister - Having finished our visit to the church, we can go to the cloister of the 16th century. Go out from the Gothic portal and then turn left proceeding along the railing; having got to the corner turn left again and go on until you reach, after n. 10 of via Carducci, an arched opening with a railing, through which we can give a look at the cloister. It has three sides, because the fourth one was destroyed during the last World War: it was leaning against the external wall of the right nave of the basilica that we can now see with its beautiful face-brick. The portico is sustained by wide and harmonious arches. In the middle of the lawn there is a cistern of *Alessandro Corsi*, Venetian with a very wide and articulated curb, surmounted by an architrave sustained by two pairs of columns. In a cartouche placed on the front of the curb there is a motto: «PUTEIS TERRA MIHI COELUM» («To the wells the ground, to me the sky»).

This is the cloister of one of the four abbeys of Ravenna founded, it seems, by Galla Placidia in 410. The monastery, of the regular canons of the congregation of S. Salvatore from 1459, it had 38 rooms, and could contain, in 1605, thirty monks.

Let's return on our steps along via Carducci until the crossing with via di Roma and let's turn left: we shall enter, in this way, in the heart of the late Roman «*Regio Caesarum*» (but the place-name is of the early Middle Ages).

The route of via di Roma is very ancient, because we think that it is the one followed by a branch of *Fossa Augusta*, a large navigable channel that coming, from North-West, crossed the suburbs of the city out of the walls of the first century so as to go out South-East in the direction of the port of Classe. Having filled the *ditch* with earth in the 5th century, and widened the town-walls, part of the space was occupied by a road that then took the name of *Platea Maior*, on which it seems military review took place and that became the axis of the new urban development (see fig. 45, pag. 195). According to another hypothesis, however, via di Roma should be the heir of the urban sector of a consular Roman street, via Popilia.

PALAZZO GALLETTI ABBIOSI - In the corner between via di Roma and via Mariani, at n. 140 of via di Roma, there is the Galletti Abbiosi building, built in the eighteenth century and widened in the second half of the nineteenth century former seat of the FEMALE ORPHANAGE GALLETTI ABBIOSI. The trimming off of the corner between the two streets was made so as not to obstaculate the curve of the tranway which connected Ravenna to Forlì starting from 1884 till 1930. The orphanage was instituted with a legagy of the owners of the building at the end of nineteenth century.

PALAZZO GROSSI - In front of the orphanage, at n. 69, there is Palazzo Grossi, of the seventeenth century, unfinished, lacking obviously of the left wing. Above the arch of the entrance door there is a marble shield. In the yard there is a little temple of the eighteenth century.

PALAZZO SERENA MONGHINI - It is at n. 67. It was built in 1725 by the architect *G.A. Soratini*, a Camaldolese monk. The portal and the balustrade window which surmounts it form a unit of very pleasant design. This is the same for every

Fig. 27 - **Sant'Apollinare Nuovo: Plan.**
1 - Pluteus of the 6th century. 2 - Transenna of the peacocks (2nd half of the 6th century). 3 - Transenna of the cross and grape clusters (2nd half 6th century).
4 - Transenna maybe of the 8th century.
5 - Chest-like altar of the 6th century.
6 - Marble chair of Roman epoch.
7 - Baroque apse. 8 - Ambo of the 6th century. 9-10 - Chapels on the side of the apse. 11 - Chapel already called of the «relics». 12 - Rasponi chapel. 13 - Pasolini chapel. 14 - Chapel of the Scala Counts.
15 - Chapel «della Vittoria».

Basilica of Sant'Apollinare Nuovo.

Basilica of Sant'Apollinare Nuovo: bell-tower and ancient cross of the parvis.

window of the ground floor, that is joined to the corresponding one of the first floor by means of a framing of whitewashed lime. Pleasant is the cyma of the ground floor gratings. The building inside preserves mosaics that were found in the Classense zone of the basilica of San Severo, with which some rooms have been floored, and a floor and other things derived from findings in the area surrounding the building, that rises on the ground of the ancient palace of Theodoric.

At n. 59 there is the ex church of Santa Barbara, of which we have a first testimony in 1109; it was closed to creed in 1806.

We are on the square of Sant'Apollinare Nuovo.

SANT'APOLLINARE NUOVO

Historical hints - The basilica of Sant'Apollinare Nuovo was erected by Theodoric, therefore it dates back to the period which goes from 493 (entrance of the Goths in Ravenna) to 526 (death of Theodoric).

Placed in the *Regio Caesarum* near the residential palace of the emperor, it rose with the name of Basilica di Nostro Signore Gesù Cristo (basilica of our Lord Jesus Christ), of whom the miracles and passion are narrated.

Of Arian faith, Theodoric wanted buildings of Arian creed (baptistery, church of Spirito Santo and others) in a Catholic Ravenna. When, after 540, the Catholic creed returned to dominate in the city with the entrance of the Byzantine army, the Arian temples were consecrated and purified. This had repercussions, especially as regards to Sant'Apollinare, above all on the name that passed to San Martin the fighter against the heretics, then on the decorations that in certain

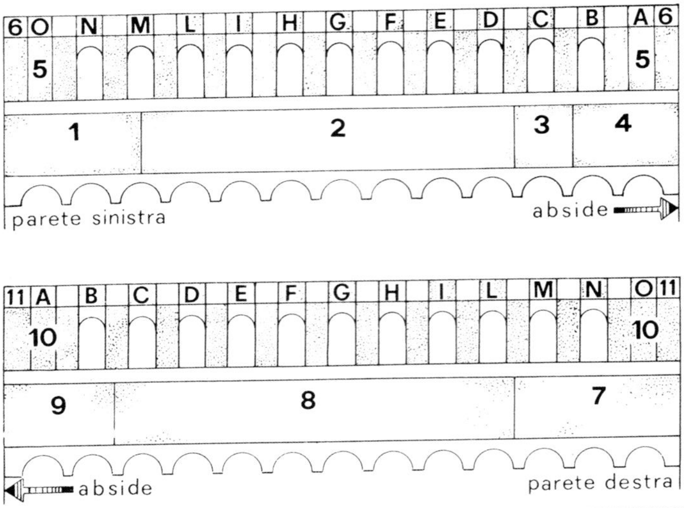

Fig. 28-29 - **Sant'Apollinare Nuovo: schemes of the mosaic decoration of the walls of the central nave. Left wall:** 1 - City of Classe. 2 - Procession of the virgins. 3 - The offer of the Three Kings. 4 - Madonna in the throne with the Infant and angels. 5 - Sixteen figures, maybe prophets, apostles, patriarchs. 6 A - Wedding of Cana. B - Multiplication of the bread and of the fish. C - Vocation of Peter and Andrew. D - The healing of the blind in Jericho. E - The adultress and the scribes. F - The Samaritan at the well. G - The resurrection of Lazarus. H - The Pharisee and the Publican. I - The offering of the widow. L - The separation of the sheep from the goats. M - The healing of the paralized man in Cafarnao. N - The recovery of the obsessed. O - The healing of the paralysed of Bethesda. **Right wall:** 7 - Palace of Theodoric. 8 - The procession of the martyrs. 9 - Christ on the throne and angels. 10 - Sixteen figures like in 5. 11 A - The last supper. B - Jesus on the mount of olives. C - The kiss of Judah. D - Christ brought to judgement. E - Christ at the Sanhedrim. F - The announcement of Peter's denial. G - Peter's denial. H - The repentance of Judah. I - Christ before Pilate.

particulars reminded too much the fallen Gothic regime, as shall be said further on while illustrating the mosaics.

Around the middle of the 9th century the basilica was dedicated to Sant'Apollinare when, from Classe, the relics of the blessed bishop, mythic founder of the Ravennate church, were transferred here, or at least this is what had been said. The attribute Nuovo (New) served to distinguish it from the little ancient church called Sant'Apollinare in Veclo (see p. 89), and not referring to the basilica of Sant'Apollinare in Classe.

Architectural characteristics - The basilica is spaced out from the street by means of a little square that carries in the middle, from many centuries, a *column with a capital* surmounted by a stone pine-cone and by a cross that once was made of marble and now is made of iron. The harmonious marble portico that preceeds the church is of the 16th century; a very simple brick façade emerges from it framed by two vertical pilasters and by the slight projection of the roof, animated by two little windows. Under the portico, on the right and on the left of the central portal, there are two epigraphs, one in praise of Constantine, the other relative to Marco Cocceio Nerva, military tribune commander of the Legion XI Claudia.

On the right side of the portico rises a beautiful **bell-tower** of the 8th-9th century (Galassi); but the upper edge of the three-mullioned windows would make us think, at least for that zone, to a period around the year one thousand (Mazzotti). The construction lightens itself going from the bottom to the top in a progression of openings that go from the thin slit to the triple series of upper three-mullioned windows, frames with saw-like teeth, with round bricks, delimit and mark the ground floor, the second landing and the passage between the windows, mullioned windows and three-mullioned windows. During the construction phase some sculptural fragments were inserted.

The architecture of the **inside** is simple: three naves delimited by two rows of twelve columns of Greek marble with simplified Corinthian capitals: the acanthus leaves of the two crowns infact, from right are reduced to five in the inferior row and to four in the superior one; the coules are arranged like a «V» («lyre motif») in which there is a leaf. Above the capitals, pulvinoes decorated with a simple cross.

The apse, much higher and deeper than the original, was built in the 16th century; on the sides, two chapels. On the wall of the nave seven little rooms open which were added in a very much later epoch. The inside receives light from the right, where the sun runs, through eight windows below and eight above, from the mullioned window of the façade and from the left wall of the central nave.

Mosaics: history and characteristics - Theodoric had decorated the basilica with mosaics, some of which carried signs of the Arian faith and personages of the Gothic court. With the return of the Catholic prevalence these parts were modified as we shall tell you further on: a real purge. However, neither the mosaics of the superior strip above the windows, nor those of the windowed strip, and those of the final piece of the wide strip above the columns were touched.

They are of Justinianean Age (Catholic), the procession of the twenty-two virgins and of the Three Kings on the left wall, and the one of the twenty-six martyrs on the right.

L - The climbing to the calvary. M - The Resurrection. N - The disciples in Emmaus. O - The incredulity of Thomas.

Basilica of ▶ Sant'Apollinare Nuovo: the port of Classe.

Sant'Apollinare Nuovo: inside before the reinstatement of ▼ the baroque apse.

1 2 3
4 5

Basilica of Sant'Apollinare Nuovo: 1, Madonna on the throne with Infant and angels.
2, The three kings.
3, Four martyrs.
4, The procession of Virgins.
5, Particular of the Virgins' procession.

MELCHIOR + SCS GASPAR

SCS MARTINVS SCS CLEMENS SCS SVSTVS SCS LAVRENT

▲
Sant'Apollinare Nuovo: the procession of the martyrs.

Sant'Apollinare Nuovo: the procession of martyrs. Saint Martin.
▼

▲
Basilica of Sant'Apollinare Nuovo: the «palatium».

Sant'Apollinare Nuovo: Christ and two angels.

Sant'Apollinare Nuovo: Christ and angels.
◄

Basilica of Sant'Apollinare Nuovo: Theodorican panels.
a - The Vocation of Peter and Andrew.
b - The cure of the paralytic of Bethseda.

The very brief temporal space that divides the Theodorican mosaics from the Justinian ones (about 50 years) doesn't stop us from noticing an important style difference: the Theodorican mosaic workers operated obviously under the influence of the Greek-Roman taste, characterized by the plasticity of the figures and by the realism of the gestures and of the scenery; while the Justinian mosaic workers expressed themselves by means of canons of different conception of art, that is called *Byzantine*, that tends to stylize, to immaterialize and therefore spiritualize the figures, placing them into an unreal golden atmosphere, that here go nearer to the musical abstraction in the repeated rythms and in the regular intervals.

Mosaics: left wall, strip above the columns - (look at scheme fig. 28 in 1-2-3-4). Looking from left to right, first of all we find the city of Classe (1), with its walls, buildings (maybe a temple, the amphitheatre, the aqueduct. But there are also structures invented in the last century by the restorer F. Kibel), the sea, the ships, the oars, the sails. It is an exceptional representation, in which life and activity testified by the ships in the sea is transferred by means of imagination also to the city, that is quite hidden by the wall. Furthermore it is the first representation of a historic city, determined, which appeared in Cisalpina. From the wall zone the Byzantine took away the images of the people of Theodoric's court: five figures were taken away, two between the port-tower and the tower which rises from the walls, three between this last tower and the door of the city of Classe.

From Classe the procession of the Virgins comes out, which occupies nearly all the wall and that we shall follow moving slowly towards the end (2). Light penetrates from the windows in front and, especially in sunny days, it lights up the gold that dominates this mosaic and that brightens itself up more and more following our movements. The bodies of the girls look towards us as if it were a frontal formation, but in nearly all the figures there are imperceptible signs of movement towards the bottom of the church: the very slight inclination of the head, the position of the arms, the leaning onto the left foot which involves a slight movement of the body.

Levitating on a green lawn from which lilies, roses and shrubs sprout, divided rythmically by palms, the procession seems to be gone through by a whiff that pushes towards the desired destination, so that the whole thing, nearly imperceptably, goes on. Maybe a spiritual inclination such as «*going towards*» has never been represented visibly with such efficacy, simply by means of the natural suppleness of the female body caught in repeated mild movements.

Nor do we have the repetition of the identical; yes it is true, there is a reproposition of the images twice, ten times, twenty times, so that the quantity transforms to quality, and we remain enchanted in the passage from one to many, but if we look with attention we shall notice that there isn't one figure the same as the other. For example, the leaning onto the left foot prevails, but not in the seventh and eighteenth figure; the bodies of many girls are slightly moved to one side, but not in all; light but perfectly perceptible the differences of position in bending the right leg; the cloths fall from the left arm with different lengths and there is a diversity of draping, the decoration of the garments is never the same, and also the colour of the crowns, the one of the diadem, and many other little particulars that show how the artist, even if he was working in a nearly fixed scheme, moved, however, with extreme freedom of fantasy.

a

b

The procession stoops nearly falls towards its destination, with the Three Kings (3), with multicoloured garments and strained faces. There is a connection between the procession and the final representation of the Madonna in the throne with the Infant and the angels with animated faces (4), by means of the angel's right hand stretched out towards the Three Kings. But everything, here, stops in its frontal stillness, the real arrival point.

In the meeting between the old and new mosaic the level of the lawn interrupts and lowers itself and it extends to the golden surface of the background.

The angels, with rich cloaks, on a lawn covered with flowers, are placed on the sides of a sumptuous throne on which the Madonna with a wide cloak of amethist colour is sitting with the Infant on her lap.

The superior part of the Kings and the two external angels were redone in the 19th century.

The mosaics: right wall, strip on top of the columns - (scheme fig. 29 in 7-8-9). Proceeding now from right to left, we notice the «palazzo di Teodorico» (Theodoric's palace) (7), in which, between the columns, we notice traces of Catholic corrective interventions to eliminate figures of unwelcome characters belonging to the Arian heresy or to the Gothic court. On the white of the columns, however, here and there, we can still find a hand, an arm. The figures taken away were substituted by soft hangings.

The great palace unfolds in its width and sumptuousness revealing at its shoulders other buildings of the city. In the middle of two lateral loggias there is a wide peristyle with tympanum in which we have the inscription: PALATIUM. At the extreme right there is a door in the room of which the footprint of a sitting figure appears, it also was purged. On the lunette there are little figures of Christ with a cross squashing a snake, and two Apostles. From the building sets off the procession of the martyrs (8) well drawn and very strongly marked on the outlines, in the creases of the cloaks, in the letters written on the cloaks. The Martyrs, solidly nailed to the floor, real human bodies, look at us and their proceeding is expressed only by the arms bent towards the left and by the position of the feet of some of them. There is no inclination of the head and no movement of the body; there is no visible final tension of figures nearer to the destination. In this wall, not favoured by light, the white of the cloak which wraps the Martyrs dominates. Only San Martin, already titular of the basilica, who leads the procession, is dressed with a beautiful dark cloak, and only the fourth figure - Saint Laurence - reveals a golden garment. All the complex is less vivacious than the one in front, because the mosaic-worker wasn't able to express himself as is possible with the variety of the decorations of the female garments.

The representation concludes with the image of Christ on the throne having at his side four angels with dark wings such as the dark dress of Christ (9) that carries in his hand a sceptre. Originally instead he had an open *codex* on which there was written: «EGO SUM REX GLORIAE». The sceptre is work of the restoration of Kibel who, around 1860, redid the half of the body, but not the head of the Saviour. Also here the two external angels were redone in the 19th century.

Remarkable are the flowers of the lawn with which the mosaic worker was able to manifest his decorative vein.

This final part, as the symmetrical one of the front wall is, as we already said, of Theodorican epoch, but here the influence, more than Greek

Basilica of Sant'Apollinare Nuovo: The multiplication of the bread and fish.

Roman, is Oriental.

The laborious interpretation of an expert gives light to the complex meaning of the procession of the martyrs: the letters that are on the cloaks of the Martyrs, of incomprehensible meaning if read, as we always did, singularly, would acquire a meaning if they were read together according to an order that doesn't coincide with those of the figures of the procession. We would obtain, in this way, the Greek words relative to Pentecost therefore we would have that the Martyrs «are the first of the Pentecost community, they redeemed themselves, they were baptised, they obtained redemption of their sins and the gift of the Sacred Spirit and now walk towards life» (Gerke). But a new iconographic reading that refers to the liturgical court ceremonial, is now proposed by C. Frugoni. In correspondence to every figure of the two processions, there is the name of the personage represented.

Windowed strips **-** (See schemes in 5-10). On the windowed strip of the two walls sixteen figures on each side are represented, of controversial interpretation (prophets? apostles? patriarchs?), well drawn with marked outlines, in frontal position, on grassy ground, solemn and fixed, carrying a roll or a book. Their head is surrounded by a halo, the faces are very varied: sometimes young, or sometimes old. Several are the positions of the hands, sometimes both on the roll or book, sometimes the right hand is raised in a blessing attitude. The rolls are not all closed, but many are partly open and some are also completely open; therefore the book in some figures is kept under the left hand instead of it being on top. All this to make you notice that also in these figures, that can give the impression of a simple repetition, in reality the artist never duplicated completely, moving, inside the adopted module with remarkable freedom. These mosaics are of Theodorican epoch.

Strips of the panels under the ceiling **-** (Look at schemes 6-11). Less evident, unfortunately, because of the distance, are the wonders of the panels high up, under the ceiling, that are of clear Roman influence. In order to admire them with ease a binocular would be necessary.

There are thirteen rectangular panels on each wall, of the Theodorican period, separated by decorative panels placed above the panels of the figures below, in which the motif of a big shell surmounted by two birds and a cross repeats itself. The panels with the scenes, in such way, occupy the space above every window, except those that are placed at the extremities of the two mosaic walls.

Observing the schemes fig. 28-29 we notice clearly that the panels with figures and scenes alternate, like a chess-board, with the merely decorative ones, so that the eye, even if it doesn't reveal maybe this particularity, always finds a resting zone, a pause, between the panels which require a careful reading.

It is discussed whether the observation order should start from the apse towards the entrance or vice-versa, we shall follow the chronological development of the facts and the miracles of Jesus starting from the apse.

On the **left wall** we have the representations of « *The wedding of Cana* (A), *the multiplication of the bread and of the fish* (B), *the vocation of Peter and Andrew* (C), *the healing of the blind in Jericho* (D), *the indication of the adultress to the scribes* (E) (who is without sin may throw the first stone!), *the Samaritan at the well* (F),

Basilica of Sant'Apollinare Nuovo: The prayer in the garden of Getsemane.

the Resurrection of Lazarus (G), *the Pharisee and the publican at the door of the temple* (H), *the offering of the widow* (I), *the separation of the sheep from the goats* (L) (of the good from the bad), *the recovery of the paralysed of Cafarnao* (M), *the recovery of the obsessed* (N) (the evil spirits transformed to pigs), *the recovery of the paralysed of Bethesda* (O).

As for the first panel, today it isn't possible to see the miracle of the water turned to wine, since Kibel restoring it in 1854, represented some baskets and not some jugs, as instead must have been originally. The ancient part is constituted by the superior half of Christ, by the hand, by the shoulder and by the head of the disciple.

On the **right wall**, always starting from the apse, are represented The Passion and the Death of Christ, excluding the Crucifixion.

The scenes narrate the «*Last Supper*» (A), *Jesus on the olive mount* (B), *the kiss of Judah* (C), *Christ brought to judgement* (D), *Christ at the sanhedrim* (E), *the announcement of Peter's denial* (F), *Peter's denial* (G), *the repentance of Judah* (H), *Christ before Pilate* (I), *Christ that goes up the Calvary* (L), *the Resurrection of Christ* (M), *the disciples in Emmaus* (N), *the incredulity of Thomas* (O).

The twenty-six panels constitute an exceptional narrative cycle as well as a splendid art gallery, that should be examined one by one. Here we shall make you notice some characteristics. A different crowding of the figures is revealed in the panels of the two walls: on the left the human figures that can be seen altogether are 47, while on the right they are more than double, exactly 99. In the scenes of the left wall there are numerous realistic notations (the boat, the oar, the net, the fish of panel C, the water spilling out of the brimful bucket in panel F, the pigs in the sea in panel N, the bed of the paralysed in panel O. On the right wall we meet scenes of major excitement and drama (B, C, I, O). Many panels acquire vivacity from the language of the hands, other distinguish themselves for particulars of the landscapes (little trees, rocks, shrubs). Remarkable is the range of colours, which touches various tones of green, yellow, black, red, blue, gold, dark blue, amethist... The critic recognizes on the two walls the work of different artists.

Presbytery - (Plan fig. 27, pag. 122). It is delimited by a **pluteus** (I) and three beautiful transenne. The pluteus, of the 6th century represents a vase from which two vine shoots emerge, on which there are two pea-cocks and a cross, Daniel in the

Basilica of Sant'Apollinare Nuovo: transenna of the peacocks (IInd half of the 6th century).

lions' pit with the breads brought from Abacuc, and the white pidgeon with crown which symbolizes help given from God to Daniel.

The **transenne**, two are of a little later than the middle of the 6th century and that is the one with the pea-cocks and the cross framed by vine leaves and grape clusters (2) and the one with ornamental motifs around a central cross (3). The last one on the right (4), with the little cross in the middle, maybe is of the 8th century.

The **chest-like altar** (5), of the 6th century is formed of four angular pilasters and by marble slabs. It has a «fenestella» that lets you see the spaces for the keeping of the relics.

The ancient table has been lost for centuries.

The four **columns** (6th century) are of porphyry, and made part of an ancient ciborium. Of the four beautiful **capitals**, those open-worked are Byzantine (first half of the 6th century); the other two formed by a circle of leaves, one of almonds and one of sacred snakes, are of Egyptian-Alexandrian type, and date back to the 2nd century A.D.

Apse - When the Minor Observants of Saint Francis took possession of the former Benedectine monastery in the 16th century, they found the adjacent basilica of Sant'Apollinare Nuovo in ruinous condition. They raised its floor, columns and arches (see the paragraph "Floor") and they made the ruined apse again, which was turned into a wide, very deep one with a big triumphal arch. This apse was then renewed in the 18th century. Because of its architectural characteristics it is known as "Baroque apse".

This apse seemed to clash with the line of the nave, so that in 1950 it was decided to rebuild what had to be, as for its dimension and line, the original, much simpler apse (see the photo on page 125). The Baroque apse was lost to people's sight.

Regarded as doubtful the result of the reconstruction, a different rule of preservation of monuments has led to the demolition of the apse, that had been remade according to the original line, and the reappearing of the Baroque apse. The map on page 122 shows the line of the two apses.

Ambo (8) - Placed under the right colonnade, sustained by a central column and four little columns standing on a base. It is of the middle of the 6th century. As the one of Sant'Agata and of the church of Spirito Santo, is formed by a base detached from the superior parts. It is of white marble; it presents in the low part a rich frieze with cones, circles, indents, above which there is a central zone with quadrangles and triangles containing pears and apples, bordered by two latin crosses on a globe.

Floor - The original level of the church is placed at 1.20 m. of depth. In the 16th century, in fact, the columns and the arches had to be lifted so as to be able to face the already stable flood, to the expenses of a wall strip that was under the mosaic zone, and that was decorated by golden stuccos or by mosaics.

Ceiling - The actual ceiling with lacunars is of the beginning of the 17th century (1611). In origin the church had another ceiling with lacunars of great beauty and splendour deriving, with every probability, from the gold reflections. When the church was dedicated to San Martin in fact, it was denominated «San Martino in cielo d'oro».

Chapels - On the sides of the apse, on the right, there is a little chapel (9). On the left there is a bigger and decorated chapel (10), built in 1690, that carries stuccoes of Antonio Martinetti and very precious marbles, like some slabs of verd antique, a jasper tablet and one of oriental black and white.

The nearest of the seven chapels of the left nave was called «*Delle reliquie*» (11) and contained the transenne, the porphyry columns, the capitals and the marble chair that are now in the presbytery. Actually the chapel preserves a marble chest placed in a vertical position, with Renaissance decorations.

In one of the sides of the chest there is the inscription: APPOLLENAis XPIis MARTIis RELIQUIE IOQ SV MI PONTIFIis HOC LOCO PIE COLUNTUR.

Because here we find ourselves in front of the mentioning of the transfer of the body of Sant'Apollinare into the church of Sant'Apollinare Nuovo, we transcribe a piece taken from «*Notizie storiche della vita e del martirio di Sant'Apollinare*» (Forlì, 1781) (Historical news of the life and the martyrdom of Sant'Apollinare): «*In the year 856, because the Saracens infested the near beaches of the Adriatic, and furthermore because they had pillaged this basilica (of Classe), Giovanni X, that others said to be VIII and some also VII, archbishop of Ravenna, took from here (Classe) the bodies of two Saints, and brought them to Ravenna in the church of San Martino in ciel d'oro, setting about the rumour that the body of Sant'Apollinare had been transferred from him for major security in this church, which from that moment was called Sant'Apollinare Nuovo*» (Guastuzzi).

The Ravennati monks then wanted to make believe that this transfer actually took place and they placed in one of their coffins a lead slab on which there was written: IN HOC SARCOPHAGO REQESIT CORPUS BEATISSIMI SACRATISSIMI APOLENARIS MARTIRIS CRISTI COLLOCATUM A IOHANE ARCHIEPISCOPO.

A reconnaissance ordered by pope Alexander III in 1173 demonstrated, instead, that the

Emilio Franceschi: Eulalia Christiana.

bones were in Sant'Apollinare in Classe, therefore the mysterious transfer in reality never took place. In any case the matter of the supposed transfer remains complicated and confused. For historical hints of the transfer of the body of Sant'Apollinare in Classe look at paragraph: «Lapidary inscriptions».

At the side of the entrance to the chapel there are two beautiful alabaster columns with serpentine capitals on which there are two marble columns of verd antique with ancient capitals.

Among the other chapels we notice the *Rasponi chapel* (12), with the big Renaissance arch in which among the other decorations crossed lion paws appear, heraldic bearings of the family. The chapel is decorated in the manner of Andrea Barbiani (1747). The following chapel, the *Pasolini chapel* (13) contains a little painting of the 14th century (Madonna with the Infant) and paintings of *Ferraù Fenzoni* («Birth of the Madonna» and «Death of the Madonna»).

In the chapel that follows (14), of the *Scala Counts*, we find another painting of *Fenzoni* («The preach of Saint Francesco D'Assisi») and a painting of *Ascanio Foschi* called «Proclamation of the forgiving of Assisi» (1612).

The last one, i.e. the one nearer to the entrance, closed by a gate, was transformed and consecrated in the memory of the war 1915-18. In the middle there is an altar. The painter *Carlo Donati* from Verona, painted on twelve tablets glorious and painful episodes of the big conflict. Inaugurated at the end of 1919, it is called «*chapel of Victory*» (cappella della Vittoria).

Crypt - The crypt, now flooded and therefore impracticable, was discovered in 1917 and it dates back to the middle of the 9th century. Of semi-annular form and therefore similar to the one of Sant'Apollinare in Classe, but maybe a little posterior to it, with barrel vault, it had the central corridor that maybe didn't lead to the church, but was divided from it by a little window. As for the crypts of the churches of Ravenna, look at the chapter on San Francesco at paragraph «Apse and Crypt».

Inside wall of the façade - The inscription that could be read in the apse of the 6th century is reproduced on it: «THEODERICUS REX HANC ECCLESIAM A FUNDAMENTIS IN NOMINE DOMINI NOSTRI JESU CHRISTI FECIT».

On the same wall mosaic panel representing a person with imperial clothing (chlamis, fibula, haloed head with a crown) hangs in which in the 19th century the inscription IUSTINIAN was inserted. The assignment is inexact, and it is mostly thought that is Theodoric's portrait.

Cloisters - Going out of the lateral door at the beginning of the right nave we can see the side of the church under a wing of the portico of the 16th century that is placed against it. The portico has only three sides.

It isn't one of the cloisters of the ancient Benedictine monastery, because of them nothing is left. It is instead one of the two cloisters erected by the Minor Observants. Many sepulchral slabs taken away from the church are kept here. The statue of Saint Anthony is of *Giovanni Toschini*.

Let's return to via di Roma and continue walking towards the left. Nearly in front of the church at n. 118, a building of the Eighteenth

Century rises, **palazzo Malagola**, with arched portal and balcony with Baroque railing. Immediately after, on the left, there is, delimited by a strong and high iron railing, the so-called Palazzo di Teodorico.

SO-CALLED PALAZZO DI TEODORICO - The façade of the construction is made up of a slightly advancing body, with a great portal above which a wide niche provided with a mullioned window that serves as balcony opens. On the sides, from the bottom, two openings with a double arch; at the height of the niche, at its sides, a decorative motif of blind arches projecting from columns standing on shelves. On the sides of the entrance door there are two pillars with Corinthian capitals (end of 5th-beginning 6th century), maybe coming from the Mausoleum of Theodoric. In the hanging loggetta two capitals are of the 6th century and two of the 8th. On the columns of the middle niche there are two capitals of the 6th century.

In the internal portico there are fragments of floor mosaics, coming from the real palace of Theodoric, which rose on the area of a preceeding majestic building. Testimony of this is given by the four floor layers that were found here and that permitted to recover floor mosaics that go from the 1st to the 7th century A.D. The palace stopped existing because of decay at the time of Charlemagne.

In the impossibility to describe all the single pieces, we invite you to notice, as well as the various geometrical representations:

— three busts with a dog, of the 3rd-4th century;

— the long fragment that represents a horse race in the circus. The central figure carries in one hand a whip and a hat. At the extreme left there is the building of the *carceres*, construction destined to keep the wagon (4th-5th century);

— the piece with the word TESSELLA (half 5th century). It is a scene of *venatio*, cruel show of the circus. Notice the foot of a *bestiarius*;

— the piece with the name of the horse (Generosus), with horse, wagon, charioteer, of the middle of the 5th century;

— wild boar hunting scene, with grass on the ground and figures, of the 5th century;

— fragment of the character with a green lizard (first half of the 5th century);

— a piece of the 5th century, with Bellerophon and the Chimera, puttos, busts with Seasons and the Latin inscription starting with: SUME QUOD AUTUMNUS... which invites to enjoy the gifts of the various seasons. Probably this mosaic decorated a dining-room.

Turning the corner of via Alberoni, on the back, we notice, one of the two remade little staired towers (and the ruins of the other) that led to the women's gallery: according to one of the hypothesis brought forward by the experts

The so-calles palace of Theodoric.

The so-called palace of Theodoric. Left door post.

on the origin and the destination of the building, in fact, the ruins before which we stand would be the narthex opposite to the church of SAN SALVATORE, a great construction with three naves traces of which were found during the excavations. This is the most acceptable hypothesis.

Therefore this severe ruin is nor the Palazzo di Teodorico nor a remainder of it. Excavations dating back to some decades ago showed that the walls we see rest on other wider walls, of an ancient building, «that must be put in connection with the Theodorican royal palace» (Mazzotti). The historian Agnello says that the church of San Salvatore Maggiore was placed where the principal door of Theodoric's palace opened.

A second hypothesis indicates the construction as a bodyguard of the 7th or beginning of the 8th century, for the soldiers that controlled the access to Theodoric's palace, at that time inhabited by the Exarchs, who had got their residence surrounded by a wall and had protected its entrance with a well supplied guard post. The construction is thought to imitate a building of Constantinople that was called «*Calce*» (that would mean *bronze*); also the one of Ravenna, in fact, took the name of «*Calce*» or «*ad Calchi*». Another hypothesis assigns it to the first half of the 7th century with the function of secretariat to the «Exarchs». According to a last hypothesis, we should be in front of the remains of a palatine chapel that was erected by Aistulf, king of the Longobards, who had entered in Ravenna in 751 and remained for a short while.

In front of the so-called palazzo di Teodorico we can see an Eighteen Century building, at n. 114 (**palazzo Spreti**), with the door surmounted by a balcony with an iron railing. Let's proceed beyond the crossing between via di Roma and via Alberoni-via Guaccimanni, noticing that in this last via, at n. 51, there is the seat of the STATE ARCHIVES, established in Ravenna in 1941 and transferred here from the building of the Franciscan cloisters in 1966.

The archive of Ravenna contains also the archives of the suppressed religious corporations, the notary archives of Ravenna and of other localities «Memorials» from 1352 to 1427 etc... On the left, at n. 47 of via di Roma there is **Bezzi house**, which rose in 1788, on design of *Camillo Morigia* and misses the right side, never built.

PALAZZO RASPONI-BONANZI - In front of Bezzi house, at n. 108, in excellent state of maintenance, there is the beautiful Rasponi-Bonanzi building, actually provincial seat of a political party. The façade with panels was modernized at the end of the nineteenth century, meanwhile the construction is of the seventeenth century. From the entrance we can go into the yard, onto which some low houses of the seventeenth century with balcony look.

Various rooms of the building are decorated with paintings of *Felice Giani* and of his school. The painter Giani (1758-1823) operated especially in Emilia and in Romagna with a group of collaborators decorating with tempera the ceiling and the walls of public buildings and of patrician houses. The critics consider him one of the most significant and original Italian artists in the Revolution period and of the First Empire. He worked also in Paris, in the Tuileries building and in the castle of Malmaison.

CHURCH OF SANTA CHIARA - RASI THEATRE - Proceeding on the left, at n. 39, very far from the road, there is Teatro Rasi, re-established thanks to recent restorations and redoings. It occupies the place of the church of Santa Chiara, famous for having kept the frescos of the Riminese school to which we send you back to the description of the National Museum (Big Refectory).

The church had been built by Chiara da Polenta in 1255. It was bought by the municipality of Ravenna in 1874 and in 1891 it was turned into a theatre that, in the first post-war period (1919), was called after the name of the Ravennate actor Luigi Rasi.

Of the ex church we preserve the apse that is visible behind the stage, from which the fourteen century frescos were torn off.

The via continues until Porta Nuova (at n. 33, the beautiful seat of the ISTITUTO MUSICALE G. VERDI), having on the right a sequence of low houses. On the left instead a square opens, already occupied largely by the barracks where there was the 28° regiment of infantry of the Pavia division, particularly dear to all the Romagnoli, many of which fought in its lines the last wars on the Alps and in Africa. Now the place has been turned partly into lawn and partly into a parking. On the square the monumental façade of Santa Maria in Porto and the elegant building of the ex monastery di Porto show themselves.

SANTA MARIA IN PORTO

Historical hints -The church and the monastery constitute a unique building, even if the monastery is more ancient than the church of more than half a century.

The religious decided to build a new monastery in town because the Venetians, dominating in Ravenna from 1441 to 1509, obstaculated the construction that they wanted to build on the

Santa Maria in Porto.

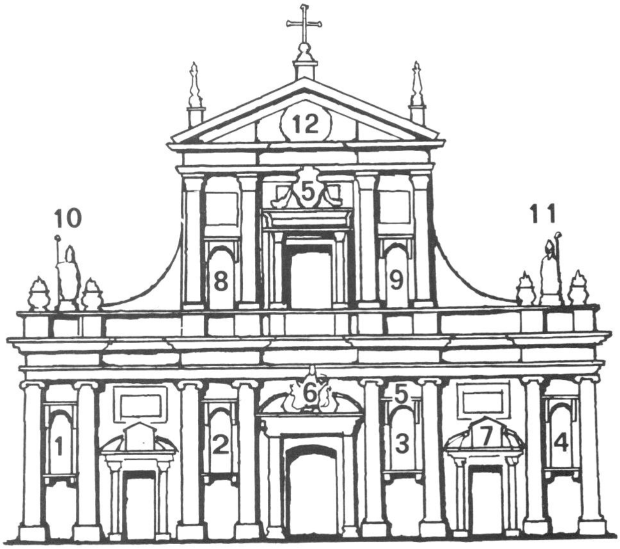

Fig. 30 - **Scheme of the façade of Santa Maria in Porto**. 1 - Statue of Charity. 2 - Faith. 3 - Hope. 4 - Humbleness. 5 - Bearings of the monks of Porto. 6 - Greek Madonna. 7 - «Aediculas» with winged putti. 8 - Saint Laurence. 9 - Pier degli Onesti. 10 - Saint Augustine. 11 - Saint Ubaldo. 12 - Monogram of Mary.

side of the church of Santa Maria in Porto Fuori («Nostra Donna in sul lito Adriano») Dante «*Paradiso*» canto XXI - v. 123).

They feared that the building could offer an easy refuge to the enemies of the Republic. The Lateranensi Canons themselves built later a big basilica. For an exact information, the constructions that rise on this area have the following chronology. *Monastery*, beginning of the building 1496, beginning of the works of the cloister 1502, entrance of the canons 1503; *Church*, beginning of the works, 1553, covering of the roof 1561, consecration 1606; *Façade of the church*, ending of the works 1784.

The monastery of Santa Maria in Porto, one of the four big abbeys of Ravenna, had in the middle of the seventeenth century a dormitory with 63 rooms for the priors, clerics, lay brothers and novices; infirmary, forestry, cellar, wheat store-rooms, stalls. In 1588 Sisto V had appointed for this monastery the number of 35 canons and 15 lay brothers.

Architectural characteristics - The façade (look at scheme fig. 30), preceeded by a staircase (1783) formed by eight steps, curved in the central part, was probably designed a first time at the beginning of the 16th century, but that project was never fulfilled. In 1695 an unknown architect designed it again and this second project was partly accomplished in the inferior part.

Having interrupted the works for some decades, there was a new project (1759) of «*Giannantonio Zane da Fusignano*», not accomplished. Finally *Morigia* intervened, he completed the inferior part on the existing traces and he conceived the superior part proposing a Neoclassical solution overcoming the Baroque.

The inferior part, of ionic order, is composed of four pairs of columns between which four statues are inserted, Charity (1), Faith (2), Hope (3), Humbleness (4), in niches with shell-like semi-vault. Above the niches there is the representation of a castle with three towers: it is the araldic emblem of the abbey, inspired from the tower of the church of Porto Fuori that was used as a bell-tower. On the façade it recurs five times and we shall find it again repeatedly also in the monastery (5).

In the three spaces that lie between the four pairs of columns three portals open, of which the central one is the biggest, with split tympana sustained by two columns. The two columns of «cipolin» marble of the central portal come from the basilica of San Lorenzo in Cesarea, of the 5th century. Between the wings of the tympanum of this portal there is the statue of 1698 that represents the Greek Madonna (6), while on the lateral portals there is a little aedicula with a winged putto overhung by a panel with a marble background (7).

The superior part of the façade, of Corinthian order, presents in the middle a window with balcony on the sides of which there are two pairs of columns with the statues of Saint Laurence (8) and Pier degli Onesti (9) inside niches. At the extremities of the façade the two statues of Saint Augustine (10) and Saint Ubaldo (11) are silhouetted against the sky, in the middle of two big flaming vases. An elegant and simple curved connection joins the two orders of the façade.

Above the two statues on the sides of the window there are two panels with palm branches; above the window the fifth coat-of-arms of the monks of Porto is placed. The façade ends at the top with a big tympanum that carries in the middle Mary's monogram inside a medallion (12). Above the tympanum the three «acroteria» silhouette against the sky, among which the

Fig. 31 - **Basilica of Santa Maria in Porto: plan 4** - «The martyrdom of San Giacomo Minore», by Scarsellino, from Ferrara (1551-1620). 5 - «Martyrdom of Saint Margaret», by Cesare Corte (1550-1613). 6 - «Madonna Assunta», by Francesco Longhi (1544-1618). 7 - «Saint Laurence», by Emilio Taruffi (1633-1696). 8 - Wooden choir of the 16th century. 9 - Great reading desk. 10 - High altar with ciborium of the 17th century. 11 - Choir-stalls of the second half of the 16th century. - 12 - Painting of Pietro da Bagnara (operating around 1550). 13 - «Annunciation», by Giovanni Laurentini, called Arrigoni (1550-1633). 14 - Greek Madonna. 15 - «Saint Catherine» by Scarsellino. 16 - Saint Ubaldo that exorcizes an obsessed», by Andrea Barbiani (1593-1650). 17 - «Santa Maria and other Saints» by G.B. Barbiani (1593-1650). - 18 - «Martyrdom of Saint Mark» by Palma il Giovane (1544-1628). 19 - Wooden crucifix of the 15th century. 20 - «San Carlo Borromeo», by an unknown painter. 21 - «The Guardian Angel», by Vincenzo Pisano, from Bologna (who worked around 1690).

central one finishes with a cross.

The general tone of the façade, all in Istria stone, except the statues that are in white marble from Verona, is Neoclassical, and testifies the passage from Baroque to the new architectural style. The statues are a good work of the Veronese *Diomiro Cignaroli* (1718-1803).

From the outside we can observe the grandeur of the whole building, from the principal body of which the arms of the apsed transept start off from the beautiful tympana and above which the drum dome stands out, 53 meters high, provided with a lantern with windows and gallery with a railing.

The architect of the church (of the façade as we already said) is not known for certainty; the experts make the name of *Bernardino Tavella* of Ravenna.

The ***inside***, solemn and imposing, has three naves with alternating pillars and Doric columns. The vaults of the main nave have spheric triangles on a squared base, those of the aisles have a rectangular base.

On the lateral walls six chapels open on each side, symmetrically the same in structure and decoration rich of precious marbles.

Inside: right nave (plan fig. 31) - In the first three chapels there are paintings of not very great value: «Two nuns with Christ», «Madonna of the Rosary», «Don Bosco». In the fourth chapel there is a good painting of the Ferrarese «*Scarsellino*» (1551-1620) that represents the «Martyrdom of San Giacomo Minore». In the fifth chapel (fig. 31, 5), the «Martyrdom of Saint Margaret», the best work of *Cesare Corte* (1550-1613), pupil of Luca Cambiaso. The two statues in the niches are of gypsum, of the eighteenth century, and represent San Pier Damiano and Pier degli Onesti.

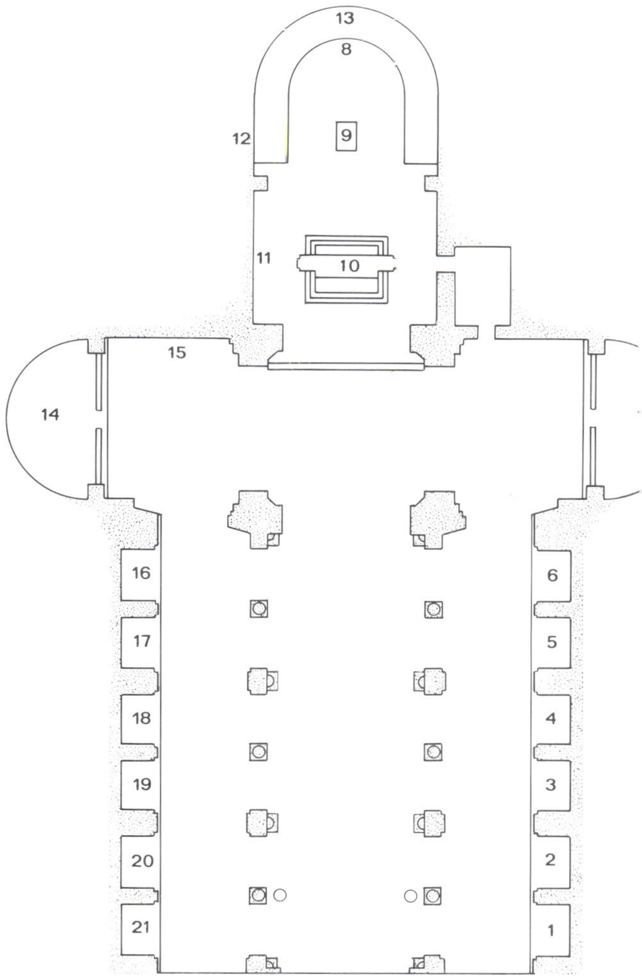

In the sixth chapel (6), there is a «Madonna Assunta» of Francesco Longhi.

Inside: transept, right wing (7) - The transept is very wide and apsed. At the end of the right wing there is an altar of precious marbles with two pairs of columns among which a painting representing Saint Laurence, by *Emilio Taruffi*, from Bologna (1633-1696).

Inside: apse **-** The apse is big and deep; the vault is formed by a big shell under which a magnificent **wooden choir** of the 16th century (8) is placed. It is reached through a little lateral door.

It is a complex of 75 stalls, of two orders, masterpiece of the carver *Marino Francese*. The second order is richer, and must be admired in its particulars. Every stall is sustained by two supports that at the bottom have the form of a paw. At the height of the shoulder of who is sitting two dividing projections stick out. On the back of every stall the prospectives of little temples are carved in which a niche which contained little statues opens. On the sides there are caryatids with noble features of the face. A jutting out trabeation acts as frieze, all decorated above which, masks, leaves and spikes alternate themselves. Very beautiful is the little carving in the middle of the choir, where the kiss of Judah is represented. On the left of the kissing scene there are three Apostles on the right two soldiers and a common man.

Behind the altar, in front of the choir there is a great reading desk (9), that only in part is a work of Marino Francese: six big prospectives of indoor places are carved.

On the previous high altar (10), redone in 1710, there is a beautiful **ciborium** in a shape of a little temple, work of father *Giuseppe Vivoli*, that started it in 1627, and of father *Ascanio Mula*, that finished it. It is made up of a base from which twelve columns rise that sustain a trabeation and the dome, covered with lapislazuli. The ciborium is sustained by two angels in white marble from Carrara. Before the altar there is a wide medallion worked by an unknown artist who wanted to represent, symbolically the speculation of Saint Augustine on the mystery of the Trinity, representing the philosopher near a child that takes water away from the sea with a shell. Remarkable are the inlaid marbles at the back of the altar. On the walls of the presbytery there are two choir-stalls (11) with beautiful balconies of the second half of the 16th century. The pipes of the organ find place in a space delimited by columns and surmounted by a rich split tympanum. The original organ of the eighteenth century, underwent various improving interventions, the last of which in 1978.

Of beautiful effect is the reproduction or repetition of the painting of *Pietro da Bagnara* (12) scholar of Raffaello, operating around 1550, «The climbing to the Calvary», that is on the left wall of the apse.

At the bottom of the apse there is the painting of the «Announcement» by *Giovanni Laurentini*, from Rimini (1550-1633) (13).

Inside: transept, left wing (14) - In it is placed, in a rich framing of marbles, the bas-relief of the so-called «**Greek Madonna**». It is a marble 118 cm. high, 62 cm. wide, in which Mary is represented as a young girl with a fluent garment and a wide cloak, in frontal position and in a praying attitude. On the sides of her head, between two discs, there are two initials in Greek letters which mean «Mother of God». The bas-relief comes from the East and dates back to the period around the year 1000, with the more precise assignement to the second half of the 11th century. The legend narrates that on the 8th April of the year 1100 to a group of religious people on the beach of the Adriatic, among which Peter the sinner, the effigy of the Virgin preceeded by two angels appeared.

The effigy, that came from the sea so miraculously, became quite soon the centre of attraction for crowds of believers, and it drew the attention of popes and emperors. Transferred to town in 1503, placed in the church where we are now, saw its cult decline when, after 1512, the one of the «Madonna del Sudore» developed. The appellative Greek derives from the fact that the image would have arrived from Constantinople so as to escape from iconoclastic persecutions.

In foreground, on the altar erected in 1626, there is a ciborium that for a long time had been assigned to Michelangelo, meanwhile it carries the date 1646, and it is of Berninian influence and it was made in Perugia by a certain Fortunato. Placed in San Vitale, it was brought here in 1900. It is a valuable work of goldsmithry.

On the right wall of this wing there is a second painting by *Scarsellino* representing Saint Catherine that contemplates an angel surrounded by terrified soldiers (15).

Here, the very famous «Madonna in trono» by *Ercole de Roberti* was placed (1450-1496). Painted for the church of Porto Fuori and from here transferred to Santa Maria in Porto in town in the 16th century, it is now in the Brera gallery in Milan, where it was transferred during the Napoleonic period.

The work is also known as «Pala di Santa Maria in Porto» and it measures 323 cm. per 240.

Inside: chapels of the left nave - Let's now pass to the chapels of the left aisle starting from the

◀ Monastery of Porto: reproductions from the collection of plaster casts (we recognize: *The boxer* by Canova, and a *Horse*, moulding from life that belonged to Canova) and show-cases of the ornithological museum.

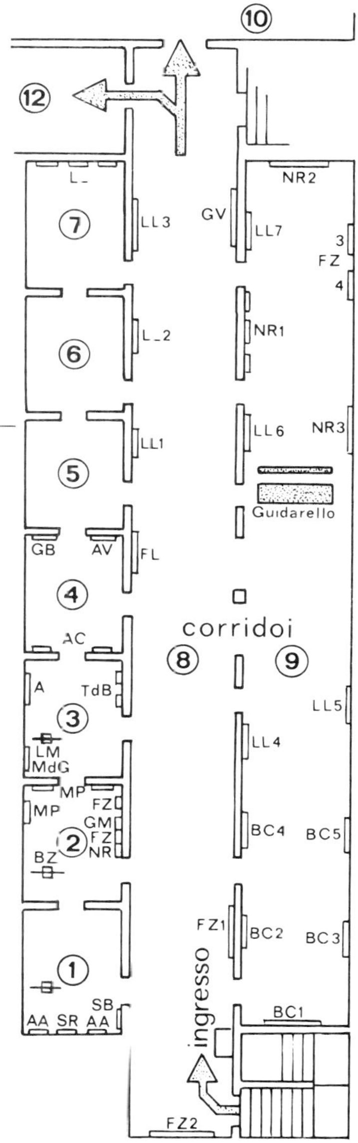

Fig. 32 - **Monastero di Porto. Civic Pinacotheca, eastern side**. The initials correspond to the following artists (alphabetical order).

A - Nicolò da Foligno called l'Alunno
AA - Antonio Alberti from Ferrara
AC - Antonio Cicognara
AV - Antonio Vivarini
BC - Baldassarre Carrari
BZ - Bernardino Zaganelli
FZ - Francesco Zaganelli
FL - Francesco Longhi
GB - Gentile Bellini
GM - Girolamo Marchesi
GV Giorgio Vasari
LL - Luca Longhi
LM Lorenzo Monaco
MdG - Matteo di Giovanni
MP - Marco Palmezzano
NR - Nicolò Rondinelli
SB - Scuola Bolognese
SR - Scuola Romagnola
TdB - Taddeo di Bartolo

one near the transept. It contains one of the best works of the painter *Andrea Barbiani* (1709-1779): «Saint Ubaldo that exorcizes an obsessed» (16).

In the following chapel (17), a painting of another member of the painting dynasty of *Andrea Barbiani*, that gave remarkable artists to Ravenna from the middle of the sixteenth century to the middle of the nineteenth century: *Giovan Battista* (1593-1650), that here presents his «Santa Monica and other Saints» («Santa Monica e altri Santi»).

The third chapel (18) contains a «Martyrdom of Saint Mark» by *Palma il Giovane* (*Iacopo Negretti*, 1544-1628), whose painting goes very near to Tintoretto's.

In the fourth chapel (19) there is a wooden crucifix of the 15th century.

In the fifth chapel, «San Carlo Borromeo» by an unknown artist. The work is indicated as the most faithful image of the Saint (20).

In the last chapel near the door, finally, a painting with an angel saving a putto represents the «Guardian Angel». It is by *Vincenzo Pisano*, from Bologna working around 1690 (21).

MONASTERO DI PORTO CIVIC PICTURE-GALLERY

Let's set off towards the building of Monastero di Porto, that in the middle has a magnificent cloister around which, in wide rooms, houses the Academy of Fine Arts, the ORNITHOLOGICAL MUSEUM AND OF NATURAL SCIENCE, and the CIVIC PICTURE-GALLERY. It was the

Monastery of Porto - Ornithological museum: a show-case. ▶

Monastery of Porto - Collection of modern mosaics: Guttuso, *Pigeons' flight*.
▼

seat of the fourth big abbey of Ravenna.

Cloister - We reach it from the square through a double portal that opens in the middle of the façade subdivided in a central body and two lateral bodies with a double sloping roof; in the façade a beautiful and rich window opens with quadrangular or arched openings.

The cloister with two loggia orders, was started in 1502. It is made up of arcades sustained by pillars in the inferior floor and by columns in the superior one. Eighty pillars and eighty columns that delimit a serene and cosy squared space. The absence of walls in the first and second order, gives to the whole great lightness. The impression is increased by the fact that all the arcades of the two orders are now closed by windows, therefore we fall nearly into a game of mirrors that send back images slightly perceptable, taking away any material certainty to what is on the other side.

The openings that give access to the green space are in the middle of every side and occupy the width of two arches. Above, a balcony corresponds. The little windows above are those of the cells that looked onto the cloister. In the mullioned window at the North the weapon of the monks of Porto is sculptured; on the one at the South, the Greek Virgin in Renaissance style.

On the eastern side the *Loggetta Lombar-*

Monastery of Porto - A reproduction from the collection of plaster casts: Gaetano Cellini, *Humanity against evil.*

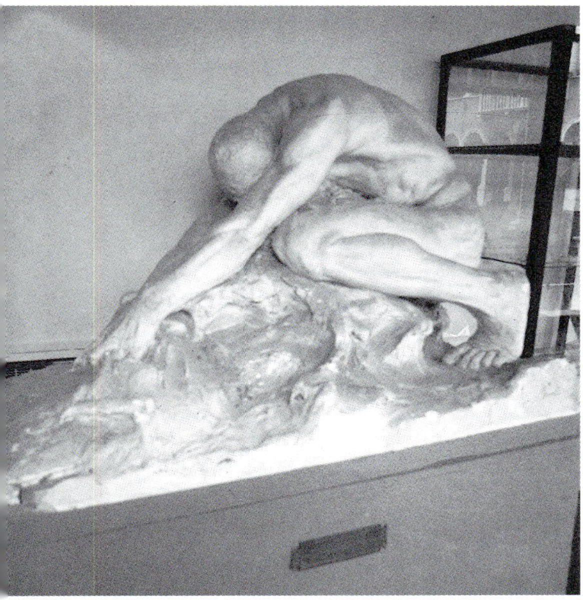

desca opens, that for the moment we shall admire from the inside, but that we shall be able to enjoy in all its splendour looking at it from the outside when we shall get to the public gardens.

Academy of Fine Arts - It was established by the municipality and by the Province of Ravenna in 1827 and it found place in a building deliberately built in via Baccarini. The actual placing dates back after 1969, date in which the cloister was restored under the care of the Municipality of Ravenna.

Collection of modern mosaics - One section of the cloister's colonnades is occupied by an interesting display of modern mosaics, conceived and prepared in the 50s. Various artists were invited to produce a pictorial work which was then to be translated into mosaic. 20 major contemporary artists accepted the invitation and sent paintings which were then executed in mosaic by the «Gruppo Mosaicisti», mosaicists from the Academy of Fine Arts. In the corridors of the cloister are hung many of the "cartoons" sent by the painters with the associated transposition into mosaic form. The schools represented include realism (Guttuso), figurative art (Chagall, Campigli, Saetti, Gentilini), non-figurative art (Reggiani, Mirko, Cassinari, Cagli, Capogrossi, Paulucci, Sandquist, abstract and stylizing; Afro, Birolli, Vedova, Santomaso, Corpora, Moreni, Deluigi, lyrical and expressionist). Mathieu did not prepare a guide-sketch but placed filaments and blocks of glass chosen at Venice on the lime with a cement mix which acts as a support for these mosaics.

The gallery of modern mosaics provides an opportunity to appreciate the potential and

Civic Pinacotheca: St. Augustine (Antonio Alberti from Ferrara).

representational effects of the mosaic vis-à-vis modern styles of painting, as evinced by artists chosen from among those whose painting is not too far removed from the aesthetic needs peculiar to the mosaic.

Gallery of plaster casts - Under the porticoes of the cloister there is also a valuable collection of plaster casts and reproductions of classical sculptures which are used as teaching aids for students at the Academy. Interspersed with the casts are a number of showcases belonging to the

Ornithological and natural science museum - The corridors house models of iguana, monitor, lacerta occellata, horned viper, python, rattlesnake, Gabon viper, spider, grass snake, turtle, together with a noteworthy collection of shells from the Adriatic, while a room giving on to the corridor houses specimens of polecat, otter, badger, rat, hedgehog, hare, fox, dormouse, squirrel, porcupine, cat, panda and three-toed sloth.

Entrance to the Ornithological Museum is gained through an entrance placed in the middle of the Northern corridor, on the ground floor. We can admire more than 1,300 specimens of the typical avifauna of the Bassa Ravennate and several mammals and reptiles.

The collection of birds started in 1906, it enrichened with various contributions and it is the result of fifty years of passionate and constant work of Alfredo Brandolini. Before reaching the actual beautiful arrangement, the collection was placed in the Polentana House of via Zagarelli alle Mura. The Museum has furthermore a conspicuous collection of shells of the Adriatic, a collection of eggs, and butterflies and a specialized library. A didactic section enriches the Museum, which houses also the National seat of the Italian Ornithologic Society.

Civic Pinacotheca - The entrance to the Pinacotheca is at the South Eastern corner of the cloister, where a stair leads to the last floor.

The collection of paintings was born in 1829, as didactic and formative support for the pupils of the Academy of fine arts, founded quite recently. Paintings were asked both to private people and corporations and at the beginning it had a remarkable flow of legacies that were then in part withdrawn by the owners and sold abroad. The pieces of the municipality and of some private people remained. Actually the Pinacoteca owns about 250 paintings, placed in a not rigorous chronological order.

Nearly half of the works exposed concern the Romagnol-Ravennate painting from the second half of the 15th century to all the 16th century.

The civic Picture-gallery is housed in the rooms indicated in the enclosed plan fig. 32-33, at pages 141 and 145.

Let's proceed in our visit indicating some remarkable paintings and postponing to a successive paragraph for some orientative hints on Romagnol and Ravennati painters of the 15th and 16th century. In the plan the paintings mentioned in the text are marked by the initials of the author and, eventually, by a progressive number per author.

ROOM 1 - *Antonio Alberti from Ferrara* (1390-1449): «Sant'Antonio Abate» and «Saint Augustine» (AA) two refined pictorial pages, of precious formal finesse. *Romagna's school of the 16th century:* «Madonna on the throne with the Infant between Saint Francis and Saint Ludovico da Tolosa. The Announcement (above); the Nativity and the Adoration (on the left); the Crucifixion and the Resurrection (on the right)» (SR), painting of about 1330. The Madonna is rather Byzantine and the other parts of the painting are of Giotto and Rimini style. *Bolognese school of the 16th century:* «Saint Francis that receives the stigmata, and Saints» (SB): delightful predella, intelligently designed.

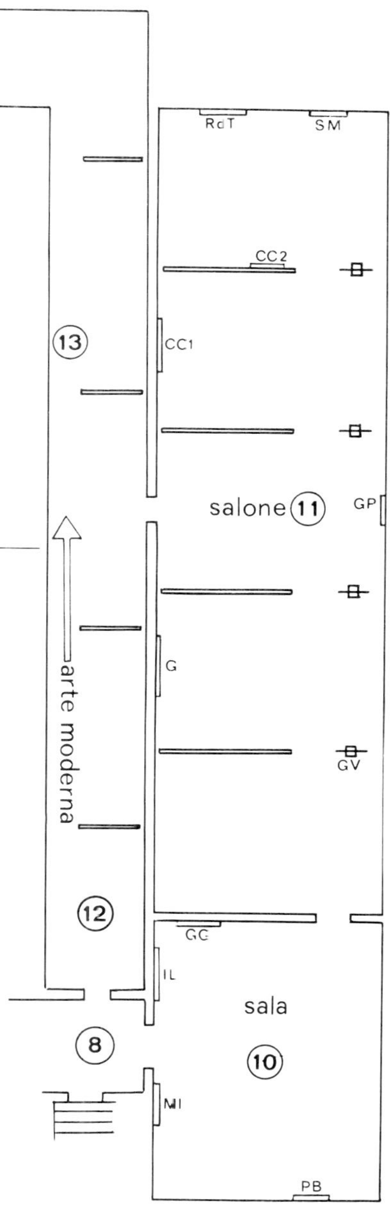

Fig. 33 - **Monastero di Porto - Civic Pinacotheca, northern side**. The initials correspond to the following artists (alphabetical order):
CC - Carlo Cignani
G - Guercino
GG - Gianfrancesco Gessi
GP - Giannantonio Pellegrini
GV - Giorgio Vasari
IL - Iacopo Ligozzi
MI - Matteo Ingoli
PB - Paris Bordone
RdT - Rosa da Tivoli
SM - Sebastiano Mazzoni

ROOM 2 - *Bernardino Zaganelli* (1465/70 - after 1509): «The prayer in the kitchen-garden» (BZ) in which the representations of the particulars is very accurate. - *Francesco Zaganelli* (1475-1531): «Madonna worshipping the Infant and Saint Francis»; «Head of Angel» (FZ) delightful fragment of a wide composition. *Girolamo Marchesi* (1471-1540): «Saint Antonio Abate and Saint Paul the hermit, Saint Jerome, four Saints, Saint John the Baptist and the Evangelist» (GM), of the juvenile phase of the painter. -*Nicolò Rondinelli* (1470-1509): «Madonna with the Infant» (NR), of the maturity phase of the painter, that shows to own the Bellinian ways. -*Marco Palmezzano* (1456/59-1539): «A martyr Saint» in which the strong and elementary style of the artist appears, but in his evolving period. «The presentation to the temple» and the «Nativity» (MP); they were the compartments of predella of a «pala»; very bright the landscapes, harmonious the figures, very beautiful the girl that carries white pidgeons in a basket.

ROOM 3 - *Lorenzo Monaco* (Siena 1370-1425): «Crucifixion and Saints (LM), very fine tablet of the maturity phase (1410) of the painter. - *Matteo di Giovanni* (Borgo S. Sepolcro 1430-1495): «Madonna with the Infant between Girolamo and Barbara» (MdG), very beautiful. - *Nicolò da Foligno called l'Alunno* (ca. 1430-1502): «Christ with cross and Angels» (A), work of the maturity phase (1499) of good quality. - *Taddeo di Bartolo* (Siena 1362/63-1422): «The Archangel Gabriel»; «The announced Virgin» (TdB); carried out around 1410, and therefore in the late period of the painter; «*but the two tablets still preserve a certain freshness in materia and in the gentle intimacy of the sacred representation*» (Martini).

ROOM 4 - *Gentile Bellini* (Venice 1429-1507): «Saint Peter and Saint Laurence» (GB), making part of a big polyptych, in which especially the sweetness of the face of Saint Laurence is very remarkable and the minute and bright description of the drapery and of the decorations of the garments. - *Antonio Ciccognara* (Cremona active in the IInd half of the XVth Century): fine and delightful Announcement divided in two little paintings that must have constituted a diptych: «The archangel Gabriel», «The virgin» (AC). -*Antonio Vivarini* (Murano 1415-1484): «Crucifixion» (AV), of the juvenile period influenced by Masolino, remarkable for the vibrations of light and for the tones of colour.

ROOM 7 - Three portraits by *Luca Longhi* (1507-1580): «Raffaele Rasponi», «Gerolamo Rossi»; «Giovanni Arrigoni» (LL). Seven pieces by *Barbara Longhi* daughter of Luca.

CORRIDOR 8 - *Luca Longhi*: «Martyrdom of Saint Ursicino» (LL1) - «Decollation of San Giovanni Battista» (LL2), one of the most beautiful works of the artist.- «Madonna with the Infant between the Saints Benedict and Paul, Apollinare and Barbara» (LL3), of the beautiful and slim figures, work of the second part of the painter's life. - *Francesco Longhi* (1544-1618): «The crucifixion between the Virgin and Saint John, Sant'Apollinare and San Vitale» (FL), it is a second-rate prolonging of his father's way of painting. - *Giorgio Vasari* (1511-1577): «Christ laid down» (GV). In the period in which Vasari was in Ravenna, mentioning in his «Vite» about Longhi, furthermore he claimed an influence of his on the Ravennate painter «*who I know how much he learned when I lived in Ravenna for two months*». The painting with which he managed to influence Longhi is this laid down Christ, painted in Ravenna in 1548, and it could be interesting to mention what Vincenzo Carrari said in the death oration of Longhi as regards to his boasted influence; he criticizes the painting (the Madonna has such proportions that, if she was to get up, she wouldn't fit in the painting; the thighs of Christ are too long; Magdalene is in an impossible position), and he affirms that if Longhi, all naturalness and spontaneousness, had copied from Vasari, he would have gone back, i.e. he would have regressed. - *Francesco Zaganelli*: «Crucifixion» (FZ1), «*it represents the highest and complete achievement on his way towards his eccentric and tortured expressionism*» (Martini); great for expressive intensity the group of the three women. «The adoration of the shepherds» in a very bad state of preservation, practically illegible; painted round about 1530, of incisive ways, was very beautiful in the group Virgin-Infant-Joseph-shepherd, and in the beautiful heads of the two shepherds that turn around (FZ2).

CORRIDOR 9 - *Baldassarre Carrari* (1460-1516): «Christ laid down» (BC1), painted at the beginning of his second stay in Ravenna, with style drawn from Palmezzano, «The descent to the Limbo» (BC2), «The capture of Christ» (BC3): in the two paintings is revealed «*his true nature of provincial illustrator, authentic and amusing, but terribly naive and poor of ideas*» (Martini). They are also of the second Ravennate stay, like the successive «Jesus put into the sepulchre» (BC4) where the artist gets sweeter and gets nearer to the Venetian style of Rondinelli «Pity» (BC5).

Monastero di Porto - Civic Picture Gallery: Tullio Lombardo, funeral statue of Guidarello Guidarelli (particular).

— *Luca Longhi*: «Christ laid down between two angels, Saint Bartholomew and the abbot of Classe» (LL4); «Adoration of the Shepherds» (LL5): the two paintings testify an ascending phase of the «Longhiana» way of painting. «Adoration of the Shepherds» (LL6); «Matrimony of Saint Catherine among the Saints Sebastiano, Jerome, Rocco and a bishop» (LL7), it is the first of Longhi's works that we got.

— *Nicolò Rondinelli*: «Madonna with the Infant between Saint Albert and Saint Sebastian» (NR1): they are three pieces making part of a triptych very praised by Vasari. «Madonna on the throne with the Infant between Saint Jerome and St. Catherine» (NR2): it documents the conquest of the «belliniano» tone, in the solemn calm of the Venetian aura and in the bright and clear sky. «Madonna on the throne with the Infant and Angels, between St. Thomas, St. Magdalene, St. Catherine, St. John the Baptist» (NR3): beautiful table with delicate chromatic timbres, airy and well-balanced.

— *Francesco Zaganelli*: «St. Catherine» (FZ3); «St. Sebastian» (FZ4).

Half way in the corridor the famous funeral statue is placed, it was sculptured in 1525 by *Tullio Lombardo* (about 1455-1532), representing *Guidarello Guidarelli*. Who he was and how he died, at the age of 33, in 1501, can be read on a chronicle of a contemporary of his from Cesena: «*Guidarello from Ravenna, very worthy soldier of the duke, having lent a beautiful Spanish type shirt of his worked in gold to Virgilio Romano in Imola for a Masquerade and since he didn't want to give it back they had a fight, the above mentioned Virgilio cut him to pieces and killed him; the Duke, who had him caught, cut his head off.*» To tell the truth, Guidarello survived a few days to his wounds and managed to make his testament, that carries the date of 6th March 1501. The «Duke» was Cesare Borgia called «il Valentino». On the beautiful face of the young soldier dressed in his cuirass, life that has just gone away, death that hasn't yet come to cancel his expression, are both present and suggest pain for an impossible return.

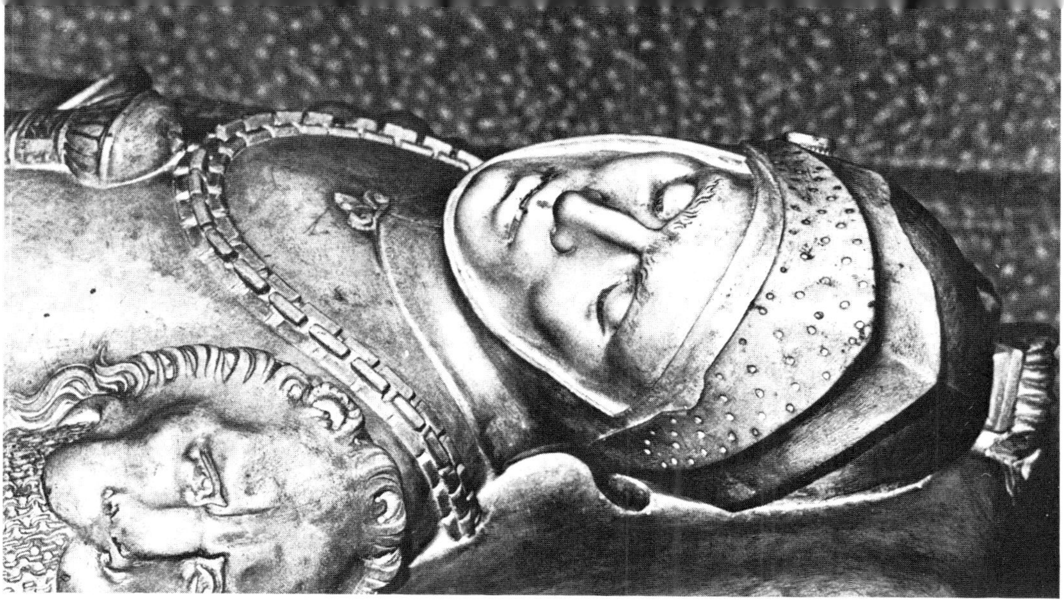

ROOM 10 - *Paris Bordone* (1500-1571): «The Redeemer» (PB), beautiful work of Tiziano inspiration». - *Iacopo Ligozzi* «Martyrdom of the saints Quattro Coronati» (IL), of which the inferior part is remarkable, against the light, with the beautiful group of the two young boys leaning against the fence. - *Matteo Ingoli* (1585-1631): «The supper-room, Saint Apollinare and the Blessed Lorenzo Giustiniani» (MI): the Ravennate painter imitates the Venetian tradition of Palma il Giovane, but in a mediocre way. - *Gianfrancesco Gessi* (1588-1649): «Crucifixion» (GG): the big crucifixion is taken from the one that Guido Reni had painted in Rome for the church of San Lorenzo in Lucina.

ROOM 11 - *Guercino* (1591-1666): «Saint Romualdo» (G), of the regressive period of the great painter, following classicizing and conventional ways of painting. The painting is of 1641. - *Carlo Cignani* (1628-1719): «Saint Benedict» (CC1), one of the nicest canvases of the painter, that inspires to a malinconic sweetness. Unfortunately the oxidation has added a lot of darkness to the falling day. «Madonna with the Infant, Saint John, Saint Theresa, Saint Carlo Borromeo (CC2). - *Giannantonio Pellegrini* (1674-1741): «Body of Darius before Alexander» (GP): «*...the sumptuous and happy description of the bright Alexander, that "far" magic all undone light, the airy leafy branch behind the curtain the brilliant and dinamic "improvisation" in the decorations make this sketch one of the most extraordinary achievements of the extraordinary maturity of Pellegrini, maybe the greatest of the Venetian painters of the eighteenth century*» (Martini). - *Sebastiano Mazzoni* (1615-1685): beautiful canvas representing «Apollo and Dafne» (SM). - *Rosa da Tivoli* (1655/57-1706): «The herdsman» (RdT): it is the painting of a famous painter of animals, very beautiful and rich of acute realistic observations. - *Giorgio Vasari*: a little drawing representing Christ that carries the cross (GV).

CORRIDOR 13 - In this part of the Pinacotheca paintings of modern artists are collected among which we indicate nine works of the Ravennate *Vittorio Guaccimanni*, especially known as an engraver.

Hints on the Romagnol - Ravennate painting - While in the architectural field, in the mosaic representation and in tomb sculpture Ravenna is a source of influence and of irradiation, in the painting field it is tributary of schools and styles that have external origin. The Romagnol painters and in particular the «Ravennati» ones don't reveal any daring, they don't carry out original researches, they take little initiative, but they work with ability and honesty, relying upon the styles of who knows and cares to carry out original and creative researches. A partial exception is constituted from Forlì.

We can indicate in *Luca Longhi* the typical Ravennate painter. He was born in Ravenna in 1507 and died in 1580, he lived therefore in the best period of Italian painting, he never went out from his town and remained a good, simple, accurate, delicate painter absorbing influences from the Emilia school, from Costa, from Francia, from Palmezzano, from Rondinelli, with some notes drawn from Raffaello through the Bolognese school. His position is well described by Vasari: «*If Longhi had gone out from Ravenna, where he has always been and lives with his family, being assiduous and very diligent, he would have managed to do very rare things, because he has carried out and carries his things with patience and study*».

At the end of the fourtheenth century, and that is after Longhi, we can make out in the Romagnol painting, some «schools». Pre-eminent the ***Forlivese «school»***, that on the trial of the glory of *Melozzo* (Forlì: 1438-1494), enumerates *Marco Palmezzano* (Forlì: 1456/59-1539) and *Baldassarre Carrari* (Forlì: after 1460 - Ravenna 1515). The *Palmezzano* overcomes the all provincial mediocrity of many contemporaries that operate in minor centres, and before falling into the *routine* of a too plentiful production, he manifests himself as a painter of great talent («The communion of the Apostles», «Saint Anthony», the magnificent «Announcement» of Forlì made him an unforgettable artist.) His painting carries the influences from Melozzo, from the Ferraresi, and through Rondinelli and then directly from the Venetians. He is represented in the Pinacotheca by means of the three little works that we saw in room 2.

The *Carrari* places himself between Palmezzano and Rondinelli; his artistic life runs between Forlì and Ravenna, where he seems to have worked around 1498 undergoing the influence of Rondinelli. He is here represented by five paintings placed in corridor 9, in which his simple and provincial style not particularly rich of ideas reveals itself.

The distinctive character of the Forlivese school is represented by the colour and the capacity of structurizing architecture and space.

The ***«Faentina school»*** is represented by Leonardo Scaletti, Andrea Utili, Gian Battista Utili and others, whose principal character is the capacity in the design more than in the colour influenced as they are by the Ferrarese school and in first place by Francesco Del Cossa. The school is not represented in the Pinacotheca.

The ***«Cotignola-Ravennate school»*** enumerates *Nicolò Rondinelli* (Ravenna about 1470-1509), *Bernardino Zaganelli* (Cotignola about 1465/70-1531), *Francesco Zaganelli called il Cotignola* (about 1475-1531), *Girolamo Marchesi (Cotignola: 1471-1540), Bartolomeo Ramenghi called il Bagnacavallo* (Bagnacavallo: 1484-1542).

Rondinelli, pupil of Giovanni Bellini great teacher of colour, has the merit of having diffused in Ravenna the style of the Venetian school at the end of the 15th century. He was called by Vasari «*excellent painter*» and may be considered as the first representative of a real Ravennate school; before, in fact, even when with the arrival of Giotto (1317) we had in Ravenna a remarkable flowering of pictorial art, especially Riminesi and Faentini artists were the protagonists. Rondinelli follows the technique of his great teacher, he is an excellent colourist, and together with Palmezzano of whom he felt the influence as time passed by, constitutes the fulcrum of the Romagnol school. In the Pinacotheca he is present with works, placed in corridor 9, where the belliniano tone can be seen especially in the «Madonna with the Infant between Saint Jerome and Saint Catherine».

The *Zaganelli* brothers, very different from each other: *Francesco* (about 1475-1531) younger, exuberant, inconstant; *Bernardino* (1465/70-after 1509), mild and sweet, operate also in Ravenna where Francesco lived from 1513 to 1531; the year in which he died. At first the sweetness, the grace, the finesse the details, of the older Bernardino prevailed, but round about 1509, Francesco prevailed, who from a juvenile period a little disconnected and scarcely brilliant in colour, acquired a more accurate style and cleaner colours, even if he remained typically Romagnolo, with characteristics of generosity, strength, redundancy and sometimes coarsness; here completely different to Longhi, that succeeded him in Ravenna. Of Bernardino in the Pinacotheca there is one only work, in room 2. While of Francesco, as well as the little work in room 2, there are two big paintings in corridor 8, and that is, the «Adoration of the Shepherds», of good level especially in the right group and in the live movement of the two figures that turn around, and the «Crucifixion»: one of the best works of the maturity of the painter, that reaches a great expressive intensity especially in the group of the three women.

Girolamo Marchesi (Cotignola: 1471-1540) and the *Bagnacavallo* (Bagnacavallo: 1484-1542) represent a moment of transition between the fifteenth and sixteenth century. The first, pupil of Zaganelli, through the teachers suffered the influence of Francia and then later, he painted in Raffaello's style, demonstrating that he is essentially an imitator. The second, more a colourist than a designer, also became an imitator of Raffaello after a first period in which the forms of the Ferrarese school prevailed in him and especially the ones of Dosso Dossi and Garofalo.

Characteristic of the Cotignola painters is the popular spirit by means of a passional and dramatic style.

Imola had no school, but gave birth to that *Innocenzo Francucci (Innocenzo da Imola:* 1490-1540) who, at first at Francia's school, suffered a very strong influence from the Tuscans and finally from Raffaello, so that, it is said, who could not have a painting from the Urbino teacher, could be satisfied with one of Innocenzo's. He isn't represented in the Pinacotheca.

In the sixteenth century the influence of Raffaello is therefore operating in Ravenna

Public gardens: the Planetarium.

(through Marchesi, Bagnacavallo, Innocenzo da Imola and the prints of Marcantonio Raimondi and Marco Dente), of the Ferraresi painters (through the Faentini, Palmezzano, the Zaganelli), of Francia.

Longhi worked in this environment, bringing his sweetness, ingenuousness, mildness, virtue that placed him in a position to imitate without effort Raffaello's style. The experts speak at least of two styles of Longhi. The first, exemplified by the «Adoration of the shepherds» by «Christ laid down», by «the Wedding of Saint Catherine» (in corridor 9), with characteristics of simplicity and delicacy of colour. The second, exemplified by the «Madonna on the throne» of corridor 8, by «Saint Agatha, Cecilia and Catherine» of the church of Sant'Agata, by «Saint Peter visiting Saint Agatha in prison» from the church of Santa Maria Maggiore, by «The invention of the Cross» of the church of San Domenico, by the «Wedding of Cana» of the Classense library, in which the composition makes the colouring richer and stronger, under the influence of Raffaello seen through the prints of Raimondi and of Dente.

Longhi was, furthermore, a remarkable portrait-painter, and in room 7 we have three essays of this quality of his, especially in the portraits of Girolamo Rossi and Giovanni Arrigoni.

Let's return in via di Roma and let's go nearer to porta Pamphilia called Porta Nuova.

PORTA NUOVA - It was built in 1580 with the name of Porta Gregoriana in honour of the reigning pontiff Gregorio XIII. It was restored and brought to the actual shape in 1653 on design, it is said, of Bernini. The restoration and modernizing works were carried out in occasion of the navigable canal that from the ancient port Candiano ended near the Porta and that was called Pamphilio, in honour of the pontiff Innocenzo X Pamphili. Also the gate (Porta) was called Pamphilia, as can be read with big letters on the frieze of the trabeation: however, neither this second name had fortune, and the people continued to call it porta Nuova, having been built in substitution to the ancient «porta San Lorenzo» that was in that zone. The big tablets on the front remind the realization of the Pamphilio canal and they were placed in 1654.

On the back of the gate above two narrow pedestrian passages opened in recent times, there are two little tablets which remind the sacrifice of two citizens of Ravenna, Francesco Segurini and Mario Montanari, who died for liberty in 1921 and in 1944

The lunette of wrought iron placed in the arch is a work of *Andrea* and *Francesco Garavini* from Ravenna who accomplished it in 1758 for the arch of Porta Alberoni, which was a little beyond the railway passage that leads to Marina di Ravenna. It was placed here when the gate was demolished in 1835.

Above a marble ball fixed to the shelf of the arch there was a marble bust of Innocenzo X assigned to Bernini. It was removed in 1758 because it threatened to fall and it was placed in the Museum where it is still today after having been placed back to its place for a few years round about 1780.

Above the gate there is the coat-of-arms of Innocenzo X sustained by an eagle.

Let's now reach the public gardens, walking along viale Santi Baldini, keeping on our left the low modern building of an elementary school.

Santa Maria in Porto and monastery.

PUBLIC GARDENS - The space now occupied by the public gardens was opened in 1866 and it was used as a race-course until 1920. It was also used as a football ground until 1931, in the same year it was destined to public gardens, realized on the project of engineer Arata. The preceeding public gardens were near the railway station.

Round about the area in which we are, the imperial building «ad Laureta», or «in Laureto» rose, built by Valentinian III.

Today the gardens house the ***planetarium***. Opened on 1st June 1985 and managed by the Town Authority's Education Department, it is equipped with a German ZK P2 telescope which shows the whole of the firmament up to the 6th magnitude (under which the sky is visible to the naked eye). The Planetarium also has projectors for the sun, moon and planets (Mercury, Venus, Mars, Jupiter, Saturn), as well as other instruments for showing eclipses, the celestial equator, the meridian and astronomic coordinate systems. It also presents a map view of the solar system, falling stars, a comet, Jupiter and the 4 Galilean satellites, and a man-made satellite. The dome measures 8 metres in diameter and the Planetarium has a seating capacity of 52.

The Planetarium also houses a conference room (seating for 56) fitted with maxi-screen videoproduction systems (VHS and U-Matic), a mechanical and photographic laboratory and a library.

The Planetarium is engaged in astronomic and scientific dissemination work in association with other national institutions and with the Astronomy Department of Bologna University.

Porta San Lorenzo and Porta Vandalaria - In the neighbourhoods it is possbile to see the remainders of the ancient gates of San Lorenzo and Vandalaria. The first is at about 160 meters from Porta Nuova and constitutes today the entrance to a condominium at n. 13 A. You can see signs of an arch; the material used is posterior to the year 1000, but the gate exists since the beginning of the town-wall of the 5th-6th century. The street that crossed it led in via di Roma.

Further on, after via Gradisca, the trace of the arch of Porta Vandalaria is very evident, that presents some walled pieces of Veronese red marble, maybe part of the jambs of the architrave. The gate cuts the walls obliquely, and it is in line with via Cerchio. It was also a gate existing at the time of the town-walls of the 5th-6th century.

From the public gardens we can admire the posterior part of the monastery di Porto and the apse part of the church of Santa Maria in Porto.

LOGGETTA LOMBARDESCA - The back façade of the monastery is formed, like the fronton, by two lateral bodies with a double slope and by a central body in which the Loggetta Lombardesca is inserted.

On the top of each of the two lateral bodies there is the coat-of-arms of the canons of Porto, i.e. the crenelated little tower that we repeatedly met during the visit to the architectural complex Monastery-Santa Maria in Porto. On one of the little towers there's the date 1503, on the other 1518.

On the two lateral bodies three big mullioned windows with balcony open (two on the left, one on top of the other, one on the right

◀ Monastero di Porto: Loggetta Lombardesca.

▶ Monastero di Porto: Loggetta Lombardesca (particular).

above); the balconies are sustained by three strong shelves finely shaped. On all the façade, finally, numerous arched windows framed like those of the balconies open, smaller quadrangular windows and, at the height from the ground, ten circular openings of brief diameter framed by stone.

The loggetta is of two orders with five arches, light, harmonious and refined. On the warm background of the brick façade it stands out as a bright jewel set in a rough stone.

The two orders of arches are bordered by two agile pilasters that from the ground interrupt themselves at the height of the first floor with a capital, to continue again towards the top and finishes with another capital that sustains the crowning cornice.

The arches of the superior part have a balustrade.

The capitals are particularly interesting: they are composed of a Corinthian capital, that in the middle of the concave façade carries a flower or a leaf of strong relief, laid on volutes of Ionic type but starting from the bottom so as to form a «lyre», inside which there are some flower motifs all difficult, with a light corbel, of very delicate design. The volutes are sustained by an acanthus leaf very elaborated. The ovule strip from which in certain «composite» capitals volutes rise, here passes behind the volutes themselves and is variously decorated. The scheme of this capital, called «*Lombardesco*», can be found in other constructions of Ravenna of the 16th century, but generally more symplified and rough; look, for example, at the portico of Casa Ghigi, in via Romolo Gessi.

In the construction of the Loggetta, as in the one of the cloister, worked marble-workers from Campione and Lombardy.

The gates of wrought iron that close the five inferior arches were made in 1907 by *Vittore Sangiorgi*.

To enjoy better the vision of the Loggetta it is more convenient to enter the garden, at least until the central fountain, so as to be able to frame the movement between the dark wings of the two holm-oak paths.

Inside the Loggetta, on the left, there is a room with decorations carried out in 1504-1506 by *Baldassarre Carrari* from Forlì.

On the right of the Loggetta, in 1913, the ornamental part of the portal of the 16th century, which constituted the entrance of the fore façade, was placed. It is an arched door, surmounted by a cornice sustained by two beautiful columns with Lombardesque capitals; above the architrave, as a cyma, the bearings of the canons of Porto, developed in horizontal sense as a castle with three towers. To see the door it is necessary to pass on the other side of the high box hedge that borders the Loggetta; and so we shall find ourselves in front of a beautiful portal marked by time, walled and half hidden by the green.

Let's return in via di Roma following the itinerary indicated in the map, i.e. going out from the garden on the right of the apse of Santa Maria in Porto (via Padre Genocchi) turning left in via Alberoni and going along it until we reach the so-called Palazzo di Teodorico that we already know. Having arrived here, turn right along via di Roma and pass onto the opposite pavement, continuing until the crossing with via Mariani, turn left.

Via Mariani is a beautiful and noble street. In the yard of the house at n. 46 there is a portico with two orders of loggias, the remainder of the eighteenth century cloister of the old Seminary, erected in the seat of an ancient mona-

The Alighieri Theatre.

stery in 1583 and closed two hundred years later. Remarkable the portal of the house at n. 21, delimitated by an ashlar-work in Istria stone with two roses in the «zocca» and a split tympanum (16th-17th century); in the yard there is a well-curb of the 16th century. At numbers 7 and 9 there is a noble palace built round about 1870, with two arched main doors with stone frames. The building at n. 26, now seat of the «Consorzio di Bonifica», is of the seventeenth century; of the nineteenth century is the one at n. 24.

PALAZZO CORRADINI - It is the building that dominates the via; it carries n. 5. It impresses you for the high portal surmounted by a balcony sustained by two big columns and three shelves. The complex is certainly not proportioned as regards to the whole façade, but if considered alone it is a beautiful example of Baroque architecture.

Above the windows of the superior floor, inserted in the architrave there are some masks. One of them strangely looks like Garibaldi.

The building has a structure of the seventeenth century; on the inside there are big rooms with decorations of the eighteenth century. In some rooms on the ground floor there is the seat of the ISTITUTO STORICO DELLA RESISTENZA.

TEATRO ALIGHIERI - Proceeding, on the right side of the road we find the Alighieri Theatre, whose side delimits a side of piazza Garibaldi.

The façade presents itself with a lobby, that we reach through a staircase, which sustains the superior order by means of lateral walls and four central columns in Istria stone with Ionic capitals. The superior order, with three balconied windows and tympana, presents four allegorical statues inside some niches.

The inside, with four orders of boxes and the gallery, is work of the *Meduna* brothers *Tommaso* and *Gian Battista.* Tommaso is the architect of the reconstruction of the theatre «La Fenice» in Venice.

Started in 1840, it was inaugurated in 1852. Important remakings and restorations were carried out for the reopening of the theatre in 1967.

SAN GIORGIO NEI PORTICI - In front of the theatre there is a little square (via Boccaccio) obtained with the demolishion of casa Bissi. A tablet placed in the wall of the façade of the Cassa di Risparmio (*«Here the ancient church of San Giorgio in Portici rose, that from 1335 to 1768 was in commendam of the "Cavalieri di Malta", closed to cult in the year 1802»*) remembers that in this place a very ancient church existed but we don't know the date of construction, certainly earlier than the 10th century. It is called *«nei portici»* because the portico that moved from the church of Santa Giustina passed there.

PIAZZA GARIBALDI - Here we conclude our itinerary. In the space occupied by the Theatre and by the square once rose houses and mean dwellings around a little square called «degli Svizzeri», because here were the quarters of the papal legate. In the little square the punitive and death sentences were carried out.

On the actual square, in front of the side of the theatre there is the Post Office building, built in 1923, and, the side of the Prefecture. The other two sides are occupied by the building of the Cassa di Risparmio, built in 1895 on design of *Arturo Gabici*, and by the side of the building of the Banca Nazionale del Lavoro. In the square the monument dedicated to Giuseppe Garibaldi is placed, inaugurated in 1892, work of the Ravennate *Giulio Franchi.* The statue first placed in piazza San Francesco, was transferred here in occasion of the restoration works of the Dantesque zone.

The bas-reliefs of the base represent, in front, Garibaldi and Anita that run away from the Austrians, on the left the battle of Rome; on the back, Ricciotti that hands to father Garibaldi the flag taken away from the Prussian regiment; on the right, the battle of Saint Anthony.

On the wall of the façade of the Post Office building there is a tablet placed in 1952 in memory of Don Giovanni Minzoni, born in Ravenna in 1885, killed by the fascists in 1923, and a tablet that carries the names of the Ravennati patriots died on gallows, in the prisons, in exile, or fallen while fighting.

On the side of the Banca Nazionale del Lavoro there is a tablet in memory of the mine searchers of Romagna; and a sun-dial of 1880.

ITINERARY OF ROCCA BRANCALEONE AND OF THE MAUSOLEUM OF THEODORIC

Piazza del Popolo - Chiesa del Suffragio - Via XIII Giugno - Municipal Tower - Via Paolo Costa - Palazzo Spreti - **Baptistery of the Arians** - Church of the Spirito Santo - Via di Roma - San Giovanni Battista - Porta Serrata - Via Venezia - **Rocca Brancaleone - Mausoleum of Theodoric** - Darsena of the city - Viale Santi Baldini - Via Diaz.

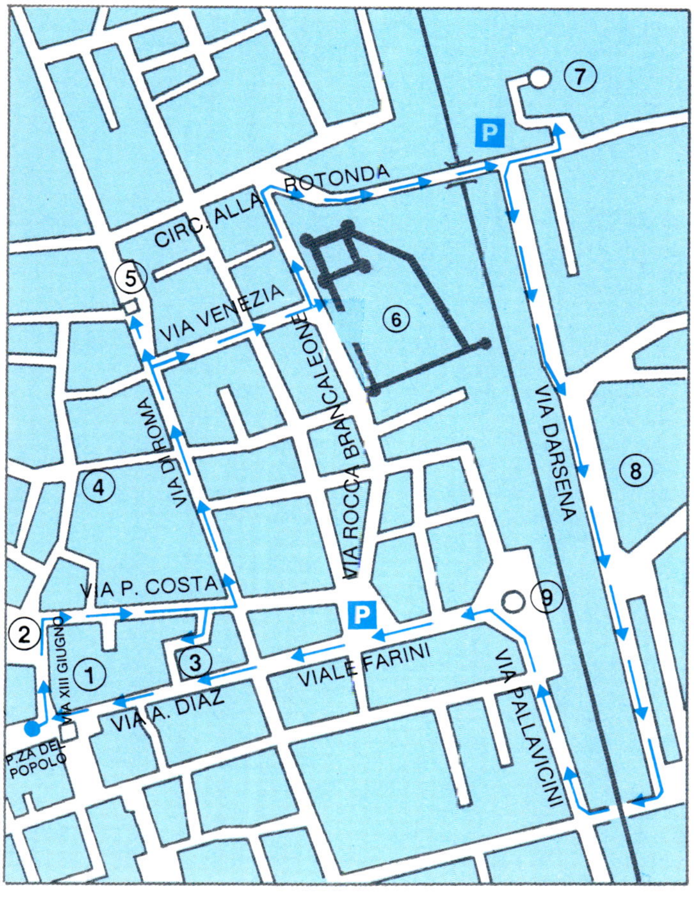

Fig. 34 - **ITINERARY OF ROCCA BRANCALEONE AND OF THE MAUSOLEUM OF THEODORIC.** 1, Church of the suffragio. 2, Civic tower. 3, Baptistery of the Arians - Church of the Spirito Santo. 4, San Giovanni Battista. 5, Porta Serrata. 6, Rocca Brancaleone. 7, Mausoleum of Theodoric. 8, City dock. 9, Railway station.

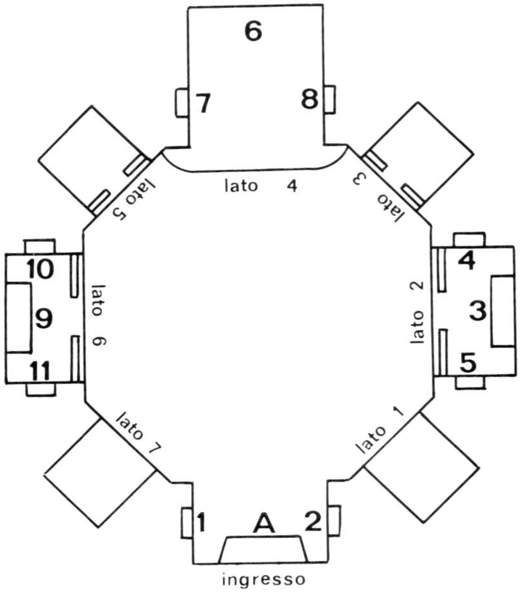

Fig. 35 - **Chiesa del Suffragio: plan.** A, «Bussolone» designed by Domenico Barbiani in 1757. 1, Statue of Faith (stucco). 2, Charity (stucco). 3, San Vitale and Angels (marble). 4, San Filippo Neri (stucco). 5, San Vitale (stucco). 6, «The Nativity of the Virgin» of Andrea Barbiani. 7, Justice (stucco). 8, Peace (stucco). 9, Pity (marble). 10, San Gregorio Magno (stucco). 11, Sant'Apollinare (stucco). The stuccos are of Antonio Martinetti, the marbles of Giovanni Toschini.

Let's leave piazza del Popolo from the north-east corner, in via XIII Giugno, where we find immediately the Chiesa del Suffragio.

CHIESA DEL SUFFRAGIO - Started in 1701, blessed in 1711, consecrated in 1728, it was commissioned by the Company or Brotherhood of the Beata Vergine dei Suffragi, which rose in Ravenna in 1635.

It is the work of *Francesco Fontana*, son of the famous Carlo Fontana, one of the inspirers of the eighteenth century architecture in Rome. Of Baroque expression and implant, it testifies to the introduction that was taking place during the first years of the eighteenth century, of a more collectedness in the often redundant style.

The façade is all in Istria Stone. The portals open in it above which a narrower body rises, connected to the inferior part by means of two volutes. On the sides of the superior part there are two statues representing «*Justice*» and «*Peace*»; in the middle, a bas-relief in which we see the souls of Purgatory and an Angel who frees one of them and comes out of the flames. Statue and bas-relief are work of *Giovanni* and *Celio Toschini* from Ravenna. The little bell-tower is of 1783. Behind the façade the octagonal form of the tambour of the dome is revealed.

The church has a central octagonal plan. A chapel corresponds to every side of the octagon; because the octagon isn't regular but it has four short sides that alternate with long ones, the chapels are alternately big and small and are divided by pylons and pieces of walls that sustain the trabeation, the tambour and the dome with eight ribs. Light enters through the rectangular windows, semiovoidal, ovoidal.

To have a good knowledge of the inside, follow plan figure 35. We enter through a «bussolone» designed by *Domenico Barbiani* in 1757.

Right after the entrance on the right and on the left, inside niches, there are two of the eight stucco statues present in the church, work of *Antonio Martinetti*. The two now considered represent «Faith» (1) and «Charity» (2).

On side 2, one of the four high altars, behind a balustrade made of gypsum, is provided of precious marbles, like the others. The sculptural part above the altar representing San Vitale and angels over a layer of clouds (3), is a work of the beginning of the 18th century of *Giovanni Toschini*. The two stucco statues in the lateral niches represent San Filippo Neri (4) and San Vitale (5). The gypsum balustrade is in front of the other high altars that, as this one, were built in 1764-66.

On side 3 there is a little chapel of the Crucifix: on the little dome and on the zone underneath we find the beautiful and delicate stuccos of *Martinetti* of neo-classical type; they represent adolescent angels that carry instruments of Passion, angels with the instruments of the Crucifixion, and two stories of Christ.

On side 4 we find the high altar behind which there is a good painting of *Andrea Barbiani* representing the Nativity of the Virgin (6). On the peaks of the dome four prophets figure: David, Salomon, Daniel, Isiah. In the centre there is also a medallion with the motif of the souls of Purgatory. In the niches at the entrance to the presbytery there are two statues of *Martinetti* which represent, looking from the left, Justice (7), and on the right Peace (8).

The choir with wooden stalls had already been in San Giovanni Evangelista.

On side 6, above the altar there is a marble group of Pity (9), it also, as the one of the altar in front, is a work of *Toschini*. The two sculptures were in San Vitale and were brought here before World War I. The two stucco statues in the niches, always by *Martinetti* represent San Gregorio Magno (10) and Sant'Apollinare (11) with a putto holding buildings of the city.

In 1789 the checked floor in red and yellow marble was done.

Going out from the church let's continue along via XIII Giugno on the right. The road is named in remembrance of the date that marks the end of the pontiff reign on the city (13th June 1858).

In front of the Chiesa del Suffragio we see **palazzo Rasponi del Sale**, now seat of the Credito Romagnolo, built round about 1770.

Further on we find a well proportioned building (**palazzo Pompili** now Ferruzzi), with elegant portal and strong gratings. On the portal we notice a marble head above which there is a Latin inscription which translated means: «*The land to live on can lack, but not the land to die on*». As crowning, the bearings of the Pompili. It is a construction of the sixteenth-seventeenth century.

Right after the church del Suffragio there is a long building (**casa Monaldini**), now seat of ENEL, with twelve grated windows, on top of the third one the inscription «IHS». In the restoration traces of an arch have been left, the only remainder of the house built in the 13th or 14th century. The house was nearly completely redone in 1783. The entrance door, at n. 3, is surmounted by a little balcony.

MUNICIPAL TOWER - It is at the end of the road on the left. It is one of the towers that rose during the Medieval epoch in Ravenna; it is 39 meters high. It was erected maybe in the 12th century, called «dei beccai» or «dei macellai» (of the butchers) later «dei Guiccioli», from 1326 it was the Municipal Tower and it was used as an observation spot on the town and its neighbourhoods. On top of it the guardians used to call with loud voice the guards that were on the alert on other towers or at the gates of the town, so as to incite them to a careful service or to signal a fire breakout. Because of a sinking of the ground, the tower has an inclination of more than two meters towards West.

At the base, two worn-out bas-reliefs, a man on horseback (3rd century A.D.), the other, behind the first, a head (Roman Age), are seen as the starting point of an ancient saying: «*To look for Mariola in Ravenna*» (Zarchê Mariöla par Ravena), that covers the meaning of «Looking for and not finding something that is near», i.e. «To be stunned, foolish». The man on horseback, in fact, looks for a woman (Maria, Mariola) who is behind him, and since he doesn't turn around he doesn't find her. There are other interpretations of this proverb, among which the hint in *Don Chisciotte* of Cervantes is quite surprising (part II, chapter X).

Near the tower there is a house built during the Venetian dominium (**casa Melandri**), and of which the arches are original, while the pillars were remade in 1905.

In via Girolamo Rossi, at the height of n. 8, there is the **Piccinini Tower**, incorporated in palazzo Spreti. At first it belonged to the Piccinini family (15th century) and then to the Ruggini family, and in 1730 to the Spreti family, of which, under the balcony with curved railing, we can see the coat-of-arms.

After brief deviation in via Rossi, let's return on our steps and set off along via Paolo Costa, admiring immediately on the left at n. 2, the big Spreti palace.

PALAZZO SPRETI - It is a work, as the chiesa del Suffragio of *Francesco Fontana*. It was inaugurated in 1711, and it is the seat of a political party. Also the balcony makes part of the big marble portal that stands on the sides, onto two shelves the motif of which is repeated on the railings of the ground floor windows. The windows on the sides of the portal have strong gratings with curved wall hooks. From the big lobby, with an imponent staircase on the right, we reach a yard in which there is an elegant loggetta (**Loggia degli Spreti**), with columns and capitals of the 15th century. One of the capitals is of the 5th-6th century, it is Corinthian.

In April 1814 Pope Pio VII, whilst returning from the Fontainebleau prisony in which he was sent from Napoleon, was guest of the Marquis Camillo Spreti in this building for three days.

CASA MAIOLI - A little further on, at n. 8, there is a little Venetian building (15th century) made up from the union of two houses, with one entrance only: remarkable is the elegant chimney of octagonal section which rises from an upside-down ashlar cone; beautiful the mullioned-windows on the last floor.

BAPTISTERY OF THE ARIANS

Let's continue along via Costa until we reach «vicolo degli Ariani», on the right, in front of n. 44, in which we shall turn so as to visit two important testimonies of the Gothic domination period: the basilica and the baptistery of Arian cult that Theodoric built for his people.

Historical hints - If we consider that Theodoric was the last most powerful assertor of that heresy, we can admit that in this place the last Arian affirmation was celebrated.

The Arian religion gets its name from its supporter, Arius. He sustained the thesis that

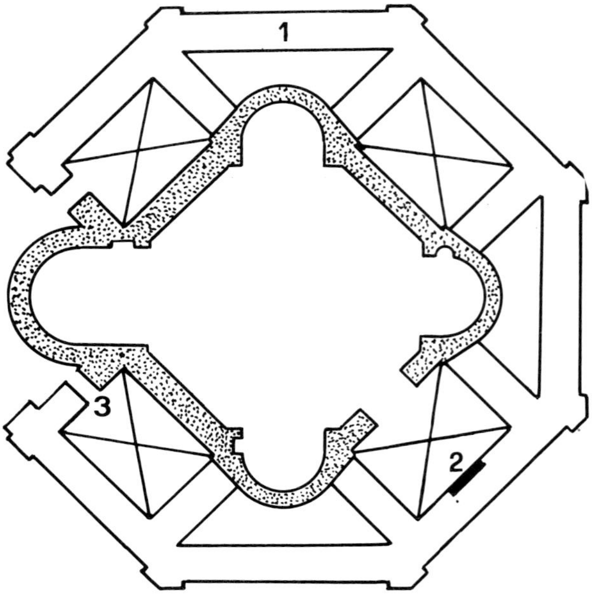

Fig. 36 - **Battistero degli Ariani: plan with the foundations of the annular ambulatory.** 1, Perimeter of the annular ambulatory. 2, Remainder of the annular ambulatory. 3, Remainder of the ambulatory arch (The dotted part indicates the base of the building as it is seen today).

Christ, having been generated, isn't eternal as his Father, therefore his nature can't be the same as his Father's. The thesis invalidates the dogma of the Holy Trinity, which is founded on the identity of the Father, of the Son and of the Holy Spirit, and denies Christ's divinity. The Arian heresy was condemned in 325 by the council of Nicea but at Constantine's death, having gone on the throne Constantius, it became the official religion of the East and it was imposed also to the West. In the 4th century the Arian religion was very popular among the Visigoths who transmitted it to the Ostrogoths, and this popularity is due also to the fact that the Arian is more permissive than the Catholic one. The heresy reached Italy and it got stronger when Theodoric in 493 conquered Ravenna.

History tells us how at first the problems of the Ostrogoths and Latins were resolved, and how later the contrasts became always worse. On one side, infact, in 523, the Eastern emperor Justin emits a decree against the Arian religion and on the other, Theodoric replies by imprisoning pope Giovanni who dies in prison. After these facts a very bitter war followed (535-553) which ended with the Byzantine success, who occupied Ravenna in 540. The Catholics, then, dispersed many vestiges of the heretic cult reconsecrating the Arian churches.

In the place where we are now the Goths reproduced cult buildings that the Catholics had erected in other parts of the city nearly a century before (basilica Ursiana, Baptistery, buildings of the bishopric). And between the end of the 5th century, and the beginning of the 6th - i.e. during the first years of their dominium - they built their basilica, their baptistery, their episcopal palace.

After the Byzantine conquest the baptistery was naturally consecrated to the Catholic cult (maybe in 559) as oratory dedicated to the Virgin Mary. Since the 8th century it was called Santa Maria in Cosmedin, from the Greek word «beauty», «ornament», maybe because the monks of a very near cenoby had enrichened it with decorations. In the 11th century the baptistery was entrusted to the Benedictines, who from the 14th century also held the near church of Santo Spirito. Round about the middle of the following century the Benedictines abandoned the place and the two buildings were entrusted to laymen.

In 1608 the jurisdiction passed to the Teatini and about forty years later an oratory, called Santa Croce was built, towards the South, of which the baptistery became the apse; in 1797 the two buildings were separated, and their junction point is marked from the arch of which there is trace in the Western apse. In that period, then, the religious orders were suppressed and therefore also the one of the Teatini, and this event brought the temple to complicated cases of property passages until the last owners, the Lovatelli - Dal Corno and Fabri families, in 1914 sold it to the Italian state. The oratory was demolished only in 1953 but still today it isn't possible to go around the whole external perimeter of the baptistery. War in the meanwhile, had provided to a last insult: the demolishion of the wall which joined the basilica to the baptistery.

This wall, of which still a good piece remains, is called **casa di Drogdone**, because the ancient building that rose on the South and South East of the church «dello Santo Spirito» (of the Holy Spirit), seems to have been used as home of Droctulf or Drogdone, a Longobard Duke who had passed on the side of the Byzantines at the end of the 6th century. But the «singular

Fig. 37 - **Baptistery of the Arians; Scheme of the mosaic vault.** 1, The Redeemer. 2, The pidgeon coming down from the sky. 3, Saint John the Baptist. 4, The Jordan or Moses. 5, Vase from which the water of the river flows out. 6, The Apostle Peter. 7, The Apostle Paul.

lifting up with tympana, decorated with crosses and marble paterae, dates back at least to the 11th century» (C. Ricci).

In 1969 excavations inside the baptistery emptying it completely were carried out. At 2,31 meters of depth a floor level was found, that must have been made of slabs of Greek marble, under which there were several tombs; on the walls traces of an ancient decoration were found and on the Southern and Western apse two little stone altars were brought back to light. Also traces of a bassin were found. The actual floor, in Furlo stone, was placed in 1977.

Architectural characteristics (fig. 36) - After the many hardships of which we spoke about, we can today see a little building with an octagonal plan with apses or big niches on four sides. A frame subdivides the construction into two parts: on the superior one there are eight windows with round arches; above, under the roof, there is a crowning with saw-like teeth. On the inferior part we notice traces of arches which document the ancient existence of an annular ambulatory (1) covered by a vault that interrupted on the Eastern side, corresponding to the bigger apse. The building that we see today, therefore is only the central part of the original one, which appeared certainly more articulated and moved. The excavation carried out around the baptistery, that we have to walk down from so as to enter, has put in evidence the remainder of the perimetral corridor; we can see it in front of the door (2), and it results to have been at least 1,90 metres wide on the sides without apses, while the passage tightened itself to a meter in correspondance of the apses.

To imagine in a better way the disappeared ambulatory let's take a few steps in the trench that goes around the temple; the signs of arches that go towards the outside can help us to imagine and add what's missing.

Decoration of the inside: central medallion - In the inside only the decoration of the dome is preserved. Anciently also the walls were full of mosaics and were decorated with marbles and stuccos.

The decorative scheme of the mosaic of the vault (fig. 37) appears as a reduction of the one adopted by the mosaic-worker of the vault of the Neonian baptistery one century older; it is made up, i.e. of a central medallion delimited by a frieze and by a large spheric zone.

On the central medallion the baptism of Christ is represented: typical scene of the baptisteries. Here we see a haloed Redeemer (1) very young immersed in the transparent waters of the Jordan, while a white pidgeon (2) coming down from the sky sprinkles him with an emanation of water (that represents the Holy Spirit) and the Baptist (3) on his left hand side puts a hand onto his head.

The Baptist has a curved stick in his hand symbol of the desert.

On the left of who looks there is the noble figure of an old man sitting down, naked till the waist, who symbolizes either the Jordan or Moses, who prefigures Christ (4). On the right side an overturned vase (5) (symbol of the river's source) from which much water flows out; in the left hand he carries a green swamp reed (symbol of the swampy place) and on his head there are two big crab chelae (symbol of water elements): all attributes of the fluvial divinities. The anthropomorphic representation of the river isn't made in a semi-lying position of the purest classical tradition, however, it is a direct derivation of it; the modification, anyhow,

Baptistery of the Arians: central part of the mosaic-worked vault.

maybe was influenced by the composition module adopted by the mosaic-worker, who needed a figure to be placed symmetrically with the one of John the Baptist so as to place Christ in the middle of the scene.

Both the old man sitting down, and the Baptist, from a composition point of view insert themselves well in the circumference and the whole scene results very well balanced and certainly built in a better way than the parallel one of the Neonian baptistery. Notice, however, that while the sitting water divinity appears in a natural and relaxed attitude, the Baptist, exactly for composition reasons, having to be standing and at the same time having to follow the round shape of the available field, appears in a very forced attitude and has no grace. If we add that Christ is rather awkward and with an expression that makes him seem rather absent, we can say that of the three figures, the best is the old man sitting down, not only for the design, but also for the soft chiaroscuro with which the volumes of the powerful chest are rendered.

The background of the scene, on top of the waters, is of uniform gold: the only landscape notes are given, therefore, by the hard steep bank of the Jordan onto which the Baptist stands and by the waters of the river, whose transparency is rendered with remarkable efficacy.

Decoration of the inside: spheric zone - The wide spheric zone that surrounds the central medallion is occupied by a procession of Apostles who, from opposite directions, advance slowly, nearly as if they were rythmizing their pace, towards a cross on a throne. The throne is decorated sumptuously. In front of the big purple cushion with golden stripes, there is the big gemmed cross with a purple draping on the limbs. It is the «*etimasia*» (preparation of the throne), a Christian iconographic motif of oriental origin, consisting of a throne surmounted by a cross or by a book, and meaning the invisible presence of Christ in the places of lithurgic meetings. At the feet of the throne there are two flowered bushes.

The whole mosaic presents stylistic varieties rather remarkable, to such an extent that some experts recognize work of at least five different mosaic workers that must have worked at successive times.

The two formations of the Apostles are led by Peter (6), on the right side of the throne, and by Paul (7) on the left. The former carries the keys, and the latter a roll, that indicates the Bible. The remaining Apostles carry a crown on the hands veiled by the pallium. In this mosaic, for the first time in Ravenna, the Apostles have their head surrounded by a halo. Peter and Paul are well characterized in their faces while the others dressed as ancient Romans, with tunic, sandals and cloak (or pallium), are nearly the same among one another, as the movements, gestures, and the foldings of the garments; this gives the whole thing nearly a dance rhythm.

All of them have some letters on the cloaks, which appear in other mosaics of Ravenna and also in mosaics of Milan, Rome, Naples etc... These letters are called «*gammadiae*», probably because the Greek sign Γ (gamma) appears frequently and so for extension all the other signs that aren't letters were called in the same way, as the orbicula, the crosses, the little squares etc... Every sign expresses one or more meanings or concepts, clear to the contemporaries but, of difficult comprehension to us, who must rebuild the reading key. Elabo-

Baptistery of the Arians: the throne flanked by the princes of the apostles.

rate attempts of interpretation look for meanings in various ways, such as the collocation of the letters (Z, initial of the Greek world «life», means «life»; H, the second letter of ΙΗΣΟΥΣ recalls Christ; Γ indicates the angular stone; N has many meanings, among which the Pentecost, or the correspondence between letters and numbers (the number of Γ is 3, and of N is 50, of H is 8...), that also carry meanings and concepts.

Between one Apostle and the other a stylized palm rises.

The nakedness and roughness of the brick on the remaining building, in clear contrast with the sumptuousness of the mosaic, creates a particular suggestive atmosphere. Maybe in this little architectural space, more than in that of other ancient monuments of Ravenna, we clearly feel the sensation of being immersed in years lost in a past age, therefore the return to the present and to its crude light, on going out, is lived for an instant as a sudden return.

CHIESA DELLO SPIRITO SANTO (CHURCH OF THE HOLY SPIRIT) - It was the church of the Arian bishops, the «*Ecclesia Matrix*» of the Goths, dedicated to «*Aghia Anastasis*»: the sacred Resurrection of the Lord. It was also called «*Anastasis Gothorum*», the Resurrection of the Goths.

As all the religious Arian constructions, also this one was reconsecrated to the Catholic cult by archbishop Agnello (557-570) after the return of the Byzantines, and it was dedicated to the soldier and martyr San Teodoro.

The aspect of the church today isn't very different from the original one. As in all the churches of Ravenna, the floor, the columns, the doors have been raised (here, in the 16th century), but the installation and the structure aren't different.

The façade is dominated by the portico of the sixteenth century, made up of five big arches in the front and by an arch on the Northern short side. The arches are sustained by eight columns in Istria stone and in Greek marble, three of which podded in the inferior part and fluted as a spiral in the superior one. Some columns present the print of a cross and must have made part of a ciborium of the church. The portico leaves the superior half of the hut-like façade free, in which a little window opens; it hides instead, an original ancient three-mullioned window.

Under the portico there are four doors, three give entrance to the church and one on the Southern short side.

On the architraves we find some Latin inscriptions that we refer here: on the left door «IMPLEMINI (s) PV SANCTO» (Fill yourself with the Holy Spirit); on the central portal «NOLITE CONTRISTARE SPIRITUM SANCTUM (Don't sadden the Holy Spirit); on the right door «SPVMS NOLITE EXTINGUERE» (Don't extinguish the Holy Spirit); on the portal of the Southern side of the portico, finally «INGREDIENTS EXEUNTES Q CUSTODI DNE DEUS (God Almighty, take care of who enters and of who goes out). The marble jambs are of the sixteenth century. Originally the church had no narthex and no quadriportico.

On the external sides there are arches following one another in which the windows open, that, in the second order, are walled. The low part of the Northern wall was redone after the last war, during which the bombings destroyed the chapels, which weren't original opened in the left nave and that haven't been redone. They had been added during the 16th and 17th century.

The church measures 26 meters of lenght and 17 of width, and the relation between these measures is rather reduced, if we can compare it with those of the other basilicas of Ravenna. It has three naves divided by fourteen columns surmounted by capitals and pulvinoes, not coming from the oriental workshops but from the work of local workers; the capitals are of Corinthian order, composed of two rows of acanthus leaves above which the volutes sustained by the corner leaves emerge. The abacus is decorated by a flower and by a little cross on each side. The side of the pulvino that looks onto the central nave carries a cross among acanthus leaves.

In the Northern nave (of the left), seven windows open; in the Southern one only six, because at half way there was a door, of which the traces still remain, which led to the episcopal buildings. Traces of ancient doors can be noticed also in the inside of the façade. The original floor is at 1.80 meters of depth, therefore the internal space had major slimness. On the walls of the central nave we can see the traces of the original six windows on each side. The ceiling is made up of lacunars.

The **ambo**, in istrian stone, is of the 6th century, and it is decorated on both faces: on every face there are laterally two crosses on a globe, while in the curved central part, there are fluted little columns which form three aediculae provided of shell and tympanum. Under the shells there is a cantharus (handled vase) with vine shoots, grapes and acanthus leaves; under the tympanum there are vegetal ornamental motifs. It is sustained by a pillar with inlaid marbles of 14th century.

Near the end of the right nave the sepulchral tablet of Cardinal Enrico Enriquez is placed, born in 1701 and died in 1756, he was the restorator of the Republic of San Marino. He was protagonist in the episode that had led the cardinal Giulio Alberoni to invade and pillage the little Republic until its submission was obtained, practically annexing it to the territories of the church and abolishing in this way the Republican liberties. Enriquez, sent by the pope, understood which abuse of power had been committed and, after having informed the Pontiff and having carried out faithfully his will, on the 5th February 1740; he gave the Republic back to the inhabitants of San Marino. After Enriquez was nuncio of the court of Madrid.

At the bottom of the nave there is a chapel anterior to the seventeenth century, where it is placed, above an altar provided of good marbles, a big painting of the Forlivese *Livio Agresti* (before 1550-1580). In it a cross stands and at its feet it collects the «colombini» bishops so called because according to the legend, they were elected by the Holy Spirit in the form of a pidgeon, represented above the cross. The legend narrates that the election used to take place in this church, and it was for this reason that the denomination of church of San Teodoro changed into church of The Holy Spirit (Chiesa dello Spirito Santo). The election by means of the pidgeon's flight and of its laying down lasted for 210 years and for 11 bishops starting from Sant'Aderito, immediate successor of Sant'Apollinare, to end with San Severo. It is just the case to notice that the church at that time hadn't been built yet.

The apse, poligonal outside, has three original windows.

The high altar is bordered by two baroque angels sculptured by *Giovanni Toschini*. The chapel at the bottom of the left nave, is also anterior to the seventeenth century, and it is provided of an altar, decorated and painted in the dome.

At the beginning of the left nave there is an ancient Greek marble sarcophagus that in the 15th century was decorated for a cardinal and it became in the following century, sepulchre of the Pasolini family.

Let's return in via Paolo Costa and let's reach via di Roma by turning left. In this part of the road, that crosses all the city within the walls, little houses, houses, palaces and buildings of different epochs and of scarce importance alternate. The house at n. 202 is of the seventeenth century. Let's return into the first street on the left (via Pietro Alighieri) and after about a hundred meters we reach the church of San Giovanni Battista (St. John the Baptist).

CHURCH OF SAN GIOVANNI BATTISTA - A very ancient church, anterior to the 9th century, it was demolished and remade as we see it today in 1683 by the architect Pietro Grossi. In ancient times the Padenna river flowed in front of it, and because of the ferry that was in front it was called «San Giovanni ad naviculam». Recently it was called «delle catene», because of the chains of iron stretched out between the stone poles that closed the square, and «della cipolla» (of the onion), from the vegetable that appeared plentiful in a fair of June. It is preceeded by a square, closed by a gate in 1929 obtained by the demolition of the portico (1634) that rose before the church.

On the façade three doors of Istria stone open. The central one has two cherubs on the sides, and a baptismal lamb in the middle medallion under which there is the inscription: NON SUREXIT MAIOR (No one major than him was born). In the big window there are two columns separated by a frame with saw-like teeth. Above the windows there are mullioned and three-mullioned windows, and in that zone the bell-tower was rebuilt in a period not preceeding the 14th century.

Church of the Holy Spirit: Giovanni Toschini, «Angel».

The vast inside, with three naves divided by pillars and sixteen columns of Greek, cipolin, verd antique, pavonazzetto recovered from the ancient church, is of Baroque style. The church is especially rich of precious marbles and it is provided of some good paintings. Let's start our visit from the right side: Holy water stoup made of peacock eyed marble.

1st Altar: painting of *Gian Battista Barbiani* which represents «Sant'Antonio Abate freed from temptation by intercession of Mary».

2nd Altar: «The martyrs Saints Crispino and Crispiniano with Madonna and Infant» by *Domenico Cignani*.

Between the columns, pensile wooden pulpit.

3rd Altar: stucco-works by *Martinetti*, and a fresco of the 14th century representing the Madonna with the Infant.

4th Altar (in the transept): four very beautiful columns of ancient green. On the front of the altar there are 11 rectangular panels of various lenght, eight of which are in marble, where jasper, agate, onyx, cornelian, lapis-lazuli etc. have been used. Vases, flowers, butterflies, birds, candlesticks, images of Saints are represented. On the side the coats-of-arms of the Gamba family. On the lateral walls of the transept the Angel of Death appears unfolding the commemorative epigraphs of Giovanni and Giacomo Gamba.

5th Altar (chapel on the right of the presbytery): altar of the cross, above which there is the lumber-room which contained the relics of St. Quirico and St. Giulitta, once contained in the little eucaristic box now in the archbishop museum.

6th Altar (High Altar): it is provided of inlaid marbles with geometrical motifs. The marble work, always with geometrical motifs extends till the walls, separating the presbytery from the choir, that can be reached through two rooms overhung by a split curved tympanum.

Sacristy: it contains a very ruined painting by *Carlo Maratta* (1625-1713) representing St. John who preaches to the crowds.

7th Altar (chapel on the left of the presbytery): big crucifix.

8th Altar (left side of the transept): it contains a painting by *Francesco Longhi* «Madonna with the Infant and St. Clement and St. Girolamo».

10th Altar: between two columns of pavonazzetto there is the painting by *Francesco Ferrari*:

Serrata Gate.

«St. Teresa d'Avila, St. Carlo Borromeo, St. Maria Maddalena de' Pazzi».

11th Altar: *Francesco Longhi*: «Madonna with the Infant and St. Matthew and St. Francis, it was painted in 1586.

At the beginning of the left nave there is a painting of G.B. Barbiani: «Madonna del Carmelo and the Carmelite Saints Simone and Andrea Corsini».

The holy water spout is in Veronese red.

The **dome** is decorated by *Francesco Ferrari* (and by a «companion» of his, maybe his son), born near Rovigo, of Ferrarese school. They are very beautiful and live paintings, of a rich and full Baroque, that narrated the story of the Carmelitan order through some pre-eminent personages and significant episodes. Above a painted balustrade overhung by many decorative elements are represented in the four partitions: Elias on a fire wagon who drops the cloak on the prophet Elyseus; the Blessed Virgin del Carmelo who hands the scapular to Saint Simon Stock; Saint Simon who dresses with the Carmelite dress the Blessed Giovanna da Tolosa; a Saint who points out the Carmelo mount to St. Giovannino. On the peaks of the dome the Carmelite Saints Pier Tommaso, Angelo, Alberto, Andrea Corsini are represented.

The church housed the relics of Sant'Ursicino, which were transferred here from the original burial, and then to the Duomo round about 972. In 1408 the Carmelite fathers settled in the church.

Let's return to via di Roma running along it towards the left.

PORTA SERRATA - At the end of via di Roma we find Porta Serrata, called also Porta Anastasia and, later, Porta Cybo, but the people for more than half a millenium call it Porta Serrata therefore this name is now the official one. It derives from an ancient legend, that many think has some truth in it, according to which the Polenta family had the gate walled so as to contrast a prophecy that wanted them to be expelled from the city through this gate.

The Venetians that took the place of the Polentas, kept it closed and the pontiff Giulio II opened it again in 1511. At that time, the gate was placed at about one hundred meters west from the actual one; it was moved when, in 1582, the legate cardinal Ferreri had the Corso — now via di Roma — which curved towards the ancient gate straightened up. The useless gate therefore was demolished. In the same year also the Roman Porta Aurea was demolished, and part of its marbles were used for the new gate, but they were very rehandled.

In 1621, while on the inside of the gate a banquet was taking place, the vault collapsed and twenty people died. In 1650 Cardinal Cybo ordered the restorations and got his name sculptured on the shelf of the external arch, as we can still see.

On the shelf of the arch that looks towards the city, Ravenna's bearings are sculptured with the inscription «**Renovata antiquitas**» («The ancient brought back to new»).

On the jambs of the two arches some of the hinges on which the big doors that closed the access to the city are still fastened.

During and after the last war the gate was isolated, as we can see now, with the demolition of the buildings next to it and that in the past housed on one side the customs buildings, on the other the mortuary.

It must be noticed that while the town walls,

Rocca Brancaleone: air view. Notice the chairs placed for opera summer shows.

having the epoch in which they accomplished a defence function come to an end, suffered a very quick degradation or were demolished here and there, the doors continued to be kept in good condition, because they were used as customs' barriers.

ROCCA BRANCALEONE

Let's return on our steps along via di Roma. Let's enter on the left via Venezia at the bottom of which we can see one of the towers of Rocca Brancaleone.

Construction - When the Venetians obtained the dominium of Ravenna depriving the power of the last of the Polentani family, Ostasio V (1441) they worried about building valid fortifications so as to give back to the inhabitants faith and security in the new government. After having repaired the already existing walls and towers, they also thought of a fortress able of consolidating their control on the city. The place was chosen carefully and with authority by a commission which had been deliberately constituted by the Venetian senate, which also prepared the project equipped with a little model.

In order to finance this exacting enterprise, at first, the profits of the duty on salt were used, by means of various taxes, with corvées and by trying to save money using materials coming from the demolition of ancient buildings. Among others, the ancient church of Sant'Andrea dei Goti and a falling building of the da Polenta paid the expenses of this.

It has been observed to this regard, that often Ravenna renewed itself by devouring itself. Just to give an example, Sant'Andrea dei Goti was built with stones and marbles of the walls of the Roman «*oppidum*» and of the temple of Jupiter; after Sant'Andrea itself was demolished to use its material for the Rocca; the Rocca, as we shall see, was dismantled to build other public buildings.

Also the Venetian government intervened directly in the financing so as to avoid the interruption of the works.

On 25th May 1457 a solemn ceremony took place of the laying of the first stone, and the works, under the direction of the noble Venetians Vitale Lando and Giacomo Cornaro proceeded with much industriousness. Already in 1460, that is only three years later, the first detachment of 25 crossbowmen arrived to guard the fortress not yet finished, but already at a good stage. The works then continued very slowly, and only in 1470 they were finished.

The big fort is divided in two parts (look at map fig. 38): the *Rocca* or *Ridotto* and the citadel.

The **Rocca** is constituted of a wide quadrilateral of 2180 square meters of surface and four imposing circular towers, of 17 meters of diameter, on the corners, joined together by wall screens of about 7 to 8 meters of thickness.

The **Citadel** occupies an area of about 14.000 square meters surrounded by walls, with a fortified wall, two circular towers at the two corners and two semi-circular ones along the wall screen. It was a little village that was made up of the houses of the garrison, the warehouses, the mill, the workshop for the preparation of weapons and other services.

The fort communicated with the outside through two fortified doors: one in the Rocca and one in the citadel.

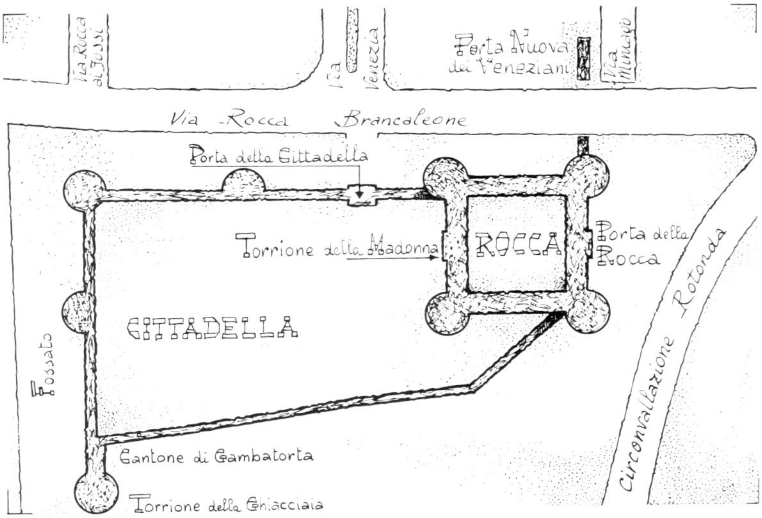

Fig. 38 - Rocca Brancaleone - Map with nomenclature.

The gate or door of the Rocca is placed on the North-Western side and it was called «*aid door*» because it was opened only in case of extreme necessity. The door of the citadel opens on the South-Western side and it opens towards the inside of the city. It is the door through which we enter nowadays, that is in front of the outlet of via Venezia. Rocca and citadel communicate by means of a third fortified door that opens in the squared tower called «della Madonna» placed half-way of the South-Eastern side of the quadrilateral of the Rocca. It was the highest tower of the whole fortress and on it the standard of the Serenissima fluttered.

On the external façade of the tower of the Madonna there is still, well preserved, a big bas-relief with the lion of San Marco and, further up, a bas-relief with some missing parts, of the Madonna (from here the name) and the Infant. The lion of San Marc was carried out between 1458 and 1460 by a valid artist that marked on the work his name: T. MARINUS MARCI CEDRINI VENETUS FECIT. The lion has its back paws in the sea-waves, the right front paw on a book, the left on the ground. The wide mane, the open wings, the long tail well express power and strenght. When Ravenna returned to the Popes (1509), the lion was taken away from its place. It was brought back in 1910, after that, in 1887, it had reappeared in San Pietro in Vincoli, in the Rasponi villa.

The bas-relief with the Madonna and the Infant, mediocre work of an author maybe of Ravenna, has never been moved. The letters I.F. are the initials of the podesta of Ravenna for Venice in 1460-61, Giovanni Falier (Johannes Faledro).

Around the fortress a wide fosse ran, still observable in its great outlines even if it is very buried, that was filled with the waters of the Montone river that flowed nearby. A moat also ran between the Rocca and the Citadel.

To cross the fosse there were drawbridges; still well visible on the three doors are the long vertical clefts inside which the levers and the tie-beams ran.

The doors were closed, from the external part, by the same floor of the lifted bridge and, from the inside part, by strong sluicegates. Every bridge was preceeded by a ravlin, that constituted an advanced defence of the doors.

In the towers and in the walls numerous «*bombardiere*» opened, i.e. a funnel-like cavities that ended with slits from which the cannon mouth of which the fortress was very provided came out. It must be noticed furthermore, even if fire weapons had been invented only since a short while, already a great variety of them existed; an inventory of that epoch infact, for our Rocca names, *bombards, little bombards, muskets, culverins, little muskets, mortars, falcons, arquebuses.* These various weapons threw stone, iron and lead balls.

It seems that the name of the Rocca derives from an ancient Venetian family.

Fact of arms - Rocca Brancaleone was involved in two big facts of arms, the second of which at European level.

The first and less important occurred in 1503 when, having the controversies between the Venetian Republic and the Papacy got bitter, on the 19th May the Duke of Urbino, working for the Pope, attacked Ravenna and its fortress (Rocca) furiously. The Duke had 32 cannons, but didn't manage to conquer the fortress, even if he damaged it rather seriously.

The second fact of arms is the famous battle of Ravenna of April 1512 that saw the French against the Spanish, with their allies. Ravenna, pontiff dominium, was with the Spanish.

After the battle, having entered the city, the French pillaged it, then they turned against the Rocca hitting it with their powerful artillery.

The commader of the garrison, prince Marcantonio Colonna, even if a worthy captain, realized quite quickly that resistance in a fortress patched up as possible after the damages suffered in the battle of 1503 was useless, and so on the 16th April surrendered to the French. The political and military events that followed the great battle of Ravenna, however, brought the Pope to re-obtain possession of the city and of its fortress (Rocca).

In 1527 the Venetians got hold of the fortress again with a surprise attack and kept if for two years, then they handed it back again to the Pontiff who kept it without interruptions until the birth of the Reign of Italy.

In 1588 the fortress suffered its last attack, nearly an outrage, on behalf of more than one thousand outlaws led by a certain Giacomo del Gallo, but even if it was in bad condition and kept by a small garrison and not very valid either, it managed to resist.

Decline - The decline of the fortress started with the attack of the Duke of Urbino in 1503. In that occasion part of the superior structures suffered big damages. When in 1512 the French set off their attack, the fortress hadn't been repaired yet, and not being able to rebut the Ferrarese artillery nor to absorb them, it suffered new and more serious damages.

Some restoration works were carried out around the half of the sixteenth century, but at this time the importance of this kind of fortress, whose straight walls weren't very suitable to hold the impetus of the artilleries, was diminishing. The governments lost interest in their preservation. In such an atmosphere the big fortress was left to deteriorate until, in 1735, since it was useless, it was dismantled in the superior structures by order of Cardinal Alberoni, to whom material for the construction of Ponte Nuovo on the Fiumi Uniti and of the lock of San Marco was necessary. After this fact, the inside of the fortress was used as a kitchen-garden and it was granted to a private citizen in emphytheusis.

From property of the pontiff state the fortress passed to the Italian state, that got rid of it by selling it to private citizens. From these, in recent years it passed in property to the municipality of Ravenna, that with opportune restorations, tried to avoid the total ruin of what was left. This aim was reached both with preservation interventions, and especially, maybe, by assigning this big fortress new functions in the social citizen texture: giving it back; therefore, a reason of life. The Citadel in this way, has been equipped with a children's park and the Rocca or Ridotto has been turned into an open Theatre.

In such a way an ancient terrible instrument of war has become a place of peace manifestations.

To visit the fortress enter freely through the door of the Citadel in via Rocca Brancaleone in front of the outlet of via Venezia. In the area before the gate, where the ancient fosse was, there is a wide parking area where you can leave your car.

Beyond the gate, there is a beautiful park with well paved paths, green lawns, a fountain with the spout coming out from four bombard balls, a little swimming pool, various games, benches, bar.

You can also walk around the ancient walls if you want to see the ancient bombards, but, especially, you can seize the opportunity of taking a few moments of rest and silence in an atmosphere full of ancient suggestive remembrances.

Having left the Rocca, let's turn right into via Rocca Brancaleone. At the end of the wall we find, on the left of the road, the remainders of a door built by the Venetians on the basis of the same project of those still existing of the Rocca and the Citadel. It was called Porta Nuova, and it was closed maybe when Pope Giulio II had Porta Serrata opened, in 1511.

Let's go towards the Mausoleum of Theodoric, that is about 600 meters far. At the end of via Rocca Brancaleone turn right into via Circonvallazione Rotonda and cross the fly-over the railway-road beyond which we see, at about 150 meters on the left, the dome of the Mausoleum rising from a row of cypresses.

MAUSOLEUM OF THEODORIC

Theodoric: historial hints - Theodoric, son of Theodemir king of the Ostrogoths, was born round about the year 454. At that time his people was settled in the Balcans on the right of the Danube as federate of the Oriental empire, with the obligation of controlling the border. The young prince remained for a decade at the court of Constantinople, until the eighteenth year of age, receiving a political education; however even if he admired the Byzantine culture, he didn't assimilate much of it and remained basically an Ostrogoth.

Having returned to his mother-land at the death of his father he was acclaimed leader of the Ostrogoths (474) and started a politics rather ambiguous as regards to Constantinople: sometimes friend and defender, sometimes devastator of imperial lands. For example, in 486 he defeated two high dignitaries of court who had rebelled against the emperor Zeno, who granted him the honour of triumph and an equestrian statue. But a year later he was marching on Constantinople pillaging Thracia. We can say that Theodoric in those years impersonates the hardship of the Germanic people who, dissatisfied of their appropriations, were in a state of continuous turmoil trying to find more favourable settlements, but they are generally unable to take linear and precise decisions.

Meanwhile in Italy Odoacer was governing, who had placed to an end the Western Empire deposing Romulus Augustulus (476). Odoacer was hated by the Oriental Court, that incited the restless Theodoric to occupy Italy.

This is how, at the end of summer 488, the great adventure of the Goths started with about 300,000 people (men, women and children), including also contingents of other Germanic people, they marched towards the heart of the prestigious fallen Empire.

In 489 Theodoric defeated Odoacer first on the Isonzo, then in Verona and arrived in Pavia. Along with the Visigoths he defeated him again on the Adda and compelled him in Ravenna, which he besieged for three years. Odoacer finally surrendered on the terms that he would be associated to the government of Italy, but a few days later he was murdered during a banquet to which he had been invited from Theodoric himself (March 493). In this way, the Gothic king became the owner of Italy, even if, for right, he was only a military commander under the service of the Eastern Emperor.

Theodoric's reign lasted for 33 years and it marked a period of peace and prosperity. The fundamental problem was to make the Roman population of more elevated civilization cohabit peacefully with the Germanic one less numerous and rougher but in possession of the power and pride due to victory.

The king tried to resolve the difficult situation keeping the Roman laws and customs separate from Gothic customs and laws; therefore he was very tolerant on the religious point of view, by building for himself and for his people new places for the Arian cult and leaving the Catholic cult undisturbed. The Roman population, then continued to dominate the economical, administrative, civil and cultural life and Theodoric availed himself always of consistant local collaborations to lead his wise government. The Ostrogoths, to come to the point, were like a population encamped among another, that worked and produced also for them and to whom they provided order and security. An example of the desire of Theodoric to establish good relations with the local people is given by the distribution of land to his people, that took place in agreement with the Romans.

Then he accomplished great public works in Ravenna and Rome, he also provided, when necessary, to large distribution of food; to come to the point, he wanted to give an image of himself as a splendid and liberal leader. He favoured art and culture cultivating the friendship of cultured Romans such as Ennodius bishop of Pavia, Simmachus, Severino Boezio, Magno Aurelio Cassiodoro; economy and agriculture were prospering. This new social situation, characterized by security and political stability, brought to a widespread affluence and to a remarkable demographic development.

In foreign politics the king of the Ostrogoths didn't worry about breaking the formal binding with the far Constantinople, but rather to enter in alliance with the near Germanic populations, getting into family relations with their leaders by means of numerous marriages, and even with wars and contrasts, which always ended favourably for him by means of lucky battles and sly agreements. At a certain moment the reign of the Goths was the strongest European power and in the first decennium of the 6th century extended its influence from the Danube to Spain.

This admirable political work, however, tottered quite soon. Composed, even with the good works of Theodoric, the brief schism between the church of Rome and the one of the East (484-519), the Latins returned favourable to Constantinople which still expressed the continuity of the Empire; to this it must be added that the emperor Justin before and Justinian then, didn't hide the intention of rebuilding the unity of the Empire, therefore Theodoric became very suspicious in regards of the loyalty of the Latins. This new mood brought him to tyrannical and repressive excesses (he condemns to death Albino, Simmaco and Boezio).

Things became worse when Justin emanated an edict which forbade heretical cults and that, as consequence, involved the Arians; Theodoric, therefore, sent forcedly pope Giovanni I (523-26) to Constantinople so that this measure would be revoked, and since the mission failed, he imprisoned the unfortunate messenger who after a few days died (May 526). Theodoric followed him in the tomb the 30th August of the same year. His fame was for a long time of an ungodly man and persecutor, but the valuation has been recently looked over and changed in the one of a wise politician who even among tragic errors and ambiguities, in the framework of times extremely hard and ferocious, gave his people and Italy a not short period of rare security.

The king wanted to rest among his people that had followed him in Italy for his fantastic

Mausoleum of Theodoric.

adventure; the place where the Mausoleum is, in fact called anciently Campo Coriandro, acted as burial ground of the Goths. The construction was carried out a little before 526.

Architectural characteristics - The Mausoleum is made of big blocks of Istria stone well squared and joined together by means of cramps and irons shaped like double swallow tails placed inside.

The structure has a central plan with two orders one on top of the other: the inferior decagonal one, wider; the superior one is narrower, decagonal below and circular on top.

The building is closed, covered and crowned by a prodigious architectural element that we have mentioned: a unique big circular stone of 10.76 meters diameter, with one meter of width and 250-300 tons of weight. The stone carries on the top a reliefed disc of about ten centimeters and of 3.75 meters of diameter, in the middle of which there is a dice. Along the circumference: twelve handles or modillions on which the names of the four Evangelists and of eight Apostles are engraved. On the top since the forteenth century there is cross, but in the stone there are traces which demonstrate that a different element from a cross had been fixed on it. It is the biggest monolith ever used for a dome.

Inferior floor - In the massive construction of ten sides, ten deep niches open, one for each side, which end in a round arch formed by a radial of eleven quoin blocks, bisegmented. that fit together by means of a toothing. A cornice at the base of the arches goes all around the monument, going out and into the niches. It is probable that a similar cornice was also at the height of the little terrace.

The door leads into a crossed room, shape already used in the Mausoleum of Galla Placidia and in the sacellum of Sant'Andrea, and it was common in ancient times. A bronze door with two leaves was sustained by hinges that rotated inside the holes of which we see the superior ones. The vault of the room, which receives a very weak light from six little windows, is a cross-vault. A big moulding placed a little higher than the external cornice goes round the naked room, decorated only by four hewn stones where shells were carved; the two shells of the entrance wall are not finished.

The destination of this room is uncertain. If it were a chapel, they think (De Angelis d'Ossat) of the existence of an altar in the Eastern wing, preceeded by transennae. If we consider it sepulchral room, we immagine (Dyggve) the collocation of the sarcophagus in the middle while in the limbs of the cross the sarcophagi of the family must have found place.

Once in the room capitals were placed, cippi, bases, Roman remainders used in the posterior construction of a cloister joined to the monastery and destroyed in 1660. Today there is only a fragment.

Superior floor - In order to get to the upper floor, in 1774 two stone stairs were built and they were placed radially at the side of the door. Since these arbitrary addings changed the physionomy of the monument, in 1927 they were taken away and a back stair was built with an iron footbridge so clearly extraneous to the construction in order not to affect its aspect. We don't know how they went up during the ancient times, but certainly not from the inside.

The upper floor, narrower than the bottom

one (about 1.30 m.) so as to permit the formation of a perimetral terrace, is decagonal till the frieze level that is above the door. From this point it becomes circular.

In the polygonal part the faces, excluding the one in which the door opens, carry slightly embedded surfaces and precisely, for each side two rectangular embeddings separated by a jutting out part which forms, on the top, a lunette above each embedding. Below every lunette there is a frieze in which a motif is sculptured which makes you think of many little lined up pincers and that has been called, for this reason, «a tenaglia» (pincer-like). Under this frieze a row of indents protudes. In every corner of the decagon, on top a little pyramid peak appears. In the first lunette of the third side a cross slightly visible is sculptured. Going around the terrace to observe the wall of the construction we notice, in correspondence of the iron bridge, a projection in relation with the internal niche that we shall see. On the wall also four big iron hooks are evident, one of which is broken, posterior to the original construction.

The circular part starts with a slightly protruding marble cornice and it ends with a powerful circle which closes and embraces the building. In this strip the «a tenaglia» motif appears again: there are 29 blocks decorated in front, 24 of which contain nine «tenaglie» each one contains seven of them, four contain four of them, and which encircle the building with a very original decorative motif and of difficult and controversial interpretation. Between the two strips in relief there is a strip in which eleven little windows open, some of them rectangular, other very little ones arched isolated or in pairs, one with a cross shape.

The architrave above the access door has eleven little brackets which sustain an element decorated with indents. On the cornice of the door a frieze with bay-leaves is sculptured. The inside room is circular, with only one arched niche provided of a cross.

In the room the porphyry tub which contained Theodoric's body is placed. On its sides it presents two false rings and, below a leonine protome. A few decennia after his burial, at the time of the archbishop Agnello (557-570), when the religious Arian buildings were consecrated to the Catholic cult, the Mausoleum presumably was violated, and the relics of the king were taken away and dispersed. On the tub we know that at least since the 9th century it was at the feet of the monument. In 1564 it was placed on the façade of the church of San Sebastiano from which, in 1633, it passed to the so-called Palazzo di Teodorico to reach, in 1897, the church of San Romualdo until, after so much roaming, in 1913 it returned to the mausoleum and it was placed where we see it now.

Above, the big stone carries in the middle inside a big shield («clipeus») a gemmed cross, with equal limbs. From the West of the centre of the cross there is a hole through which the rope of a bell, placed on the top of the dome at the time when the Mausoleum was incorporated in a church, passed. But what is more remarkable is the long split that is connected to an ancient legend. It is said that he would have died struck by lightening, therefore, to escape his destiny, he got himself built a mausoleum with a monolithic covering as refuge in the case of a thunderstorm; the sad prophecy, however, would have taken place all the same, because lightening broke the stone and burnt the king. It is one of the legends which flowered around his great personage and that generally tend to depict him as a man oppressed by remorse for his cruel misdeeds and uselessly intent on escaping from the right divine rage. On this regard, remember of the famous «Leggenda di Teodorico» of Giousé Carducci, who founds the Germanic Odinic legend of the demoniac hunter and the Catholic one of the revenge of the souls of Simmaco and of the pontiff Giovanni.

In reality, however, the split which lights the fantasy must have had a more prosaic origin; it is thought, in fact, that it came out during the arranging works. As to sustain this last thesis we add the argumentation, to tell the truth a little weak, that the two hewn stones which are on top of the ideal line which passes in the middle of the two doors aren't at the same distance from that line, breaking a symmetry that they wanted but they couldn't affect because of the breaking of the block.

Technical and interpretative problems - The whole building places problems: technical as regard to the transport and the placing in loco of the dome; aesthetic, as regard to the embedding motif and the reliefs of the decagonal part of the upper floor; semantic, on the interpretation of the whole building and of some of its parts as the monolith and its hewn stones; historical, regarding the derivation of the structure and historical-philosophical proposed by the deep sense of the construction.

The **transport of the monolith** was carried out placing the stone onto a platform of big trunks which was then placed onto a barge to cross the Adriatic. On the ground the shifting took place by means of sliding which was facilitated by the rolling bodies underneath. The stone was then brought to a height a little superior to the building letting it slide along an inclined floor deliberately prepared. Then it was lowered until it stood onto the last circle of stones of the Mausoleum, maybe by means of a piston system which slowly went down into cylinders full of sand while the sand itself was

Mausoleum of Theodoric: particular of the pincer-like frieze.

taken slowly out from below; it is a technique still used in a phase of construction works of certain highway viaducts composed by prefabricated elements.

This is the most recent thesis which excludes the **hewn stones** as structures used for dragging and lifting; to get to the point, as handles. They would instead, be decorative elements and should allude to twelve little sarcophagi (Tabarroni). Or else they should represent the projecting extremities of the poles which sustain the top of the tents as they built them, for example, the Barbarians represented on the column of Marcus Aurelius in Rome (Ferri). Another hypothesis wants the hewn stones to symbolize a crown (Cecchelli); or, finally, that they recall the armed head of a soldier with the task, therefore, of giving the monument the sense of a savage power (Guberti).

The *monolith* can represent the vault of the sky, or else can witness a return to the memory of the Goths' motherland and to its megalithic civilization.

The **structure**, has a central plan with two orders one on top of the other and it can be historically collocated moving from the fact that this module has its first origin in the hut and that it reached the Romans through the Etruscan tomb architecture of the 8th and 7th centuries B.C. From the Etruscan tumulus, infact, the tombs of the Republican Rome derive till the great imperial mausoleums as the one of Augustus, of Hadrian (Castel Sant'Angelo), or like the one of Cecilia Metella.

According to Guberti, while the central plan of two superimposed orders places this mausoleum in the Roman cultural area, the monolith covering and the frieze «a tenaglia» would connect it with the Nordic-Germanic art; the hewn stones of the covering monolith, then, would be elements of Assyrian derivation. And since among these characteristics the one that majorly imposes itself is the central plan of two orders, the mausoleum would essentially be of Roman conception, spirit and philosophy. The sense of power that it expresses is however due to the mouldings, to the friezes and especially to the form of the dome bristling with hewn stones: it would derive, that is, from «Germanity», by the war power, by the original barbarousness of the Goths. Therefore, to get to the point, the building is a meeting of the Roman world and the Barbarian one, in conclusion a stone expression of what Theodoric had fate to live and to express in his destiny and in his political vicissitude.

The problem concerning the **rectangular embeddings** of the upper floor can be considered resolved by accepting the thesis that, on the basis of the careful examination of part of the wall taken into consideration, asserts that the building as we see it today isn't completed (De Angelis d'Ossat). The superior portico would be missing constituted at the base of the perimetral terrace and, in the external part, by a row of little columns (where there is a railing now) sustaining a roof which joined to and stood onto the building exactly according to how the wall traces reveal; a portico similar to an ambulatory which interrupted only in correspondence with the door of the cell.

Historical hints from 540 to our days - After the return of the Byzantines the mausoleum, having taken away the body of the king, was used for the Catholic cult, and from the documents of the ninth century we have the first news about the construction of a light house that was placed against it.

Near the mausoleum a monastery was later built «*ad farum et ad regis memoriam*» denominated Santa Maria della Rotonda, (see page 10) demolished in 1660.

We mentioned a bell whose rope was pulled from the superior room; infact for a while it was attached to a church, and the quadrangular notches on the entrance door of the upper room served exactly to hold the beams of the roof of the church that used the superior floor as a choir. After the disappearance of the monastery and of the church, other buildings were placed against the construction. The latter, in the meanwhile, started to silt up, to such an extent that in 1748 the first elements which emerged from the ground were the round arches of the niches of the lower floor, which were therefore nearly completely buried.

From 1748 preservation works started, by means of digging out and drying up, and now we can admire it solitary in its intact power, a challenge to time and to the caducity of things.

Let's return to town going up the fly-over again and keeping our left before running into it. We shall pass along the dock of the city, terminal of the Corsini canal which joins Ravenna to the sea for a lenght of about 11 kilometers. In the dock merchant ships moor for the transport of manure, coal, cereals, carob, etc. On the quays several industrial buildings rise.

After the covering up of the Port of Classe, Ravenna was able to enjoy the usufruct only of landing places for little ships. These landing places, however, which in the 8th century were five (porto Candiano, porto della Foce del Ronco, porto Blacherno, porto Padoreno placed near the Mausoleum, porto Leone) didn't consent the loads to reach the inhabited area, making it necessary to use land transport. Therefore in 1652, a navigable canal was dug, called Pamphilio, which reached the city near porta Nuova. But this channel silted up and in 1735 another one was dug which is the one whose dock can be seen.

This work was wanted by the dynamic Cardinal Alberoni and was carried out on the project of the hydraulic engineers Eustachio Manfredi and Bernardino Zendrini. The excavations started in 1735 and, since they took place under the pontificate of Clemente XII, the canal was called Corsini from the surname of the Pope. In occasion of the works a statue in honour of the Pope was erected which is now in the second cloister of the National Museum. The population, however, called this new harbour with the name Candiano, ancient name which the Ravennati had already used to name other harbours. The channel was opened in October 1743, the dock in July 1746.

Actually Ravenna disposes of a big industrial port which opens on the Corsini channel a few kilometers from the city.

Let's continue turning right (nearby there is the church, today desecrated, of the Saints Simon and Giuda, built between 1898 and 1900, that contains a canvas by the Ravennate painter Camillo Maioli, representing the two Saints), and let's cross the railway road Ravenna-Rimini, which in order to be carried out compelled the demolition of a long piece of the town-walls. Beyond the railway crossing, we keep our right again for Viale Pallavicini until the railway station, built in 1836 and built again after the last war. Let's continue on the left along viale Carlo Farini running along the basilica of San Giovanni Evangelista. Let's then go into via Diaz and reach Piazza del Popolo from which we set off.

A lost basilica: San Vittore - On the 4th of Semptember 1944 an Anglo-American air bombing destroyed one of the oldest churches in Ravenna, the basilica of San Vittore. It certainly existed in the first half of the 6th century (in someone's opinion it would date back to the 5th and even to the 4th century), but it was rebuilt in Romanesque style (Testi Rasponi maintains in the 10th-11th century).

It was not a big building (round 25 meters in lenght, little less than 15 meters in breadth), originally with three naves, it was then reduced short before 1591 to the only central nave, much later (1906-1907) it was brought back to its primitive form by rebuilding the two lateral naves and with the construction, at that date, of a little bell-tower like the one of the Church of Saint John and Paul (see on page 87). Some researchers consider it as the prototype of many churches and especially of a lot of «pievi» (little country parish churches).

Nowadays on the floor of a warehouse at No. 83 Via Girolamo Rossi, near Porta Serrata, we can see, marked in light marble, in the place where the basilica rose, the perimeter, the line of the apse, the bases of the pillars.

ITINERARY OF THE CATHEDRAL

Piazza del Popolo - Via Cairoli - Via Romolo Gessi - Palazzo Baronio - Casa Ghigi - Palazzina Diedo - Santa Giustina in Capite Porticus - Palazzo Vitelloni - **Museo Arcivescovile** (Archbishop Museum) - **Oratorio di Sant'Andrea - Battistero della Cattedrale** - Piazza Duomo - **Duomo** - Via Porta Aurea - Sant'Andrea Maggiore - **Porta Aurea** - (*variant*: - Walls - Madonna del Torrione) - Walls - Monumento alla Resistenza - Park of Peace - Porta Gaza - Via Nino Bixio - Via Giovacchino Rasponi - Piazza Kennedy - Palazzo Rasponi Murat - Palazzo Rasponi dalle Teste - Piazza dell'Aquila - Palazzo Pasolini dall'Onda.

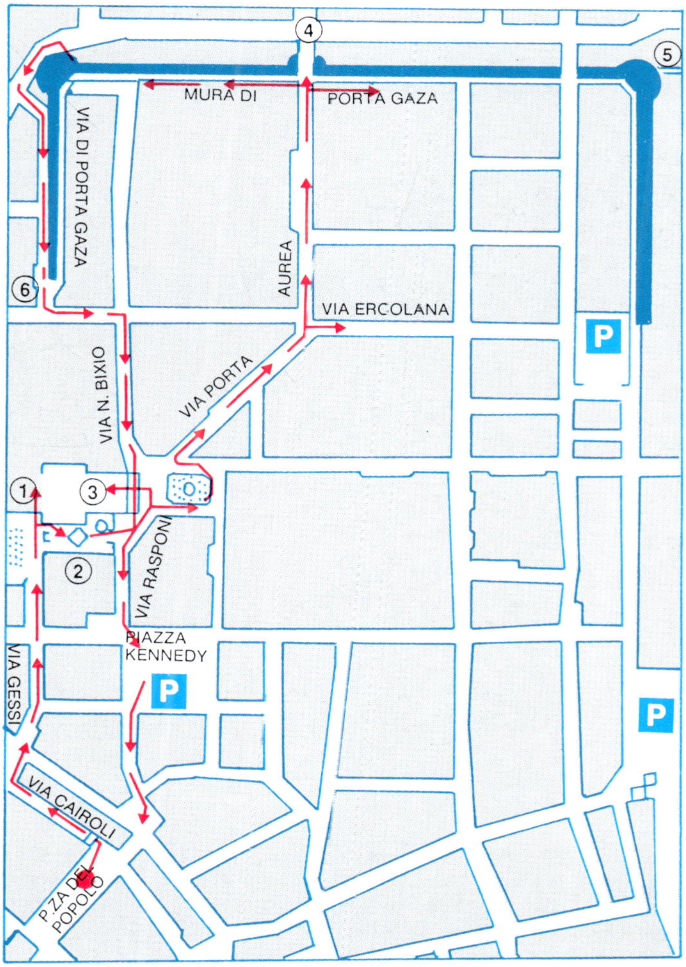

Fig. 39 - **ITINERARY OF THE CATHEDRAL.** 1 - Archbishopric, entrance to the archbishop museum. 2 - Baptistery of the Cathedral. 3 - Cathedral. 4 - Port'Aurea. 5 - Madonna del Torrione. 6 - Porta Gaza.

Balcony of the Palazzina Diedo.

From piazza del Popolo let's go into via Cairoli passing under the big arch on the side of the palazzetto Veneziano and run into via Romolo Gessi which we will run through towards the right.

In the piece of road between via Cairoli and via Mentana it seems that Odoacer had got his palace built, «*super flumen Padennae*»; that piece, in fact, was occupied by the Padenna river.

CASA SUCCI (n. 9-7-5) - At the corner of via Mentana, going right, there is a house of the end of the 16th century with subsequent transformations. The corner little balcony is of the Renaissance. The two doors are of the seventeenth century and carry, one the cross of the order of Santo Stefano, the other the monogram of Christ.

CASA GHIGI - At n. 11. It is a building of the 15th century provided of a beautiful portico with five arches sustained by four columns with lombardesque capitals and two pillars, one of which is an ancient print with the «Madonna del Sudore». The floor of the portico is a cobbled paving with geometrical shapes. On the roof, two big round chimneys. On the entrance door a little tablet is sculptured with the coat-of-arms of the family which had the house built: three strips, respectively with three, two, one star. In the Eighteenth and Nineteenth Centuries the house was the seat of an inn (Locanda della Spada d'Oro) and it housed Chateaubriand, Lamennais, Thiers. Actually it is the seat of several municipal offices, among which the office register, whose big room occupies the ancient yard of the house.

PALAZZO BARONIO - It is at n. 16, in front of casa Ghigi. It was started off in 1744 in the place of an ancient tower which during the works was built again, it was designed by the architect Domenico Barbiani for the Guiccioli family, who sold it to the Baronios in 1788. The façade is in Baroque style; from the vestibule we enter, on the right, through a portal, into a big staircase. The entrance still has its original floor with bricks disposed like a fish-bone. In the rooms, paintings of Felice Giani and his school. Above the portal at n. 16 and above those at the corner of via Guidone (now at n. 14 there is the entrance of a shop) there are two baroque balconies.

PALAZZINA DIEDO (15th century) - «*It is a little Renaissance jewel, one of the most beautiful buildings of the Venetian period. All of it is in face-brick, it has a white balcony of Istria Stone with three decorated brackets which sustain it. The door of the balcony is mullioned and the central marble column sustains the two little arches the cornice of which is in brickwork*» (Foschi). On the arch of the portal, the coat-of-arms of the Diedo family made up of

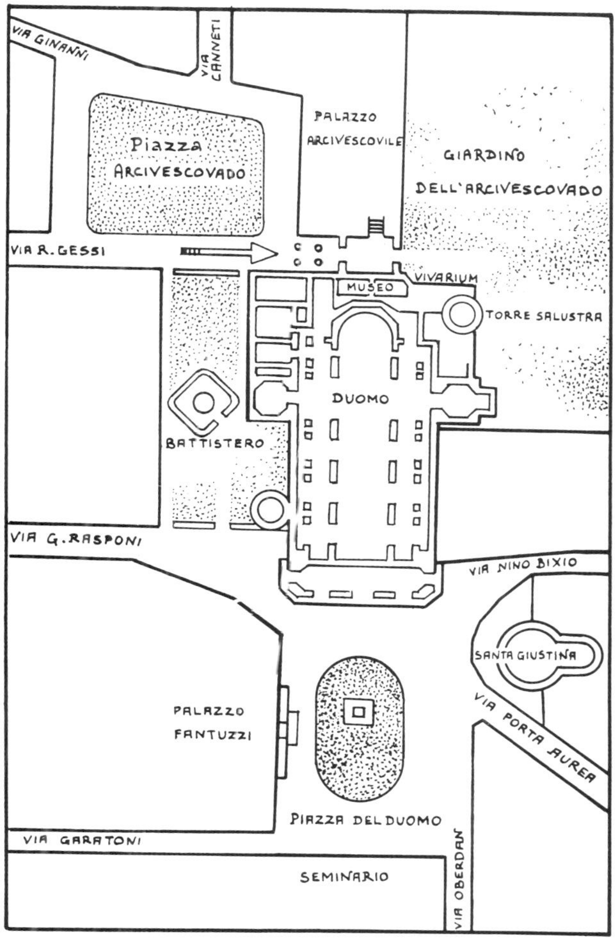

Fig. 40 - Map of the zone of the Cathedral.

two horizontal strips. 1574 the palace was the theatre of a gloomy event: Girolamo Rasponi with a gang of acolytes of his, carried out a carnage in which several members of the Diedo Family died to revenge a missed matrimony between a Diedo and a Rasponi girl.

SANTA GIUSTINA *IN CAPITE PORTICUS* - Beyond the «palazzina Diedo» there is a big modern building in the façade of which, conveniently restored, the little façade of the church of Santa Giustina *in Capite Porticus* is incorporated. It presents, at the crowning, elegant little arches on pilaster strips. The façade is of the 15th century.

The original little church, whose remainders have been conserved and worthly presented inside the modern building, is of the 13th century and it his at about four meters of depth. The nave with the apse is the only visible part; on the lateral wall the niches open and we can see traces of empty spaces. We can also see the beginning of a portico which ran along the actual via Romolo Gessi, passed the Padenna at the Apollinaris bridge or «Ponte Coperto», and continued along the actual via Gordini and via Mariani.

PALAZZO VITELLONI - BANCA D'ITALIA - The corner between via Romolo Gessi and via Guerrini, on the right, is occupied by the big massive structure of Palazzo Vitelloni, now seat of the Banca d'Italia. It was built in the seventeenth century in extremely severe forms and without decorations. The window on the first floor was originally the entrance portal which could be reached by means of external stairs. Above there is a long balcony with Baroque railing, sustained by five brackets.

The building was constructed by Ginanni-Maroncelli family; it belonged in the 19th century to the Vitelloni family, then to the Guiccioli and tothe Rasponi, who in 1868 sold it to the Banca d'Italia.

The side on via Gessi stands on a scarp, delimited on top and under by a cordon and a base in Istria stone.

Let's cross via Arnaldo Guerrini and enter in the last part of via Gessi until the little Arcivescovado square; the railing on the right delimits the space on which the «Battistero della Cattedrale» rises and which we shall visit in a short while.

PIAZZETTA ARCIVESCOVADO - It was a famous place in the past. Much wider than today, because it comprised also of the space occupied by the I.N.P.S. building, it was called «*campus communis*». It was delimited by the archbishop palace, by the water course called Lamisa which marked the Southern side (zone of via Ginanni) and by the municipal buildings which before the actual collocation were near

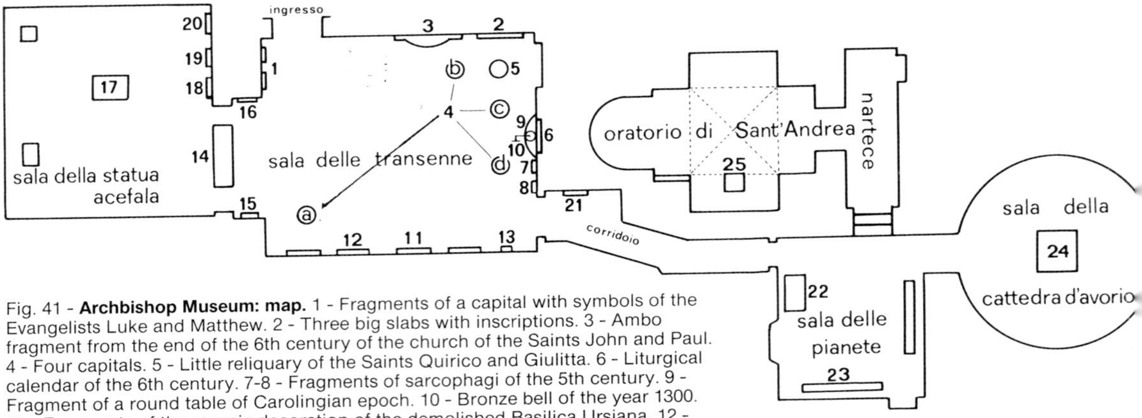

Fig. 41 - **Archbishop Museum: map.** 1 - Fragments of a capital with symbols of the Evangelists Luke and Matthew. 2 - Three big slabs with inscriptions. 3 - Ambo fragment from the end of the 6th century of the church of the Saints John and Paul. 4 - Four capitals. 5 - Little reliquary of the Saints Quirico and Giulitta. 6 - Liturgical calendar of the 6th century. 7-8 - Fragments of sarcophagi of the 5th century. 9 - Fragment of a round table of Carolingian epoch. 10 - Bronze bell of the year 1300. 11 - Fragments of the mosaic decoration of the demolished Basilica Ursiana. 12 - Transennae of the middle of the 6th century from the Basilica Ursiana. 13 - Fragment of the mosaic floor of Basilica Ursiana.
14 - Sarcophagus of the 5th-6th century. 15 - Stelae of Antifonte. 16 - Stelae of Valeria Maria and of Flavius Anastasius. 17 - Acephalous statue of the 4th-5th century. 18-19 - Relief fragments with putti. 20 - Relief fragment with female figures (Roman Age). 21 - Marble Christmas Crib (bas-relief) of the 15th century. 22 - Silk cloth of the 8th century. 23 - Planet said of Angelopte. 24 - Ivory Throne. 25 - Oratory of Sant'Andrea -Silver cross of the archbishop Agnello.

the Cathedral, because the municipality was under the authority of the archbishop. The square, placed immediately outside the Roman Town-walls, became later, in the 15th century, a market place for oxen. Still before the first years of nineteenth century the place was called «Piazza dei buoi» (i.e. Oxen square) even if the market didn't take place anymore for quite some time.

In 1980, during works in the yard of the seat of the Banca Popolare, adjacent to the little square, various remainders, that go from the 3rd-2nd century B.C. to the middle ages, were found at a depth of 7meters, precisely: a) a brick wall, probably the most ancient town-wall of Ravenna, in which a tower stands out, all of the Republican Age; b) parts of a Roman house, of which three phases of construction were pointed out, the first of which is of the 2nd century A.D.; c) a thermal implant relative to the first bishop's palace, made up of 6 tubs of various forms and dimensions. The implant is of the 5th century A.D. and it was used at least until the 10th century; d) a tower of masonry and limestone blocks with rectangular foundations, referable to the first municipal building of the town.

The floor mosaics of the Roman house were recovered and three thermal baths rebuilt at the National Museum.

PALAZZO ARCIVESCOVILE - The actual archbishop's palace doesn't coincide with the ancient bishop's palace, started during the time of Bishop Orso, continued by his successors and finished by Maximian. Of that ancient building and of others which rose near the «Basilica Ursiana» we give you a few outlines adapting the hypothesis of De Angelis d'Ossat.

Around the ancient basilica which had been built by Orso, now substituted by the Duomo, there were religious buildings, and a first bishop's residence, placed on the Western side of the church, inside the Roman walls. Furthermore, there was a building referable to bishop Pietro II, outside the walls near the apse of the basilica and to the Salustra tower, called **Tricoli**, most probably because it was divided into three parts in height with very evident architectural elements. The construction of this building started in the first years of the 5th century and it continued for many decades; the oratory of Sant'Andrea made part of *Tricoli*, which still exists and which we shall visit.

On the South of the basilica there was then another splendid place erected by Neon and called «**Quinque accubita**». The *accubita* are semi-circular divans which were placed inside niches. It was therefore a building in which there was only one big rectangular room, with big niches for each of the long sides, as well as for one of the short sides. It was used as meeting room, it was decorated with marbles and by a complex of mosaic pictures.

In the enclosure of these buildings there was a stretch of water with fish and the thermae, vast and decorated, fed by the near Lamisa ditch.

In the 8th century a building was added to it, called «**vivarium**» placed against the Salustra Tower. It is a double floor construction, still existing, with various series of arches, niches, holes, maybe for the placing of animals, such as fish, amphibians, reptiles on the lower floor; quadrupeds and game on the superior one; birds closed by nets on top (Gerola).

Of these ancient buildings something has remained in the actual building, like the oratory of Sant'Andrea, the «*vivarium*» but the relations between the new constructions and the old ones are not very known as also the icono-

Archbishop Museum: liturgic calendar.

graphy and the development of these buildings.

The actual Arcivescovado comprises a part dating back to the year one thousand with successive additions. The portico with columns from which we enter to reach the staircase and the Museum is of the 17th century and of the same time is the «Sala Gialla» (Yellow Room) placed above the portico.

ARCHBISHOP MUSEUM (Museo Arcivescovile) ORATORY OF SANT'ANDREA

The little precious museum was born to collect objects which made part of the basilica Ursiana demolished in the first half of the 18th century, and it has gone more and more enrichening itself with contributions of various provenance.

To visit if follow the map fig. 41.

Room of the transennae - It is one in which we enter. Right after the entrance, on the right, two **faces of capital** are hung of the type called «of the two zones», that in the inferior part carry acanthus leaves moved by the wind. On the superior part a winged lamb and an angel appear, symbols of the Evangelists Luke and Matthew (1). On the inscription the bishop Pietro II is remembered and this consents an exact dating (from 494-519).

On the wall of the entrance door, hung on it, there are several inscriptions and, by the window, **three big slabs** (2). The one on which the inscription starts with: «CRUX SCTA ADIVVA NOS IN IUDICIO...» (*«Blessed cross (Santa Croce), help us in the day of Judgement»*), is the front of the sarcophagus of Gregory and Mary (end 8th - beginning 9th century). A second slab called of Arrenia Cirilla (D.M. ARRENIAE CYRILLAE) carries, on the left of the epigraph, a voluted cross with two stylized cypresses under the pole, while on the right there is a double knotted ribbon enclosing two rosettes (end of 8th - beginning 9th century). The third slab finally, whose inscription starts with: «HIC REQUIESCIT IN PACE VIR SBL (sublimis) SEDA IGNUCUS...» it is the front of the sarcophagus in which the body of the eunuch Seda was placed in 541, assigned to the rooms (CUBICULARIUS) of Theodoric. In the lateral «ediculae» of the slab there were two figures of dead people, that were chiselled, and this indicates that the sarcophagus is pagan (3rd century) reused in the 6th.

On the left of the slabs (3) there is the **fragment of an ambo** of the last years of the 6th century which comes from the church of Santi Giovanni and Paolo. It is composed of twenty whole tiles inside each of which animals are sculptured (lambs, deer, peacocks, pidgeons, fish), at the base. In the four lateral wings there are, on top, Saint John and Saint Paul; below four animals on each side. They are representations of little artistic value and of mediocre make. The inscription says that the ambo was erected by a certain Adeodato during the fifteenth indiction (596-597). The indiction is a chronological period of 15 years, used since the 4th century to indicate dates with more precision. This ambo, as the one of the Duomo that we shall see, is formed of a single marble wall while others are composed of more parts.

Of the interesting four capitals with animals, two come from the church of San Marco (4-a-b), one from Mantua (4-c) and one from the church of Sant'Apollinare in Classe (4-d). Those in which a superior circle with rams follows an inferior circle of acanthus leaves are of the second half of the 5th century. On every façade leaves, vegetables, fruit and a hawk with an animal in its claws, or else profiles of birds jut out. The two capitals that instead of acanthus leaves have vine-shoots with grapes are of the Justinean Age. A little piece of horn missing from one of the rams was found during works carried out in 1973-76 in Sant'Apollinare in Classe, and it is now exhibited at the National Museum.

Near the window, on a base that permits its rotation, there is a beautiful little «**capsella**» (5) (reliquary of the Saints Quirico and Giulitta) which carries on its four faces the following scenes.

— Representation of «*Traditio Legis*» (Christ hands the book of law to Peter who accepts it with his hands covered by the pallium. On the left there is Paul).
— Daniel in the lions' pit while from a rock the prophet Abacuc hands two loaves and a fish.
— The offering of the Three Kings, with oriental garments, inclined towards the naked Child held by the Madonna who is sitting down.
— The pious women at the sepulchre and the Ascension of Jesus. In the centre Jesus flings himself towards the right, holding a cross on his shoulder, while a hand comes down from above and grabs his wrist. On the right there is a construction of big blocks with four square merlons. The container was used to keep relics and it was closed by a lid sliding in two grooves. It comes from the Basilica of San Giovanni Battista and it should date back to the year 450. Tradition says that Quirico and Giulitta were martyrized in 304 in Tarso, and their relics were brought to Auxerre and then to Ravenna at the time of the emperor Valentinian III (424-455), where Galla Placidia must have placed them onto the high altar of the Church of San Giovanni Battista.

In the middle of the wall with the window there is a **liturgical calendar** (6) of the 6th century. It is a marble slab of 95 cm per 90 which served to determine Easter day for a period of 94 years and precisely from 532 to 626. Easter, in fact, is a mobile holiday, and while the Eastern Christians calculated the day according to the Lunar calendar, gathered from the Jews, the Western Christians calculated it according to the solar calendar; from here many controversies to determine the day to celebrate this important festivity. The council of Nicea (395), as well as condemning the Arian religion, decided, unsuccesfully, that all the Christians were to celebrate the Easter festivity in the same day and the way to determine it was defined in the Easter tablets elaborated by Teofilo d'Alessandria and completed by Dionigi il Piccolo in Rome.

The calendar of Ravenna carries a cross, in the middle of which 19 sectors of rays branch off which contain the information. Being impossible to clarify completely the reading of the complex slab, we limit ourselves to give some indications that will make it possible to have a more careful observation of this important archeological piece. The letters *LV* on the external part, repeated at every segment, mean «*moon*» (lunar cycles). The letters AN, immediately underneath, indicate the year of the various nineteen year cycles (AN 1, for example, is the year 1 of the first nineteen year period). The inscription PAS III ID AP LV XX which appears exactly above the central cross on the third band of writing from the extreme circumference, means, PASCHA 3 IDUS APRILES LUNAE DIE 20 («Easter 11th April, last quarter of moon»), which is the indication of the date of Easter day.

On the right of the Easter tablet there is a **sarcophagus fragment** (7), which shows two little lambs looking towards a disc with a cross on which there is a little lamb representing the *Agnus Dei* (first half of the 5th century). Nearby, on the right, another fragment of sarcophagus with nine rows of roundish flat tiles (8) (middle of the 5th century).

Under the Easter tablet there is the fragment of a **round table** of Carolingian epoch above which a bronze **bell** (10) of the year 1300 which carries the name of pope Bonifacius VIII.

On the wall in front of the entrance there are some **fragments of mosaic decorations** of the apse of the demolished Basilica Ursiana (11). They are the few remainders of a big mosaic dating back to 1112 which covered the apse and the triumphal arch of the very ancient church, and which was demolished without tight need in 1734 at the epoch of the construction of the new temple. This mosaic can be described in the following way:

Triumphal arch - Above a row of sixteen ecstatic, praying figures of Saints and Angels with Christ in the middle, representing the Ascension. On the lateral peduncles, two episodes of the life of Sant'Apollinare.

Archbishop Museum: «The falling putto», bas-relief of Roman epoch.

Archbishop Museum: acephalous statue (end of 4th - beginning of the 5th century).

Apsidal Conch - Above, three scenes of the Resurrection (The Angel shows the women the empty grave - Christ descends to the Limbo - Peter and John go to the sepulchre). Below, in the window zone, the Virgin, the Baptist, St. Barbaziano and St Ursicino. At the extremities, two facts of Sant'Apollinare's life, among which martyrdom. More under, 18 figures with Sant'Apollinare in the middle and on the sides the «colombini» bishops, those i.e. elected by the flight and the laying down of a dove.

The six fragments that we see here are: the Virgin, with a long dress and a wide cloak, in a praying attitude, which occupied one of the zones between the windows; the head of St. Barbaziano (below) and the one of St. Ursicino (above), on the left side of the Virgin. Furthermore the head of St. Peter on the right above and the one of St. John, below; finally, the head of a personage that on the mosaic placed the lid on St. Apollinare's tomb, in the Martyrdom scene.

On the same wall, below, we notice several **transennae** of the middle of the 6th century (12) open-worked very well, they too coming from the Basilica Ursiana, where maybe they enclosed the «bema» or «*schola cantorum*». Very high up, on the left, there is also a very little floor fragment of the ancient Basilica (13), of the beginning of the 5th century.

In the passage between the transennae room and the one of the acephalous statue (look at map), a **sarcophagus** of Greek marble is placed, of the «columnar» type, that can be dated to the end of the 5th - beginning of the 6th century (14). On the *front* in the middle there are two peacocks who quench their thirst from water that flows out of a «cantharus» (jug); above them, two shells carrying a «*chrismon*» in the middle surrounded by a crown. The central scene is bordered by two niches on each side, with a shell, delimited by tortile columns, carrying two crosses and two palms. On

Archbishop Museum: The Virgin in a praying position.

a

a - Archbishop Museum: The ivory throne. St. John in the centre, and the Evangelists.
b - Archbishop Museum: The ivory throne.

the *sides* the niches contain Latin crosses. At the back seven little columns form six niches, all with a shell, in which two palms are symmetrically inserted, two crosses, two sheep. The original lid, maybe was lost. The sarcophagus is the twin of one of the sarcophagi of Sant'Apollinare in Classe.

In the same passage, near the sarcophagus, on the left there is a little stele which, as well as the ones in front, can be considered the most ancient Christian remembrance in Ravenna (15). It is the **stele** of a young boy, **Antifonte**, who died at the age of 17 years, 5 months and 12 days, on which the Good Shepherd is represented near a tree. It is a very naive representation in light relief (end 2nd - beginning 3rd century). In front there is a **stele of Valeria Maria** (16) in which, on the side of the acroteri, the letters MM are engraved (MeMoriae), two fish opposed to a «clipeus» with monogram of Christ. It is anterior to the 4th century. Underneath there is an inscription which remembers a boy who died at the age of seven, **Flavius Anastasius**; at the end of the first line there is the chrismon; it is of the first half of the IVth Century. These three pieces come from the zone of the basilica of San Probo in Classe.

Room of the acephalous statue - Having passed into the little room, that we called of the acephalous statue, notice at first a big sculpture of dark porphyry, without head (17). It is a piece of rare power for the contained strength and the composed virility that it expresses, even if mutilated. The personage is represented in the act of putting his sword back into its sheath, mantled by a wide «clamys» (short surcoat), held on the right shoulder by a decorated fibula from which some little strings hang. Under the «clamys» the tunic is tied by a belt (go onto the right side) decorated by precious stones, from which a pendant hangs down. The head, the neck, the left hand, the inferior part of the legs are missing. In 1869 the right hand was found by some laundresses in the Santerno river near Imola. Among the various hypotheses on the personage represented in the statue, there is one that sees in it emperor Theodosius, father of Arcadius and Honorius. The sculpture could be of the end of the 4th - beginning of the 5th century, and it seems to have been made in Egypt.

On the walls of the little room **fragments of reliefs** are hung: two putti with a vase full of fruit (18) perhaps fragment from Cerere's throne, a falling putto fragment from Bacchus's throne, made with nice realism (19), some female figures very well drawn (20) (relief of the offering women going to a temple). As well as with the famous relief of the Giulio-Claudia family at the National Museum and with the two reliefs of Neptune's throne in San Vitale they offer a good testimony of Roman sculpture in the first centuries in Ravenna.

In this room a **silver cross** is placed of the archbishop Agnello (25). It is 1.28 meters high and 1.22 meters wide. It was built a little after the half of the VIth Century. The decoration is made up of fourty images (20 on each side; 5 per limb) of haloed Saints. The images of the

b

transversal limbs are original of the 6th century both on the recto and on the verso, as well as a few others, while the ones of the inferior limb on both faces are an integration of 1559. The big shield (clipeus) with the praying Virgin is of the 16th century; the other, with the Resurrection of Christ is of the 1559 restoration. On the whole, a magnificent work of silver foil embossed work.

Let's return in the transennae room and let's enter in the **corridor** which opens in the corner on the right. Immediately after the door, on the left there is a little marble Christmas crib in relief. It is of G. Boni da Mantova, made in 1493 (21).

The room of the chasubles - Having gone through the corridor, we enter into the chasubles room, in which ancient liturgical materials are exposed.

The first on the right (22) is a silk cloth, of purple colour, of the 8th century. At the bottom there is the big chasuble of Angelopte (23) in dark blue BROCATEL which, according to the judgement of a great expert, dates back to the 12th century (Braun): the epoch is deduced by the richness and by the type of design and by the motif of lunettes in the embroidery. The lining of thick reddish cloth is a restoration adding. San Giovanni Angelopte was archbishop of Ravenna in the 5th century, therefore the attribution of the chasuble, of many centuries posterior, is completely wrong. Angelopte means: «He, who saw the angel».

Room of the ivory throne - Let's now pass in the room of the ivory throne, obtained in the Roman tower of Porta Salustra. The circular room, contains mainly the very famous throne of Maximian (2). It is an ivory that «*constitues undoubtedly the most beautiful of which the ancient world has handed down to us*» (Bovini). It was built for bishop Maximian, we think around the middle of the 6th century as a gift of Justinian to tell the truth it is a masterpiece of the early christian ivory sculpture, and even only a glance is sufficient to notice the beauty of the reliefs and the elegance of the drawings of the figures and of the decorations.

There are ivory tablets which cover a little throne that without them would be, also for dimensions, very modest. Some tablets, that had been lost in the past, were given back by the Museums to which they had been brought; some others are missing maybe for good. The tiles should be 39; 27 are present without counting the decorative parts.

The experts underline that the whole thing was carried out by four artists whose pieces can be distributed in the following way:

artist A - Five figures on the front of the long bench;
artist B - Anterior and posterior part of the back;
artist C - Sides of the throne;
artist D - Decorative strips which form the arrangement and separate the panels.

Let's describe the various parts considering the above mentioned subdivision.

Oratory of Sant'Andrea, vestibule of the chapel: Christ warrior.

Front of the bench - The artist inserted the figures of John the Baptist and of the four Evangelists in alternating wide and narrow «aediculae», framed by tortile little columns surmounted by shells. Saint John holds the clipeus with the symbolic image of the Redeemer (the lamb); the Evangelists hold the *codex* with their left hand, while with his right hand the first one blesses in the Latin way, the second one touches the *codex*, the third makes an oratory gesture. Notice the richness and the variety of the pleats of the tunics and of the pallii, as well as the diversity in the attitudes of the figures.

Above and below the five figures there are two very rich ornamental friezes, made of vine-shoots with various animals inserted in the volutes (peacocks, deer, goats, lions etc...). On the superior frieze there is a monogram that many experts, but not all, interpret as «*Maximianus episcopus*».

Back - Three panels miss in the internal part: the theme is made up of the life of Jesus: the Announcement, the demonstration of Mary's virginity with the «water proof», Joseph's dream and the journey to Bethlehem, the Christmas crib and the obstetrician Salome with her dry hand before the Virgin lying on the bed, the Madonna with the Infant.

On the outside of the back, where 9 panels are missing, we have the following representations: on the two top ones the baptism of Christ and the entrance to Jerusalem; on the three of the row underneath, the refection of the crowd, the multiplication of the loaves and of the fishes and the miracle of Cana's wedding; on the third row, the healing of the born-blind, the meeting of Christ with the Samaritan at the well. The author of these panels reveals some flatness in modelling and a certain tendency to pictorialism deriving from Hellenistic influences and recalls.

Sides - Under the arms there are five panels on each side, carried out with a deep and resolute carving, rich of life and movement. The panels that are on the side of the left arm of who sits down contain the following scenes: Joseph's brothers who announce his death to their parents, Joseph lowered into the cistern while a lamb is killed the blood of which will be used as a proof of Joseph's death, Joseph sold to the merchants, Joseph sold to Potiphar, Joseph tempted, accused, imprisoned.

The panels that are on the other side contain: Joseph on the throne who receives his brothers, the wheat jest, Joseph who explains his dreams to the Pharaoh, Jacob who embraces again his son Joseph, the dream of the Pharaoh.

Friezes - The carver who worked at the decorative part demonstrates a rich and fervid fantasy and, in the research of the «chiaroscuro» effects, a delicate pictorial sensibility.

The place of the missing ivory panels is occupied by wooden tablets covered with parchment. Of some of the lost panels we know the subject.

Oratory of St. Andrea - We get to it through the chasuble room.

It was the private chapel of the bishops built during the widening of the building between the years 494-519 (bishop's palace of Pietro II); in full Theodorican period. We know that also in the Arian bishop's palace there was a private chapel.

Before coming to the real chapel we pass through a **narthex** of rectangular plan with bar-

Architectural complex of the Duomo: **vivarium** (8th century).

rel vault. The walls of the narthex are covered, below, by white marbles, above which there is a long Latin inscription - twenty hexameters - originally in mosaic and painted with tempera like mosaic. The first verse says:

«*Aut lux hic nata est, aut capta hic libera regnat*» (or light was born here, or captured, here it reigns freely).

A verse which expresses in a very suggestive way the polichrome luminosity of the mosaic rooms, vibrating of reflexes and of unimaginable change of colours. At the end of the right wall there is a short strip of original mosaic.

Having gone a few steps in the little narthex, turn around to admire the **lunette** above the door through which we entered. The scene represents Christ warrior that tramps onto a lion and a snake, motif present in other places of the early christian Ravenna; the lion and the snake are symbols of evil annulled by the divine force. Unfortunately, the figure from the bust down-wards, is redone in tempera like false mosaic. On the book that Christ holds in his left hand veiled by a pallium there is written: «*Ego sum via, veritas et vita*». Also the barrel vault has been quite redone. The decoration represents a flowered lawn with hens, doves, ducks, peacocks and pheasants.

From the narthex we pass to the **chapel**, that is a little room with Greek cross plan with a cross-vault. The limb in front of the entrance finishes with an apse redone at the beginning of this century. The vault is decorated with false mosaic, with a starry sky around a central cross.

In the vault, above the intersection of the four limbs there are four angels markedly lanky that, with raised arms, sustain a central disc with the letters I and X interlaced, Greek initials of *Iesus Christos*.

Between the four angels there are the symbols of the Evangelists and that is: the angel, the eagle, the lion and the calf that the visitor has already met or will meet in other decorations of Ravenna, from the early christian mosaics to the frescos of the 14th century.

In the intradoses of the four arches at the sides of the central vault some medallions with portraits are mosaic-worked. Underneath the arch of the little apse there are the busts of Christ with those of Peter and Paul, Jacob and Andrew, James and Philip. The mosaic is in excellent state of preservation and the work which was certainly made by a skilful artist, shows a beautiful face of Christ, an intense look of Paul, a sad expression of Peter.

Also in the underarch in front of the apse Christ and the Apostles are represented, while under the other two arches there are the busts of Saints on the sides of a medallion which contains the letters alpha and omega. Also the two symbols of the end and the beginning are very frequent in the Ravennate iconography.

In the lunettes there are paintings of Luca Longhi very retouched.

Torre Salustra - The round room that houses the ivory throne is as we said in the Salustra tower, visible from via De Gasperi as well as the superior external wall of the Sant'Andrea chapel. The **vivarium** of which we spoke about a little isn't visible and it is at the feet of the two constructions, inside the garden of the archbishopric closed to public. In the garden there are also two columns of pink granite with

Archbishop chapel: mosaic particular of the vault of the vestibule.

carved crosses, maybe belonging to an ancient ciborium; they come from one of the seven altars that were in the church of Sant'Agata.

The tower is of remarkable historical interest because it is one of the two (the other one rose South-West to this one) towers which delimited the Salustra Gate. From here the *cardo* branched off that with a route of 480 meters crossed the Roman city till the opposite gate called, in the Early Middle Ages, «*Posterula Latronum ad Summum Vicum*» (look at the diachronic map of Ravenna fig. 45, page 195).

The examination of the mortars and of the bricks reveals that the tower, until the offset, is coeval to the walls of the square city, i.e. probably of the first century, while the superior part is of the 6th century. Its dimensions, in section, are like those of the base of the disappeared towers of Port'Aurea. This offers a concrete testimony in order to imagine, and rebuild graphically, the aspect of the most famous roman city gate, demolished in 1582.

The building houses also the ARCHBISHOP ARCHIVES and the LIBRARY, «*very famous for its ancientness and for its contents*» (Bernicoli). The library had its origin towards the middle of the seventeenth century and it is equipped with more than seven thousand books. The archive, modernly arranged and equipped in 1959, contains five papyri and 13,000 parchments from the 8th century onwards. In the same seat there are also the CAPITULAR ARCHIVES.

CATHEDRAL BAPTISTERY

Historical hints and external characteristics - From the Archbishopric square, through a little gate, we enter in the zone where, on the side of the Duomo, the bell-tower and the baptistery rise.

We can suppose that the latter was built by bishop Ursus, in the first decades of the 5th century, along with the basilica which rose on the area of the actual Cathedral. It is also called «*Battistero Neoniano*» from bishop Neon who brought substantial renewals. Furthermore Neone got the baptistery splendidly decorated with the mosaics of the dome and with the inlays of polichrome marbles on the inferior part. Or else it is known as «*Battistero degli Ortodossi*», to distinguish it from the «*Battistero degli Ariani*» built by Theodoric more than half a century later.

It has an octagonal plan. The original level is about three meters below the actual one, therefore the four ancient doors are buried, and of them we can only see, from the outside and from the inside, the superior part of the arches on the sides between the four little apses. The experts practically agree in saying that originally a portico connected the Baptistery to the basilica Ursiana. Now we enter through a Renaissance door with jambs and a marble architrave; this last one has the French motto «EN ESPOIR DIEU» engraved «*In vain we have searched a reason for it*» (C. Ricci).

The superior part is lightened by pilaster strips not very jutting out which finish in pensile little arches. Between the two right pilaster strips, on the left side of the door, during construction, a little marble fragment was inserted (IIIrd A.D.) of Roman epoch with a cavalier carrying the victor's crown in his hand: the only «coquetry» in the extremely severe aspect of this big octagonal prism of ancient bricks.

Baptistery
of the Cathedral
and bell-tower.

Inside: general decorative scheme - All the surface of the inside walls is richly decorated with stuccos, inlays of polichrome marbles and mosaics: different techniques that integrate themselves perfectly to give life to an extraordinary united and harmonic complex.

The basic decorative scheme is conditioned by the octagonal shape and by openings carried out in the walls; in this way, we have a first circle of eight arches that cover the strip from the floor to the base of the window; a second circle of eight arches which cover the strip from the base of the windows to the base of the dome; finally the dome completely decorated with mosaics according to a radial scheme that, starting off from a central medallion, embraces two wide spherical zones.

All the mosaic decoration is characterized by the use of a chromatic palette extraordinarily rich both in the basic colours, and in their shading.

The primitive floor, as we have already observed, is three meters below the actual one, that is the fourth. The third floor is the one on which the four perimetral little columns stand, about half a meter under the actual one, as we can see from the perimetral excavation left open (6). Considering this, we can well imagine how much more was the internal impulse of this construction, that we are now admiring as if we were on a stage at three meters of height.

Inside: first order of arches - Let's start with observing the first strip of arches and its decoration. The arches rise from little marble columns crowned by capitals, two of which are of Italo-Byzantine type. The others are Corinthian surmounted by impost stones with the shape of an upsidedown truncated pyramid, slightly shaped with a straight cyma, between two smoothe listels, with a decorative motif that ends in the edges with an acanthus leaf. The intrados is mosaic-worked with motifs recurring also in other monuments of Ravenna: festoons with leaves and fruit, ribbons with fanciful volutes etc...

The big lunettes of the four arches interpolated to the four little apses are covered with tarsiae (*opus sectile*) composed of porphyries, serpentines and oriental white marbles, which form ornamental motifs with panels containing lozenges and circles.

In the South-East apse there is an ancient **cippus altar** (6th century). It is composed of two lateral little pillars with two wide grooves each, on which two capitals stand which sustain a trabeation decorated with a little cross in the middle and by vine-shoots and two pidgeons on the sides. The central part is composed of two spiral columns, onto which an arch stands, adorned by ovules, which frames a shell. Outside the arch there are two long leaves with a pine-cone in the middle. Under the shell the «*fenestella confessionis*» opens. Also the table is ancient, and it is upside down, therefore the plane is in contact with the cippus. Of the four little columns which sustain it, the anterior ones are of the 18th century, the posterior ones of a few decennia ago.

In the North-East apse there is a wonderful marble **roman vase** that maybe was used for ablutions. Under the vase, upside down, there is a Corinthian capital of the end of the 5th century, with an only crown with four acanthus leaves with big dentils. The cauli form a V and make up the spiral volutes. In the centre of the «lyre» motif a cross appears.

In the little South-West apse in 1963 the **cross** of the 7th century that was on the top of

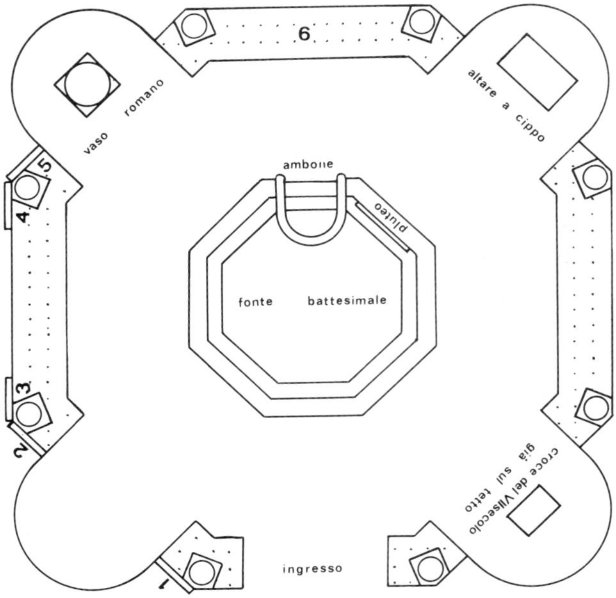

Fig. 42 - **Baptistery of the Cathedral: plan**. Stucco-work strip, above the «aediculae». 2 - «**Traditio legis**» scene. 3 - Christ warrior tramping on a lion and a dragon, symbols of evil. 4 - Jonah between the two sea monsters. 5 - Two cocks peck some wheat seeds from a container. 6 - Perimetral excavation until the base of the corner columns.

the roof was placed. Below it there is a Ionic capital missing from one of the columns of the «loggetta».

Above the little apses there are some mosaic **latin inscriptions** that, with every probability, indicate the argument of the mosaic representations that maybe coated the apse vaults; we remember that originally the apses were more than five meters high. We present the text of these inscriptions, nearly completely remade during the restorations of the second half of the last century. (In cursive the original letters; because three of the inscriptions are interrupted in the middle by a monogram, in its place we shall leave a space).

Inscription above the arch on the right of the door whilst looking:

IN LOCUM *PASCUAE*   IBI ME CONLOCAVIT
SUPER AQUA REFECT   *IONIS EDO*CAVIT ME

The monogram inserted in the middle most probably can be read, MAXIMIANUS. The inscription taken from Psalm XXII (1-4), means: *The Lord has placed me in a place where food and drink to restore me is abundant.*

The inscription on the arch above the Roman vase:

UBI *DEPOSUIT IHS* VESTI   *MENTA SUA* ET MISIT AQUAM
IN PELVEM *ET* LABIT PEDE   S DISCIPULORUM SUORUM

The monogram inserted in the middle is read probably, NEON EP (iscopus) FAMULUS (servant) DEI (of God). The inscription is a summary of a passage of John's gospel (XIII, 4-5), and it remebers the episode that preceeded the last supper, when «*laid aside his garments' Christ poured some water and washed his disciples feet*».

Inscription on the arch above the little cippus altar:

BEATI QUORUM REMISSAE SUNT
*INI*QUITATES
ET *QUORUM* TECTA SUNT PECCATA
BEATUS VIR CUI NON IMPUTAVIT DOMINUS
PECCATUM

The inscription is taken from Psalm XXXII (1-2) and it means: *Blessed is he whose transgression is forgiven, whose sin is covered; blessed is the man unto whom the Lord imputeth not iniquity.*

Inscription on the arch above the cross:

IHS AMBULAS SUPER MARE   PETRO MERGENT MANUM
CAPIT ET IUBENTE DOMN   O VENTUS CESSAVIT

The monogram inserted in the middle is of difficult and problematic reading. The inscription is the summary of a passage of Matthew's Gospel (XIV, 25-32): «*And in the fourth watch of the night Jesus went unto them, walking on the sea, they were troubled, saying, It is a spirit; and they cried out for fear. But straightway Jesus spake unto them, saying, Be of good cheer; it is I; be not afraid. And Peter answered him and said, Lord, if it be thou, bid me come unto thee on the water.*

And he said, Come. And when Peter was come down out of the ship, he walked on the water, to go to Jesus.

But when he saw the wind boisterous, he was afraid; and beginning to sink, he cried, saying, Lord, save me.

Baptistery of the Cathedral, central medallion: Christ's baptism.

And immediately Jesus stretched forth his hand, and caught him, and said unto him, O thou of little faith, wherefore didst thou doubt? And when they were come into the ship, the wind ceased.».

The general content of the inscriptions refers to the sacrament of baptism and to the dogma of the remission of sins.

Also the mosaic part which completes this first strip above the arches and until the base of the windows has been remade quite a lot in the last century, when wide zones of original mosaics were lost in occasion of the nearly total redoing of the arches which weren't safe anymore.

The decorations of this side represent volutes of acanthus which rise from the bases of the arches and end at the top of the arches after having left an oval free on which, on a golden background, a white virile figure appears with a tunic and pallium.

Inside: second order of arches - The strip of arches which includes the windows is decorated especially with **stucco-works** dating back with every probability, to the first decennium of the second half of the 5th century, when the dome was erected at the time of bishop Neone.

The little columns are surmounted by Ionic capitals and by flared pulvinoes; the eight on the corner sustain the arches on which the dome stands; those placed on the inside of every arch divide the background surface into three niches of which the middle one is wider and frames the window, while the two lateral ones contain «aediculae» with virile figures seen from the front. On the whole, a light and elegant gallery made up of twenty-four little columns. Above the corner columns there is a jamb stone decorated by a Latin cross surrounded by acanthus leaves.

The personages that appear in the «aediculae», carrying rolls or showing open books, probably represent the prophets of the Old Testament. The figures are slightly reliefed and result definite, more than by the projecting part, by grooves more or less deep: more drawn or graffited, to come to the point, than modelled. Well relieved, instead, are the hands and the heads.

The faces have an expression like of terror or of amazement, because of the eyes open wide and the pupils rendered with circular and deep holes full of shade. Looking around we receive the impression of being in the middle of an astonished parade of human larvae. The best of these figures, certainly due to the artist who influenced the authors of the others, is the one above the niche of the Roman vase: it has on top, two cocks pecking wheat grains from a container (5). The figure of the prophet, with the right leg slightly bent and with the body slightly flexed, has an open book in his left hand and raises the right one in an acclaiming attitude.

Every «aedicula» is surmounted by a triangular or semicircular crowning in the middle of which a shell with the mussel is placed, alternatively at the bottom and on the top. Above the tympana of the «aediculae», and however still inside the niches, pairs of animals in front of a «cantharos» are represented and also four very nice scenes of the Old and New Testament: *Daniel in the lions' den* (1); the scene of the «*Traditio legis*», in which Christ gives Paul the task of evangelizing people and Peter the cross (2); *Christ warrior with cross and book tramping on the heads of a lion and of a dragon symbols of evil* (3); *Jonah between two sea monsters*, one of which swallows him while the other gives him back (4).

Above the little arches, the lunettes of the superior archivaults were also decorated with stuccos, eliminated around 1880 as undue addings of recent epochs; of them the prints on dark backgrounds and some pieces below are left. They are arabesques with vine-shoots and grapes coming out from vases; peacocks and deer. All the stuccos were most probably coated with colours.

The pendentives at the base of the dome are decorated with mosaics of plant-shape motifs which, from the middle of every spheric triangle of the vault, expand with the shape of sumptuous candlesticks of cactus plants right until the first spheric zone of the dome, that in this way is divided in eight sectors. In such way the big decorative complex of the dome is intimately connected to the spheric triangles and through the latter, to the decoration below.

Inside: dome - central medallion - The composition of the decoration of the dome, having been planned out on a radial scheme, gives the impression of being animated by a rotating movement. The illusion is particularly reinforced in the Apostles' zone, represented while moving forward with rythmic pace.

The central medallion is like the wheel-hub. The scene of Christ's baptism is represented, customary, we must say for baptisteries. The Redeemer is immersed in the waters of the Jordan till his waist, the transparency of the waters is rendered with rare efficacy, if we think that mosaic is not certainly a technique favourable to such illusionistic effects. The Baptist is standing on his right (on the left of who is looking) on the rocky bank of the river, from which, however, tender little plants rise: the saint wears the traditional skin and holds a rich cross in his left hand, while with his right hand pours water on the Redeemer's head by means of a flat bowl (patera): this is a particular arbitrarily introduced in the last century by a restorer but not convalidated by tradition; originally, therefore, the Baptist nearly certainly only placed his hand on Christ's head.

From the sky a white pidgeon with open wings flies down. On the left of the Redeemer (on the right of who is looking) the personification of the Jordan advances, immersed till his chest (but there are people who see a patriarch of the Old Testament, such as Moses, who prefigures Christ), carrying on his hands a green cloth to dry Christ with when coming out of the waters.

The composition of the scene inserts itself badly in the tondo, of which wide portions remain completely empty. Under this point of view, the scene of the medallion of the Baptistery of the Arians is made in a better way.

Observing the mosaic carefully, we shall isolate a zone which results pale in regards to the rest, including the heads of the Baptist and of Christ, and the pidgeon: that zone was remade in the last century.

Inside: dome - zone of the apostles - Around the medallion a large strip goes around with the images of the twelve Apostles, who in two rows led by Peter and Paul proceed carrying a crown on veiled hands. The offering carried on the hands or received by hands covered by the pallium, of which there are innumerable examples in the early christian Ravennate iconography, is a custom of the Oriental courts. It symbolizes both the respect for the offerer or for the receiver of the offering and the respect for the thing received.

The attitude of the figures is such to give the impression of a proceeding with a musical rhythm; the illusion is emphasized by the rhythm division of the composition. The figures alternate regularly which create its significative part, and the pauses, enlivened by the chandeliers, act like the accompaniment. The illusion is also underlined by the colour of the garments that are alternatively white for the tunics and gold for the pallia and gold for the tunics and white for the pallia.

The heads of the Apostles, with very strong features, stand out against the hanging edges of the cloth which surrounds the medallion: the halo will appear only later, in the dome of the Baptistery of the Arians.

Between one Apostle and the other a flowered candlestick rises drawn with golden tesserae which strongly contrast with the indigo of the background. On the tesserae, for the diversity of the inclination with which they were immersed in maltha, the light vibrates with ephemeral and always varied reflexes: infact, only a little shifting of the observer is enough to «light» tesserae that before were in the shade and to «turn off» others that before were shining. For the letters of the pallia, we send you back to the hint that we did, describing the mosaic of the Baptistery of Arians.

Inside: dome - zone of the thrones and of the altars - It is the external strip of the big wheel of the dome. It is divided in eight sectors by the candlesticks which rise from the peaks below. In every sector an exedra bordered by two brief porticoes is represented. In the exedrae alternatively thrones and altars are represented and in the lateral porticoes, still alternatively, gardens (viridaria) and empty seats: gardens (viridaria) with thrones, seats with altars. These motifs repeat themselves with slight variations. The altars, composed by a base and by four lateral columns and by a central one which sustain the table, are «*the most ancient example surely datable of table altar*» (Mazzotti). Notice furthermore the beauty of the transepts and of the plutei of the gardens (viridaria).

Baptistery of the Cathedral: the Apostle Peter.

Even if this strip doesn't present any human figure, it doesn't have only a decorative function, but it is rich of symbolic meanings, maybe of not easy interpretation: it seems clear, however that the artist tried to express with figurative means some abstract concepts very important for Christianity.

The four thrones, that aren't empty, but covered by a cushion surmounted by a cross, would indicate that they had been prepared for the Redeemer in function of judge of men, as it is said in the Apocalypse; the lateral «viridaria», in this way would be the gardens of Paradise.

The empty seats, at the sides of the altars on which an open gospel is placed; would indicate that in heaven a place for the elected has been prepared. All the complex would symbolize the sovereignty of Christ Judge and the promise of a fair reward to the good.

Inside: baptismal font - In the middle of the room there is an octagonal tub of the sixteenth century, a redoing of the primitive one, with reused marbles, like the fragment of pluteus with the lamb that faces a cross, of the 6th century. On the side of the tub in front of the door there is an ambo of the third quarter of the 5th century, taken from a single marble block, equipped with two little steps, on the sides of which there are two little columns with capitals. On the ambo the bishop took place to administrate the baptism which was composed of three phases:

a) exorcism and renunciation to Satan;
b) triplex immersion in the baptismal tub, to symbolize the three days in which Christ remained in his tomb;
c) unction or confirmation.

Leaving the polychrome atmosphere of the Baptistery, we can stop with profit in the surroundings and look for good shots for our photos, combining in the most various ways the forshortenings offered by the baptistery itself, from the bell-tower and from the dome of the Duomo. The light is more favourable in the morning.

PIAZZA DEL DUOMO - Let's now go to the adjacent square of the Duomo, onto which the following buildings look. *Southern side*: Duomo, *Eastern side*: Farini building, *Northern side*: seminary, *Western side*: houses and church of Santa Giustina.

In the middle of the square there is a green zone with a column of grey granite erected in 1605. In 1659 the statue of the Virgin was placed on it, work of Clemente Molli, in occasion of the end of one of the frequent pestilences. The column is made up by three pieces and it is of Roman epoch.

Palazzo Farini before it was palazzo Fantuzzi. It is a beautiful building with a big door, it is made of ashlar of Istria stone, with square openings for the cellars and attics, and two rows of windows. We reach the big door by means of a little frontal staircase with six steps bordered by strong pillars, and by two lateral flights. It dates back to the beginning of the seventeenth century.

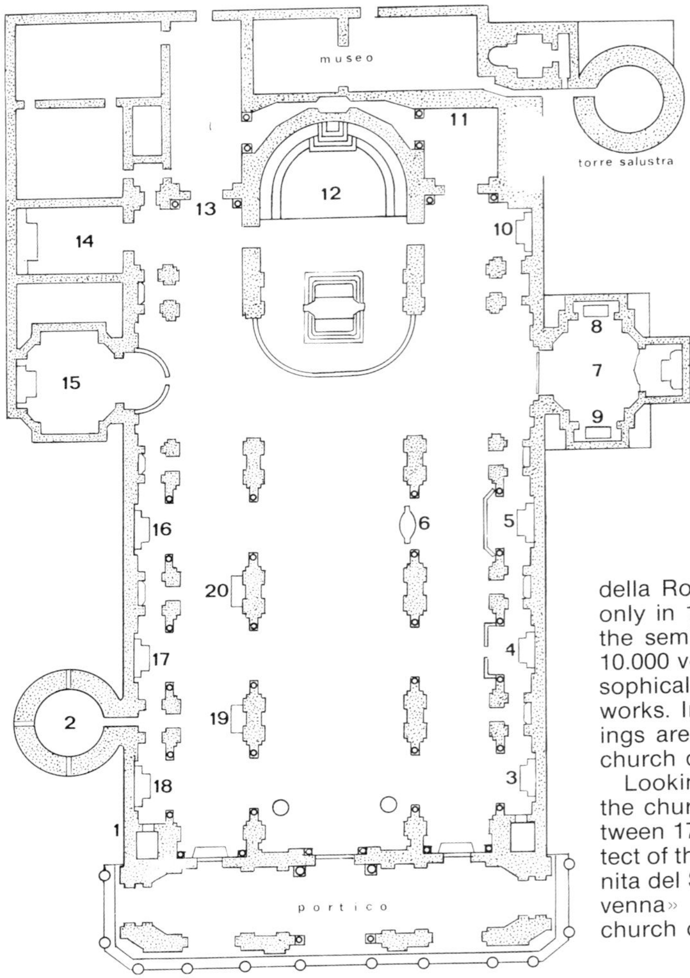

Fig. 43 - **Cathedral or Duomo: plan**.
1 - Remainder of a wall of the preceeding construction. 2 - Bell-tower. 3 - «Saint Christopher», of Antonio Rossi (1700-1753). 4 - Sarcophagus-altar of the bishops Esuperanzio and Massimiano (1st half 5th century). 5 - «San Pier Chrisologo and the Saints Romualdo and Pier Damiano», by Giuseppe Milani (1716-1798). 6 - Ambo of the 6th century. 7 - Chapel of the Blessed «Vergine del Sudore» (the Virgin of sweat). 8 - Sarcophagus of San Rinaldo. 9 - Sarcophagus of San Barbaziano. 10 - «Martyrdom of Saint Ursicino», of Cesare Pronti (1626-1708). 11 - High relief of Mark the Evangelist, of Matteo da Ragusa and Giovanni Antonio da Milano (15th century). 12 - Apse. 13 - Lunette by Guido Reni: «Elijas in the desert». 14 - Winter choir. 15 - Chapel of the sacrament with paintings by Guido Reni and helpers. 16 - «Saint Peter who is sending St. Apollinare to Ravenna», Filippo Pasquali (17th century). 17 - Painting of the «Resurrection». 18 - «Jesus between St. Anthony and St. Jacob», by Joseph Wicar (1762-1834).

The **Seminary** is a building with twelve windows on the ground, six on each side of the door, above which there is a row of thirteen little windows. This part of the façade is divided in rectangular shapes; a wall strip divides the thirteen windows of the upper floor that has a balcony in the middle. The inscription under the cornice (SEMINARIUM SANC RAVENN ECCL ANNO MDCCCCXXX ANTONIO LEGA ARCHIEP RENOVATUM ET AUCTUM) commemorates the renewal and widening works of 1930. Until 1929 the right side was occupied by the church of San Girolamo, that in that year was demolished, with the consequent widening of the Seminary. Of the church a chapel is left decorated between 1756 and 1757, by Domenico Barbiani with paintings of cartouches, shells, cornucopias, festoons, flowers, fruit, plates, vases etc, typical motifs of the artist.

The seminary was established in Ravenna in 1567 by the Cardinal Archbishop Giulio Feltrio della Rovere called «Cardinale d'Urbino» but only in 1779 it was placed in this building. In the seminary there is a library of more than 10.000 volumes. It contains theological, philosophical, juridical, ascetic and agiographic works. In the Seminary also numerous paintings are kept, some of which come from the church of San Romualdo.

Looking on the right of the Duomo, there is the church of **Santa Giustina**. It was built between 1747 and 1750 by Buonamici, the architect of the Duomo, on behalf of the «Confraternita del Sacramento della Metropolitana di Ravenna» that moved here abandoning the church of Santa Giustina in Capite Porticus.

DUOMO

Historical hints and façade - On the place occupied by the Duomo the first big Catholic church of Ravenna rose, originally it was dedicated to the Resurrection of the Lord, erected by bishop Orso at the beginning of the 5th Century and, from the name of the founder, it was also called Basilica Ursiana. In this church, for the first time in Ravenna, the Christians could gather together in a very numerous group, while until that moment they had gathered only in little chapels. In Classe instead basilicas in which they could gather already existed.

It had five aisles, without entrance-hall, with a semi-circular apse in the inside and polygonal on the outside, without transept, coated with marbles, adorned with mosaics and stuccos. As time went by it underwent restorations, rearrangements, redoings that transformed it

Cathedral: dome.

to such an extent that many of its original charachteristics were changed and make it assume those of a basilica of the 9-10th century. Its demolition in 1733-34 was however an inconsiderate decision brought to conclusion, under the will of archbishop Farsetti, by the architect Gian Francesco Buonamici, that in its place built the actual Duomo. The church was rich of traces of a very ancient past: it is enough just to think that inside among many elements and original pieces, there was also a marvellous mosaic composed in 1112.

Of the original Basilica Ursiana (5th century) the marble screens of the 6th century have been preserved, now in the Archbishop Museum, and some re-used columns of which we shall speak about later. The piece of wall between the corner of the façade and the bell-tower, where a walled door appears (fig. 43, 1) is indicated as the remainder of the primitive Cathedral, but most probably it is a re-handling of a later epoch when, around the year 1000, the columns were raised and maybe the perimetral walls were redone. Furthermore, but not of the original Basilica Ursiana, we have the crypt of the 10th century, it cannot be entered because it is constantly full of water, it was built in order to transport there the bodies of the bishops from the Classense basilica of San Probo; the bell-tower of the 10-11th century; a few fragments of the 1112 mosaic.

The actual church is preceeded by a wide **portico** of Doric order that opens in front with three arches.

The powerful pillars are run by pilaster strips which rise from a high base of Istria stone and end with capitals formed by moulding as sustain of a stone strip. The wider, central arch, stands on two columns of pink granite 4.80 m. high, coming from the ancient basilica. Above the arch, on a tablet, there is a big inscription commemorating he who finished the church adding the portico:

FERDINANDUS ROMUALDUS GUICCIOLUS
ARCHIEPISCOPUS
TEMPLUM ABSOLVIT PORTICUM ADIECIT
ANNO MDCCXLV

On the two sides, the portico is opened by a big arch formed by two pilaster strips like those in front.

The architecture of the portico presents itself with a beautiful pictorial aspect for the neat standing out of the elements in Istria stone, on a background of brick-red colour of the plastered parts.

Around the portico a stone pavement runs delimited by eleven pillars.

Above the portico, in arrears as much as its width, the superior part of the façade of the central nave rises, crowned by a curved fronton. In the middle a wide window opens.

On the left of the portico the cylindric **bell-tower** is silhouetted against the sky which presents four building phases. The most ancient is the one of the narrow windows -, two of which start off from the ground (but you must remember that the original level is two meters below the actual one); the second one, broader, presents mullioned-windows and walled openings and, in the inferior part, holes framed with radial bricks; the third is the one with the superciliated three-mullioned windows (year 1038), while the final part (bell cell), was remade after that a fire of 1658 had destroyed it.

Shifting onto the right or onto the left of the square you can see the dome of the transept which stands onto a high cylindric tambour di-

Cathedral: ambo.

vided by eight pilaster strips. These delimit 8 panels in which the crowned windows open, alternatively, by a triangular and curved tympanum. Inserting themselves in the pilaster strips of the tambour above the cornice, the big ribs of the dome start off, covered by oxidized copper plates of a beautiful dark green and crowned by a lantern. It was erected in 1780/82 by Giuseppe Pistocchi from Faenza in the place of the one of Buonamici. It is 47.40 meters high.

Inside the portico, in every one of the four big pillars, a high empty niche, opens, about two meters high and, on the opposite side, other four niches open in the façade of the church. Three rectangular doors interpolated by plastered pilaster strips give entrance to the temple. The wider door is crowned by a split curved tympanum and is bordered by two columns of Greek marble coming from the ancient basilica Ursiana.

Inside - Wide, solemn and full of light, but cold, the church is divided in three naves. It is provided of a transept whose arms are made up by two pre-existing chapels, added to the basilica Ursiana in the 17th century. In the crossing of the transept the bright oval room of the dome opens with the elevated tambour that we already saw from the outside.

The subdivision between the naves is stressed by three wide arches on each side, divided from one another by means of a wall and sustained by columns of Greek, grey and «cipollino» marble.

Above the arches two wall strips run, one with an ornamental festoon, the other with an inscription, all around the church, which says: «VICTIMAE PASCHALI LAUDES IMMOLENT CHRISTIANI AGNUS REDEMIT OVES CHRISTUS INNOCENS PATRI RECONCILIANT PECCATORES MORS ET VITA DUELLO CONFLIXERE MIRANDO DUX VITAE MORTUUS REGNAT VIVUS ALLELUIA † SANCTE APOLLINARIS SACERDOS ET MARTYR CHRISTI DEPRECARE PRO PLEBE TUA QUAM EX GENTIBUS ACQUISISTI NOS AUTEM POPULUS TUUS ET OVES GREGIS TUI INTERCEDE PRO NOBIS AD FILIUM DEI» («Father, death and life clash in an extraordinary duel, the maker of life lives again triumphant over death, alleluia. Oh St. Apollinare, priest and martyr of Christ, pray for your people that you won from paganism. We are all your people and the sheep of your flock. Intercede with the son of God for us»)

Higher up there is a trabeation from which the barrel-ceiling branches off with three windows on each side. Opposite to every arch, in the three minor naves, a chapel (three on each side) opens. Every chapel opens with a wide arch also sustained by columns; three little domes on each side form the ceiling of the minor naves.

On the floor marbles of various type have been used, taken from the demolition of the Basilica Ursiana; often, they are sections of columns, little columns, pillars, capitals; of the latter we can recognize very well a few Corinthian abaci.

Right nave - *First altar* (3): a painting representing St. Christophorus of *Antonio Rossi* from Bologna (1700-1753), placed between two columns of pavonazzetto.

— *Second altar* (4): (altar of the Crucifix - 1701). A **sarcophagus** is placed here. The inscription says that it contains the relics of the two bishops **Esuperanzio** and **Massimiano** (the

The Cathedral with the homonymous square.

latter placed in 1809). On the *front*, solemn on smoothe background the figure of Christ in a praying attitude and the figure of Paul with a book and of Peter with a cross in an acclaiming attitude appear. On the sides, two palms, and in the edges two tortile little columns. On the *sides*, on the left, there are ornamental motifs and a cross, on the right the monogram of Christ. On the *back*, not visible, two peacocks with monogram in the centre and two cypresses on the sides. The sarcophagus dates back to the second decennium of the 5th century.

— *Third altar* (5): a painting of *Giuseppe Milani* (1716-1798) from Parma representing «San Pier Crisologo and St. Romualdo and St. Pier Damiano».

— ***Ambo*** (6): in front of the third altar, among the columns, there is a «pyrgos» ambo, i.e. «tower», made up of a single piece from the base to the top, like the one of St. John and St. Paul of which we saw a part at the Archbishop Museum, and the one of which a fragment is still extant in the National Museum.

In the tower-like ambos a vast decoratable area is available that in what we are observing is divided in thirty six panels for each of the two faces. Inside each panel, divided from the others by two decorated frames, an animal is represented and precisely, from the top, lambs, peacocks, deer, pidgeons, ducks, fish, all looking towards the middle. The animals are represented without a real relief, nearly like some flat shapes, as the Byzantine taste imposed that had abandoned the strong relief of Roman origin. The dating of the piece is known with all security since, in front, there is the inscription: «SERVUS XPI AGNELLUS EPISCOP. HUNC PYRGUM FECIT» and on the back: «...PI AGNELLUS EPISC. HUNC PYRGUM...». The piece, therefore was worked between 557-570, espiscopal period of Agnellus.

To go up into the ambo there are two stairs with steps plus three little steps placed spirally. The two worked faces would be two enormous sarcophagus lids adapted to become part of an ambo (Gerola).

***Chapel of the Blessed* «Vergine del Sudore»** (7) - It constitutes the right arm of the transept. It was erected in 1630 in the hope of holding back plague that, in fact, didn't touch Ravenna even if it had spread in all Italy. It is a sumptuous room, paved and coated with precious marbles. To reach it ask the sacristan to open the gate.

In the chapel there is a little **tablet** (35 cm per 20) representing the Virgin carrying the Baby in her arms. It is of the fourteenth century, of Riminese school, and it was worshipped in the Duomo until the end of the 15th century. It is said that it bled for the first time when it was hit by a drunk man, and a second time during the pillage of Ravenna (1512), and that it sweat («**Madonna del Sudore**» [Madonna of sweat]) in procession in 1630. When it was placed in the chapel, the tabernaculum of Roverella, that is now in San Carlino was used as niche.

Later it found a more sumptuous collocation when the Roman sculptor *Pietro Bracci* (1700-1773), follower of the «Berninian» tradition, author of the beautiful statue of Clemente XII placed in the second cloister of the National Museum, in 1759 designed the altar of precious marbles, with sculptures and bronzes carried out, later, by Roman and Ravennati artists.

The dome is frescoed by *Giovan Battista*

Barbiani (1656) and represents «The Virgin between the celestial chorus».

Andrea Barbiani frescoed the four Evangelists in the pendentives, the stuccoes are of *Martinetti*; the iron gate was drawn in 1844 by *Gaetano* and *Angelo Ferrari*.

In the chapel, on two sides, two of the most beautiful sarcophagi of Ravenna are placed: the one of St. Rinaldo da Concoreggio and the one of St. Barbaziano.

Sarcophagus of St. Rinaldo (8) - Rinaldo da Concoreggio was archbishop of Ravenna and died in 1321. The sarcophagus that contains his relics is of the first half of the 5th century (around the years 420-430) and it is of imposing dimensions and decorated with reliefs of high artistic level.

In the *front* it presents a Christ on the throne, under which the four mystic rivers of the Earthly Paradise gush out. Christ holds his right hand out to Paul and holds with his left an open book; Paul stretches out towards the Lord with veiled hands offering a crown, while Peter, as well as the crown, carries a cross on his shoulders. Behind the two Apostles there are two stylized palms. Pale clouds in the sky; two little corner columns close the panel.

On one of the two *sides* a vase with rich going out of vine-shoots, on the other the monogram of Christ.

On the *back* with a rather rough technique, vine-shoots and peacocks are sculptured which face a big disc with *chrismon* from which the Apocalyptical letters alpha and omega hang. The lid is of the barrel type, covered by lanceolated leaves. In the *lunettes of the sides*, on one side the chrismon in a garland, on the other two lambs in front of a cross.

Sarcophagus of San Barbaziano (9) - It comes from the church of San Lorenzo in Cesarea. It is of the second half of the 5th century (De Francovich says it is datable to 440-450). In 1658 the relics of the confessor and adviser of Galla Placidia, Barbaziano, were placed here.

In the *front*, inside five niches with little columns and high capitals (the lateral little columns are double surmounted by an eagle), decorated by shells with deep relief, there are Christ in the middle with halo and an open book in his left hand, Peter with a cross, Paul with a book in his hand; the two Apostles hold their right hand in an orant attitude. In the lateral niches; two vases with plants with three leaves.

On the *sides*, in every niche there are two tripod candlesticks with lit candles: between them a cross with a monogram.

On the *back* two lambs face the *chrismon*. The *lid*, carries in the middle a crown containing the monogram, alpha and omega and four rosettes. On the sides of the crown, two big decorated crosses. In the *lunette*, on one side a vase with lily branches, on the other side peacocks with crown and monogram. Curious the particular of the animal - a rhino? - under the crown.

— *Fourth altar* (10): it is placed beyond the transept; it carries a painting of *Cesare Pronti* («Martyrdom of St. Ursicinus») between two columns of ancient African marble. In front of the altar there is the sepulchral epigraph of **father Antonio Cesari**, born in Verona in 1760, linguist and literary man, who made a reedition of the Crusca vocabulary adding many words to it. He died in 1828 in the college of nobles of Villa San Michele in Ravenna. The medallion was sculptured by Enrico Pazzi.

A little beyond, in the ambulatory (11), there is a highrelief of Mark the Evangelist, work of *Matteo da Ragusa* and *Giovanni Antonio da Milano*. It was the altar-piece of the apse of the church of San Marco and it was ordered in 1492 by the podesta Marco Bragadino. It was placed here in 1837.

Apse (12) - It houses four big paintings of some among the best painters of the beginning of the nineteenth century. From the left to the right, we have: «St. Severo enters in the sepulchre» *of Gioacchino Serangeli*, a Roman (1768-1852).

«St. Apollinare makes a temple of Apollo collapse» of *Giuseppe Colignon*, from Florence (1776-1863).

«St. Pier Chrisologo dying near the altar of St. Cassiano in Imola» of *Pietro Benvenuti* (1769-1844), painter of great drawing and compositive ability, however full of rhetoric.

«St. Orso consecrates the basilica built by him» of *Vincenzo Camuccini* (1171-1844), Roman neo-classical painter influenced by Canova. The altar was built on behalf of the archbishop Guiccioli and it is coated of green marble, of alabaster and of oriental black and white marble. The golden bronzes (1760) are of *Bartolomeo Borroni* from Vicenza.

Left nave - Returning along the left nave towards the entrance, before reaching the left arm of the transept, looking backwards we notice, above, a lunette with a painting of Guido Reni: «Elias in the desert to whom an angel brings bread and wine» (13).

— *Winter choir* (14): before the transept; built in 1852. On the altar there is a painting of an unknown artist: «Madonna, St. Orso and St. Rinaldo» in which beyond the balustrade, a view of mounts and towers appears. Above the painting there is a little oval canvas representing St. Gregorio Magno, Always in the choir

Fig. 44 - Conjectural reconstruction of Porta Aurea.

there are three lunettes by *Carlo Bonone* i.e. «Magdalene in the Pharisee's house», «Esther's banquet», «Mardocheo's triumph». The first lunette on the right, finally, is a «Deposition» of *Marco Palmezzano*, with Christ between the Madonna and the Evangelist Mark. On the right, in the painting, a little view of Ravenna.

Left arm of the transept - chapel of Sacrament (15): it was built on behalf of the bishop Pietro Aldobrandini on design of *Carlo Maderno*. The works started in 1612 and finished in 1620. Richly decorated, it has its major quality in the painting for which *Guido Reni* was called, who came to Ravenna with some worthy disciples of his (*Gian Francesco Gessi*, *Giovanni Giacomo Sementi*, *Bartolomeo Marescotti*). Also if they worked «alla gagliarda» (vigourously) in order to leave the city as soon as possible, they left very beautiful paintings. Completely and only of the master of arts is the oilpainting «Moses and the picking of manna», which is one of his best works.

Of Reni and of Gessi is the fresco of the dome: «The Redeemer and the archangels in glory». In the middle there is the Redeemer, around which a garland of cherubs' heads rotate; in the Southern zone the archangels are painted: Michael dressed as a warrior with his right hand raised holding a lance.

Gabriel that holds a lily, Raphael with female looks. Kneeling near Raphael there is Tobiolo with a fish. In the Northern zone two big angels are represented. The rest of the painting is occupied by putti who carry the instruments of Passion.

Again of Reni and of Gessi is «Melchizedec that blesses Abraham and his victorious people» in the two lunettes. Of Sementi are the «Prophets» in the four pendentives of the dome, «the theological and cardinal Virtues and some angels» in the twelve partitions of the underarches, and eight Saints in the eight partitions of the pillars.

Of Marescotti it is said that he mixed the colours and kept the brigade cheerful.

In the chapel some important restoration works were carried out in 1930: a new lunette was opened, the floor was remade with good marbles on a design imitating the ancient floor, the altar was remade with polichrome marbles and the ancient precious ciborium has been preserved; finally, the paintings and the stuccos were restored.

In the three chapels which separate us from the exit we find, between two columns of pavonazzetto (16), a canvas of *Filippo Pasquali* from Forlì, who died in 1696, pupil of Cignani; «St. Peter who sends St. Apollinare in Ravenna so that he converts it to Christianity» is represented.

In the following chapel (17), there is a baroque «Resurrection» in which Christ leaves the sepulchre, four soldiers fall heavily on a background of angels and clouds.

In the last chapel (18), finally above an altar with columns, there is a very nice picture of the painter *Joseph Wicar* (Lilla, 1792-1824) representing «Jesus between St. Anthony and St. James», on the background the city of Ravenna is represented.

The paintings of the two naves that we have just illustrated have been recently restored.

Monuments of the archbishops Guiccioli and Codronchi: they are leaning against the first two pillars of the left nave. The first one is de-

Fig. 45 - **Diachronic map of the city of Ravenna.** (The contemporary presence of monuments and topographic elements of different epochs and not always still existing will favour the reading of the map and an easy comparison between the city of today and the ancient one). On the map we notice the MUNICIPAL OPPIDUM which constitutes the first rational nucleus of the city, whose walls most probably already existed in 43 A.D., the year in which Porta Aurea was built and that could also date back to the Republican epoch. The OPPIDUM has the shape of the Roman **castrum**, with the **cardo** crossed as a rectangle by the **decumanus**. Its special dislocation, however, is anomalous, because the Roman **castrum** was usually oriented on the North-Southern axis (cardo), while in our case there is a deviation of about 45°. This is due nearly certainly to the characteristics of the place, rich of river courses, that didn't allow the usual choice. In this way the course of the North-Eastern side is anomalous, in fact instead of being straight, it leans against the courses of the two Padennas so as to exploit it as a natural defence or as natural ditch for the walls which, probably had been raised also near their banks.

The presumable ancient **decumanus** is still live in the actual via Port'Aurea until the crossing with via Ercolana - via Guidarello. From this point the rest of the **decumanus** has disappeared from the city's topography. Maybe it finished in Porta Asiana, on the actual via Cavour, beyond which the little Padenna river crossed on the bridge «of Augustus» or «of Austro», and then joined on the actual route of via Salara.

The actual via Oberdan retraces the course of the ancient «**cardo**», but, as regards to it, is a little towards North-East. It went from Porta Salustra, near the Duomo which still incorporates some remainders of it, to a little gate, called in the Early Middle Ages **Pusterula Latronum**, which was round about in the point in which via Oberdan goes out into the Circonvallazione Fiume Montone Abbandonato.

The addition where in the 5th and 6th century the complex Santa Croce - San Vitale - Santa Maria Maggiore rose, was ground destined to religious institutions, but the installation started at least during the 4th century, *extra moenia* (outside the walls).

The addition indicated as REGIO CAESARUM, that can be considered as the directional zone of the Gothic-Byzantine period, was territory property of the imperial Ravenna, where we had installations, still *extra moenia*, since the 2nd century.

The two little zones A and B, near the episcopal curia, finally, were incorporated in the 5th century.

The construction of the walls that, inserting themselves in those already existing of the OPPIDUM, included in the urban area the installations that had already formed outside the first town walls, took place during the 5th century. Widening works were started by Valentinian III (418-455) son of Galla Placidia and carried on by Odoacer (about 434-493), so that Theodoric found the town nearly completely sur-

---

dicated to the archbishop Ferdinando Romualdo Guiccioli, who brought to accomplishment the actual Cathedral, and it is of the sculptor *Ignazio Sarti* (1857). Above there is a well done angel representing the Christian virtue. Underneath there is a very accurate bas-relief, nearly a photograph which illustrates the presentation of the prototype of the Cathedral's portico to the archbishop. Notice with how many details the sculptor has made even the embroidery and the lace of the garments.

The second monument is dedicated to archbishop Antonio Codronchi; the architecture is of *Cristoforo Michelini*, the statues were sculptured in 1826 by the Ravennate *Gaetano Monti*; there is finally, a medallion of *Cincinnato Baruzzi* from Imola.

SANT'ANDREA MAGGIORE - Let's set off along via Port'Aurea, on the side of the church of Santa Giustina. Having reached the crossing with via Ercolana, on the right, we are in the zone where the basilica of Sant'Andrea Maggiore rose, dating back to the 6th century, in which bishop Maximian was buried. It was a church with three naves of which some parts remain, of the 11th century, incorporated in the walls of the houses at n. 31 of via Ercolana. In the warehouse at n. 33 there is a pulvino of the right nave and the lines of the arches are drawn; on the corner of the house at n. 29 there is another pulvino, and also in the kitchen-garden of the Capuchins. The church was demolished at the beginning of the last century. Near the church, in the 14th century, a monastery of Benedictines with cloister was built.

PORTA AUREA AND WALLS

Porta Aurea - Let's proceed along via Port'Aurea whose route, from the crossing with via Ercolana, coincides with the one of the supposed «decuman» of the Roman Ravenna (fig. 45, pag. 195), that from Port'Aurea reached Porta Asiana 720 meters far.

In this zone the **amphitheatre** and the **temple of Apollo** rose; Andrea Agnello, in fact, says that the temple of Apollo was «*ante portam quae vocatur Aurea iuxta amphitheatrum*».

After the great prison building which rises on the right (inaugurated in 1900), we reach the two uphill slopes that lead to the walls, at the feet of which, on the right and left side of the road, you can see two very low circular ruins: they are the traces of two towers which bordered Porta Aurea.

The gate was built in 43 a.D. under the emperor Claudius and it was demolished in 1582. It had two passages framed by semicolumns which carried a trabeation on which two tympana rose. Above a gallery ran (fig. 44). The gate couldn't be closed. It therefore had a celebrative function more than a defensive one. The internal structure was in bricks, while on the front it was decorated with marbles of which some fragments are at the National Museum, among which the two «paterae» that can be seen in the figure on the sides of the two arches. Other marbles were re-used, re-handling them, in the construction of Porta Adriana and of Porta Serrata. The graphic restitution that we propose here can be considered quite trustworthy, if not in the particulars, at least in the general aspect of the monument. To build it we used the contribution of several ancient rounded by walls. Having conquered it, he installed himself with his Goths in the wider area of the recent inglobations, where he accomplished the great constructions of his palace and of his churches. It must be said however that as regards to the walls other chronologic hypothesis exist.

Excluding limited expansions in the form of villages that occurred in the Medieval period, until a few decennia ago Ravenna was contained within the limits established in the 5th century.

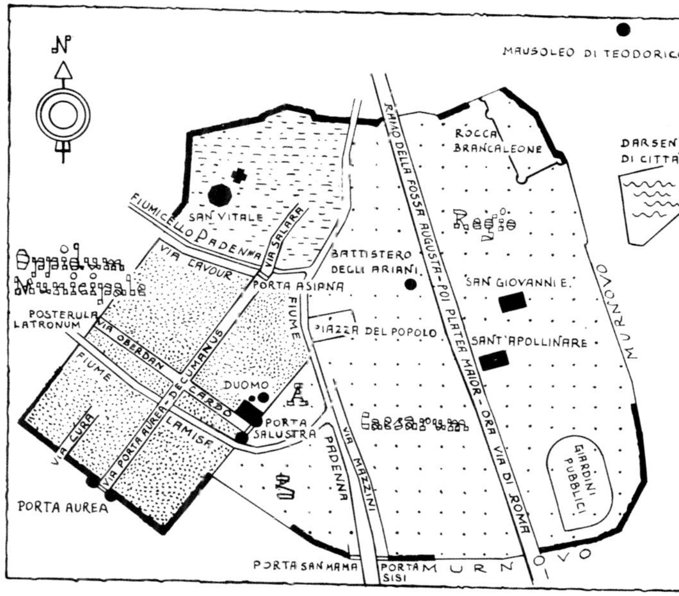

drawings, work, among others of Sangallo and Palladio, who saw the gate a few decennia before its demolition. We also considered the most recent historical and archaeological contributions. The aspect of the gate was handed down by an ancient seal of the city of Ravenna.

The width between the towers is of 18,65 meters. At five meters of depth the street paving lies made up of big blocks of trachyte. If the gate still existed, it would emerge from the street level from the jambs of the arches upwards, therefore the «paterae» would be at man's height.

Walls - The time of building of the walls in Ravenna is disputed. There are at least two different opinions about that. According to the first, the traditional one, city walls rose in the 1st century a.D. (maybe before), they had the shape of a not regular square, that surrounded a rather narrow area. These walls would have been then enlarged in the 5th century by Valentinian III and Odoacer, including so a much larger area. This thesis is illustrated in fig. 45, that follows completely this version.

According to the second thesis, it is impossible that the walls we know nowadays had been built in the 1st century A.D. «It is rather unbelievable the conjuncture of a construction of the walls at the time of Claudius. These would have defended a tenth of the town excluding nothing less than the military harbour with its large docks, Classe, Cesarea» (A. Roncuzzi). Besides, an excavation made in 1970 by A. Roncuzzi near Porta Aurea (Golden Gate), until the base of the walls, would demonstrate that they date back to the 5th century, because the level of the town in the 1st century lies over one metre beneath this base.

We are taking this opportunity to remind that in Ravenna, beneath the level of the present situation, we can locate three other levels: one lies at a depth of 7 metres, dating back to the 5th century B.C.; a second one between six and four metres, from the Roman age; a third one from four metres to one metre and a half, from the Byzantine age. The circle of the walls was kept intact until 1863, when a large piece was demolished in the Eastern side to make place for the railway station. The construction of the gas workshop determined the demolition in the Northern part near Porta Serrata and in 1921 the piece that goes from porta Adriana to via Oberdan. The last brief demolished piece is the one that allowed the outlet of via Cura in the Circonvallazione al Molino.

VARIATION - The itinerary proposed would bring us now to follow the walls towards the left going out, but for who wishes to see all that remains of the piece of the Roman walls on the South-Western side of the ancient town we suggest a brief variation. Go right up the little slope that leads on top of the walls. It is a path shaded by olm-oaks, pine-trees and cypresses. On the right proceeding there is the building of the prisons; a box hedge and a long row of pine-trees divide us from the town. Having passed the prisons, below the walls there are houses both on the left and on the right.

After about two hundred meters, we go down into via Cura, that we shall cross so as to climb up the opposite side until we reach the back of a little church, where the town-walls turn in a rectangle towards North-East. It is a pleasant place, with pine-trees and cypresses (itinerary, pag. 171).

ZANCANA TOWER - In this corner of the town-walls, in 1496 a powerful tower was built, called

Park of Peace: mosaic by Josette Deru.

Zancana tower by Andrea Zancano, Venetian podesta. It was a fortification work not devoided of beauty, as is demonstrated by the presence of a circle of elegant marble «brackets», of which we still see the remains, which must have constituted a pleasant decoration on a rough brick background. The tower took the place of a little castle that in turn had incorporated a tower already existing in the 14th century.

In 1730 the Zancana Tower was demolished until the wall level so as to build a little church, called then Madonna del Torrione, which had to house worthily an image of the Madonna del Sudore.

To enter the church, it is necessary, to return in via Cura, turn right, leave the ring-road and enter into via Fiume Abbandonato, right again. After a few steps, the first gate on the right leads into the church-square.

SANTA MARIA DEL TORRIONE - The church is a baroque construction with octagonal plan brought to the actual shape through various building phases. In 1761 the sacellum of the Virgin was redone and decorated as we see it now; in 1769 the lateral chapels were built and in the same year the little bell-tower is given as already extant. In 1789 finally, the whole central body was remade and its decorations too. After, the church was used as garrison of the custom guards and as lazaret for the infective sick people. In 1927, having re-established the parish seat, the image of the Madonna del Sudore was brought back that for a period of 43 years had been housed elsewhere.

In the central body, the paintings of the dome are work (1791) of *Giuseppe Cuppini* (perspective and ornamental decorations) and of *Giuseppe Santi* (figures): in the middle there is a glory of angels from which decorative festoons branch off and come downwards with medallions carrying emblems of the Virgin, like the star, the monogram, the crown and the pidgeon. At the base of the dome seven little oval windows open that give the inside a suffused light.

In the chapel at the bottom and in the lateral ones the pictorial decorations are of *Domenico Barbiani*. In particular, in the pendentives of the little dome above the high altar we see four cartouche shields («clypei») with the representation of other symbols of the Virgin: a little temple with dome, a well with buckets and pulley, a fountain, an open tower, crenelated and windowed. The walls are decorated in geometrical partitions with vases and masks.

The stuccos, typically baroque, of the bottom wall around the reliquary of the Virgin are of *Giuliano Garavini*: they represent a glory of angels with God that holds up a globe.

Underneath the venerated image there is the inscription: MONSTRA TE ESSE MATREM.

Let's now return on our steps going back on the walls until Port'Aurea, where we shall continue our itinerary climbing up the walls on the opposite side of the road.

From Porta Aurea to Porta Gaza - Walking along the path on the walls, we reach, after a hundred meters another corner of the Roman city, in which the Venetians built a twin tower to Torre Zancana, called **Torrione dei Preti**. It had two floors and, like the other one, it was equipped with bombards. Now it is breached and ruined.

From the tower let's proceed till Porta Gaza walking on the walls or on the street underneath. As soon as we pass the tower we find the

Park of Peace: mosaic by Edda Mally.

MONUMENTO ALLA RESISTENZA (Monument to Resistance) - It is a work of the sculptor Gio Pomodoro, inaugurated in 1980, commemorating the massacre of 12 partisans and patriots, which took place on the 25th August 1944, on the Allocchi bridge (from the name of a family from Ravenna), now called «ponte dei Martiri» (bridge of Martyrs), today a place completely transformed by the new road arrangement.

The sculpture lies on various levels and it is articulated in elements which represent the defeat of reason (the T, as representation of reason in the form of the Carthesian axes, upside down and broken), in contraposition with the element constituted by the round block of Trani stone, which represents work, transformation (millstone, wheel), the optimism of will. On the base on which the round block stands the cardinal points are engraved: NORD (North), SUD (South), LEVA (East), PONE (West). The last two terms recall the «*levare*» (removing) and «*porre*» (placing), acts of the sculptor but also of any other human work.

The months of the year and the square which intersects them put in relief the four seasons. «The whole thing creates a map of knowledge acquired by men through hard labour» (G. Guberti).

This is the point in the tour that takes us nearer to the

Park of Peace: mosaic by Jerry W. Carter

PARK OF PEACE - whic can be reached by going down Via Mario Montanari, then turning right and going down Via Cassino for about one hundred metres. The park is situated between Via G. Marconi and Via Marzabotto.

The Park of Peace is a relatively contained area of public parkland which houses mosaics made by artists from various parts of the world on the theme of peace. For those who might wish to digress from the tour to visit these mosaics, we have provided below some general remarks, taken from an illustrated book, on the meaning of each of the works, together with the names of the artists:

— Claude Rahir: This mosaic is of semicircular arrangement and is composed of minerals from all over the world. In the centre is a cube of Carrara marble from which water falls, «the secular and religious ideal of man in close contact with nature is expressed by the com-

Porta Gaza.

position-landscape of pebbles, gravel and crystals».

— Margaret L. Coupe: Warship and men in uniform for atomic tests off the coast of New Zealand. Huge whales exposed to radiation.

— Jerry W. Carter: Pictures of the earth (the blue planet denoted by a huge curved line) transmitted by space vehicles. A reflecting surface expresses the energy released by the meeting of matter and anti-matter. Very small white circles on the top edge represent the solar system. Bright red blotches warn of the nuclear threat.

— Alexandr Kornoovkhov: A stele of stones, marble and enamels.

— Mimmo Paladino: Around and among the branches of a three hover figures, shapes, bodies, heads, masks and bars - images of a past, existing, imaginary world.

— Josette Deru: Young people under a tree, symbol of life, bedding small plants, symbolizing man's ties with the earth.

— Edda Mally: Two wings of a dove, one stretching towards the sky, the other shattered, representing the evil of war.

— Bruno Saetti: Saint Michael with large wings, under a huge sun and resting on the demon.

Let's now return to the Monument to the Resistance and move down Via Porta Gaza to

PORTA GAZA - Mentioned for the first time in 1186; walled in 1590; it was remade in 1750 by the archbishop Ferdinando Romualdo Guiccioli «as ornament and convenience of the town», as can be read on the Latin epigraph placed on the attic.

In 1798 it was walled again and at the beginning of our century it was used as entrance to a powder magazine of the army placed in the terminal part of todays via of Porta Gaza. Later the low constructions of the powder-magazine were used as pidgeon houses for carrier-pidgeons of the army: in the neighbourhoods, in via Nino Bixio, there was, and there still is today, a garrison.

The name of the gate maybe comes from the family of Gaza counts who had a castle or forthouse in the neighbourhoods. The term should belong to the Longobard linguistic area, in which the term «*garbagium, gagium, gazium, gajum*, means forest, woods». The gate is where the primitive Roman town-walls were abandoned to insert, in North-East direction, one of the widenings of the 5th century. If the Roman walls in this point hadn't been destroyed, they would lead us in a straight line to the tower of Porta Sallustra.

From Porta Gaza, climbing for some ten meters to the feet of the walls, we can try to make out the **crenelations of the ancient walls**. They aren't very visible. They are revealed by the bricks which, not interpolating themselves, make a vertical continuing line in some points which reveals, in fact, the closing of the spaces between one crenelation and the other, when the walls were raised and the crenelations were incorporated.

The Roman crenelations were 1.20 meters high, with a space of about one meter between one and the other.

We remind, here, that in the mosaic of Sant'Apollinare Nuovo you can see the crenelated walls.

PIAZZA KENNEDY - Having passed Porta Gaza we turn left in via Santa Teresa and right in via Nino Bixio and we return in piazza del Duomo. Having arrived here, passing under the portico of the Duomo, we go along via Giovac-

Palazzo Rasponi delle Teste: portal.

chino Rasponi and we reach piazza Kennedy.

To open this big square, in 1930 they had to demolish several houses, occupy a garden which made part of the palace Rasponi dalle Teste and eliminate the remainder of the basilica Sant'Agnese (5th century) of which we have preserved some fragments in the yard of the above mentioned building, as we shall see. The place witnesses and illustrates a historical period of Ravenna: the one in which the rich and powerful Rasponi family, with its various branches, prevailed from the 16th and 19th century, even if they never actually kept a real signoria. It was a family, however, with which pontiffs and princes had continuous contacts.

On the square, infact, one in front of the other, two of the numerous palaces or Rasponi houses scattered around the town face each other: the side of the Rasponi-Murat palace and the Rasponi dalle Teste palace. On the corner of the square, at the insertion of via D'Azeglio and via Garattoni, a third Rasponi building appears. On the other two sides of the square there is the «Casa del Mutilato di guerra» (house of the mutilated of war), of Fascist epoch, and on the other side, the Della Torre palace and other houses.

PALAZZO RASPONI-MURAT - Built in the 15th century by Giovanni Balbi, it belonged to a very ancient family of Ravenna, and passed later to the Rasponi family, it has the façade that looks onto via Guerrini. The wall of the building stands scarp and it is crowned by big «barbicans» which sustain a beautiful row of little arches. The door is surmounted by a little balcony of the eighteenth century. Beyond the hall, a yard with an ancient well and two marble wash-basins. In front of the palace, beyond the little square, a door designed by *Camillo Morigia*, who carried out remarkable interventions in the building itself, leads to the garden, widened in 1780 by the Count Marco Fantuzzi, who became owner of the building. After a few transfers, the palace returned again to the Rasponi family in 1847, bought by count Giulio who had married the princess Luisa Murat, daughter of Gioacchino king of Naples and of Carolina sister of Napoleon. He got the ceilings painted by *Gaetano Ferrari* (also interventions of *Felice Giani*). The inside preserves rooms, library, sitting-rooms, bedrooms, furniture, antiques, works of art of such level that the prince Carlo Murat, visiting the building a few years ago, affirmed that «in Paris not one building of the Ist Empire that can be compared to this one exists» (Foschi).

PALAZZO RASPONI DALLE TESTE - 70 meters long, 24 meters high, it is the most beautiful building of the town. Built in the first years of the eighteenth century , maybe on design of the Ravennate architect Luca Danesi it is called «dalle Teste» because on the architrave of the windows of the first and the second floor there are alternatively a Moorish bandaged head and a lion's head, which make part of the bearings of this branch of the Rasponi family. On the window-sills, furthermore, there are two crossed lion paws with powerful drawn out claws (the rasponi) which make part of the bearings of every branch of the family. The sumptuous portal surmounted by a beautiful balconied window, bordered by two elaborate volutes, and the cornice of the windows, are of Istria stone. On the second floor, on the corners, there are three beautiful balconies, of which two on the sides of the façade and the third on the corner via D'Azeglio-via Longhi. Remarkable the pillars of the balustrades with very nice varied figures. The building is crowned all around by a harmonious cornice and it is surmounted by two big chimneys. The hall and the staircase are work of the Camaldolese *Giuseppe Antonio Soratini*. In the garden of the building two columns are preserved, a pillar, pulvinoes and capitals of Greek marble, remainders of the basilica of Sant'Agnese, erected in the 5th century.

PALAZZO RASPONI - It rises next to the Rasponi dalle Teste palace. The aspect of today is the result of a work carried out by Morigia in 1789 on a preceeding construction. The portal, of imposing aspect, carries a lion's head on the architrave and is surmounted by a balcony whose door ends with a triangular tympanum. Under the eaves, there is a frieze in which roses and the Rasponi emblems appear (moorish heads, lion paws). In the inside, some rooms preserve paintings of Felice Giani. The stuccos above the doors are of *Benedetto Fiandrini*.

PALAZZO «DELLA TORRE» - Placed on the corner between piazza Kennedy and via Garatoni, it can be dated to the 18th century. It was inhabited by the Della Torre counts, originally from Florence, relatives of Dante Alighieri. The building incorporates the remainders of an ancient tower and is the seat of a branch-office of the Monte dei Paschi, after a very recent restoration and re-arrangement.

Near the zone where we are now there was the **Forum** of the Roman Ravenna. Remembrance of it is in the name of **Santa Maria in Foris**, a church which rose at the beginning of via Pasolini towards via D'Azeglio. Here, at 20 meters from the crossing, near the civic number 59, above the fourth window, more than three meters of height, there is a tablet nearly two meters long, about ten centimeters high which marks the place. Near the Forum there was the **Basilica d'Ercole**, the statue «**Ercole orario**», of which we have already spoken about describing the sculptures in the Venetian columns of Piazza del Popolo, and the **miliarum aureum** of Ravenna capital, decorated column from which they measured the distances of the roads which branched off from the town and which marked, therefore, the centre, the *umbilicus* of the city itself.

PIAZZA DELL'AQUILA - PALAZZO PASOLINI DALL'ONDA - Let's now set off along via Giovacchino Rasponi in the North-Eastern corner of the square and let's reach piazza XX Settembre, called by the Ravennati piazza dell'Aquila because of the eagle placed on top of the column of grey granite that is in the middle of the square. The column was erected in 1609 in piazza Maggiore, now called del Popolo, on design of *Francesco Longhi* and brought here in 1673; the eagle is the bearing of cardinal Bonifazio Caetani.

In the past the square was called «delle garnelle», «della legna» (of wood), «del vino» (of wine), «Foro Asinario», indicating the commercial activities which it housed.

The Pasolini dall'Onda palace looks onto the square erected in the 17th century. It underwent numerous transformations. The last restoration of 1905 gave the façade the seventeenth century aspect that we see today. On the architraved door there is a balcony with a marble balustrade. In the park of the building there are big secular trees. The rooms are rich of ancient furniture, historical relics, two important libraries, paintings (Felice Giani and his school), portraits, marble busts, prints.

ITINERARY OF CLASSE

Via di Roma - Ponte Nuovo - The port and the city of Classe - The excavations of Classe - Basilica of **Sant'Apollinare in Classe** - Column of the French (Colonna dei Francesi) - Garibaldi's hut (Capanno di Garibaldi) - Santa Maria in Porto Fuori - Mirabilandia.

Sant'Apollinare in Classe: air view.

This itinerary has as principal aim the basilica of Sant'Apollinare in Classe, but it will also allow us to get to know places where the city of Classe rose with its big port.

To arrive to the basilica, you can catch a line of urban transport (a bus) that leaves from the centre of town, or else a local train of the Ravenna-Rimini line, or else you must have a car. In such case go along via di Roma, go out through Porta Nuova and continue by following the road directions for Rimini. The road which runs through the suburb is called Cesarea; immediately after the inhabited area it takes the name of Romea Sud.

THE BUILT-UP AREA OF CESAREA - In the zone of this first part of our route in the early ancient times the built-up area of Cesarea rose which, from little extraurban nucleus, widened to such an extent to join practically Ravenna with Classe, even without ever rising to the dignity of city. For the geographical relations between Ravenna, Cesarea and Classe, we quote this passage of the Arian bishop Jordanes, who towards the middle of the 6th century wrote «...The city of Ravenna glories itself and rejoices for its triple denomination and collocation: that is, first Ravenna, last Classe, in the middle Cesarea between the city and the sea».

During the residence of the emperor Honorius in Ravenna (that goes from 402 to 423, year of his death), in the village of Cesarea a big cemetery church was built dedicated to St. Laurence (**San Lorenzo in Cesarea**), «*mirae magnitudinis*», decorated with very beautiful mosaics and a great variety of marbles. It was demolished around 1553 and part of the material was recovered and re-used in the construction of the church of Santa Maria in Porto.

The place where the church rose was marked, as commemoration, by a column surmounted by cross. This gave origin to the place-name Crocetta that we still find in the denomination of a road of the zone. The Crocetta (little cross) was a hundred meters beyond the via Mangagnina, on via Romea, on the left, more or less where n. 50 is. It was thrown down by unknown people during the night on the 25th July 1875, and now it is in the National Museum.

THE PORT AND THE CITY OF CLASSE - Continuing along the road which leads to Rimini we reach the territory where the waters which constituted the port of Classe opened. To orient ourselves we must keep an eye on the map fig. 46 taking as observation the top of the Ponte Nuovo which crosses the Fiumi Uniti (1).

Beneath us the river flows; before us towards the sea, there is the bridge of the railway (2), whose projection cuts the horizon on the left towards Ravenna, on the right towards Rimini. All around there is a country landscape. The road that goes down from the bridge divides in two at a little less than one hundred meters from our emplacement, on the right for Cesena (via Dismano), on the left for Rimini (via Romea). From this last one via Marabina turns left like a rectangle, which runs at the feet of the right bank of the Fiumi Uniti, reaches the railway and passes underneath.

If we look around to scan the horizon, running along the railway ballast towards Rimini, at a certain point we meet far away the bell-tower and the dark massive structure of the basilica of Sant'Apollinare in Classe (3). Having framed the basilica, looking towards the left along the embankment of the railway, we can make out under it a low unshaped ruin, the remainder of an ancient bell-tower of which we shall speak about later (4). Basilica and ruins are the only ancient elements, even if not coeval, they are now visible above the ground level. To this we must add what existed and that we haven't got today, taking knowledge, even if quite a summary one, of the results of the excavation campaigns carried out in the zone.

Here there was the water basin which made part of the port of Classe: the big naval Roman base of the upper Adriatic. Here around us the ships moved, moored, weighed anchor. The ships were made of wood moved by oars.

The «Classis Ravennas» i.e. the Roman fleet that Augustus established as permanent fleet in Ravenna (there was another one in Miseno, in the Campania region and other fleets were placed in other areas of the Empire), it was made up of 250 ships that had the duty to defend the port from the enemies and therefore they were war ships (naves longae) or else they were cargo ships for goods for the army (naves onerariae).

The ships had five (quinqueremes or penteres), four (quadriremes or quadrieres), three (triremes or trieres), two (biremes) oars, or even only one order of oars (actuariae). The little ships used in the river fleets were called *lusoriae*. Among the biremes there were the *liburne*, fast ships with a pointed stern, provided with rams, with 70 oarsmen and 180 soldiers, called in this manner because they were used by the Liburni, a population from Illyria (Liburnia).

It mustn't be thought that the quinqueremes and quadriremes had five or four rows of oars. No Roman ship, just as no Greek ship, had more than three orders of oars i.e. three rows on each side. Already on a trireme to be an oarsman of the superior order meant to work harder and therefore they had better wages. In the triremes there were 170 oarsmen, 31 on each superior level with longer oars and 27 on each of the lower levels. The levels were three. There were therefore 85 oarsmen on each side. The quadriremes were called in this way because 1) At the upper oar there were two oarsmen while at the two lower ones there was one oarsman at each; or else 2) the ship had only one row of oars with

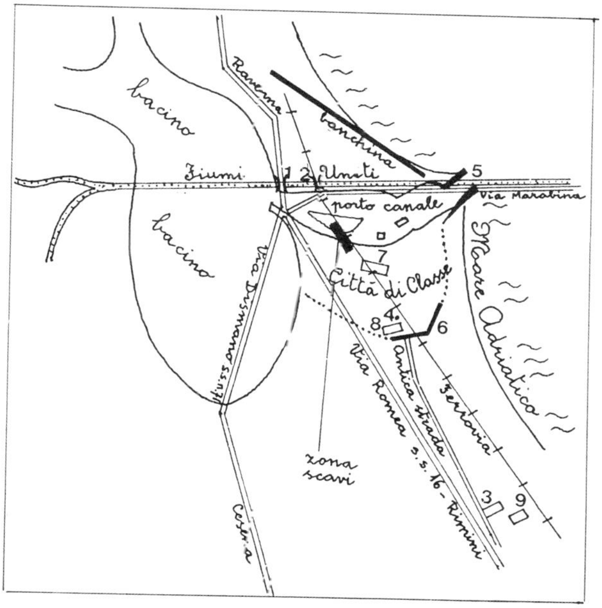

Fig. 46 - **Diachronic map of the zone of the port and of the city of Classe.** 1 - Bridge on the Fiumi Uniti. 2 - Bridge of the railway on the Fiumi Uniti. 3 - Basilica of Sant'Apollinare in Classe. 4 - Ruin of the bell-tower of San Severo. 5 - Docks of the ancient port of Classe. 6 - Singled out sectors of the walls of the city of Classe. 7 - Basilica Petriana. 8 - Basilica of San Severo. 9 - Basilica of San Probo.

four oarsmen for each oar; or otherwise 3) the ship had two rows of oars with two oarsmen for each oar. The quadrireme had two oarsmen at the upper oar, two oarsmen at the middle one, and one oarsman at the lowest. The quadriremes most probably had a total of 232 oarsmen, the quinqueremes had 286 The draught of the hull was minimal, maybe one meter and a half, and therefore the ships were not suitable for rough seas and therefore liable to sinking. A trireme could reach a maximum speed of about 21 kilomters per hour that could be maintained only for 5-10 minutes and it most probably took about thirty seconds to reach the highest speed from standing start.

The weapons with which a war ship was provided were: the ram, and in this case the ship was long and narrow with a relation between length and width of 10 to 1 (a ship 40 meters long was 4 meters wide), or with catapults, weapons based on the elastic strength of ropes made of sinews, more than on flexible arches that flung stones and arrows, the latter made of tree branches with metal points. The catapults, that were maintained on the wider and more stable ships could fire at more than 200 meters of distance. As the thickness of the hull was only 3,5 centimeters it wasn't difficult for the arrows to break through and hit the oarsmen that were inside.

Historically, the ram appeared around the year 800 B.C., the catapults around 332 B.C. the quadriremes in 400 A.D. ca.; the first quadrireme was built in 399 B.C. In the passing of centuries, larger and steadier ships with catapults prevailed over the agile and narrow ones with rams, then later, for tactic reasons smaller and faster ships prevailed. During the last great naval battle of ancient times (the Battle of Actium 31 B.C.) Anthony's heavy ships with 8, 9, 10 oarsmen for each group of oars were defeated by the lighter and faster ships of Octavianus, and this type of war ship was certainly the kind that made up the fleets in Ravenna and Miseno.

Every ship was designated with the name of a god (Mercury, Minerva, Apollo, Neptune) or an allegorical one (Constantia, Victoria, Fides) or with the name of a river (Danubius, Padus) or of an animal (Aquila, Castor, Taurus). The supreme command of the fleets was the emperor's who would appoint his representatives with the title of *Praefecti* who belonged to the equestrian order. Between 71 A.D. and 127 A.D. the fleets of Ravenna and Miseno received the title of *praetoria*. Among the officers of the fleet we find the trierarchs and the navarchs that were terms which designated the commanders of the ships. Among the petty officers (principales) we mention the *gubernator* (the helmsman), who as well as holding the rudder, made up of two oars at the stern, had to observe the sky to fix the route, he had to know the shallow waters and the rocky areas, the beaches and ports; the *proreta*, who stayed at the prow would point out to the *gubernator* the presence of rocks, shallows etc.; the *nauphylax* (guardian of the ship), the *hortator* (who would regulate the rhythm of the oaring), the *optio* (the captain's lieutenant), the *coronarius*, who prepared crowns that were to be used to engarland ships etc.. On every ship there was an M.D.

The crew was made up of oarsmen (remiges), sailors (nautae) and of soldiers (classici milites). No component of the crew was a slave since there weren't any slaves on Roman ships. The sea soldiers were mostly *peregrini* (i.e. inhabitants of one of the Roman Empire's provinces, who remained *peregrini* for all the military

Chapel of San Savero:
fragment of inscription.

service, but at the moment of demobilization, after a service that lasted from 26 to 28 years they could obtain Roman citizenship) and those in Ravenna came especially from Dalmatia, Pannonia, Thrace.

The docks of the port, now buried under more than three meters of ground are at about one hundred meters beyond the bridge of the railway (5). They are 50 meters away from one another. As we can see on the map figure 46, the mouth contained exactly the actual riverbed of the Fiumi Uniti, with all the right embankment, and the via Marabina. It is to be noticed, however, that there is no relation between the river of today and the ancient port, because the actual mouth was artificially obtained in the 18th century. The docks run a little transversally in regards to the banks of the river. At the beginning of the docks presumably the towers of the light-houses were placed.

The Southern dock continued towards land with a wide arched quay which reached till the point in which the roads divide for Cesena and for Rimini, before the end of the descent of the roads. Along this quay the portual warehouses, the deposits, the shipyards rose. Behind them, towards the South, there was the «civitas» and that is the place of the civil houses, of the meeting places, of the associations, of the markets and of artisan shops. The city was protected by wide town-walls (6) which went a little beyond the low bell-tower ruin that we see under the embankment of the railway. A piece of this wall was revealed during preceeding researches: it is several meters wide and it can be dated back to the 2nd-4th century A.D. It is maybe the one that compelled Theodoric to besiege Odoacer for three years and that appears on the mosaic which represents Classe in the basilica of Sant'Apollinare Nuovo where the city shows its rich buildings a little above the high wall, nearly an unreachable mirage for the Goths afflicted by years of tiring marches, battles and by the hard life in the open.

Can we imagine the houses, the noise, the fervent life of these places? The coming and going of the ships, of the people; the trading, the works, the events, the voices of this town full of people coming from all the parts of the Empire? How can we think about the existence of such a world in the silence of the landscape of today?

> . . . . Or dov'è il suono
> di quei popoli antichi? or dov'è il grido
> dei nostri avi famosi, e il grande impero
> di quella Roma, e l'armi, e il fragorio
> che n'andò per la terra o l'oceano?
> Tutto è pace e silenzio, e tutto posa
> il mondo, e più di lor non si ragiona.
> (Leopardi, «La sera del dì di festa» vv. 33-39)

Classe was the biggest naval Roman base of the Adriatic and of the Oriental Mediterranean, with its 250 ships and ten thousand «classiari» as the marines, sailors and oarers were called. They came especially as we said from the coast zones of Italy, Syria, Egypt, Balkans and we can still see the sepulchral «stelae» at the National Museum and read their names and qualifications: Anario Felice, graduated sailor of the

Excavations of Classe: some terracotta lamps.

ship Sphinx, Apella, helmsman of the ship Neptune, Plator son of Abacalli. The funeral stelae were found along the sand slope which was the cemetery of the city and that ran parallel to the railway, beyond it, from the Fiumi Uniti till St. Apollinare in Classe.

Classe was a bishop's seat, and even if it passed in Ravenna after 402 when the imperial court established here, its importance continued. Therefore big basilicas rose such as the Petriana (7), San Severo (8), San Probo (9), St. Apollinare (3) of which we shall speak about and churches such as St. Eufemia, San Sergio.

In Classe the military authority had seat, while the political and administrative power were in Ravenna. The city underwent the seiges of Odoacer in 476; of Theodoric in 491-93; of Belisarius 540. Then it was pillaged and finally destroyed by Liutprand, King of the Longobards in the 8th century. So Classe disappears, the sea goes further away, sand accumulates, the abandoned buildings deteriorate and collapse, the lowering of the ground and periodical alluvions act in such a way as to bury every remainder under a thick blanket of ground. Nature gets the upper hand. Where the superb Roman quinqueremes moored now the plough traces its grooves.

Only the basilica of Sant'Apollinare overcomes unharmed the centuries and resists isolated in the silent countryside to speak to us about those ancient times.

We now give some hints on the ancient basilicas localized and in part dug, then we shall go towards the one of Sant'Apollinare.

BASILICA PETRIANA - Started off by bishop Pietro I Chrisologus (429-449) finished by his successor Neon, it was the vastest of the churches of the zone of Ravenna, measuring 78 meters per 40, it was even bigger than the Ursiana. It was called Petriana because its construction had been started by Pietro I. It had three naves, preceeded by a quadriportico on whose area now the railway passes, and it was decorated by mosaics, marbles, paintings. It collapsed in the 8th century after an earthquake. It was discovered in 1964 by G. Cortesi which revealed its plan.

BASILICA OF SAN SEVERO - Built nearly attached to the walls it is localizable by the ruin of its square bell-tower, which we already mentioned. The area on which it rose, half way about from Ponte Nuovo and the Basilica of Sant'Apollinare, is now fenced. The excavations show the semi-circular apse, the «pastophorium», quadrangular room of the 10th-11th century near the apse, the whole plan.

Started off by the archbishop Pietro III (570-578) it was finished by his successor the archbishop Giovanni II (578-595), it had 3 naves, it measured 54 m. per 27, and it was preceeded by an atrium.

It was erected in honour of San Severo, the last of the «colombini» bishops. Large parts of the floor are today in Ravenna in the Rasponi crypt, in the National Museum, in the palace Serena-Monghini.

It rose in a place called *Vicus Salutaris*. Against the church on the Southern side, there was a cell of more ancient construction, in which the relics of the Saints were preserved until the basilica was built.

In the 15th century it was demolished because it was ruined and in its place a smaller, new church was built (1468) which, renewed in the 18th century, later abandoned resulted definitely destroyed round about 1820. The square

bell-tower of which a ruin remains, is maybe of the 12th century.

BASILICA OF SAN PROBO - It is at 190 metres South-East from the apse of the basilica of Sant'Apollinare. We think it was built by Probo II bishop of Ravenna in the second half of the 4th century, but Cortesi says that: «the analytic exam seems to suggest us the primitive implant of the basilica must not be dated back before the 5th century». The title of San Probo was assumed according to someone because of the name of the builder, according to others because of the relics of Probo I that the archbishop Maximian, after having accomplished big arrangement works (for example, he had the façade decorated with mosaics) had placed here. It measured about 70 metres of length and 32 of width with transept with apsidal extremities and it was preceeded by a narthex and a quadriportico. It had a primary importance as regards to other suburban churches of Classe even if the bishop Orso, at the beginning of the 5th century, built in Ravenna the Cathedral (Ursiana) and the episcopal seat. In it the bodies of the ancient bishops of Ravenna were buried then they passed at the end of the 10th century, in the crypt of the Ursiana. After this transfer the church was abandoned, it became the shelter for livestock and for hunters until, pressed by the surrounding forest, it was devoured by it and it disappeared. The plan was drawn by Cortesi in 1964. In the zone the most ancient Christian epigraphs were found of Emilia Romagna: the stele of Antifonte, of Valeria Maria and the epigraph of Flavio Anastasio, now in the archbishop Museum.

BASILICA NEAR THE «CA' BIANCA» - Found nearly by chance by Cortesi in 1965, is about 2 kilometres south of the basilica of Sant'Apollinare in Classe and at about 800 meters from the statal road Adriatica uphill. It is reached by going along the right bank of the drain Castelladella. The excavations show a basilica with three naves that were paved by marble slabs, to which they added two ambulatories paved of mosaic (another hypothesis: the church was widened by three to five naves), four «pastophoria», the quadriportico before the façade, a baptistery, the semi-circular apse inside and with five faces on the outside. The primitive implant of the church dates back to the second half of the 4th century.

It has measures similar to those of Sant'Apollinare Nuovo.

The prints left on the paving certify that the church was provided of «bema», of a ciborium and of an ambo. The existence of a church in this place is extraordinary, because documents which speak about it don't exist, except a laconic and controversial passage of Andrea Agnello (9th century). The name of San Demetrio has been mentioned. The denomination «Cà Bianca» refers to a farm-house nearby.

THE EXCAVATIONS OF CLASSE - Since 1974 excavations have been carried out in the zone of the excavation in fig. 46 page 203, that corresponds to a little rectangle drawn with dotted lines.

The excavation interests part of the island in the port, the channel between the island and the city, a sector of the city. Considering that it is the layer of the 5th-6th century, belonging to the Gothic and Byzantine period, we shall say that the following were brought to light:

a) in the island, a road and part of two buildings;

◀ A street of the ancient town of Classe. Its bed is formed by slabs of volcanic stone (trachyte)joined together. We can just see the two long ruts let by the carts. On the left there are remains of the warehouses (No. 2 and 3 of Figure 47), beyond which there was the secondary branch of the Port-Canal.

Excavations at Classe: in the foreground the building with basin; in the background a warhouse (No. 1 and 2 of Figure 47). The two buildings looked onto the secondary branch of the Port-Canal.

▼

b) in town, a street paved with trachytes, 5 meters wide, maybe it was the principal road of the port zone of Byzantine Classe, it was practically parallel to the channel, with buildings on both sides, both between the road and channel both on the opposite side.

Beyond the road, the warehouses, the porticoes, the landing stages made up of steps on the channel, sewerage drains, and a kiln for ceramic. The excavations consent to recover a lot of material, such as ceramics, glass, metal objects, goldsmithery, amphorae, oil-lamps, ambers, bricks coins.

The schematic map in the nearby page (fig. 47) can be useful also for a visit in loco.

The excavation is on the right of via Marabina, before the railway projection.

There is a project of creating an archaelogical park that should valorize these discoveries connecting them to the basilica of Sant'Apollinare.

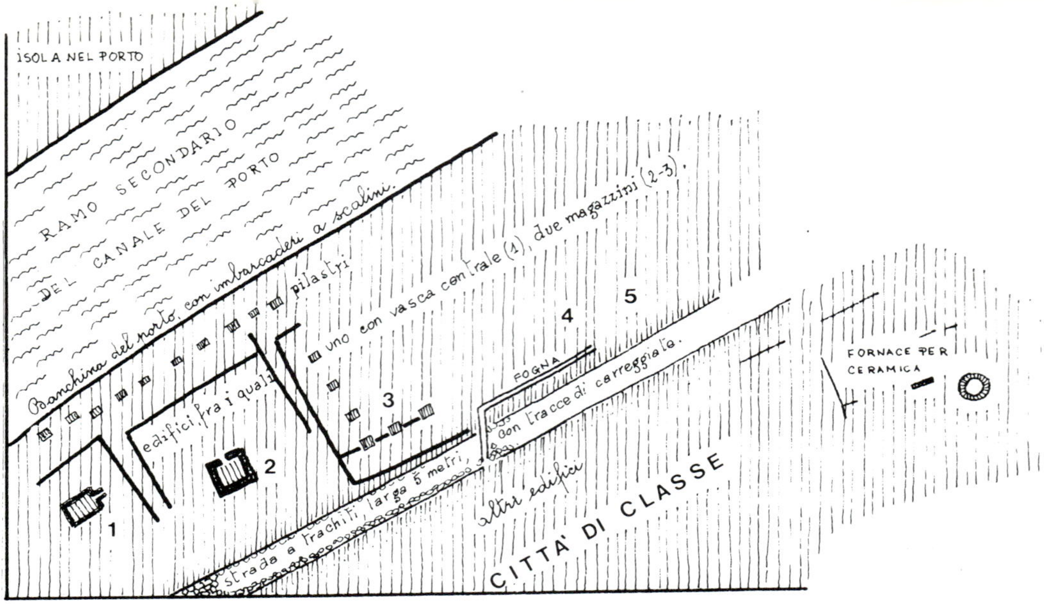

Fig. 47 - Indicative scheme of the excavations in the port and in the city of Classe.

Excavations at Classe: a sewer of the town that flows from the street, visible in the background, into the canal.
▼

SANT'APOLLINARE IN CLASSE

Historical hints and external aspect - It is placed at about five kilometres from the centre of Ravenna. It rose outside the city of Classe. The construction was financed by that Giuliano Argentario that in the same period provided to the expenses for the erection of San Vitale. It was wanted by Ursicinus bishop of Ravenna from 535 to 538 and it was consecrated on the 9th May of 549 by the archbishop Maximian that had consecrated S. Vitale one year before.

It was dedicated to Sant'Apollinare, the first bishop of Ravenna and his relics were transferred here.

The entrance was preceded by a big quadriportico, whose foundations were individuated exactly. One of the sides of the quadriportico was against the church (ardica). On the sides of the ardica two towers rose maybe of two floors. Of these ancient elements only the little Northern tower is left, even if very rehandled and falsed during reconstruction and restoration. The actual portico has nothing to do with the ancient ardica, because it was built entirely in 1908-1909 without considering the traces, still existing and known, of the ardica itself.

Above the portico a three-mullioned window which lightens the austere façade of brickwork.

Along the sides of the church the numerous windows are framed by a row of arches not very jutting out which confer to the perspective remarkable dynamism. Notice that the bricks with which the church was built are the same as those of San Vitale and of other structures financed by Giuliano Argentario.

Very moved is also the posterior part where, in the middle, the great volume of the apse di-

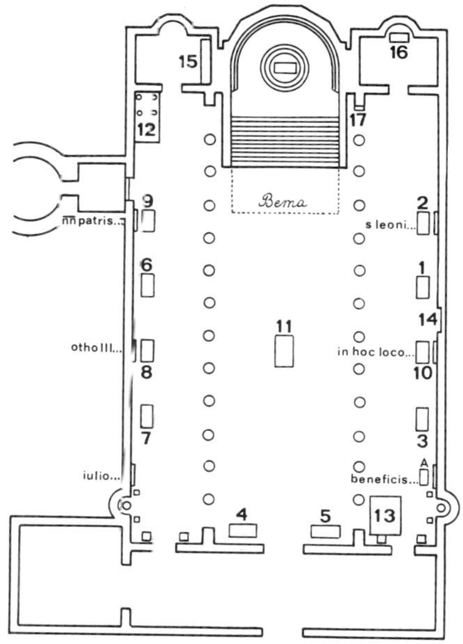

Fig. 48 - **Basilica of Sant'Apollinare in Classe: plan.** 1, 2, 3, 4, 5, 6, 7, 8, 9, 10 - A Sarcophagi (for the illustration of each sarcophagus, look at the text). 11 - Altar composed by pieces of different epochs. 12 - Ciborium of St. Eleucadio (9th century). 13 - Remainder of a floor mosaic (6th century). 14 - Remainder of the floor mosaic of the central nave (6th century). 15 - Wooden choir. 16 - Cippus altar. 17 - Book of indulgences (1468).

vided on seven faces juts out and on the sides the chapels of the «prothesis» and of the «diaconicon», which end with a little apse made up by five faces.

The **bell-tower**, that rises on the Northern part, 37,50 m. high is joined to the church by an original little passage restored in 1901, when the sacristy was demolished. It starts off from a low squared base and it goes upwards in a cylindric form. Two orders of slits follow (and in this zone there are red and yellow bricks and an ornamental strip of little brickwork squares, they are yellow and red, too), two orders of wide windows, one order of mullioned-windows, three orders of three-mullioned windows.

As date the 10th century is indicated. Mazzotti says it isn't posterior to the beginning of the 10th century, while he places the zone of the three-mullioned windows round about the year 1000.

It is maybe the nicest bell-tower of the Ravennate zone presenting itself as a prototype of the round tower. The openings, that widen while going upwards, lighten its imposing dimension: an enlightening not only aesthetic but also physic. In the shade of the mullioned and three-mullioned windows the stone columns stand out which sustain the little arches.

The building underwent after a beginning of great splendour, a slow decline that got worse during the centuries until it reached periods of abandon, when the monks transferred to Ravenna after the pillage (1512) of the abbey that rose near the basilica, and when the Napoleonic decree of suppression (1797) sent the Camaldolesi away from Ravenna who, even if from far, in some way provided to the maintenance of the Church. Fortunately there have been also periods of great restoration fervour: the first from 1719 to 1775 (in the hall there is a tablet commemorating the works); the second from 1888 (demolition of the slums placed against the monument, lowering of the roof of the portico to free the three-mullioned window of the façade). Then from 1899 to 1909, during which, under the guide of Corrado Ricci, the Southern side was nearly completely rebuilt; the windows were re-opened; the prothesis and the diaconicon were restored by lowering the external walls, opening the windows again and re-arranging the little apses; the atrium was thrown down and remade and the tower was completed, giving it a tympanum (but in origin the roof was pyramidal) three-mullioned windows and windows in the superior part and three-mullioned windows on the Western and Northern sides.

Under the portico there are marbles and inscriptions taken from the church. The principal door has the door posts and the architrave of marble. From the architrave the bronze hooks still jut out on which anciently veils were hung during celebrations. Above the central portal of the façade you can see the ancient hollow bricks and, higher up, the holes in the wall which sustained originally the beams of the narthex.

On the door on the left the original inscription that commemorates the foundation, the construction and the consecration of the church has been reproduced. It starts with «† BEATI APOLENARIS»...

Inside: global look (plan fig. 48) - The interior of the basilica, divided in three naves, is wide and full of light.

The twenty-four very beautiful columns of Greek marble with transversal veining came

+SANCTVS
APOLENARIS

The Basilica
of Sant'Apollinare
in Classe.
◀

1
2 3 4

Sant'Apollinare in Classe:
1 - St. Apollinare (detail).
2 - General view of the apsidal zone.
3 - Bell town.
4 - St. Apollinare as an orant.

Sant'Apollinare
in Classe: Moses.

from the Marmara sea. They stand on square bases, of marble too, with faces decorated with geometrical motifs.

The **capitals**, very nicely worked, are of the type «*acanthus leaf moved by the wind*». The leaves are bordered with rows of little holes which introduce in the light mass, a sprinkle of deep shade, of pleasant pictorial effect; the pairs of leaves open like «butterflies» in the joining point. Above the capitals, the classic pulvinoes of truncated pyramid figure upside-down and swollen, with a cross on the façade that looks towards the central nave.

The **ceiling**, that in origin was lacunared, is now trussed. The tondi that are above the arches represent the chronological series of bishops and archbishops of Ravenna, and they were carried out in 1775 by Antonio Cantoni, G.B. Roberti from Forlì and Domenico Barbiani. Recent restorations have given back the original colours.

At the bottom the vast exedra of the mosaic worked apse opens, it is framed by a sumptuous arch coated with mosaic decorations too. We shall first consider the apse and the arch and later we shall pass to other aspects, less spectacular but not less interesting than this extraordinary monument.

Inside: arch of the apse - The mosaics of the apse date back only in part to the epoch of the church. However of the middle of the 6th century are those of the vault of the apse and the four characters placed between the windows.

On the superior register of the arch, in the middle there is a medallion with the haloed portrait of Christ in a blessing attitude. On the sides, immersed in a group of many coloured clouds and looking towards the middle, there are; two on each side, the symbols of the Evangelists: the eagle for John, the angel for Matthew, the lion for Mark, the calf for Luke. They carry the sacred book. The representation of the Evangelists by means of their symbols is quite frequent in the iconography of Ravenna. The mosaic of this register is of the 9th century.

On the inferior register, largely broken into by the curve of the arch, two towered towns are represented with gemmed walls, Jerusalem and Bethlehem from which, six on each side, twelve white sheep come out representing the Apostles. The motif of the two towns can be found also on the arch of the apse of San Vitale. This mosaic dates back to the 7th century.

On the two sides of the apse, under two slim palms of the 7th century too, which have a decorative function but not devoid of symbolic meaning (they are the symbol of Resurrection and Heaven), the archangels Michael and Gabriel are portrayed. They carry a labarum on which the acclamation to God «*Blessed, Blessed, Blessed*» is written three times in Greek.

At the feet of the arch two half-length portraits. They are Matthew on the left, and an Apostle not identifiable on the right, datable to the end of the 11th century - beginning of the 12th century.

The decoration of the intrados of the triumphal arch is very rich (of the 7th century): on the top there is a cantharos, and on the surface, blue cocks, parrots appear and brown colour birds, quails, pidgeons.

To the mosaics of the triumphal arch a meaning of solemn celebration of the son of God and of his church is given.

Sant'Apollinare in Classe:
the Archangel Michael.

Inside: apse - The decoration of the vault of the apse is divided in two zones. In the higher one in the middle a big disc stands out containing a cross decorated with gems that is silhouetted against the sky sprinkled with ninety-nine stars.

In the crossing of the four limbs inside a crown of pearls, there is Christ's face with a beard.

At the extremities of the horizontal limbs of the cross there are the symbolic letters Alpha and Omega. Above the vertical limb there is the Greek word 'ίχθυς (fish) whose letters are the initials of the words which make up the Greek sentence, «*Jesus Christ son of God the Saviour*». Under the cross there is the Latin sentence «*salus mundi*». Connecting these various parts, we can obtain the following speech: «*Jesus Christ son of God the Saviour, beginning and end of life, salvation of the world*».

The disc is surrounded by a sky full of clouds, the figures of Moses (on the left) and of Elias (on the right) come out. Also three lambs; one on the left and two on the right looking at the cross also make part of this decorative strip.

All the scene can be interpreted as a representation of the transfiguration of Christ, carried out with a mixture of figurative elements sometimes symbolic, sometimes realistic. The big cross of the disc, in fact symbolizes Christ transfigured; the three lambs are the Apostles Peter, Jacob and John, who were present at the miraculous event on Mount Tabor while the two prophets that welcomed Christ in heaven are represented in their realistic human aspect. This type of inversion, for whom the characters that at the moment of the event were still in life are represented with symbols, while those that had already lost their corporal consistence are represented in a realistic way, maybe has a meaning and we like to interprete it as an expression of a mutual integration of Earth and Heaven, of what is material and what is spiritual.

Moses and Elias, i.e. Law and Prophets, having finished their mission, hand over their post to the son of God. Peter, Jacob and John add the testimony of Earth and Heaven. The hand of God, high above the cross, stands to confirm the Divinity of the Son.

On the band below a wide lawn extends itself on which little plants, little trees, shrubs, flowers, stones, birds are arranged, with a decoration rhythm so regular that it appears naive in its freshness.

In the middle the majestic figure of Apollinare rises with his arms in a praying position, in the middle of his flock symbolized by twelve sheep, six on each side, that intervalled by white lilies, go towards him. It has been very discussed if a unitary interpretation of all the representation of the apse vault is possible, and if so how the figure of St. Apollinare surrounded by believers may be inserted in the big theme of the transfiguration.

For the general program that presided over the creation of all the mosaic, Gerke's interpretation of which we here give a schematic illustration will help us. The mighty gemmed cross in the starry sky that hovers among the busts of Moses and Elijah is the dominating character. Instead of the disciples, frightened on the ground, Peter, John and Jacob appear as white lambs, separated from the transfiguration scene. Elijah is like an angel, beardless; Moses is a beardless youth. In Classe, the Tabor event isn't represented personally, but as an idea. The superior zone of the apse in Classe is a

VRSI CINVS

B M
LICINIAE VALERIAE
FAVSTINAE ITALICAE
DORMIENTI IN PACE
QVAE· VIX· ANNO VNO
MENSES· VI· DIES· VI
FILIAE DVLCISSIMAE
PARENTES CONTRA VOTVM

1 2
3 4 5

Sant'Apollinare in Classe:
1, Bishop Ursicino.
2, The gemmed cross.
3, Inscription of the sarcophagus of the little girl Licinia Valeria. 4, Remainder of a fresco in the narthex, maybe 14th Century.
5, Particular of the mosaic of the apse.

representation of the «Metamorphosis» (in Christian tradition Jesus revealed for a short time his glory to Peter, Jacob and John transfiguring himself in front of them: his face shone like the sun and his clothes were as white as snow. At his side Moses and Elijah appeared. The mountain to which the episode refers is Mount Tabor in the Esdrelon plain. Here the deep meaning of the story of Mount Tabor is revealed: Christ is left behind and appears between Moses and Elijah for the first time like the one who was crucified. For the first time we find in an apse, a Palestinian-type of representation of the Crucifixion. What here is announced to the three lambs is the salvation of the whole world enclosed in the cross. In this way we can understand, considering the meaning of Heaven's gate that the *Crux invicta in coelo stellato* gives, the presence of Gabriel and Michael, who announce the *Sanctus, Sanctus, Sanctus* on tablets: the land is a Holy Land. In the apse, above the cross, there is the Pantocrator (almighty, omnipotent) medallion between the four symbols of the Evangelists, towards which, the twelve lambs that are coming from Bethlehem and Jerusalem turn, therefore the whole *Corpus mysticum ecclesiae*. The cross above the Tabor is the Golgotha cross and also the one of the Last Judgement.

St. Apollinare among the twelve lambs: the lambs are the baptized who go to the Supreme Shepherd of the Church, as disciples to Christ. St. Apollinare, who here represents the Shepherd is in the middle of Heaven as Christ's cross in the starry sky. He collects Christianity around Christ.

During recent restorations, having the mosaic of the six sheep on the right been detached, the sinopia below was discovered, (now exhibited at the National Museum) and, with a certain surprise, we got to know that the starting idea didn't foresee the row of sheep but a motif with big peacocks. Also the peacock is a symbol and it often recurs in the iconography of Ravenna both on sculpture and mosaic: look, for example, in this same church at the sarcophagus of the archbishop Theodorus (plan n. 2).

In the interspaces of the windows the Saint bishops Ecclesius, Severus, Ursus, Ursicinus are represented. The faces of the four characters are very expressive and well characterized to such an extent that they can be considered as portraits. On their head there is a crown hanging from three cords. They have tunic and pallium and hold with their left hand, covered with the chasuble, the holy book, while their right hand is blessing (6th century).

The mosaics of the apsidal vault are separated by those of the window zone by an ornamental decoration in which many «A»'s of lapidary character stand out, the initial of Apollinare.

On the left and on the right of the windows there are two big square panels. The one on the left commemorates an important event for the Ravennate church: the handing to archbishop Reparato by emperor Constantine IV (Pogonatus), of a series of fiscal immunities in favour of the clergy and of a kind of ecclesiastic protectorate and of *privilegium fori* for founders of churches and monasteries. The personages represented in the mosaic are the emperor Constantine IV (Pogonatus), dressed as Justinian in the mosaic of San Vitale. On his right there are his younger brothers Heraclius and Tiberius, officially associated to the throne.

Near them, a youngster holds a ciborium. On the left of the emperor a bishop with halo, a tunic, chasuble and pallium (maybe Sant'Apollinare) that keeps a hand on the shoulder of a figure without nimbus in episcopal clothes (Reparatus), who with veiled hands receives a role on which there is the inscription PRIVILEGIA. Near Reparatus there is a glabrous ecclesiastic personage. Two deacons follow, one with a thurible, the other with a box of incense. The inscription under the composition, that starts with «HIS IGITUR...» was translated by C. Ricci: «*So that Reparatus could take part to these merits, the room got a new decorum and it glows forever*».

We remind you that Reparatus was archbishop of Ravenna from 671 to 677 and who a few years before, in 666, not yet bishop, was protagonist of a very important event for the church of Ravenna: the handing, from the emperor Constans II (Pogonatus), father of Constantine IV, of the privilege of «autocefalia», which fixed in front of the court of Constantinople a dignity equal to the one of Rome, without however disowning the spiritual primate to Peter. In that period head of the church of Ravenna was the archbishop Mauro.

The mosaic, as the opposite one, can be dated back to the second half of the 7th century. Unfortunately it underwent some restorations and additional touches rather inexperienced during the course of centuries and sometimes it was even distempered.

On the panel in front the sacrifices of Abel, Melchizedec and Abraham are represented. On the left Abel offers a lamb; in the middle behind the altar on which there are two breads and a chalice there is the priest Melchizedec with a little golden paten in his hands; on the right Abraham with his son Isaac as offering. The scene is well done, but it has weak colour and it is hard in the drawing. It is certainly inspired to the one of the big lunette on the right of the presbytery of San Vitale, but it doesn't have neither its naive freshness nor the chromatic

Sant'Apollinare in Classe: sarcophagus of the archbishop Theodorus, side (5th century).

and formal liveliness. Also the scene in front remembers the one of Justinian's suite on the left wall of the apse of San Vitale.

On the altar of the eighteenth century, rich of marbles, the relics of Sant'Apollinare are contained in a little box. The beautiful circular base of the altar made up of three steps is of 1725.

Of the eighteenth century is also the coating of the inferior part of the apse. The inscriptions on the tablets of Greek marble commemorate the life of St. Apollinare, the transfers and the surveys of his relics. The marble chair placed at the end of the apse, in the middle, is made up with parts of Archbishop Damian's chair, who died in 705.

The stair which leads to the presbytery and to the apse is of 1723 and it substitutes two preexisting lateral staircases dating back to 1173.

The two rooms on the side of the apse (*diaconicon* and *prothesis*, i.e. the *pastophoria*), contain a wooden choir (15) and a little cippus altar (16).

Inside: the sarcophagi - The two lateral naves were coated by precious marbles. Those that still existed, in 1449 were brought to Rimini by Sigismondo Pandolfo Malatesta for the decoration of the church of San Francesco.

On the two naves eleven sarcophagi were housed on which it is useful to stop for a unitary discussion about this important artistic manifestation of the first centuries, since no other church of Ravenna encloses so many significative examples and of periods so different from one another: they go in fact, from the 5th to the 8th century.

The Christians continuing the Roman custom, placed their dead in marble sarcophagi, that in Ravenna had these distinguishing characters:

a) the sculptural decoration generally takes up the four sides of the sarcophagus, and not only three.

b) The arrangement is not crowded, as in the Roman sarcophagi, but the figures sculptured are placed one quite distant from the other.

c) The arrangement often is divided by architectural elements too, therefore we find columns, pillars, arches, shells, friezes.

As in mosaic representations, with the arising of the Byzangine sensibility the relief of the figure little by little diminishes and flattens and the human figure changes into symbol. For example, from the figure of Christ in relief with human realistic features, we reach the flat abstraction of the *chrismon*, passing through the allegorical representation by means of a lamb.

Of strong Roman influence, and therefore with a resolute relief and with human figures, are therefore the first sarcophagi like the one of the *Traditio Legis* at the National Museum, the one of Prophet Elyseus in the Quadrarco di Braccioforte, the two sarcophagi in San Francesco

Sant'Apollinare in Classe: St. Severus.
◄

►
Sant'Apollinare in Classe: the handing of privileges to the church of Ravenna by emperor Constantine IV Pogonatus.

to which the one of the Twelve Apostles of this church (1) connects itself, the three sarcophagi of the Duomo, the sarcophagus of Isacio in San Vitale. They are all of the 5th century.

Starting from the end of the 5th century the fascination of plasticity and of volume diminishes and the allegorical representations start substituting the realistic ones: vase with handles appear, pidgeons, peacocks symbols of immortality, sheep, palms symbol of Eden (like in the two sarcophagi of the wings of the Mausoleum of Galla Placidia dating back to the end of the 5th - beginning of the 6th century), the *chrismon*, abstract symbol of Christ (as we can see here in sarcophagus 3, then always flatter like in the sarcophagi here in 4 and 5).

The school of the sarcophagi of Ravenna takes place during a period of three centuries. It is a local school that shows originality, vivacity and freshness, even if re-elaborating elements of various provenance. The working of the sarcophagi in Ravenna starts around the half of the 2nd century A.D.

Let's now describe the sarcophagi of this church with the date according to Bovini. The number order follows the chronological order and it corresponds to the numeration written in plan fig. 48 at page. 278.

A) - ***Sarcophagus of Licinia Valeria***. It is of the 4th century. Very poor. It carries only an inscription on which we read about a little girl who lived only for 1 year, six months and six days, FILIAE DULCISSIMAE, to whom the parents, CONTRA VOTUM (i.e. against what is wished), dedicate this sepulchre. In the sarcophagus however the bodies of two little girls were found.

1) - ***Sarcophagus called of the Twelve Apostles***. On the *front*, in the middle, we see Christ on the throne with a high back holding an open book in his left hand and in his right the *Nova lex* that is given to Paul who receives it with veiled hands. Peter, with the cross presents the keys. The other figures are Apostles too, two of which raise their right hand in an acclaiming gesture and two carry triumphal crowns. On the *sides*, three Apostles on each side with different attitudes. On the *back*, in a very accurate

execution, we see vine-shoots with wide volutes and grape clusters, in front of which there are two beautiful peacocks which face a disc with a cross. The barrel like lid is decorated with big monograms made up by a cross, by an I and a X, initials of the Greek words which mean Jesus Christ. On the two lunettes of the sides, two pidgeons with a cross in the middle. The sarcophagus connects itself for its style to those of San Francesco; in it a live sense of the relief is present. It is of the half of the 5th century (De Francovich: 430-440).

2) - ***Sarcophagus of the archbishop Theodorus***. The *front* has a disc in the middle with a monogram in which the apocalyptical letters are inserted: at the bottom there are two roses. On the sides two big solemn and proud peacocks, behind which there are volutes of vine-shoots with grape clusters pecked by two pidgeons. At the extremities there are two little pillars and, above, there is a long frame with a motif of aquatic leaves. On the sides volutes, flowers and pidgeons are sculptured. The central part is occupied by a vase from which a cross emerges overheaded by a pidgeon in a nose-dive position. On the *back*, wide volutes with grape clusters which are eaten by pidgeons and a rabbit. The barrel-like *lid* has three crowns on each side with monogram, alpha and omega. On the *lunettes of the sides of the lid* we have the repetition of the volute, pidgeon and cross motif.

Even if on the façade there is a symbolic representation, the sarcophagus is of the 5th century, between 450 and 475. It seems to have been carried out by the same sculptor of the sarcophagus of the Twelve Apostles. It was reused in the 7th century to house the mortal remains of archbishop Theodorus, as can be read at the base of the lid.

3) - ***Sarcophagus with six niches***. The four faces of the sarcophagus present a niche architecture made up of spiral columns with Corinthian capital and shell on the superior part of every niche. On the front the middle column is missing and in its place there is a vase with a water spout with which two peacocks placed on a relieved base quench their thirst. On the

Sant'Apollinare in Classe: front of a sarcophagus of the 6th century - particular.

other niches a cross or a palm except in the central part of the *back*, where there are two lambs sniffing a palm that substitutes a little column. The semi-cylindric scale-like lid presents a frieze with flat ovules. On the lunettes of the lid there is a shell on one side, on the other a garland, the *chrismon*, pidgeons. The sarcophagus is the twin of the one that is at the archbishop Museum. It is of the end of the 5th - beginning of the 6th and the relief of the front is still strong.

This sarcophagus, like the one in the right wing of the Mausoleum of Galla Placidia, was sculptured while Theodoric was in Ravenna and we know that at that time a sculptor named Daniele worked who could be the author of the two sarcophagi.

4) - ***Sarcophagus on the left of the entrance***. On the *front* it carries two big lambs which face a cross from whose limbs alpha and omega hanging from a little chain come down; behind the lambs there are two palms. On one of the *sides* there is a lamb with its head looking backwards which preceds a monogrammatic cross toward which a pidgeon flies carrying a crown. On the other side the Mount with the four mystic rivers is represented, on which there are two pidgeons and a monogrammatic cross; in the middle of the rivers, a lily. On the *lunettes of the lid*, on one side there is a pidgeon with a vase from which vine-shoots come out; on the other a cross with two pidgeons. This sarcophagus is of the beginning of the 6th century, and in the flattening of the relief the taste which will get very popular is pre-announced; look for example at the ambo of the Duomo sculptured a few decades later.

5) - ***Sarcophagus on the right of the entrance***. On the *front* (in this sarcophagus the front is considered to be the side of the four niches) it presents four niches divided from one another, the two central ones are delimited by pillars, the two lateral ones by spiral columns. In each one there is a beautiful shell. Two crosses and two palms, inside the niches, and three pidgeons between the arches complete the arrangement. On the *back* there are three niches, they too are distanced from one another, with arches sustained by little columns; the central arches lowered and surmounted by a tympanum. On the lateral niches there is a cross; in the central one a double curtain, collected at the bottom, on opening itself a cross can be seen. On one of the *sides* there is the *Agnus Dei* on the mountain from which four rivers flow down; on the other there is a cantharus with shell and two little pidgeons placed on a high sustain. The arches above these two representations are lowered. The lid is decorated only on the sides, on one of which there is a garland with monogram and pidgeons and on the other two peacocks that face a vase from which vine-shoots come out. We are at the first decades of the 6th century and the relief is rather flat.

6) - ***Sarcophagus of the lambs with cross***. The sarcophagus is maybe work of a rough artisan, which represents two flat lambs that carry a cross. In the middle there is a disc with monogram. We are in the middle of the 8th century. The lid is maybe of the 6th century, as the better style with which the cantharus and peacocks were carried out indicates.

7) - ***Sarcophagus of the archbishop Felix***. In the middle of the *front* there is a niche formed by little columns sustaining a tympanum with

acroteria; containing a monogrammatic cross and the letters alpha and omega. Outside the aedicula there are two lambs surmounted by a cross. Behind the two lambs, two niches with pointed arch; from each of the arches a lamp hangs. More outside two candlesticks with a lit candle and finally a little column on the left and a pillar on the right. Along all the ridge of the *lid* a very long limb of a cross runs and four garlands with monogram and with alpha and omega. The inscription says that in it the body of the archbishop Felix is kept S(an) C(t)ISSIMI AC TER BEATISS(imi). The sarcophagus is of the third decennium of the 8th century.

8) - ***Sarcophagus with lambs and a bay leaf garland***. On the *front* there are two lambs behind which there are two palms. The lambs look towards the central bay wreath which encloses a cross, from the base of which two «lemnisci» which end with an oak leaf. On the *sides*, two little pillars with decorations. The sides of the sarcophagus present each three little pillars that sustain two arches, the former and the latter decorated with rough pearls. In the spaces formed in such way a leaf decoration is included. The *lid* has three crowns with monogram. The sides of the sarcophagus are of the 8-9th century: the lid and the front are of the end of the 6th.

9) - ***Sarcophagus of the archbishop Giovanni***. Inside a rectangular frame three crosses are placed, in deep-set spaces they are separated by a zone that carries the inscription: HIC TUMULUS CLAUSUM SERVAT CORPUS DN(domini) JOANNIS SCISSIMI (sanctissimi) AC TER BEATISSIMI ARCHIEPISCOPI. Also on the *right side* there is the repetition of the cross motif. Having the archbishop Giovanni died in 748, the sarcophagus should be of the half of the 8th century.

10) - ***Sarcophagus of archbishop Gratiosus***. It is similar to the one of Giovanni in its *front*. On the *back* there are three crosses slightly reliefed. It must have been sculptured about fourty years after the preceding one having Gratiosus died in 788.

Inside: lapidary inscriptions - On the walls of the church several inscriptions are placed about whose contents we shall give a few hints later.

The one that is behind the sarcophagus n. 9 and that starts with NN PATRIS... (i.e. (i)N N(omine) PATRIS) is very long and speaks about the archbishop Giovanni «*junior in nomine quintus*» (Giovanni V) and of his donation; dates back to 731.

The inscription that starts with OTHO III... commemorates the penance done in basilica by emperor Otho III in the year 1001.

Sant'Apollinare in Classe: the ciborium of St. Eleucadius

The iscription that starts with IULIO PAPAE II commemorates the visit that Giulio II with 12 cardinals, paid to the basilica.

On the right wall the inscription that starts with S. LEONI... commemorates the works carried out in the church by pope Leo III who repaired the roof, the quadriportico etc...

The inscription that starts with BENEFICIS AC MUNIFICIS... remembers the benefits done in favour of the church by the archbishops Mauro, Reparato, Damiano, Sergio, Giovanni V, Giovanni VI, Valerio and Domenico.

We left for last the inscription, of the half of the 6th century that starts with IN HOC LOCO STETIT ARCA BEATI APOLENARIS... which allows us to give a hint to the burial problems of the first bishop of Ravenna.

The saint, after martyrdom (3rd century), was buried, sources of information say (i.e. *Passio S. Apollenaris*, an apocryphal document of the 5th-6th century), outside the walls of Classe, «*in arca saxea*». Having accomplished the basilica, bishop Maximian transported here the body of the Saint in 549 and in the place of the primitive burial he made set an epigraph IN HOC LOCO STETIT ARCA... that now is in front of us. Where was that place? Opposite the tablet, on the external part of the church against a wall under ground, a loculus was found and it was thought that it was the place of primitive burial next to which later the church was built. There are however reasons that go against this hypothesis. Above that loculus another one was dug, on the perimetral wall, and it can be seen through the grating under the tablet. It was thought to have contained, before the transfer of 549 the body of the Saint.

After a few transfers inside the basilica and

its collocation in the crypt, the bones were brought to Ravenna (1650), before in an oratory of the Camaldolese Monastery, then (1651) in San Romualdo, finally (1652) in the Duomo. Two years later they were brought back into the crypt of the basilica of Sant'Apollinare in Classe, then (1655) at the bottom of the nave. Then (1723) they were temporarily placed in the chapel at the bottom of the left aisle while the works for reconstruction of the staircase were carried on. In 1725, having finished these works the bones were placed inside the high altar.

From 1511 the bones had been placed in a sarcophagus that is now in the crypt. As regards to a transfer of the bones in Sant'Apollinare Nuovo that was to have taken place in the 9th century we send you back to the third itinerary, Sant'Apollinare Nuovo, paragraph: «Chapels».

Inside: wall of the façade - On the sides of the two doors that border the central one four columns of oriental black and white marble, that formed part of a ciborium erected by the archbishop Domenico Ublatella (889-898). The capitals aren't the original ones.

Inside: lateral niches - At the beginning of the lateral walls there are two big niches or apses (one on each side), rebuilt on secure traces and both have on each side two columns. They are the four porphyry columns of the ciborium erected by abbot Orso after the half of the 9th century on the altar in the middle of the church. The actual bases and capitals are of the eighteenth century. The dug capital - now a baptismal font - behind the iron gate is maybe one of the original ones of the Ublatella ciborium. It is of the 5th-6th century, Corinthian with acanthus with big indents. It stands on a column base of the 6th century. The inferior zone of the column is square, decorated by «V» like notches that in the middle form a Greek cross; a circular zone follows decorated subsequentely with a vegetable motif, a palm motif, a ring of little circles, a circle of pods.

Inside: little altar in the middle of the central nave (11) - It is here since the 9th century, and it is made up with pieces of various epochs: of the 6th century, for example are the cippus with fenestella that sustains the table and the altar itself. The epigraph on the marble plane remembers, but it is a late legend, that the archbishop Mauro in the 7th century placed in the middle of the church the relics of Sant'Apollinare that, found again in 1173, were then brought in the crypt, already built to contain the mortal remains of the Saint. Recent studies, instead date the construction of the crypt to the middle of the 9th century (Mazzotti).

The inscription on the back of the altar remembers how San Romualdo, praying at the altar, after two visions of Sant'Apollinare became monk in 927. The actual arrangement of the altar is of the 18th century.

Inside: ciborium of Sant'Eleucadio (12) - Proceeding towards the bottom of the church along the left nave we notice the blind arches of the nine doors (three on each side in the walls, three on the façade) which opened in the walls. The only one which is used today, as well as those of the façade, is the door which leads to the little passage of the bell-tower.

At the bottom of the left nave placed in a corner there is a very important and beautiful ciborium, that was once placed in complete visibility in the church of Sant'Eleucadius of

The pinewood of Classe.

Sunset in the pinewood.

Classe and that was brought here after the year 1000. It was sculptured between 806 and 810 it is integer apart from the modern brick and stone bases on which the columns stand.

The columns, for a third with pods, for the rest grooved with spirals, carry capitals that remember the Byzantine basket-like shape, and sustain archivaults minutely decorated with a band of wicker interlacings very much next to one another and complicated along the curve of the arch and with peacocks, cantharus, crosses and pidgeons, vegetal motifs on the triangles. The inscription reveals that the ciborium was done in honour D(omini) NI N(ostri) J(e) H(s)V XPI(sti) ET S(an)C(t)I ELEUCHADII while Valerius was archbishop.

Under the ciborium there is a little altar (**altar of St. Felicola**) with some pieces of the 7th century (fenestella framed by spiral little columns, two lambs and a cross in the lunette), and others (columns and table) in cement, on which some sculptures were carried out that until 1901 were spread in the basilica: the front of a sarcophagus, beautiful sculpture with Christ in the middle on the Mountain of Paradise slightly sketched and seven of the Twelve Apostles, of the end of the 4th century; a little arch of the 9th century; a little statue of the Madonna of the 15th century. Two panels hang on the wall under the ciborium, representing the Announcement, are work of the 7th century according to some people, of the 10th century according to others. A curiosity: the left hand of the Madonna has six fingers.

Inside: fragment of the original floor - Under the ciborium there is a fragment of the original floor. Another fragment is at the beginning of the right nave (13). It is divided in two parts both of the 6th century. It carries the names of the donators GAUDENTIA and FELIX. Recent restorations have pointed out the original parts of these fragments, separating them from the remade parts by means of a lower row of tesserae with a lighter colour. A third fragment, coming from the central nave leans against the wall of the right nave, protected by glass (14).

In 1953 the «**bema**» coeval to the basilica was discovered, that extended until the height of the third column, contained the altar and it was delimited by plutei, transennae, little pillars.

Inside: book of the plenary indulgences - At the bottom of the right nave, against a pillar of the first arch, an open marble book is placed on a pedestal; it is of 1468. It indicates the plenary indulgences connected to the basilica. The inscription says, in vulgar «LA SUMA DELE INDULGENCIE CONCESE A QUESTA ECLESIA PER SANCTO GREGORIO PAPA NEL MEXE DE MAGIO E PERFINA L'OCTAVA DE SANCTO SIMONE IUDA TOIANDOLE OGNI 5 ANI CXXXIII CCCCLXVIII».

◀ The column of the French: particular.

The column of the French.

Inside: crypt - Nearby there is one of the two entrances to the crypt which rose round about the middle of the 9th century (Mazzotti) to receive the relics of Sant'Apollinare. It has a semi-annular form. In the middle of the semi-ring a corridor starts off and it goes towards the axis of the church, and originally it led into it (fig. 21, pag. 102).

Nearby the basilica, in the post war period, the statue of Augustus was placed, brought to Ravenna in 1937 and placed at that time in Piazza del Popolo (at that time called Vittorio Emanuele) in the atmosphere of the «reconstruction of the Empire» after the fascist conquest of Ethiopia. The statue is a copy of the existing one in the Vatican Museums in Rome.

COLUMN OF THE FRENCH - It rises on the right bank of the Ronco river where the battle of Ravenna took place, fought on April the 11th 1512. To reach it we must get to the big road ring that surrounds Ravenna, on the point in which it overgoes the Ronco, and then continue for about 200 meters along via Argine Destro of the Ronco river.

The battle of Ravenna saw on one side the French army, made up by French, Swiss, Spanish soldiers of the Navarra reign, Lanzichenecs and two formations of Greeks, commanded by Gaston de Foix representing Louis XII; on the other the army of the Sacred League, formed by Jule II, made up by Spanish, Italians, Greeks of the reign of Naples.

Coming from Budrio, Massalombarda, Cotignola, Conselice, Russi the French army surpasses the Montone river and comes nearer to Ravenna, at that time tied between two rivers: the Montone river (that bordered the city on the North) and the Ronco (that lapped on the South). An attempt of assaulting the city was effected (9th April 1512) by means of the artillery that placed at 200 meters from the walls, shoots on the zone between Porta Gaza and San Mamante. The assault that costs 1500 deaths between the two parties doesn't manage because of the heroic resistance of the besieged.

In the meanwhile the army of the League, coming from Faenza, gets nearer to Ravenna surpassing the Ronco near Barisano and camps (10th April) on the right of the Ronco, near Ponte Cella (Molinaccio locality). The French abandon the besiege and go against the enemy army, therefore also going on the right embankment of the Ronco by means of a bridge thrown between porta San Mama and porta Sisi.

On the 11th April 1512, Easter day, the battle takes place, extremely cruel, historically relevant for the new use of the artillery and because one of the last greatest cavalry fights took place. Victory was obtained by the French, who however lost their captain, Gaston de Foix, twenty-three years old. After the battle in which legendary personages fought (Baiardo, il signor de la Palisse; also Ludovico Ario-

Garibaldi's hut.

sto was present) a terrible pillage of the city of Ravenna followed.

The column was erected, in remembrance of the battle, in 1557, by Cardinal Pier Donato Cesi. First placed at about fifty metres from the bank of the river, where it was supposed that Gaston de Foix had fallen, later towards the middle of the 19th century it was placed on the bank of the river so as to make it more visible, and it was restored in 1972.

It is a pillar of Istria stone with Ionic capital surmounted by a cube on which there is a sphere. It is decorated on the four sides by a very nice bas-relief «sculptured with incredible knowledge, and exquisiteness of art» (Ghigi). Of the epigraphs on the base, the one that starts with VIDEBIT HOSPES informs the foreigner that the stone commemorates the immense massacre of the armies of Spain and France; the one that starts with GESTA FUERUNT indicates the date of the battle (11th April), since the pope was Julius II; the one that starts with HANC PETRAM attests that the marble was donated by Pier Donato Cesi; the one that starts with PAULO IV PONT MAX, remembers that Cesi erected it after having visited the place while he presided Emilia, and the pope was Paul IV. On the tondi of the bas-reliefs, the inscription starts with HEUS VIATOR says that Gaston de Foix assaulted Ravenna and threw its walls down; the one that starts with HINC POST speaks about the getaway of the Spanish after the death of Gaston de Foix, and of the pillage of Ravenna; the one that starts with HEU CLADEM HORRENDAM remembers that in the terrible massacre nearly twenty thousand men died and the one that starts with REIECTUS AB OPPIDANIS says that Gaston, having been sent back from the walls of Ravenna, crossed the river and defeated the army of the Pope and of Spain.

GARIBALDI'S HUT (Capanno di Garibaldi) - It's about 8 kilometers from Ravenna; we reach it from via Romea Nord following the road that leads to Porto Corsini and Marina Romea until the touristic sign «Capanno di Garibaldi» from which it is far about 200 meters. The route crosses the industrial area, in which big complexes dominate, and it borders the «pialassa» of the Baiona, on which the ancient pine-wood of San Vitale looks.

After the falling of the Roman Republic, Garibaldi passed Terni, Todi, Orvieto, San Marino, and came to Cesenatico where he embarked himself with 250 men on thirteen «bragozzi» (fishing-boats), with the intention of reaching Venice. Intercepted by an Austrian naval squad, and gunshotted, he moored at 8 kilometers from Magnavacca (Palazza Locality). After various movings, during which, in the Guiccioli farm, at Mandriole, Anita died, he then came to this hut from which he was brought to Ravenna (Borgo Sisi) and then to Castiglione, Case Murate, Coccolia, Forlì, Tuscary, Genova escaping in this way from the Austrians.

The hut was built in 1810 for hunting use. It was bought in 1867 by the «Società Unione Democratica» it then became property of the «Società Conservatrice del Capanno di Garibaldi» (a society preserving Garibaldi's hut). It was burnt in November 1911, and it was faithfully rebuilt.

A REBUILT BASILICA: SANTA MARIA IN PORTO FUORI - A basilica destroyed by air bombings and rebuilt in 1952 is situated at Porto Fuori, almost 3 km. in a bee-line to the East of Ravenna. One can reach the basilica from Ravenna (road for Punta Marina, then to the right in Via Stradone for 2.5 km. Or: new road on the left side of Fiumi Uniti) or from Sant'Apollinare in Classe (road leading to the seaside for about 6 km.).

The basilica had a great religious and artistic importance, and although it was nearly completely rebuilt it is worth visiting it.

It was built near the seaside at a time when this was not so far from the town as today, there was one of the harbours which always linked Ravenna to the sea. It might be the church which Dante calls of «Our lady on the Adrian shore» (Paradise, canto XXI, v. 123).

The date when the church was first built is disputed. Here is for you a synthesis of different chronicles:

According to what is generally maintained: - 1096-1131 (end of the 11th-beginning of the 12th century) construction of a basilica with nave and two aisles, 19 m. long.
- 1175-1187 (end of the 12th) costruction of the never completed bell-tower.
- 1246-1314 (middle of the 13th-beginning of the 14th century) rebuilding of the basilica, by prolonging it until a length of 49.30 m., with a new façade, a four-sided portico, a large cloister.

According to Mazzotti: - 9th-10th century, construction of a basilica with nave and two aisles, 19 m. long.
- beginning of the 12th century, lenghtening of the basilica, new façade, bell-tower, four-sided portico, large cloister, monastery with refectory, chapter-house, dormitory, etc. hospice for pilgrims, house for the «portuensi» lay sisters.
- beginning of the 14th century, new lenghtening of the basilica (49.30) m.).

Short after 1350 the basilica was provided with some very important paintings of Riminese School.

Religious importance - The function of the basilica, where a little religious community had formed already in the first half of the 11th century, had to be, at the beginning, to help sailors with their ships giving them assistance and shelter. Since the first years of the 12th century it took on an extraordinary religious prestige having become the seat of an own congregation, under the authority of which several churches were, not only in Italy. In the heart of this movement there was Peter the Cleric, who because of his humility made call himself «the Sinner». He formulated the rule which became the base of the «portuense» reform and the rectory of Santa Maria in Porto Fuori was considered as its «mother». Round Peter a centre of Marian piety (the «Greek Madonna» was venerated, about whom we wrote on page 140) of Roman faith formed, which proposed a religious reform for canon regulars (Mazzotti). Renowned visitors were Henry V (1112), Lothar (1133), Frederick I (1177), Henry VI (1200), Frederick III (1468) together with an endless crowd of other Princes and Lords of great or less great fame «and everybody came with generous offerings so that a very rich treasure was made up» (Tarlazzi).

When the Venetians forced the «portuensi» monks to move to Ravenna (see page 137) the abandoning of the whole building (cloister, monastery, etc.) started and the ruin of all parts of it, excepted the church with the bell-tower, followed soon.

Restoration work took place in 1921, 1938, 1942, but a bombing by the allies (on 5h of November 1944) destroyed what still remained.

Artistic importance - In the second half of the 14th century the church was provided with a fine fresco cycle, an important work by masters from Rimini (for the «Riminese School» see page 22). Here you find a very brief not complete summary of the represented subjects: *Madonna with the Infant, four Saints and Saint Julian - The Redeemer between the Antichrist and Angels - Blessed and Damned* - In the vault of the central chapel: *The Evangelists, four Doctors of the Church, Saints - The Virgin's Coronation and Death - The slaughter of the innocents* (from a small balcony two figures appear, presumed Francesca from Rimini and Sister Chiara da Polenta) - *The Virgin's Birth and presentation to the temple* (two figures talking together were regarded as Guido Novello and Dante Alighieri, with beard) - *Saint Paul - The Blessed Rainaldo, archbishop of Ravenna - The incredulity of Saint Thomas - Saint John that baptizes a king - Peter the Sinner that heals blind, crippled, sick people - The same that meets the poor - Saint Sisto Pope in jail with the Saint Deacons Agapito and Felicissimo - The same people before a king - Christ that converts Saint Matthew - Saint Matthew taken to the Heaven by two angels - Saint James from Compostella.*

The frescos were destroyed, excepting just some fragments, by the bombing.

What we can see today - A visit to Santa Maria in Porto Fuori is not useless (if it is closed, ring for the parish priest). The rebuilding of the church on the foundations of the old one was completed in 1952. Indoors 9 fragments of the frescos, now transferred on canvas, are placed together with an important sarcophagus from the 5th century not damaged at all by the bombing, a ciborium from the 16th century of Istria stone supported by two columns of Greek marble and an altar-piece by Gaspare Sacchi, representing the Ascension, coming from the former church of Santa Maria delle Croci (Sant'Apollonia). One of the nine remained fragments is almost unintelligible (entrance wall on the left). Beginning from the one near the entrance on the right, we have: *a woman Saint - The slaughter of the innocents - Saint Sisto Pope in jail with Saint Agapito and Felicissimo, Deacons - A woman Saint - Saint James from Compostella - A martyr woman Saint - Saint Sisto, Agapito and Felicissimo before a king - Peter the Sinner, that heals blind, crippled, sick people.*

The **sarcophagus**, placed at the end of the church on the left, is one of the oldest in Ravenna. According to different opinions it might date back to the 3rd century (Dütschke), between 350 and 370 (Goldmann), the 4th century (Toesca), the first half of the 5th century (Bovini), the 5th century (C. Ricci, Galassi). De Francovich, from whom we got the expressions you can read between inverted commas, maintains it would date back to the first decennium of the 5th century. On the **front** we can see Christ giving the Law to Saint Paul («Traditio Legis», see on pages 52, 103, 104, 176, 192, 218) in a realistic «airy but unconnected» representation which develops «free within its frame, without architectural divisions», «with heavy figures, badly dressed in clothings that tend to widen in the sides». On the **back** there is on the contrary an abstract representation: in the middle we can see a big disk with a cross «in which the abstract concept of absolute is admirably represented in symbolic form».

On the sides of the disk there are two palms and two pigeons flying towards the disk, «alluding to the souls living in Paradise». The sarcophagus has a semicylindrical lid with flat roof tiles.

In the sarcophagus the body of Peter the Sinner (Ravenna 1050-1119) was put on 23rd of March 1119 when he died. His bones are in a small case from the 18th century, that we can't see, on which it is written as follows: «Ossa beati Petri Damiani de Honestis dicti peccatoris». But this Peter was not the Great Pier Damiani (Ravenna 1007-Faenza 1072) nor he belonged to the degli Onesti family (a great family of renown in Ravenna between the 9th and the 16th century). In reality Peter the Sinner «was just a humble canon, nothing more than father of the canons at Porto» (Mazzotti) and perhaps he never attained the priesthood.

At the end of the church, on the right there is a moulded image of the Greek Madonna. A capital with expanded leaves of Verona marble is used today as a baptismal font.

Outside the basilica, towards the apse, there is a column with capital of Verona marble, on which we can see a statue of the Virgin dating back to the 11th century, damaged by the bombing. Interesting are also the ruins of the eastern side of the **cloister**, that show us some doors and a mullioned window with two lights with an arch above it. The cloister was still undamaged in the 18th century.

MIRABILANDIA - Recently built (1992), Mirabilandia lies few kilometres south of Ravenna, along the Adriatica trunk-road (SS. Adriatica). It is the wonderland which got its name from the Italian word *Mirabile* meaning worthy of admiration and the German word *Land* «region».

This is a more than 40-hectare amusement park offering recreation, fun and entertainment, including playgrounds for children, adolescents and adults, restaurants, a theatre, shows, special effects, games, scenes, streams, ponds, fantastic attractions, animation and a majestic roller coaster.

At present Mirabilandia is Italy's state-of-the art amusement park.

From design to plan to works

Any kind of builder (a town-planner, an architect, an engineer, an artist, an artisan...) before producing an object (a machine, a tool, a building etc.) draws its parts and the whole of it. The object therefore is studied under every point of view, the top, its side, the outside, the inside and the whole structure. This is the reason why we have drawings, sketches, schemes, plans, prospects, sections.
The designs are useful to the builder, but they are useful also to those who observe the construction in order to understand it better. This is why maps of certain parts of the city, building plans, mosaic schemes have been enclosed in the Guide. In order to enrich the collection we now add some illustrative TABLES that carry designs* that refer both to big monuments and to very little objects. We trust they will be useful to understand and know better the works of art that Ravenna is so rich of.

PLANS:

they are horizontal sections of a structure. It's as if the building were cut horizontally at the point that we want to underline and it is observed from the top.

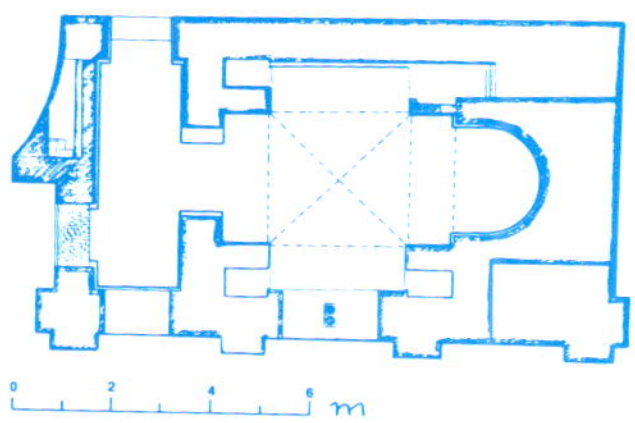

Plan of the archbishop chapel (narthex and oratory of Saint Andrea) to compare with the plan at pag. 174. The oratory is on the third floor of a building of which hereunder we have its section.

SECTIONS:

they are graphic representations of the building as if it were cut vertically. The vertical sections serve to show internal parts of sectioned structure.

Section of the Baptistery of the Arians (plan and photo of the baptistery at pag. 156).

Section of the building that on the higher floor is made up by the Oratory of Saint Andrea (archbishop chapel, p. 180) leaned to the building is the section of the so-called «vivarium» (page 174).

* The designs are taken from FELIX/RAVENNA (F.R.) AND from CORSI DI CULTURA SULL'ARTE RAVENNATE E BIZANTINA (C.A.R.B.).

PROSPECTS:

They present the outside of the building.

View of the tomb of Dante. (Plan of the dantesque area p. 94).

View of the so-called palace of Theodoric, former church of S. Salvatore (description p. 136). Designs by the ravennate engineer L. Nabruzzi (1766-1849).

SCHIZZI:

By means of design we can also make sketches, that are rapid drawings that have the function of giving the idea of the object that's represented (Here we can see the Sketch of the «stele of Longidienus»: instead of the sculptures there are the names of the people portrayed), described at pag. 49), ...

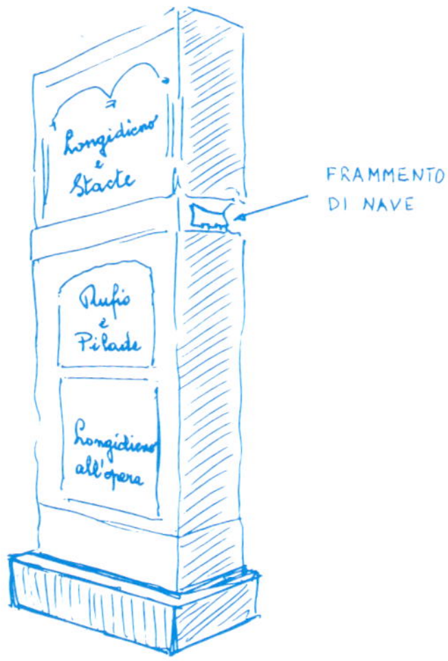

RECONSTRUCTION:

of missing parts, based on existing traces. For example, in the sketch of the stele of Longidienus you can see the fragment of a piece of ship. The design here shown, represents an hypothesis of rebuilding of the missing part..

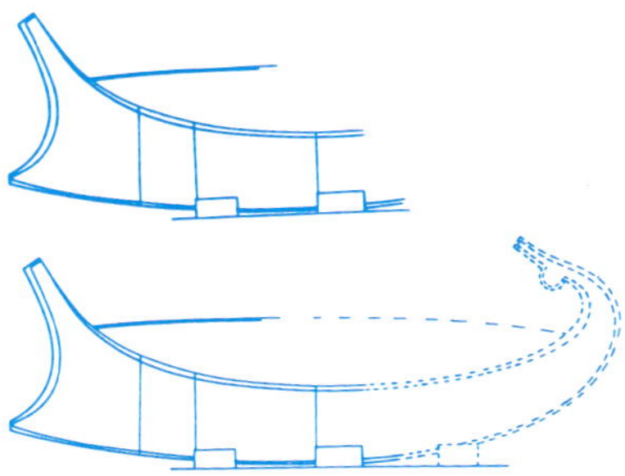

Another example of reconstruction is the hypothetical design, made on the parts of a sinopia discovered below the mosaic in Sant'Apollinare in Classe (see pag. 63).

Thanks to design we can rebuild the various moments of the ideation of a work by means of the initial scheme that is quite simple in regards to the complexity of the final work. Here we can see one of the ornamental motifs on the floor of the Basilica of San Vitale in front of the steps at the entrance to the church.

1st phase

2nd phase

3rd phase

Design of very little objects such as brooches, buckles of Roman, Byzantine and Barbaric Ages, preserved in the National Museum of Ravenna. They were used to close cloaks, belts, shoes etc. They are made of bronze and they are about 4-8 cm long. A, E and F are complete. B, C, D are missing of needle and spring (taken from M.G. Maioli, Fibule Romane, bizantine e barbariche del Museo Nazionale di Ravenna. FELIX RAVENNA - 1976).

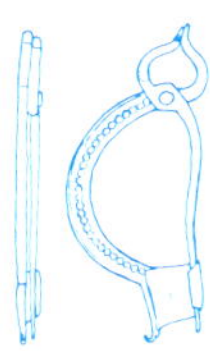

A

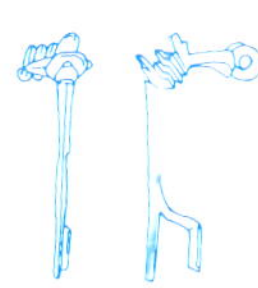

B

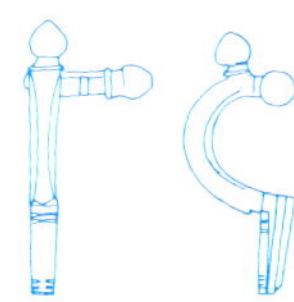

C

D

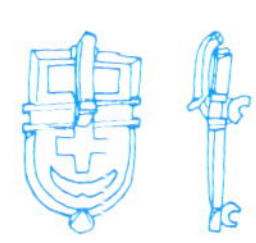

E

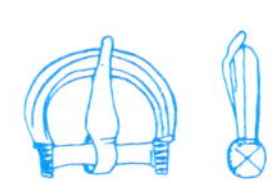

F

Sometimes designs can explain better than words. In the two drawings we can see which part of the building of Sant'Apollinare Nuovo was sacrificed in order to build the higher floor (see pag. 134 at the paragraph «Floor».

From a description of Andreas Agnellus (9th Century) it has been possible to create hypothetically, in this scheme, the plan of the «edificio neoniano» (neonian building) called «Quinque accubita» (see pag. 174). In his description Agnellus speaks about the mosaic decoration of the room. The themes of this decoration can be seen in the scheme. He specifies also that the scene of the flood was placed on the wall «*parte ecclesiae*» (i.e. the side of the Basilica Ursiana referring to

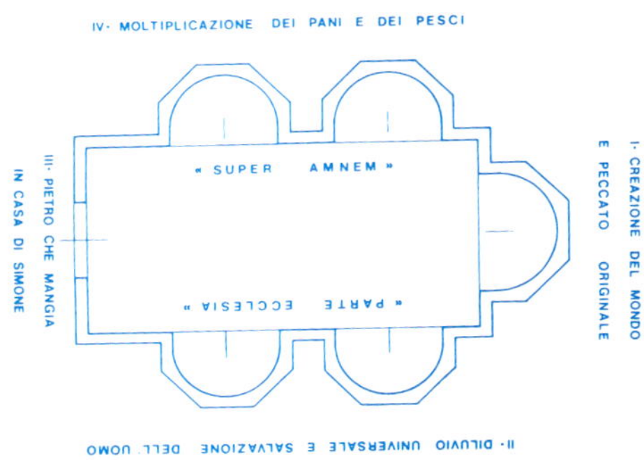

TABLE IV) and the one of the miracle on the wall *super amnem* (i.e. from the side of the watercourse called Lamisa, of which pag. 105, 173, 174).

On the TABLES that follow we present drawings regarding:

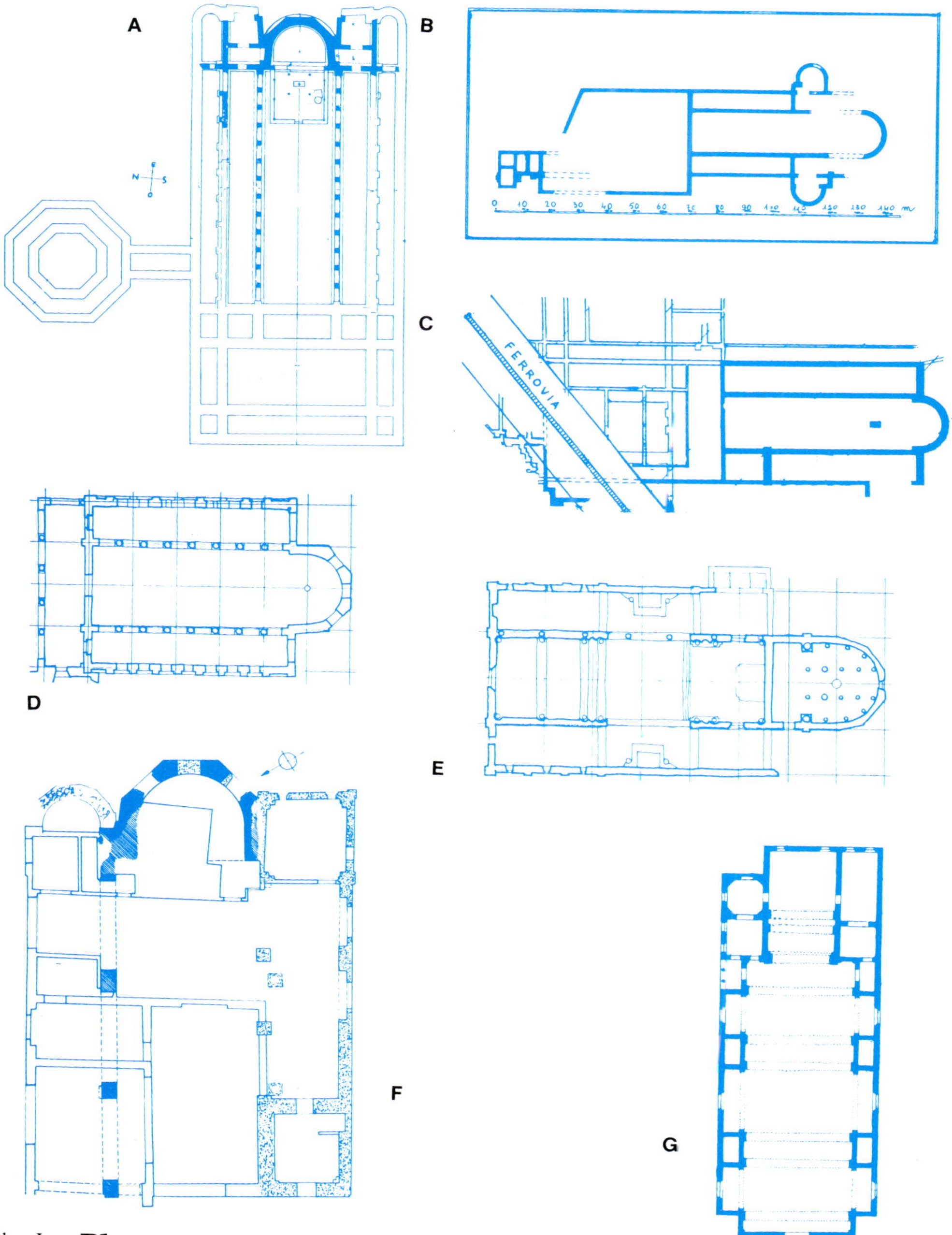

Table I - **Plans**

A: *Basilica nearby «Ca' Bianca»* (4th Century) pag. 206. B: *Basilica di San Probo* (4th-5th Century) pag. 206. C: *Basilica Petriana* (4th Century) pag. 188. D: *Chiesa dello Spirito Santo* (5th-6th Century) pag. 159. E: *Basilica di Sant'Andrea Maggiore* (6th Century) pag. 194. F: *San Michele in Africisco* (6th Century) pag. 18. G: *Chiesa di San Domenico* (13th Century) pag. 88.

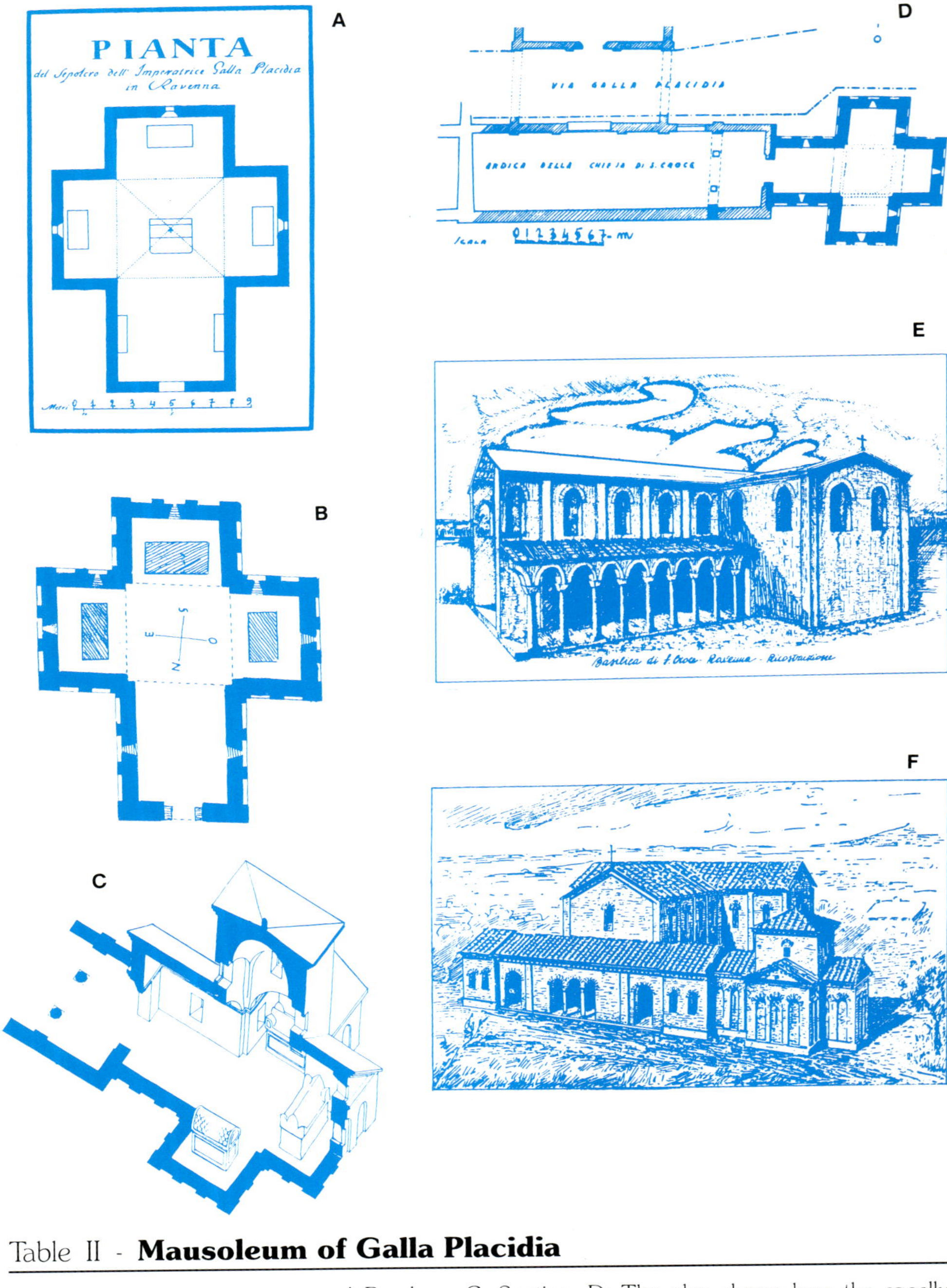

Table II - **Mausoleum of Galla Placidia**

A-B: plans. C: Section. D: The plan shows how the sacellum was connected to the narthex of the church of Santa Croce. E: the design presents a reconstruction of the Church of Santa Croce. F: the design presents a reconstruction of the position and aspect of the three elements: Holy Cross (Santa Croce), narthex, Mausoleum.

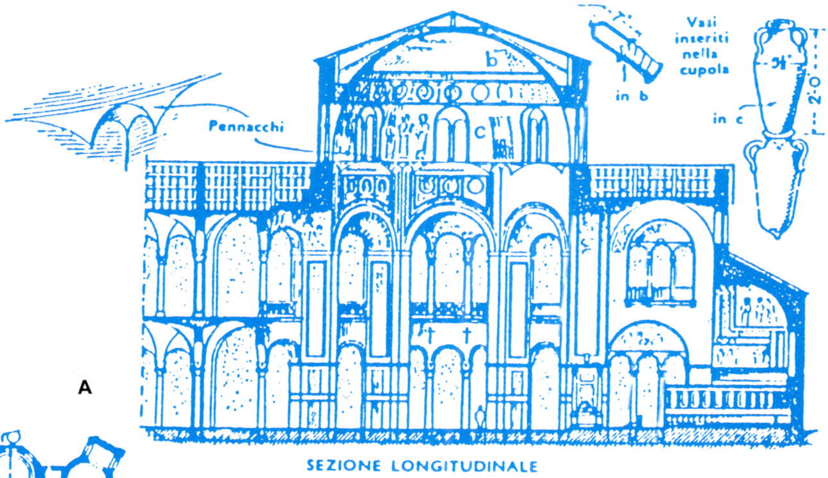

A

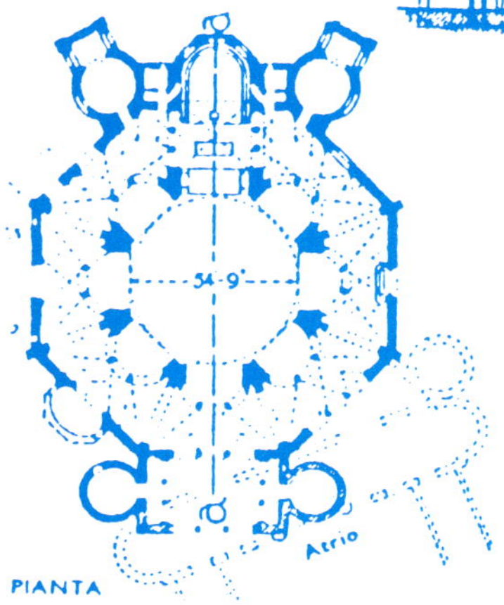

B

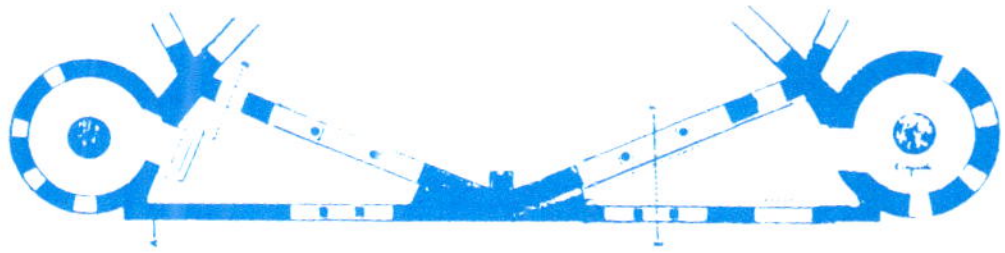

C

Table III - **San Vitale**

A: Plan and longitudinal section.
B: Plan of the triangular rooms of the women's gallery.
C: Sketches of the plan ar.d of an elevation carried out by the architect Antonio da Sangallo il Giovane (1483-1546).

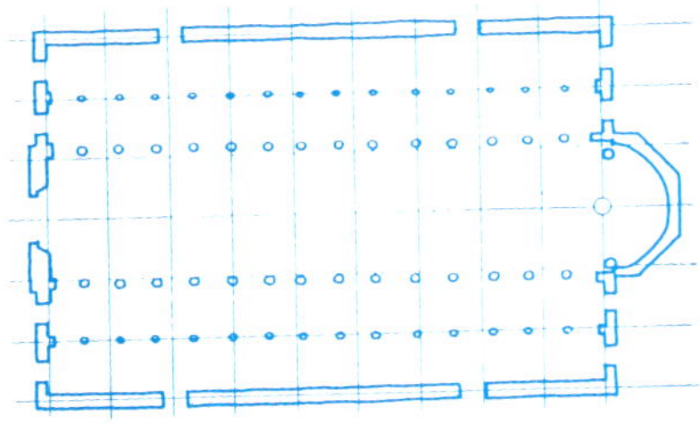

A

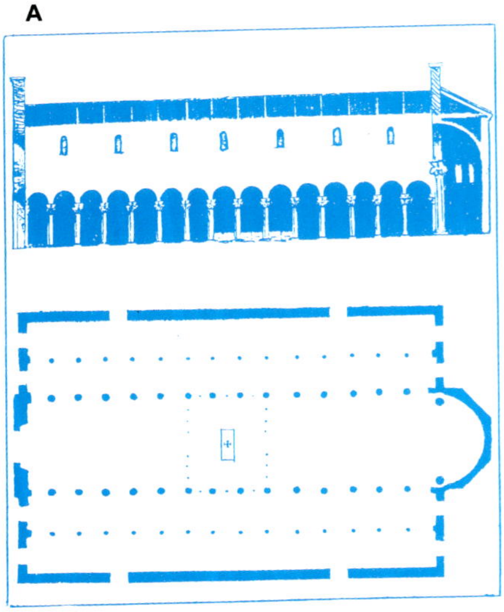

B

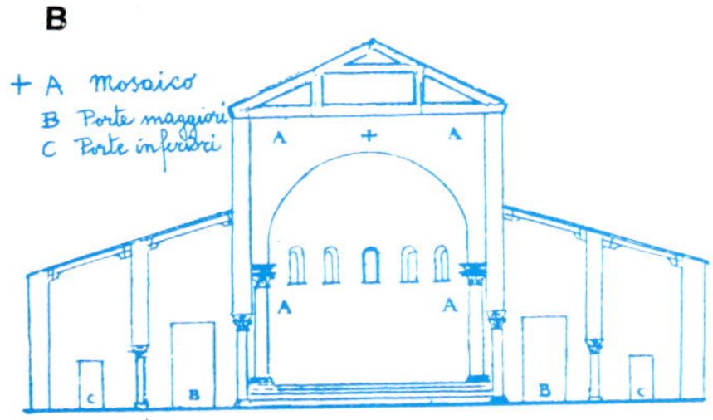

C

D

E

Tavola IV - **Basilica ursiana**

A: plan of the basilica. The generating element of the plan is the square. The surface of the basilica can be subdivided in 54 squares (6 in width, 9 in length) with side measuring 594 cm. The length of the lateral naves corresponds to the side of a square, that of the central nave to two squares (F.R. 1962).
B: Vertical section and plan.
C: Section (nave and apse).
D: Mosaic of 1112 described at pag. 176-177.
E: Prospect and plan of the ambo of bishop Agnellus (pag. 191).

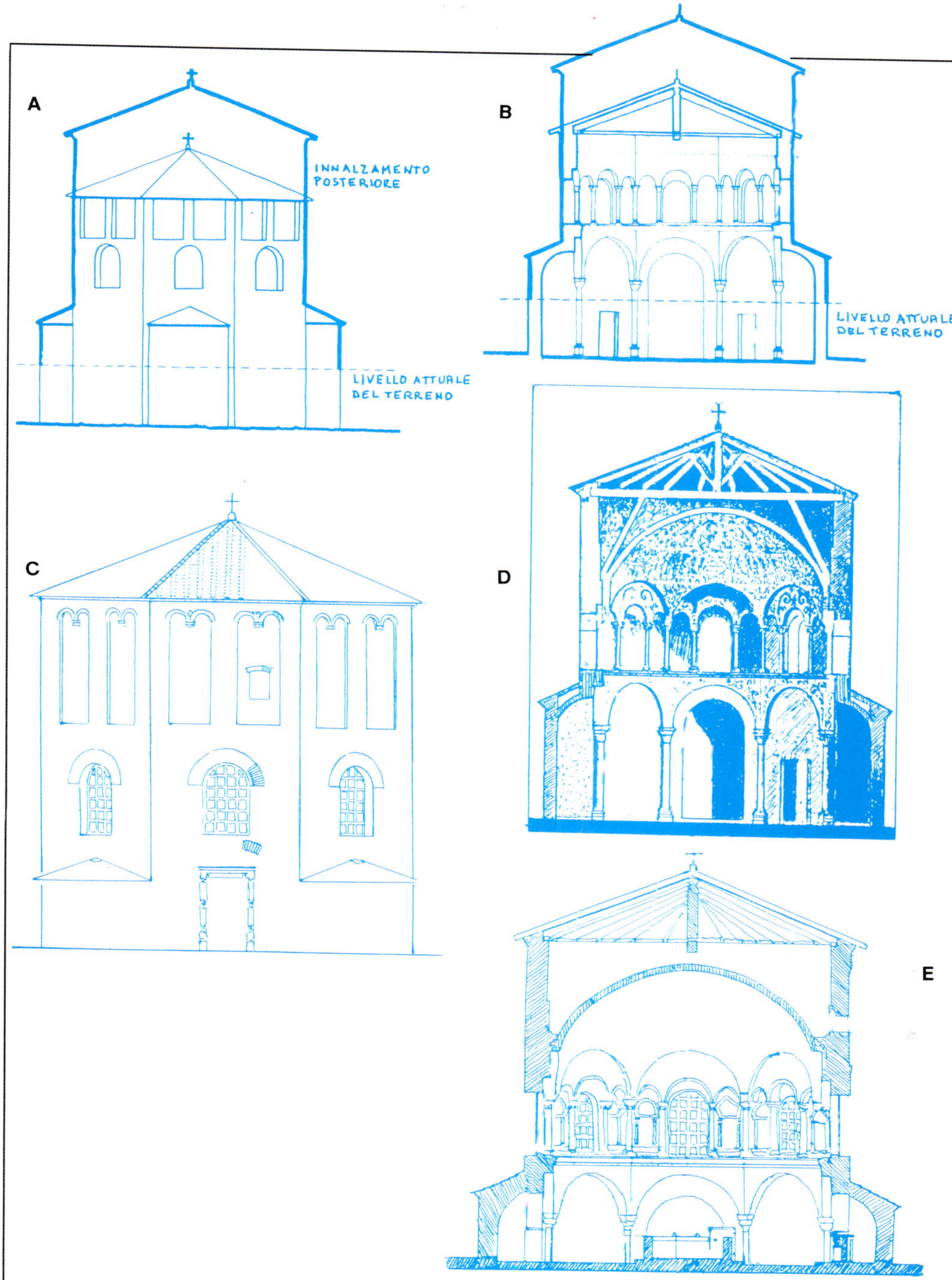

Table V - **Neonian or Cathedral's baptistery**

A-B: Prospect and section. It is emphasized the ursian building and the neonian addition (see pag. 182 and 185) (CARB XXXII).
C: Prospect.
D: Section.
E: Section.

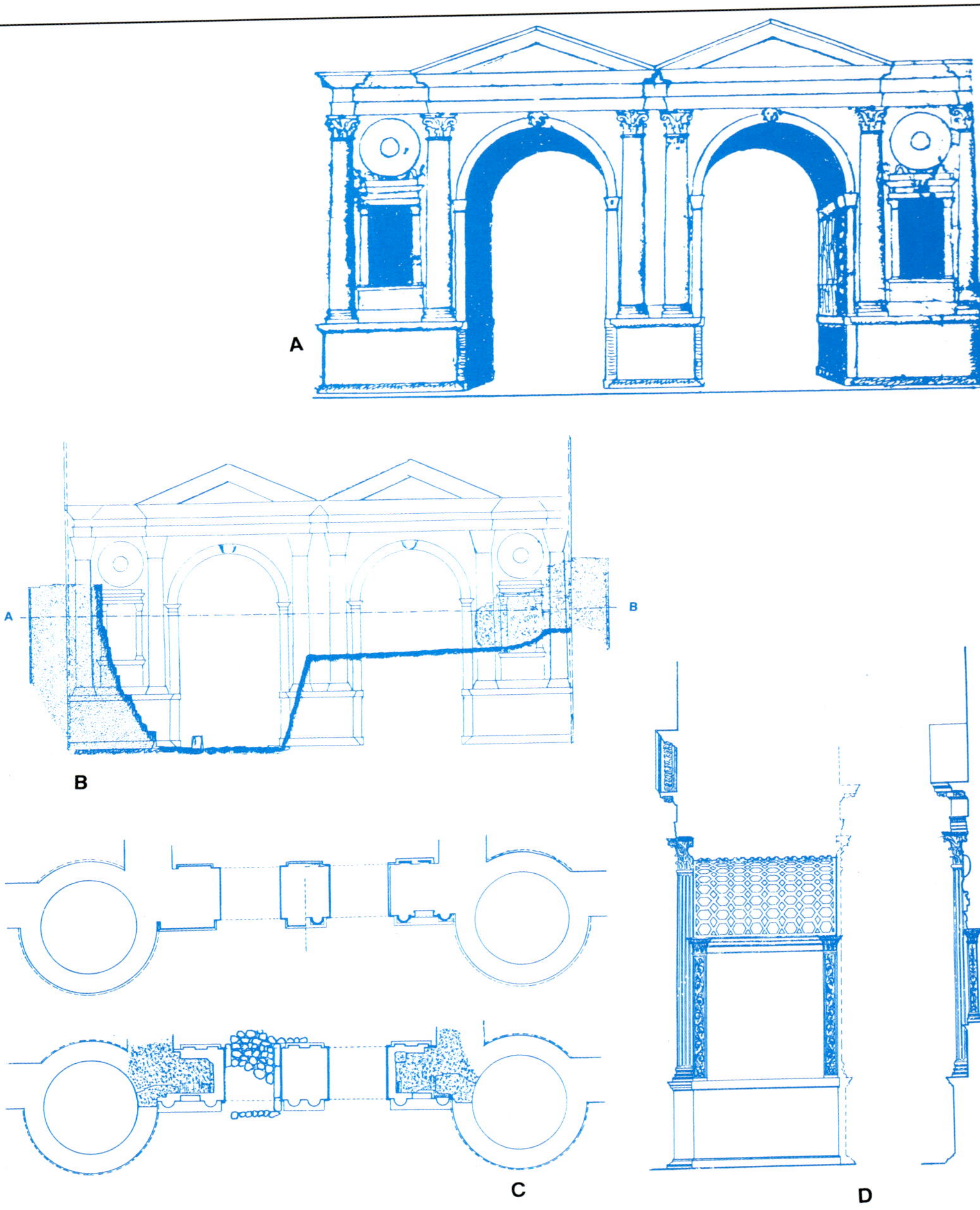

Table VI - **Port'Aurea**

A: Port'Aurea designed by Andrea Palladio (1508-1580).
B: The excavation of Port'Aurea. The dotted line A-B shows today's street level. The dark line delimits the excavation. The gate was demolished in 1582 (pag. 194).
C: Plan.
D: Section.

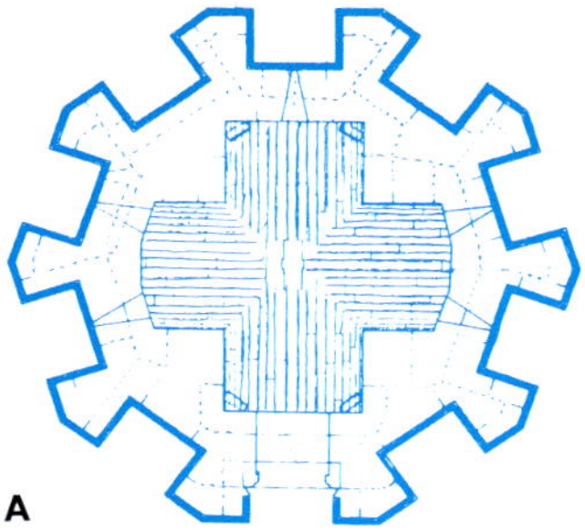

A

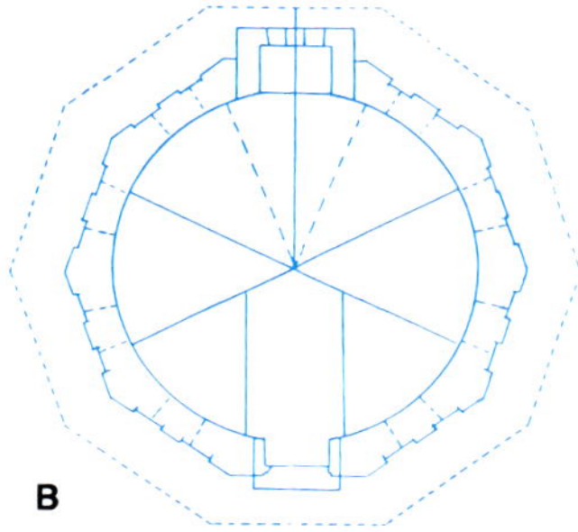

B

C

D

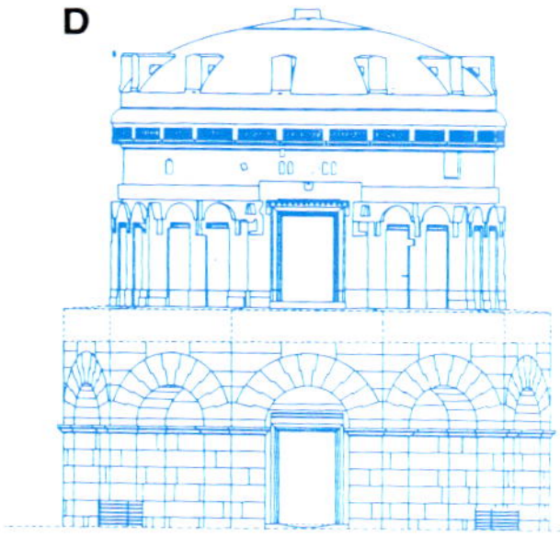

E

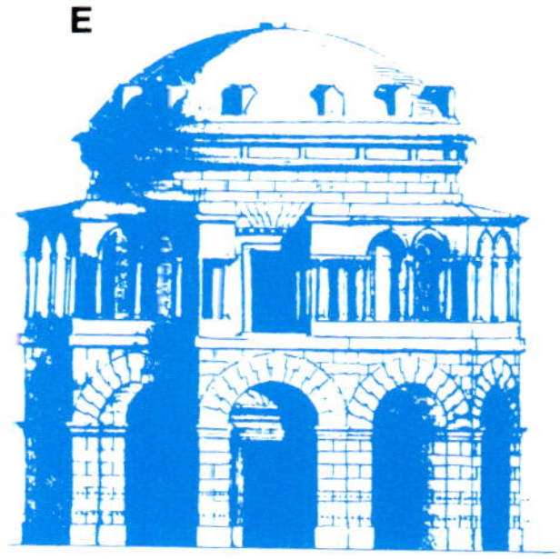

F

G

Table VII - **Mausoleum of Theodoric:**

A: Plan of the lower area.
B: Plan of the upper room.
C: A drawing of the Mausoleum (from an article of Carlo Cecchelli in F.R. 1956).
D: Prospect.
E: Reconstructive prospect of the open gallery.
F: Graphic reconstruction of the open gallery - Prospect and plan.
G: Reconstruction (and partial section) carried out by the architect Giuliano da Sangallo (middle of the 15th Century - 1516).

A

B

C

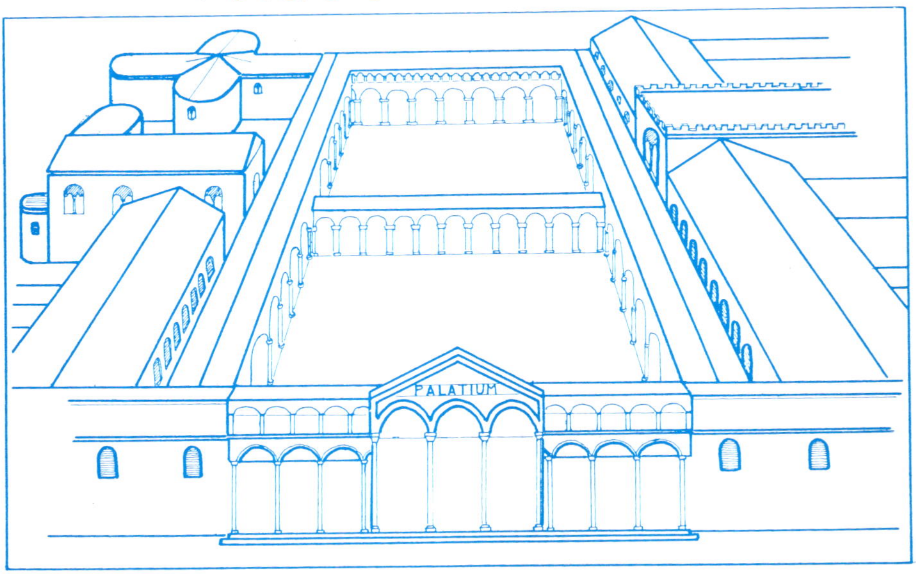

Table VIII - **Reconstruction of Theodoric's palace**

Carried out by Dyggve (A) and by F. Benoit (B) starting from the mosaic in Sant'Apollinare Nuovo (pag. 131).
C: reconstruction of a part of the building based on excavations (by G. Savini).

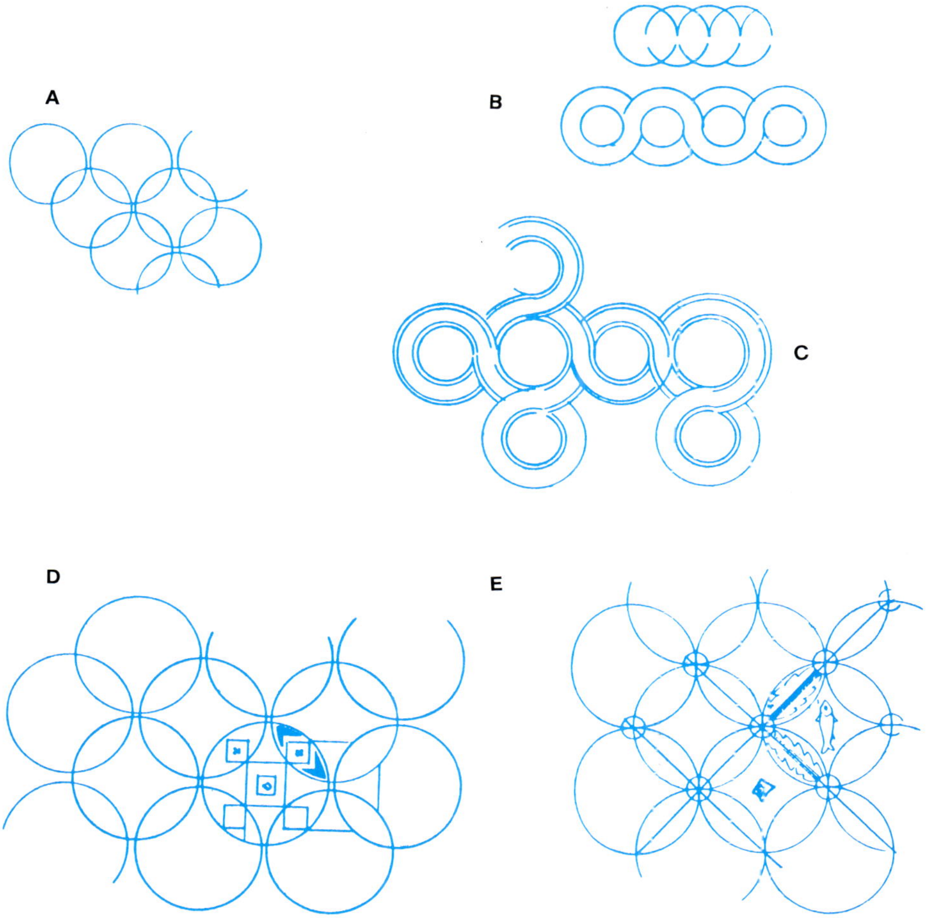

Table IX - **Ornamental patterns**

Schemes of ornamental floor motifs. Scheme A: *crypt of San Francesco*: circles that intersect forming ovcidal motifs. Scheme B: *Basilica of San Vitale*, on the edge of one of the floor triangles. There are strips of little arches that cross each other. Scheme C: *Basilica of Sant'Apollinare in Classe*, inserted on the wall of the right nave, protected by glass: enrichment of the arch motif that cross each other. Scheme D: *ambulatory of the Basilica of San Vitale*: circles that intersect forming ovules, in which little squares are inserted in contact with a bigger square in the centre. Scheme E: *crypt of the little tower in the garden of «The Palazzo della Provincia»*; coming from San Severo: series of circles that intersect creating ovoidal forms and squares with concave sides. On the squares various figures appear: little crosses, fish, birds, ducks, snakes etc. In the ovules a leaf motif with rigid nervation is inserted (from R. Farioli; *Mosaici pavimentali d'età paleocristiana degli edifici di culto di Ravenna*, XII CARB., 1965).

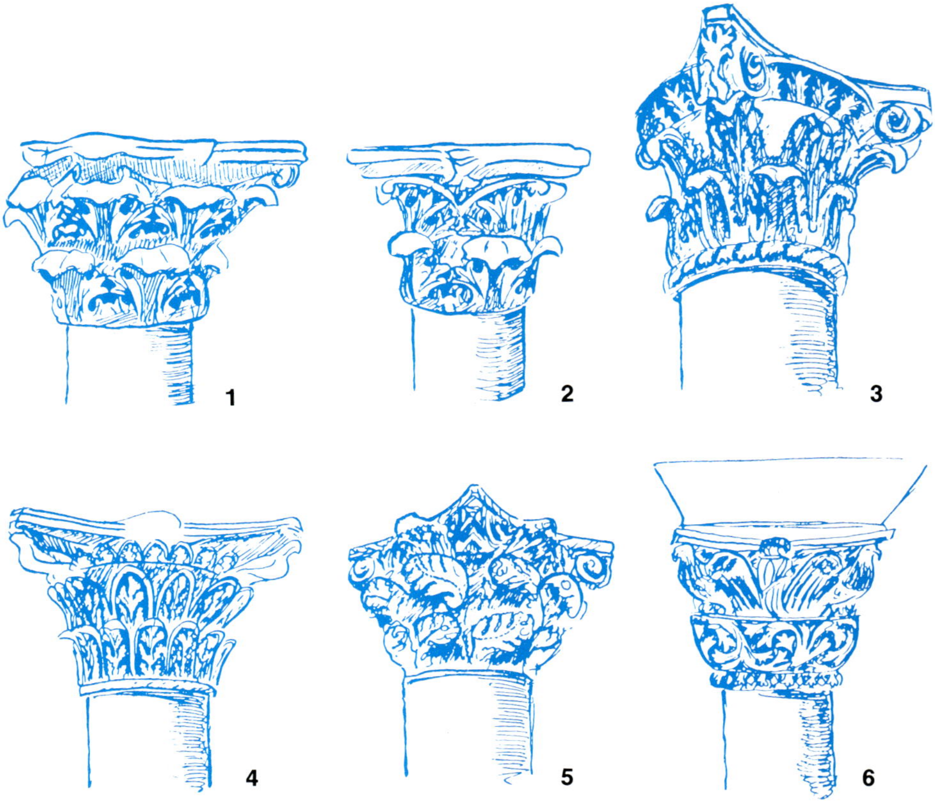

Table X - **Types of capitals**

1 - Corinthian capital (the Corinthian capital presents acanthus leaves).
2 - Corinthian capital of «lyre-type» (above the acanthus leaves there is a sort of «V». In Ravenna there are several types of Corinthian Capitals (pag. 94, 112, 123, 141, 145, 169, 204).
3-4 - Theodosian capitals with overlapping leaves (this type spread at the epoch of the emperor Theodosius II). For Ravenna, pag. 52, 60.
5 - Capital with «leaves moved by the wind» (the acanthus leaves are represented as if moved by the wind). For Ravenna, pag. 52, 80, 194.
6 - Two zone capital. On the upper part some birds are represented. For Ravenna pag. 161.

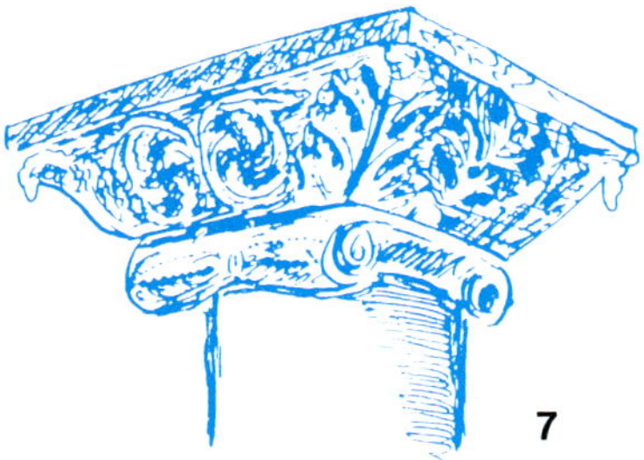

7

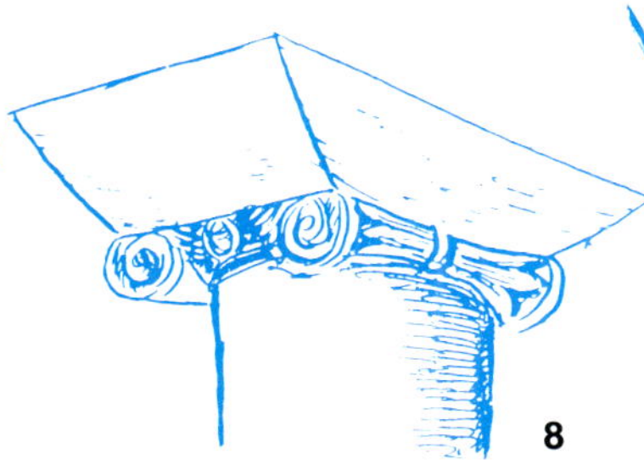

8

9

10

11

12

7-8 - Impost-Ionic capitals (there are the ionic motif, the volute, above which there is the impost, a shaft of an upside-down pyramid). For Ravenna pag. 51.
9-10 - Impost capital very finely decorated
11 - Basket-like capital with doves (for the basket-like capital see pag. 52, 54, 204).
12 - Capital with pulvino in the Basilica of Saint Vitale (pag. 32, 53). The drawings of the first ten capitals are taken from R. Farioli; *I Capitelli paleocristiani e paleobizantini di Salonicco* (in XI CARB. 1964). The authoress underlines how from a classical capital, here not shown, in which the acanthus leaves were represented in a naturalistic, live realistic way we pass to a semplified, geometric leaf to get to an abstract capital, purely decorative and ornamental.

DICTIONARY

ABACUS, generally a quadrangular tablet, that makes up the superior part of the capital and sustains the architrave. It may be Doric, Ionic, Corinthian.

APSE, a semicircular or polygonal building covered by a basin-like vault, that closes the central nave in Roman basilicas or in Christian churches at an extremity.

ACANTHUS, a plant with prickly cleft leaves. It is used in the Corinthian capital, the invention of which is credited to Kallimachos, who saw in Corinth a basket covered with acanthus leaves on the tomb of a youth.

ACEPHALOUS, headless.

ACROTERIO, a prominent part placed on the top of a pediment.

AGGETTO, the jutting out part of a building.

ALPHA and OMEGA, alpha is the first letter of the Greek alphabet, omega the last. To understand their meanings see: apocalyptical letters.

ALLEGORY, we have an allegory when we capture the hidden sense different from what words openly express.

ALTAR, see cippus, table, chest.

AMBO, an elevated tribune or pulpit used in early Christian and medieval basilicas placed before the presbytery. It derives from the ancient word that means «to rise».

AMBULATORY, a wide corridor; a covered place to walk in.

ANCONA, a painted altarpiece called also «pala». The term probably comes from a corruption of a Greek word that means «image» and it also indicates marble sculptures or terracotta ones, placed on altars.

ANSA, handle of a vase.

APOCALYPTICAL LETTERS, the letters Alpha and Omega used in the Apocalypse as symbol of the eternal essence of Christ. «Ego sum alpha et omega, principium et finis» (Ap. 1, 8).

APOCRYPHAL, not authentic. Particularly the non-canonical book of the Ancient and New Testament.

ARA, altar.

ARCHITRAVE, that part of an entablature which rests immediately on any sort of support that can be pillars columns or walls. It is practically a trave that carries out the function of an arch.

ARCHIVOLT, ornamental contour which follows the curve of an arch.

ARCH, a curved structure that rests on columns, pillars, walls and that supports the wall weight. It is a ROUND ARCH when the curve of the intrados is formed by a semicircumference. It is a POINTED ARCH when the curve of the intrados is formed by two circumference arches that create a peak.

ARCOSOLIO, it is a sepulchre dug in tufa or directly into a wall surmounted by an arched niche. Arcus » arco; solium » sarcophagus.

ARDICA, see narthex. It is a term particularly used in Ravenna to indicate the portico of a basilica.

ARM or coat-of-arms. It is the complex of figures that characterize the earmark of people, families and corporations.

ARMILLA, in architecture, an arch structure made up of two radial masonries of the same height.

ASHLAR, a stone that is worked in order to receive a regular shape.

BACCELLATURA, decoration obtained with convex elements or concave grooves.

BADALONE, a long lectern in the church choirs.

BANCALE, a big bench with a back.

BARBICAN, a support, a reinforcement or prop. It comes from the Arab word b-al-baqara, that means «cow's door» and its function was to protect the cattle's paddock.

BASILISSA, queen.

BECCATELLO, a bracket placed to sustain little terraces, galleries etc.

BEMA, from the Greek «rostrum» or also «step», «walk». In the early christian basilicas, the elevated part in regards to the floor of the church containing the presbytery and apse.

BUSSOLONE, swinging door at the entrance of buildings, theatres and churches.

CANTHAROS, an urn with a rounded deep body provided with two handles and a pedestal which is generally narrow and long.

CAPITAL, the finishing element of a column, between the column trunk and the trabeation.

CAPSELLA, a little box where relics and the Eucaristic bread and wine were kept.

CARYATID, figure of a woman (or man) used as a column or pillar.

CHEST-LIKE ALTAR, an altar whose communion table is held up by four angular little pillars, between which there are the marble slabs that form the chest.

CAISSON CEILING, when the ceiling is made up by a crossing of rafters that delimit spaces called lacunars.

CASTRUM, Roman military camp.

CASULA, ancient name for the sacerdotal chasuble.

CAULIS, the stem or stalk in plants.

CENOBY, monastery or however a place where monks live together. It derives from two Greek words that mean «life in common».

CLOISTER, a typical convent yard, with quadrangular plan, closed by a wall and run along all its perimeter, or only partly by a portico. In the middle there is generally a well.

CHRISMON, religious Christian mark used as symbol of Christ. It is made up by «chi» (X) and «rho» (P) that are the first two letters of Christ's name in Greek.

CIBORIUM, a fixed structure that can be found outside or inside a building, and is made up of a cover that rests on four or more columns to protect statues, altars or tombs. Bernini's monumental one is very famous in St. Peter in Rome with intertwined columns.

CIMASA, from the Greek word «little wave» crown moulding of a trabeation, of a pedestal, of a bracket with curved profile.

CINERARY (vase) a vase made in order to contain the ashes of the dead.

CIPOLLINO, deriving from the word «onion» for veinings that are similar, it is a light, rather white marble with areas of different colours majorly green or grey (cipolin).

CHASUBLE, a liturgic robe worn by the priest during Mass. It could be a complete mantle or cut laterally in order to let the laces to be tied around the waist, pass.

CIPPUS ALTAR, altar under whose communion table there is the element that sustains in the central part (cippus) and that sometimes contains a little cell for relics.

CLAMYS, it is a quite short and light surcoat, wrapped to the body by a buckle. It was made up of a rectangular piece of material, cut semi-circularly in one of the short sides, that could also be closed on the chest or on the shoulders.

CLASSIARIUS, soldier, sailor or oarer of the Roman military fleet.

CLIPEUS, leather shield of the Roman soldiers; metal or marble disc that was hung as vow in temples. Clipeatae images: portraits in a clipeus.

CORBEL, projection from a wall supporting a structure.

CORINTHIAN (order), it is one of the classic architectural orders: the trunk of the column is grooved, and the capital is decorated with acanthus leaves (see acanthus).

CORNICE, the part that crowns the buildings, jutting out. It juts out very much and sustains the projection of the roof.

COTTO, brick or tile made with clay undergone to the action of fire in a furnace.

CRATER, a big jar used to prepare a mixture of water and wine; it has a very wide mouth, a large and short pedestal, and two handles.

DECUMANUS, one of the two lines and precisely the eastern/western one, that divided a city, a territory assigned the colonists or a military camp, into four areas.

DIACONICON, a little room placed at the side of the apse in which precious objects of the church are kept.

DORIC (order), one of the classic architectural orders; the column doesn't have any base, it is grooved by vertical grooves, it ends in a capital made up of a square rock (abacus) surmounted onto a spreading shape (echinus).

EARLY CHRISTIAN, it means «ancient christian» the term is used in relation with the first periods of Christianity.

EMBRICE, a tile used in roof-coverings called «in Roman way». It is a trapezium-like tablet, with lifted up edges on the two obliquous sides. The embrici are placed in parallel lines.

ENOTECA, it literally means «wine deposit».

EPIGRAPH, an inscription on bronze or marble in memory of the dead or to commemorate men or events. It derives from the Greek word «to write on».

EROTE, a little putto that belongs to Eros' suite.

EXARCH, governor sent by the Byzantine emperors to Ravenna (another was in Africa) from the end of the 6th to the middle of the 8th Century.

EXEDRA, any architectural structure with semicircular shape (square, gardens, fountains, etc.).

EXTRADOS, the upper curved surface of an arch or vault.

FENESTELLA, a little window that allowed the first Christians to see or touch the tombs of martyrs and saints through a little partition that divided the tombs from the crowds of believers. After some time the fenestella was used for the confessions. The «confession» is the place where the relics of a Saint or confessor are kept (inside the altar or crypt), opening in the central cippus of the altar that puts the little relic cell in communication with the outside.

FIBULA, buckle, safety pin.

FORMELLA, a tablet of various shapes (quadrangular, polygonal) used for ornamental applications, that can be decorated with paintings and reliefs.

FRIEZE, architectural element made up of a strip, generally it is horizontal, with ornamental motifs or figures.

FRESCO, painting carried out with colours mixed with water, on a wall that has been prepared before with sand and lime and always kept cool during the work.

FUSERUOLE, architectural ornament made up of a series of spheric elements alternated variably.

GAVALO, sector of a wooden wheel.

GREEK PATTERN (meander), ornamental motif made up of lines that meet in right angle, they intertwine, stand side by side.

HALO, a bright disc placed behind some characters in images of Pagan gods or in the Christian religion, in the images of the Holy Virgin, angels, apostles, saints and characters of the Old Testament.

HERMA, a stone pillar surmounted by a sculptured head or bust.

ICNOGRAPHY, synonym of «plan».

ICON, sacred image painted on wood, typical of Byzantine Art.

ICONOGRAPHY, discipline that studies and analyzes the graphic elements and the subjects of a work of art, with the intent of stressing the relations of the work with the tradition to which it belongs.

IDRIA, vase for water with three handles.

IHS, the name of Jesus made up fro I, from «eta» (the long Greek e) and from the Latin termination «S» of Jesus.

INDULGENCE, act with which the church remits, in part or completely the punishment for sins committed.

INTERCOLUMNIATION, the distance between the adjacent columns.

INTRADOS, the surface that delimits the inferior concave part of an arch, of a vault or of a dome.

IONIC (order), one of the classic architectural orders. The column has a base made up of three elements, while the capital is decorated with volutes that roll up laterally.

JAMB, it is a wooden or marble finishing etc., of vertical edges of a door, a balcony or a window on the side where there are the fixtures.

LACUNAR, ceiling with the framework of the rafters open. Lacunar is precisely the space between the rafters.

LANTERNA, a little construction, generally circular, that is placed on top of the dome and finishes it.

LATIN CROSS, while the Greek cross has the vertical pole that is exactly the same in length as the horizontal, the Latin cross has the vertical pole longer than the horizontal one. In the Latin cross the vertical pole surpasses, on top, the horizontal one, whilst on the «crux commissa» it forms a sort of a T.

LATICLAVIUS, it is a tunic hemmed in purple that was worn by the Roman senators and also by the members of their families.

LEMNISCO, a little ribbon with which the Romans decorated their crowns.

LESENA, a slight relief of the wall with decorative functions, in marble or brick that can also be made up in base, capital or shaft.

LIBERTUS, a liberated slave that often continued to live with his patron with economical and respect obligations.

LIBURNA, a very light and fast ship with a long stern, provided with a ram, a mainmast and two orders of oarsmen.

LOBBY, a room on the ground floor that from the entrance door of a house leads to a yard or stair.

LYRE (motif), a drawing with the shape of a «V» similar to the musical instrument. The instrument is formed by an harmonic box from which two arms come out, joined together by a transversal board.

LOGGETTA, a building or part of one, that is open towards the outside by means of columns and arcades.

LUNETTE, portion of a semi-circular wall, with a linear horizontal base.

MATRONEUM, women's gallery in ancient Christian basilicas.

MAUSOLEUM, a funerary building or monumental tomb. Its name derives from Mausolo, that was a satrap from Caria who got himself a tomb built enumerated among the seven wonders of the world.

MEGALITHIC, megalith in Greek means «large rock» and megalithic is the prehistoric period in which monuments were built with heavy rocks.

MENSA, communion table of the altar held up by four or more feet, often with a central cippus that contains relics sometimes.

MITRE, the little cap that the Pope, the cardinals and bishops generally wear in solemn liturgical functions.

MOULDING, it is an architectural structure with a continuous profile, made up of rectilinear or curved elements, grouped together variably.

MULLIONED WINDOW, window divided in two by a vertical bar.

MONOFORA, window whose light has no subdivisions.

MONOGRAM, intertwining or ligament of letters that make up a word.

MONOGRAMMATIC CROSS, it is a cross from which the first two letters of the Greek name of Christ are drawn. See: chrismon.

MONOLITH, a single block of stone.

NARTHEX, open portico or closed vestibule in front of the basilica. Originally it is the side of the quadriportico adhering to the façade of the church.

NAVE, in the churches it is the longitudinal subdivision of the internal space, delimited by columns, pillars or walls. Usually the naves are three, separated by two rows of columns.

NECROPOLIS, in Greek it means «city of the dead». It usually indicates a grouping of pre-Christian tombs, but it can also regard Christian cemeteries.

NICHE, a recess in the wall generally ending in the top with a sphere. It may contain statues.

OBLATION, in liturgy, the offering made by the faithful especially in relation with the Eucharistic celebration of which today we find some traces in the collection during the offertory.

OGIVE, Ogival, the term with which a pointed arch is called but it really means the diagonal ribs of a vault.

OPPIDUM, a little fortified town.

PALIOTTO, the covering of the altar, generally of very preciously embroided material, but also of precious metal or marble, gypsum adorned with gems and ivory (altar piece).

PALLIUM, Roman mantle of rectangular shape, often preferred to the toga. The term also meant a rectangular piece of material that could be more or less large. Today it is a liturgic robe with the shape of a large ribbon of white wool, 5 cm wide with two strips that end in fringes worn around the neck. The ecclesiastical pallium is worn only by the Pope or by some authorized bishops.

PALMETTE, vegetal ornamental motif mad up by petal or lobes.

PASSETTO, a small, narrow passage.

PASTOPHORIA, the two rooms of the prothesis and diaconicon.

PATEN, the little plate used for the bread in the Eucharist.

PATERA, a sort of a short bowl, without any handles used by the Romans during sacrifices. In italian the term «padella» was derived.

PEDIMENT, crowning front of a building of triangular shape. The inner triangular space is called tympanum.

PEDUCCIO, as the corbel, it creates the impost of the arch, of the vault, of the trabeation. Generally it assumes the shape of the capital.

PENDENTIVE, it is the part of a wall, generally of triangular shape with the top upside down, with the sides made up by the curves of the archivolt.

PERGAMO, a high platform used for talks, debates etc.

PERGULA, architectural element made up of columns or pillars that come out from a parapet, to which lamps or festoons were hung. The «pergula» separated in the churches the part destined to the believers from the presbytery.

PYRGUS, Greek word that means «tower».

PLINTH, element that holds the base of the column. Square base at the feet of the walls of a building.

PLUTEUS, a slab of stone but also of wood or metal worked in bas-relief (while the transenna is open worked) used to create internal enclosures in sacred buildings.

POSTERGALE, the back part of a seat.

PRESBYTERY, the place reserved to the bishop and clergy in Christian basilicas, placed in the remotest part of the church. It ends with an apse. The term is also used as synonymous of apse.

PRIMICERIUS, means «first in degree» for example, the first of the notaries or the priest that presided the subdeacons.

PRONAOS, means place «in front of the temple». In Greek temples it is the entrance.

PROTHESIS, a little square room, made up in the left side of the apse, by the opposite side of the diaconicon where the sacred species were kept and everything was prepared for the functions.

PROTIRO, a little fare-part that in many churches preceeds the entrance. It is generally made up by a vault sustained by columns.

PROTOME, the front part (neck and head) of an animal.

PULPIT, ancient wooden, marble or stone seat used by the Greeks and Romans. In the middle Ages it designated the bishop's seat placed in the apse.

PULVINO, the element that stands above the capital and holds the weight of the arches.

PUTEALE, a small circular wall that protects the mouth of the well on which the rope to take the bucket up ran. Often the puteali are made in stone and marble and are decorated.

QUADRIPORTICO, square hall, surrounded by a portico with columns that in ancient times was built in front of Christian churches.

RACEME, it is a sort of flowering said also «cluster». The flowers are represented like on a branch.

RECTO, it indicates the front, for example, of a sheet, of a coin and also of a sarcophagus etc.

REVERSE, the behind of a sheet, coin or sarcophagus.

RIVELLINO (ravelin), it was a defence, detached and quite advanced to protect a castle or however a fortification.

SACELLUM, little closed sacred place.

SACRISTY, place made up of one or more rooms attached to a church very often near a choir and in communication with it. In it the sacred paraments, the liturgical books etc., are kept; in it the priests put on their sacred clothes before celebrating their liturgical functions.

SARCOPHAGUS, a marble, stone or wooden container for the dead. It means «meat» and «eat» from a legend which in Asso, in Troade, the sarcophagi made with local stone would consume the corpse in little time.

SYMBOL, mark, image or object that represents another.

SINOPIA, drawing on a wall, in red earth called sinopia (from SINOPE on the Black Sea), that was used by the artist to prepare the execution of mosaics or frescoes.

STELE, an oblong slab of rock or marble that indicates a burial (funerary stele).

TAMBOUR (of the dome), the architectural part that is immediately under the dome, it is cylindrical or prismatic, whether it is a dome of cylindrical or polygonal plan.

TABLE ALTAR, an altar with little columns or pillars that hold the communion table.

TELAMON, male figure used in architecture to sustain trabeations or cornices.

TEMPERA, painting technique that makes use of different substances (glues, gum, milk, etc.) to agglutinate the colours.

TESSERA, each little stone of a mosaic.

TIBURIO, external covering of a dome in the shape of a right prism with pyramidal covering.

TYMPANUM, the triangular space inside the fronton.

THYRSUS, a stick surmounted by a enclosure of ivy leaves, attribute of Dyonisus, of satyrs and bacchantes.

TRABEATION, architectural element placed horizontally on pillars or columns. It is made up of an archivolt, frieze and cornice.

TRANSENNA, a marble stone or bronze slab, openworked placed as closure of windows or as parapet of various spaces.

TRANSEPT, transversal nave which gives to the church plan the shape of a cross. The word derives from «trans septa», that means «beyond the enclosure».

THREE MULLIONED WINDOW, a window divided in three parts by two pillars or little columns.

TRUSS, scaffolding to sustain the roof.

TUNIC, a robe that was worn directly on the body, sewed on its sides with openings for the head and arms.

UMBRACULUM, a sort of shell used in ancient art to give more dignity to the people it overhangs.

VESTAL, a priestess of the goddess Venus who always kept the fire in her temple lighted. Extensively it can refer to whoever preserves something sacred and precious.

VIRIDARIUS, an ancient Roman garden. Pleasant place with flowers and trees.

VOLUTE, ornamental motif made up of a spiral winding of geometrical or naturalistic motifs.

WEB, the spheric triangles of a vault with square, rectangular or polygonal based.

WELL CURB, well parapet.